Building
Your Own
Home

Above: Border Oak Design & Construction Ltd

Building Your Own Home

The essential guide for anyone wanting
to build, renovate, convert or extend
their own home in the British Isles

David Snell &
Murray Armor

Seventeenth Edition

EBURY PRESS
LONDON

5 7 9 10 8 6

Text copyright © Ryton Books and David Snell 2002

Ryton Books and David Snell have asserted their right to be identified as the authors of this work in accordance with the Copyright, Design & Patents Act 1988.

First published in the United Kingdom in 1978 by Prism Press

Updated editions: 1980, 1981, 1982, 1984, 1985, 1986, 1987
Revised editions: 1983, 1988, 1989, 1990, 1991, 1993, 1996, 1999

This seventeenth revised edition published in 2002 by Ebury Press
Random House 20 Vauxhall Bridge Road, London SW1V 2SA

Random House Australia (Pty) Limited
20 Alfred Street, Milsons Point, Sydney,
New South Wales 2061, Australia

Random House New Zealand Limited
18 Poland Road, Glenfield,
Auckland 10, New Zealand

Random House South Africa (Pty) Limited
Endulini, 5A Jubilee Road,
Parktown 2193, South Africa

The Random House Group Limited Reg. No. 954009

A CIP catalogue record for this book is available from the British Library

ISBN 0 09 188619 8

Designed by Jerry Goldie Graphic Design

Printed and bound in Singapore by Tien Wah Press

Acknowledgements

Jeanne, Charles and Katie Armor; Mark Brinkley, author *The Housebuilder's Bible*; Robert Capper, Harrison & Clarke solicitors; David Charlton, Accountant; Joe Checuti, Forest of Dean DC; Raymond Connor, Buildstore; Ken Dijksman, author and planning officer; Karen Fardell, Entrepreneur; John Greene, Border Oak Design & Construction Ltd; Christopher Heath, Custom Homes Ltd; Peter Harris, Ascent Publishing; John Hay, Buildstore; Martin Hocking, editor *Build It*; Michael Holmes, editor *Homebuilding & Renovating*; Nick Jones, BRECSU; Mary Ludden, Magic Media; Bruce MacDonald, Design and Materials Ltd; Sam Malcolm, Buildstore; Gary McGee, Carson McDowell, Belfast; Dante Mutti, Design and Materials Ltd; Moussa Maimh, IPPEC; Mairead Sherlock, A.L. Goodbody, Dublin; Tom Somerville, Design and Materials Ltd; Tom O'Sullivan, Key Properties, Bantry; Jason Orme, *Homebuilding & Renovating*; Julian Owen, architect, Janet Parker, DMS Services Ltd; Beverley Pemberton, Design & Materials Ltd; Robert and Ruth Pennicott, Landbank Services Ltd; Ian Pitts, gardener; David Ransley, Accountancy Services; David Robbins, Robbins Systems; Cynthia Scott; Linda Snell; David Taylor; Alan Tovey, Basement Development Group; Jenny de Villiers, DMS Services Ltd; Gunnel Westley, Scandia Hus.

And all of the people who have put up with telephone calls from me, whilst I sucked their brains dry for information, often without their realising what I was doing.

Contents

Foreword

For almost a quarter of a century, *Building Your Own Home* has been widely regarded as the benchmark title for what has come to be known in the British Isles as the self-build movement. The work of the late Murray Armor, and now his successor David Snell, has served as a beacon, lighting the way ahead for literally tens of thousands of successful self-builders, and helping to nurture the development of a movement that has grown from around 2000 projects in 1978 to over 16,000 a year in 2000. For anyone considering building a one-off house – still a very real break with the accepted way of doing things today – the discovery of the existence of this book was and is a very important step, one which helps to legitimise their ambition and, in the eyes of friends and family, to reaffirm their sanity.

The strength, reassurance and inspiration offered by the advice and case studies contained within this book's many pages goes some way to explaining its importance in so many people's lives. I am always staggered to notice just how many people have a copy tucked away on their bookshelves. Although the successive updated editions of this title have now all but extinguished the original words, the spirit of its creator, Murray Armor, is still very much in evidence. In common with so many who go on to build their own home, Murray was a determined individualist, a maverick, complete with that essential sense of purpose, who managed to weave his way amongst society at every level, unbridled by tradition, conformity or prejudice. He was as comfortable amongst leading politicians and opinion formers as he was amongst disadvantaged group self-builders. It was his work more than any other – inspired by the lack of help and advice experienced when building his own home back in the mid 1960s – that helped to create the identity of a self-build movement, transforming it from a disparate group of individuals going it alone, to the modern mainstream industry it is today.

If Murray was the pathfinder, then up front amongst those who followed was David Snell whom Murray saw as a kindred spirit. David built his first house, for his bride-to-be, Linda, in 1970. Despite seven successive self-build and renovation projects, they recently celebrated their 30th wedding anniversary and even have plans to build again. David has been advising self-builders for 25 years now and has built up a wealth of knowledge and experience that is probably unrivalled. He has a wisdom on all matters of house building –

and much else in life – that is tempered by failure as well as accomplishment. He is the first to acknowledge that his career has not been all success – having tried his hand at development, he has been wrong-footed by the vagaries of the property market and the building industry on three separate occasions. It was Murray Armor's bequest of this title that encouraged David to put his days as a paid self-build consultant behind him and become a full-time writer and journalist, a role in which he would be able to share his hard-won knowledge with a wider audience. David is now Contributing Editor on the monthly self-build magazine, *Homebuilding & Renovating*, and the building expert on *The Daily Telegraph's* property clinic, Bricks and Mortar. He also helps to organise and run self-build courses in conjunction with Worcester College of Technology and is an accomplished seminar speaker.

In this new fully updated 17th edition of *Building Your Own Home*, David has for the first time extended the breadth of the book to cover renovation and conversion projects and address those issues relating to the self-build movement in Scotland, Northern Ireland and Eire. The book can now legitimately claim to be truly comprehensive.

Michael Holmes
Editor, *Homebuilding & Renovating* magazine

Something which readers may not notice at first, is that the book is written entirely in first person. This is an unconventional idea – more conversation than text book – but one which somehow makes the advice and information more accessible and gives it all a more personal tone.

Introduction

Main-stream television advertising now extols the benefits of a major building society's new self-build mortgage. I have to confess to a wry smile whenever I see it. When I first joined Murray Armor in 1976 and we travelled around the country talking about self-building, the whole thing was considered slightly wacky and the domain of hippies. Those who wanted to self-build had to run a gauntlet of prejudice and ridicule with building societies, architects, banks and builders merchants all seeming to conspire to deter them.

Those early pioneers weren't deterred, of course, and the industry as a whole, for that is what it has now become, has burgeoned to the point where approaching 16,000 new individual or self-built homes are started each year, representing over 8% of the total number of completions and up to 25% of new detached houses and bungalows. Add to that the countless conversions and renovations carried out by private individuals and self-building becomes main-stream big business. No wonder banks, building societies and builders' merchants now fall over each other to work within and play their part in its success, often inventing a history for themselves that they don't really deserve. No wonder that architects have completely changed their tune and now actively encourage the free expression that self-builders bring to the design board. And no wonder that companies with innovations or inventions first try them out and then watch them gain full acceptance, by reference to the self-build market.

The industry has come a long way in the last three decades and with maturity comes responsibility. Those working within the industry have recognised this fact and acknowledged that a sector that can claim to build more houses than some of the larger developers put together, should be able to speak with a single voice. Petty rivalries and commercial considerations have been put aside in order to do this. Within the lifetime of this edition I therefore fully expect to see self-build being able to lobby on equal terms for the changes in planning laws that are necessary to maintain and increase the supply of land.

So what is self-build? Well, for a start, many of those who succeed in creating their own homes wouldn't put themselves in that category and some even express complete surprise when they are referred to in that way. The term obviously includes those who end up with a new home built on a green field site as well as those who undertake the (perhaps more onerous) task of converting a wreck of a barn, or some other non-domestic building, into a dwelling. And to a large extent, it includes many who buy up an existing house and renovate, extend and adapt it to fit in with their own ideals. In short it includes all those who, rather than just accepting what developers and the market wish to foist upon them, take charge of the production of their new home to standards and ideals that they set themselves.

Is it all, therefore, down to money? Well, much of the media, outside that directly involved with self-building, still clings to that belief, and television programmes and newspaper articles always seem to home in on that aspect. Building for yourself does offer considerable savings, with demonstrable gains in equity of between 15% and 50%. This often leads to the assumption that it is these cost savings that motivate the self-builder and that they build cut-price homes. Nothing could be further from the truth and, although smaller and cheaper homes are built by self-builders, by far the largest number of them are four-bedroom, double-garaged properties built, and fitted out, to a very high standard indeed. In a quarter of a century of involvement with self-builders, I could probably count on the fingers of one hand those people whose sole motivation was cost-cutting and,

Above: An unashamedly modern house that nevertheless harks back to design features and details of a previous age. (Potton Ltd)

when I think of them, there is no doubt in my mind that this small group form the least successful of self-builders, at least in terms of the satisfaction achieved. By far the greatest motivation for self-building is, and always has been, the desire to achieve and create one's own individual living environment from within one's own resources, and the fact that quite huge increases in equity are often made seems almost incidental.

The new self-build home is an expression of the individual, and it will, almost invariably, be built to the highest standard. At the very least the standard will be several levels above the property developer's lowest common denominator. Self-builders come from all walks of life, from manual labourers through to highly paid professionals, from soldiers through to vicars. Some are more successful than others but any measure of success has to be related to an almost

Above: Within this book you should either find your ideal design or the seeds of inspiration that will lead to it.

complete lack of failure. Some have advantages in that either the pattern of their work allows them to spend more time on site, or the nature of their employment means that they can take advantage of accommodation during the build period. Some of them have skills that are directly attributable to their self-build, whilst others possess little or no knowledge of building. What the most successful, undoubtedly, have in common, is a capacity to get things done, to see beyond the immediate problem and to seek out the solution.

It starts and ends with management and the critical paths of that management are set down in the following chapters of this book. Whether you are intending to get out there with a shovel and a trowel to do everything yourself, or whether you are planning to go to the Bahamas until a builder gives you a shout and tells you that it's all over and it's all right to come home and move in, management is still the key. Management of your ideals, tailoring them to your needs and your resources. Management of your own skills and the husbandry of other people's skills. All of this needs to be carefully evaluated and thought through before ever site is bought and before ever pen is put to paper or sod first turned.

'Does one have to have a lot of technical knowledge to self-build?' is an almost constant refrain from would-be self-builders. Not at all. Of course, if you've got a good grounding in the general sequence of events then that's all to the good but the facts are that, in the main, you're going to be employing people for the skills they possess. Your job, therefore, is going to be the management and co-ordination of those trades and of all of their ancillary requirements. No lay person can, in the short timeframe between deciding to self-build and its execution, learn all that there is to know. All self-builders can learn enough to know what questions they should be asking and to understand the answers. All self-builders should learn that, if they're not happy with the answers or, if they feel that they are heading in the wrong direction, they should stop and seek another opinion or another choice. All self-builders should temper any knowledge that they might gain with (what is the ultimate skill in self-building) the ability to manage people and situations. Learning about bricklaying to the point where you can chat with your bricklayers about the type of

Above: The initial drawings should excite the imagination and convey a true impression of the finished home, as this sketch from Potton Ltd does.

sand they would prefer, or the additives they want you to get for them is fine. But if that knowledge leads to you standing behind them in a white coat barking instructions, don't be surprised if the relationship very quickly breaks down.

So, how do you increase your knowledge? Well, you're at the very beginning of a book that will, by its end, have given you much of what you need to know about self-building. Nevertheless, there's a lot more that you can do and what follows is a short list of suggestions. What I would warn against is taking single-interest or narrow-perspective advice too much to heart. Always keep the bigger picture in mind and remember that what the successful self-builder has to do is balance out all of the advice, some of which may be conflicting, most of which is probably appropriate, and all of which needs weighing up with just one objective in mind – your new home.

Books

I wouldn't want to pretend for one moment that this is the only worthwhile book on the market on the

subject of self-building. There are many other books that will sit beside and complement this book, among them *The Housebuilder's Bible* by Mark Brinkley and other titles by Rob Matthews, Speer and Dade and Ken Dijksman. It is unlikely that you will find them in your local bookshop: the best place to obtain them is through Ryton Books, tel: 01909 591652.

If you are using a library to obtain books of this sort, ignore anything written more than five years ago. Also ignore American books unless you propose to build in America.

Useful books in a different category are the Building Regulations and the NHBC and Zurich Custom Build handbooks, both of which are considered invaluable by some self-builders and ignored by others. The Building Regulations are published in sections, so you can buy only those which are of interest to you. You may find the various illustrated commentaries on them easier to read than the regulations themselves. All are on display at the Building Bookshop at the London Building Centre in Store Street, London WC1.

Magazines

Apart from the first edition of this book in 1978, nothing has influenced the homogeneity of the self-build industry more than the monthly self-build magazines and their various spin-offs. The two major publications, *Homebuilding & Renovating* and *Build It,* and one lesser known one, *Self-build & Design,* are all available at most newsagents or by subscription. They are essential reading because, as well as detailed case histories about other self-builders, they contain a whole host of information and features. Most importantly they also carry a great deal of advertising which can help to keep you up to date with what's available and what's going on in the self-build business.

Exhibitions

The exhibitions, sponsored by the major magazines, both national and regional, are not to be missed by the serious self-builder as they feature hundreds of firms providing all sorts of services, from manufacturers and package-deal companies through to architects and financial agencies. In addition, there is a rolling programme of seminars, with advice centres on hand to help with any queries that you may have. *Build It* magazine runs two major national exhibitions, one at Alexandra Palace in London every September and another in Scotland. In addition, they hold at least five large regional shows throughout the year, advertised in the magazine. *Homebuilding & Renovating* magazine runs the National Homebuilding and Renovating Show at the National Exhibition Centre (NEC) every spring, with another show in the summer at Sandown Park and two further shows in the autumn at Harrogate and Edinburgh. Details and precise dates are widely publicised within the magazine itself.

It is remarkable just how many self-build projects can trace their origins to, or really be got off the ground, either as a direct result of a visit to the shows or through the information gained at them. Sometimes the visits are almost accidental, sometimes they are planned long in advance but, in so many instances, the shows seem to have been the catalyst for the eventual self-build and the means by which many self-builders make their choices.

Show houses

Potton have a show village of three houses available for inspection, by appointment, with regular seminars. Scandia-Hus have a group of fully furnished show houses at their offices and prospective clients are welcome to visit at any time, but preferably by prior appointment. Most of the other package-deal companies do not have show houses but can arrange for you to visit the finished homes of some of their clients.

The Association of Self-builders

I can probably do no better than to paraphrase the association's own words: 'The association was founded in 1992 to bring together a potentially disparate group of people who have an immense amount in common. It aims to encourage an exchange of ideas, experiences and knowledge through a national newsletter, occasional national gatherings and regular meetings of regional groups.' This is an association formed by ordinary self-builders. It's not everybody's cup of tea but it does publish a lot of useful information and it has arranged discount facilities with national builders' merchants. If you want to talk with and meet other self-builders in order to exchange ideas and knowledge, something that I continually preach, then it is worthwhile considering joining this association.

The Internet

The major magazines each have their own website. *Homebuilding & Renovating* are at the address www.homebuilding.co.uk. From the home page you can find out all about the magazine, read articles from current or back issues and get information on forthcoming shows and exhibitions. As well as their 'Plotfinder' service, they also have a 'Products and Services Directory', which provides comprehensive listings in alphabetical order covering every aspect of self-build. There is also a discussion forum at which self-builders and potential self-builders can air their concerns and ideas, often joined by acknowledged experts from

Above: Exhibitions are where many would-be self-builders learn that they can realise their dreams.

Right: The dedicated self-build magazines are an essential pre-requisite for the serious would-be self-builder.

within the industry. *Build It* can be found on www.self-build.co.uk. Once again you can view issues of the magazine, together with features on readers' homes and all of the latest news and features on self-build. There are also sections on finding land, finance and house design and, as you would expect, they too have a Products and Suppliers' Directory with a database containing all of the products and services that can help to turn your dream of self-building into a reality.

Buildstore, which started life as The Self-build Advisory Service, have branched out to cover practically every aspect of self-building. They can be found on www.buildstore.co.uk. This company pioneered the Accelerator mortgage scheme that is discussed in greater detail in Chapter 1 but they preceded that with their on-line plot-finding service called 'Plotsearch'. Their website contains full details of their financial services and products, including mortgages, insurances and a warranty scheme. They also have 'Buildplan', where account cardholders enjoy trade prices, together with important advice and assistance, through their bulk-buying power and special arrangements with leading builders' merchants. For those who are not on-line they publish regular newsletters that are issued free with the magazines or handed out at the various exhibitions.

Self-build courses

Homebuilding & Renovating magazine, in conjunction with Worcester College of Technology, run four-day courses every autumn and spring, covering all aspects of self-building. Although largely classroom-based, the course is highly interactive, incorporating a visit to a plot, as well as a renovation or conversion opportunity, together with a tour around a timber-frame factory. The subjects covered include finance, finding and assessing development opportunities, legal issues, building regulations, planning and home design. In addition, there is the option of a three-day extension for practical and hands-on training in bricklaying, carpentry, plumbing and electrics. With no more than 25 people on each course and with many major contributors to the magazine, including the writer of this book, giving the lectures, it is an undoubted opportunity to gain essential knowledge. You can get further information by telephoning 01905 619031 or by looking at the magazine's website.

Constructive Individuals (tel. 0207 515 9299 www.constructiveindividuals.com) run weekend courses in self-build project management, looking at the building process with particular reference to building with subcontractors. From time to time they also run three-week accommodation courses where up to 20 students can gain hands-on experience of building a house from empty foundations to a weathertight and carcassed shell, including making and erecting the timber frame on site and first and second-fix plumbing and electrics.

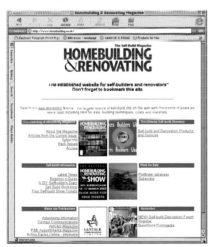

Above: The Internet is playing an increasing role in self-build as in every other aspect of our lives.

Right: Self-build companies such as 'Buildstore' are predominantly web-based.

1. MONEY MATTERS

There are some who will wonder at the first substantive chapter being about finance, when for most people thinking about self-building the availability of land seems the most important first hurdle. Well, important as that may be, finance is where it all starts, and setting the budget, working out how much you can pay for the land and just how much the project as a whole is going to cost is where it should start. In some cases, if the budgets do not work out, it can also be where the whole thing finishes or, at the very least, is put on the back burner until the time and the finances are right and available.

Building for yourself is about spending money. It's also about spending huge amounts of money compared with the average person's normal expenditure. It's about spending that money so that you get exactly what you want and it's also about spending it so effectively that you end up with a bigger or better house than the money would buy on the open market. How you manage this money is as important as the management of the whole of the building work, and far more hazardous. The Building Inspector, the warranty inspector, your architect – all and any of these will be concerned to see that nothing untoward happens with the construction but far fewer checks are in place to prevent a financial incompetent from wilfully steering their self-build ship onto the rocks. Having said that, most of the reputable companies working within the self-build market will ask the relevant questions at an early stage and, as long as they're told the truth, will try to steer you in the right direction. This has every bit as much to do with their interests, of course, as it has with yours, as they will want to be assured that they are going to get paid. No self-build venture can be entirely risk-free but if you follow the paths laid down in this book and use and listen to common sense and professional advice, rather than ill-informed pub talk, you are most unlikely to have any major problems. It is a fact that self-build disaster stories are few and far between.

Setting the initial budget

At the risk of being patronising, the total budget for any self-build is made up from the cash that you have available to put into the project, plus any equity you have in your existing property, should you decide to sell, and the amount you are able or prepared to borrow.

However, investing all that you can possibly afford in any particular project might not always be the right thing to do. Obviously, you'll want to get the best and the most out of your self-build but you do need to think carefully about what you build. Let's suppose that the most any property could possibly sell for in your area is around £150,000. If self-builder 'A' builds a 145 square-metre house with a 36 square-metre garage, all of which is valued at that £150,000, but then self-builder 'B' comes along and builds a house 45 square metres bigger with a triple garage, he might be very disappointed that although he's spent 30% more than Mr 'A', his increased value might not be greater than 3%!

In similar vein, if a plot comes up in a street full of large 5-bedroom Victorian houses, it might not make sense to contemplate building a small 2-bedroom bungalow. Not only would it look lost and incongruous, but you would never be achieving the potential of the plot, which, in any case, would almost certainly have been indicated by its high price in the first place.

That is, unless that's what you planned for in the first place – that this is your decision and to hell with the values! After all, that's what self-building is all about – informed choice.

In reality, much of this can be academic, as nowadays the planners will be very concerned to see that what you're proposing fits in, in proper planning terms. But there are times when it breaks down and the controls are a little lax. You can see this clearly on the self-build sites where councils like Chesterfield sold off single self-build plots in the late seventies. Self-builders, for all the right emotional reasons, tried to get as much as they could into their plots and, in many cases, built right up to both boundaries. As a result, looking along the street it's difficult to see where one house ends and another begins, even though they're all detached.

Well, that's the warning against over- or under-spending on your project, but for most people, having understood the principle behind that warning, reality will mean that they are having to juggle the total amounts that they can afford between the various component parts of their new home, such as land cost, building costs, fees of various sorts and the one which is often forgotten, the costs relating to the borrowing of money.

So, what proportion should be allocated to each of these categories? The land cost is likely to be the least movable object. Finding a plot is the first hurdle in the race and it's the one at which most self-builders fall, which is why the next chapters are devoted to its finding and acquisition. In this book it would not make sense to state definitive figures on land costs because they can vary hugely from area to area, and I obviously hope to cover the whole of the United Kingdom. In the examples that follow, I have had to make assumptions on land cost. To check their appropriateness to your circumstances or area, look through the back pages of the major magazines catering for the self-build market such as *Homebuilding & Renovating* and *Build It*, where plots are often advertised.

More detailed discussion of the effects of design and choices of external materials on building costs will be made in Chapter 5 but when setting the initial budget, it is necessary to make some fairly basic

TYPICAL AREAS OF HOUSES AND BUNGALOWS

Up to 65 sq. metres
Holiday chalets, tiny 1- or 2-bedroom bungalows. Granny annexes.

65–75 sq. metres
Very small 2- and 3-bedroom semi-detached houses. Small 2-bedroom bungalows.

75–85 sq. metres
Small 3-bedroom bungalows with integral lounge/dining-room.

90–100 sq. metres
Large older semi-detached houses. Pokey 4-bedroom modern estate houses. 4-bedroom bungalows with very small bedrooms. 3-bedroom bungalows with separate dining-room. Luxury 2-bedrom bungalows.

Around 120 sq. metres
Many modern 4-bedroom estate houses. Detached houses and bungalows with the possibility of a small study, a utility room and/or a second bathroom.

Around 150 sq. metres
Comfortable 4-bedroom family houses or bungalows, often with en-suite facilities to master bedrooms, studies or family rooms and a utility room.

Around 185 sq. metres
Large 4- and perhaps 5-bedroom houses and bungalows with the possibility of en-suite facilities to more than one bedroom and with a separate family room.

All of these sizes exclude garaging accommodation, which can have the effect of adding 30–40 sq. metres.

assumptions. There are of course always going to be regional variations in building costs, particularly in hot spots such as Greater London, but at this stage, when all you're really trying to do is assess the potential of any project in relation to your budget, it is necessary to generalise in order to demonstrate the principle. For up-to-date information on costs, you could do no better than to follow the 'Average Build Costs Guide', published monthly in *Homebuilding & Renovating* magazine.

For the purposes of this exercise, therefore, let's assume average figures of £550 per square metre if you're going to be building with subcontractors, plus a fair amount of your own DIY, or £580 per square metre if you're going to be managing subcontractors with little or no physical input of your own. If you're going to be using a builder for the whole job then you should budget around £680 per square metre but if you're prepared to consider using a builder only as far as the weathertight shell and then managing subcontractors for the finishing trades, then this figure could be reduced to about £620 per square metre. These assume a fairly standard design with a fairly ordinary choice of external materials but, as I've said before, you've got to start somewhere and we'll build up on the possible variations as we go through these sections.

Next, you've got to make some assumptions on the probable, or hoped-for, size of your new home and here you can use the information in the box on page 17 or you can study books of plans, such as *The Home Plans Book* (Ebury Press) by the same authors, where over 330 designs are featured by reference to size.

Supposing you're interested in a house of 140 square metres. If you elect to build this with subcontractors then your rounded-up guideline budget cost is £81,500 and if you decide that you want to get it built by a single builder then that will rise to £95,500. To keep things simple, let's also assume that you've decided that you can undertake this project using subcontract labour.

Let's also assume that your budget is £150,000. You've added up the money that you think you'll have left when your house is sold. You've added up the savings that you and your spouse have decided to invest in your new home and you've added up the amount of the mortgage the two of you expect to receive in order to come up with this figure. The house you're hoping to build of 140 square metres at £580 per square metre, is going to cost you roughly £81,500 and if that's deducted from the total budget, you're left with £68,500 to go out and spend on the land. Off you go on what is probably the biggest shopping trip of a lifetime and, lo and behold, the only plots you can find are on the market at £75,000. Something's got to give. If the vendor of the land won't come down in price then you've got to trim your ideas on the size of your new house and, if we work the figures backwards, that means that you've only got £75,000 to spend on the actual construction. If we divide that figure by the £580 per square metre, that means that your new home has got to be around 129 square metres instead of the 140 you were hoping for.

In similar vein, let's assume that on your next shopping trip you have better luck when you find a plot for sale at £65,000. However, on further investigation you find out that, whilst it's a lovely plot it was once the site of the village pond and that the foundations will have to be piled at an extra cost of roughly £7,000. Again we work the figures backwards and end up with a total left for building of £78,000. Now that's better than with the more expensive plot but it still means that you've got to trim your sails and think in terms of a house of 134 square metres.

All of this assumes that there are only two financial elements in a self-build project: the land and the building costs. But we all know that there is a further part to the equation that goes to making up the eventual value of your new home: the equity that any developer of property might hope to gain. In days gone by, when plots were more plentiful, there was a simple rule, often quoted and still relevant in parts,

INITIAL BUDGET

Total funds available	£150,000
Land cost	£75,000
Available for building	£75,000

Anticipated costs: £580 per sq. metre
Max size of home: 129 sq. metres

AMENDED BUDGET

Total funds available	£150,000
Land cost	£65,000
Additional ground work costs	£7,000
Available for building	£78,000

Anticipated costs: £580 per sq. metre
Max size of new home: 134 sq. metres

Above: New build can capture the timeless elegance of traditional design with all of the comforts of modern living. (Potton Ltd)

called the third, third, third rule. This supposed that the plot price would form roughly one third of the value of the eventual house with the build costs accounting for another third and finally the increase in equity or profit making up the last third. It was an ideal and even in the best of times it was only a starting point with regional variations in build costs and things like scarcity of plots in particular areas distorting it, but if you refer to the figures above, it still holds some relevance.

That the formula remains at all useful is by very careful reference to its extremes of distortion and their relevance to your chosen area. In parts of the realm where land is readily available, and property prices are relatively low, the principle reduces the average plot price to something like a quarter of the market value

of the finished property. In areas that enjoy high retail values with low plot availability, the plot price can equal or exceed half the eventual value.

Those in the industry are used to doing these calculations in their head and in many cases can do so without consciously analysing or questioning their assumptions, but for the lay person coming to the self-build table it's necessary to go through the essential stages of valuation carefully. Starting off with the piece of land, imagine (possibly but not necessarily by reference to the planning permission) the finished dwelling on it and then investigate the market value for such a property in the region and in similar locations.

That might seem difficult but it's the type of calculation that most homeowners repeatedly make in the comfort of their own homes or at dinner parties. If it's one that you don't feel capable of making, then spend time looking in the windows of estate agents for similar properties and making a note of their values. Alternatively, HM Land Registry give details of recent

The self-builder's savings – a comparison with developers' costs

Developers' costs

1. Land cost
2. Interest on land cost over a long period
3. Design and planning fees
4. Site labour costs

5. Labour overheads – cost of labour between profitable jobs, in periods of bad weather, holidays. Training Board levy, N.I. etc.
6. Materials at trade prices
7. Up to 10% of materials damaged/wasted/stolen on site
8. Office overheads
9. Staff costs and staff overheads
10. Expensive general contractor's insurance, NHBC warranties, Trade Association Levies
11. Sales costs
12. Provision for bad debts
13. Interest on building finance assuming worst sales situation
14. Corporation Tax or other revenue involvement
15. Return required on capital

Self-builders' costs

1. Land cost
2. Interest on land cost over a very short period
3. Design and planning fees
4. Site labour costs, which may be as low as the developers' or could be at premium rates
5. No labour overheads

6. Materials probably at trade prices
7. No site losses

8. No office overheads
9. No staff
10. Cheap simple site insurance and the premiums for your chosen warranty scheme
11. Nil
12. Nil
13. Interest on building finance kept to a minimum
14. Nil
15. Nil

property transactions and average prices of the various differing types of house in each postal area.

You'll then need to calculate the average size of these similar properties and relate that to what you're intending to build or what you realistically believe your potential plot could support. Using the average building costs published monthly in *Homebuilding & Renovating* magazine you can then work out the probable build costs and by deducting that figure from the assumed market value you get to the maximum amount that can be allocated to the land purchase. Of course that doesn't allow any gain in equity and if that were to be the norm in any area then there would be no incentive for any builders or developers to remain in business. So this is where the self-builder has to start to make realistic assumptions.

A developer might hope to make around 30%

profit but even they have to take a long-term view and there are times when they will be prepared to take less. Realistically, self-builders are probably more interested in getting what they want for the money they have rather than making an immediate profit and this is where they should have the edge on the developer. In certain areas and in certain situations they could even decide to spend right up to the finished value of the property or trust to inflation to make sure that they stay on the right side of the cost/value equation.

Does this all seem complicated? Well, it probably is at first but it is absolutely essential that anyone buying a building plot learns how to juggle the figures like this and, although the figures might change, the principles remain. Really first-class and constantly updated information is always available in the national monthly self-build magazines, not just with the tables they publish but in their Case Histories which contain a load of information on costs that you can use to arrive at your budget projections. Information of this sort is invaluable, as is information gained at first hand from other self-builders who are well down the road on their projects and are probably more than happy to share their experiences with a like-minded individual and his family. Bear in mind that these costs only reflect that one job and that you need to take extraneous costs and peculiar circumstances into account but bear in mind also that it all adds up to your essential store of information.

Obviously, the figures given in the tables are averages. In Greater London, costs could go as high, and maybe even exceed £1,100 per square metre for really high-quality houses built with a top-notch builder, whereas in the more far-flung corners of the realm, a self-builder putting in a large degree of his own labour could hope to achieve figures as low as £335 per square metre. Peculiar circumstances apart, however, building costs remain remarkably consistent, irrespective of whether it's a house or a bungalow. For either very small dwellings or extremely large ones the figures won't work at all. For properties within the normal ranges, however, the economics of scale that are undoubtedly gained by the larger dwellings are then matched by a corresponding increase brought about by the natural use of more expensive fittings and fixtures.

How much can you borrow and where from?

First of all, not all those who build an individual home need a mortgage and a great many people are able to finance their project from cash resources or the proceeds of the sale of their existing homes. For those whose equity in their current home is sufficient to cover the costs of their project, essentially what they need is short- rather than long-term finance and this is some-

thing that high-street banks are usually far better at providing than building societies. In fact banks are perhaps the unsung heroes of the self-build market, for whilst they have never entered it with the publicity blazes of various building societies down the years, they have quietly worked away at providing all sorts of financial assistance to those creating their own home.

Banks, of course, look at loan-to-income ratios and are concerned at the exposure of cost to value. But in general they are able to look at the bigger picture; to consider the application and the applicant in the round and base their decisions on proven track record or demonstrated ability.

Average Build Costs

In 2000-2001 national average costs for average-sized houses and bungalows, built on single sites by individual self-builders, on normal strip foundations, including fittings and fixtures appropriate to the size of dwelling, central heating, double glazing, connections to drains or septic tank, short length of drive and no landscaping were:

When built by a well established NHBC builder, working from his offices, following a formal invitation to tender and a formal contract: £680 per square metre and upwards.

When built by a reputable small builder, NHBC registered, working from home, usually a tradesman himself, following an informal approach and contract established by offer and acceptance: £640–£720 per square metre.

When built by a reliable small builder to erect the shell with subcontractors on a supply and fix basis finishing off the building: £565–£650 per square metre.

When built on a direct labour basis by a private individual using subcontract labour without providing any of the labour himself: £550–£610 per square metre.

When built on a direct labour basis by a private individual using subcontract labour plus a reasonable amount of DIY: £510–£580 per square metre.

N.B. The area of a building is arrived at by measurement of the internal dimensions of the building on each habitable floor.

Building societies, on the other hand, have dipped in and out of the self-build market like reluctant partygoers, never sure of whether to complain about the noise or go in and join the fun. In the decades tracking the rise in popularity and the emergence of modern-day self-building and renovating, the names that have come and gone are legion and those with longer memories cannot perhaps resist a wry smile when they see mainstream building societies advertising self-build mortgages and experience on the television. In many ways the bad name that self-build finance gained in previous decades was due to the lack of understanding and a shortfall in basic knowledge by the societies that entered this market at half cock. It took some time for them to appreciate that the land had a value all of its own without the building and that, once finished, the cost to value, more often than not, demonstrated a healthy equity gain.

Prior to 1987, banks and building societies normally required anyone building for themselves to find their own money to buy the site, following which they would lend the money for a house to be built on it, with the land itself as the security. When the house was built this loan was repaid by taking out a mortgage in the usual way. It was very common for a bank to lend the building finance, and for a building society to issue the mortgage on the finished property, with the two of them hopefully working closely together. However, this didn't always happen and the stools that many fell between were the insistences of both lenders that they should each have first charge on the land. This meant that a very high proportion of borrowers had to sell their existing house in order to finance the site purchase and building costs.

In 1987, when it seemed that the rise in property values would go on for ever, the National & Provincial Building Society launched a '100% finance' scheme for self-builders who had an existing home. This involved transferring their current mortgage to the National & Provincial, who after a careful assessment of their proposals, would lend them a further sum to cover the entire cost of both buying the site and building a home on it. The interest on this further loan was rolled up with the capital, so that no additional repayments were required until the new house was occupied, the old house was sold, and the special self-

builder's mortgage could be converted to a standard mortgage. This scheme attracted a four-figure total of borrowers in a very short while, and everything went well until the housing market collapsed in 1989, when borrowers who had completed their new homes found that they could not sell their old properties.

This caused serious problems for both the society and its borrowers and the situation attracted widespread publicity. The National & Provincial withdrew its scheme, to the disappointment and near despair of the large number of people who were proposing to take advantage of it to finance their new homes. Other building societies, and in particular the Birmingham Midshires, had similar schemes up and running at the time and they too pulled out, although they were not as heavily committed and avoided large losses. Self-

Above: Swedish building technology married to Norfolk design to create a home that is a compliment to the landscape. (Scandia-Hus Ltd)

Left: Self-build finance has become very much more user friendly.

build lending began to curry bad favour with financial institutions and the situation went from bad to worse as self-build group after self-build group failed in the wake of the housing market crash, leaving even more lenders with serious bad debts.

The memory of this lingers on and since that time it has been nigh on impossible to borrow 100% of the eventual value of any completed self-built home from a mainstream financial institution. However, there are alarming signs that the consistent rise in property values could trigger the emergence of similar schemes. Undoubtedly this would be welcomed and for a short while it could even assist a great many people to build their own homes successfully. But it would never last and the chances are that history would repeat itself.

Those responsible building societies that now promote themselves within the self-build movement offer many packages, but in general they boil down to the requirement that the borrower should sell their existing house and repay the old mortgage, following which the building society will lend a proportion of the cost of the land, plus a further proportion of the building finance required, up to a maximum of 95% of completed value. They get around the problem of seeming to require potential customers to sell up and move into temporary accommodation by saying that they have no objection to the provision of a self-build mortgage for the new house in tandem with the mortgage on the existing house, so long as the potential borrowers can demonstrate their ability to service both mortgages.

In practice, this means that only the seriously rich, those with an extremely small existing mortgage or those with an enormous income relative to their borrowing requirement can benefit, as the way it works is to deduct from the applicant's income the cost of the existing mortgage and then to treat the remainder as the total gross income. Now, all of this may seem unfair at first glance, but remember, it wasn't just the building societies who got their fingers

burnt when everything changed so very quickly in 1988/89, it was ordinary people, and all of these new precautions are there to prevent you coming a cropper just as much as they are to protect the financial institutions.

The essential difference between a self-build mortgage and any other mortgage is the existence and distribution of stage payments. Apart from that, the remaining criteria are the same in that your borrowing capability is based on an income multiplier, governed by a maximum ratio of loan to eventual value (usually 95%).

The typical income multipliers are $2\frac{1}{2}$ times a joint income or 3 times a higher income plus 1 times a lower income. For sole earners the figures vary between 3 and 4 times income.

As I've said, the principal difference between a self-build mortgage and any other normal mortgage is not in the way they end up, but in the mechanics available for stage payments. If stage payments are not available, or are so limited and back-pedalled in nature as to make them all but useless for the build process, then this is not a self-build mortgage and you should perhaps move on to another lender.

Most of the building-society lenders in the self-build market at the time of writing are prepared to advance monies against the land purchase of between 75% and 85%. This means that if you already own the land, they will give that percentage of the valuation in order to get started on the build. On the other hand, if you're buying the land, you will need to demonstrate that you have the necessary deposit and the building society will then release the remaining monies to coincide with the purchase of the land.

Building societies normally offer stage payments for the construction in four or five stages. In most cases these are issued in arrears and they won't normally release monies until the relevant stage has been reached. This is where the problems can occur for those on a tight budget, for the lenders will then require that the building is inspected, usually by a surveyor appointed by them, and that the certificate is received before any funds are actually authorised for release. Even if they agree to accept the Stage Completion Certificates given by the warranty company or the Architect's Progress Certificates, this

BUDGET FOR SINGLE EARNER

Cash savings	£5,000
Equity in existing home	£40,000
Income £30,000 p.a. x 3 =	£90,000
Total budget	£135,000

BUDGET FOR DOUBLE EARNERS

Cash savings	£5,000
Equity in existing home	£40,000
Joint income £50,000 x 2 $\frac{1}{2}$	£125,000
Total budget	£170,000

can take an inordinately long time which can seem even longer if you're being hassled every day for money by a large bricklayer or you have an intransigent package-deal company which will not release materials until they have the money in their hands. However hard you try to jump the gun and prearrange the surveyor's visit this never seems to go to plan and the 'stop/start' that this creates is often a feature of those self-builds where stage payments are being used up to the hilt and there isn't a cushion of money to carry things forward. Try to make sure that your lender knows just how critical the timing of the receipt of monies is to you and, above all, make your builders and subcontractors aware of your particular problems before they crop up rather than afterwards; you'd be surprised just how helpful a tradesman can be if he knows that the money is going to be there and, on top of that, he knows that its getting there is reliant on his reaching a stage in the construction of the building.

Many of the package-deal companies and, in particular, those where there is a bespoke or manufacturing element, require their monies up front or in stages in advance of any deliveries. In addition, stage payments are often front-loaded to the point where the company can take their margin and leave a 'cost to complete' in their books. None of this needs to cause too much of a problem just as long as you've allowed for it all in your cashflow. If you're making large payments in advance of deliveries, make sure that either the payments are made into a client's deposit or that you have established the existence of an insurance-backed bond, of which more later. Certain of the larger and more reputable companies have long recognised that the self builder does, sometimes, need a bit of help over the financial hurdles and they have recognised, too, that it's a question of *when* the monies will arrive rather than *if*. These companies have various schemes on offer, which can help you and, at the same time, guarantee their payment when the money finally comes through.

All of which welcomed the arrival of the Accelerator mortgage schemes introduced by Buildstore Ltd. whereby, for a fee that whilst significant is nevertheless a tiny percentage in the scale of most self-build budgets, the stage payments are given in advance. This scheme, operated through several building societies, has come to the aid of many a self-builder, enabling those with limited funds of their own to self-build and easing the cash flow of others. It has also made a few of the other building societies operating within the self-build market recognise the need for advance payments and include them in their product. An up-to-date schedule of which lenders are offering what is published monthly in *Homebuilding & Renovating* magazine.

Of course, this type of loan has always been available for those using banks where a project is financed through an arranged overdraft facility. But there is no doubt that the Accelerator enables people to self-build who don't perhaps have the clout and the track record with a bank.

Two cautions. First of all, do not be tempted to borrow further from any other source without disclosing it to the principal lender. Secondly, do not be tempted to exaggerate the cost of the land so as to gain an advantage. In other words, if you are buying a plot for £60,000, do not tell the lender it is costing £80,000 in the hope that you will get a 75% loan, which will be equal to the whole of the real cost. This is sometimes advocated by those who should know better or who will even offer to arrange it for you. It is dishonest, and a recipe for potential disaster.

How to approach a lender

Despite all the leaflets outlining just what a building society or other lender is able to offer you and just how their product is tailored to the needs of the self-builders, when you sit in front of a manager, you are being assessed as to whether you are capable of doing all you say you are planning to do. Of course they'll look at your finances, your borrowing capacity and any track record. But more than that, they'll be weighing up whether you can actually pull this thing off; something which may be beyond their own capabilities and full understanding.

This lack of understanding can sometimes have a profound effect on just how they treat your enquiry. Despite strenuous efforts by head offices, news of the benefits of self-building does not always seem to filter down to branch level. Managers earn their reputation head office by arranging mortgages that are simple, straightforward, and generate no problems of any sort. Normally these are ordinary mortgages on ordinary homes bought on the open market. A proposal linked to a house which is yet to be built, and which may be being built on what they regard as a DIY basis is often not in the category that they are used to handling. You have to persuade them that your proposals carry no risk of any sort, and that you are very well able to handle everything in a completely risk-free way. So, how do you do this?

Treat your application in just the same way as you would if you were applying for a job. Set out your CV or project plan clearly and concisely, detailing all of the cost elements that we have discussed above. Allow for contingencies. Back up any cost assertions with additional information and/or brochures. Make sure that you have detailed the warranty arrangements you will be taking out, that you have listed the costs of site insurances and that you have allowed, within your budget, for the finance costs that you will be experiencing. That last one is bound to impress them, by the way.

Above: The introduction of the accelerator mortgage scheme has enabled those with modest equity to self-build successfully.

If you know that you will only be able to borrow 75% of the project cost, explain where the other 25% is coming from. Produce a tentative programme for the work, and once more, if you need to, back this up with additional information, maybe in the form of magazine articles or copies of this book with stories of others who have done what you're setting out to do.

Types of mortgage

Another issue here is the choice that has to be made between endowment and repayment mortgages, the early redemption arrangements and of course the interest rates. The pros and cons are always changing, and magazines such as *What Mortgage?* provide useful up-to-date information.

A repayment mortgage is one where the interest and principle are paid off over the period of the loan, leading to a demonstrable reduction in the outstanding balance on each annual statement. Most are issued as variable-rate mortgages where the rate rises and falls as the economic cycle progresses. In times of low or medium interest rates this is usually favourable, but in times of high interest rates, considerable hardship can be caused. As a result, the societies introduced various fixed-rate schemes. In one you pay interest at an agreed rate for a fixed period of usually between two and five years and at the end of this period the rate reverts to the current variable rate. Capped-rate mortgages offer a fixed rate but, if the variable rate falls below a certain level, allows your payments to be reduced accordingly. With discounted rates you pay a lesser amount for the first few years but then your mortgage converts to a higher rate, which might be useful for those starting off with a lower income in the expectation of a greater one. However, this type of mortgage can store up trouble for those whose outgoings are rising but whose income remains static.

With an interest-only mortgage, you do not pay back any of the capital until the end of the loan period and instead, you pay interest only at a variable rate, plus fixed premiums into an investment option that pays off the principal at the end of the term. The most usual form off interest-only mortgage is the endowment mortgage where an endowment insurance policy is taken out with automatic life insurance to clear the debt in the event of prior death. The advantage of this type of mortgage is that it is more portable but the disadvantages have been demonstrated in recent years by the failure of some of the endowment policy options to generate sufficient funds to clear the mortgage.

Pension mortgages link the payments to a pension plan that, at the end of the term, pays off the principle and leaves sufficient funds for a subsequent pension. The advantages are that tax relief is given on the basis of the payments being part of a pension plan but the disadvantages are that, once the mortgage is repaid, there may be an insufficient capital amount to provide an adequate pension income. The advice must be to examine all of the options available at the time of taking out the mortgage and to discuss the merits with an accountant who will be able to relate each product to your specific or expected circumstances.

Family money and Inheritance Tax

Wealthy families with inherited money have their own attitude to it. They tend to consider their funds as family assets, and use trusts and other devices to ensure that it passes smoothly down the generations with the minimum interference from Inheritance Tax. Often this is their favourite topic of conversation, and very boring it can be, too! In contrast, those whose modest capital has always been kept in the building society until they inherited a couple of houses with telephone number values, tend to keep their affairs very much to themselves. They may refuse to face up to the fact that they cannot take it with them and that the taxman is lurking.

Inheritance Tax is often described as a voluntary tax, because if most people make appropriate arrangements at the right time, nothing at all needs to be paid. However, this involves giving money away in one form or another, and just try discussing this with Aunt Lucy who, after a lifetime of being careful with money, is now worth a cool £500,000. If she is able to take a realistic view of things, she should be able to continue to enjoy her present standard of living indefinitely and ensure that her favourite niece and nephew use her money for a new house so as to avoid Inheritance Tax. This all depends on her seeing her capital as a family

Above: These surprisingly readable leaflets are available from your local tax office.

asset. If she does, there are various ways of going about it. If very large sums are involved, it is appropriate to make specialist arrangements, which will cost money but can be cheap at the price. Finding the right professionals to handle this may not be easy, since they should be totally independent and not people who are wanting to sell you some sort of financial service. A large firm of accountants is probably best.

The simple way of obtaining help with the cost of your new home from, say, an elderly relative, is for them just to give you the money that they intend you to have some day. Gifts given during the lifetime of a person are known as Potentially Exempt Transfers (PETs) and if the donor lives for a total of seven years following the gift, there is no IHT liability. However, if a donor dies before the seven-year cut-off point, tax will become payable on the total value of the estate on death, including gifts made within the seven-year period prior to death, for anything above the threshold, currently £250,000.

If tax is payable on gifts made within the seven-year period because they exceed the threshold, they may be subject to what is known as 'Taper relief'. This has the effect of reducing the tax payable on a sliding scale for gifts made between three and seven years prior to the donor's death. Additionally, gifts made by an individual, so long as they do not exceed £3,000 in any one year, are exempt, although if Aunt Lucy didn't give away anything in the year before, she can backdate her gift and give you £6,000. In addition, outright gifts, which can be classed as normal expenditure 'out of income', are also allowable, as are some gifts made on the occasion of a marriage. Here, parents can each give a further £5,000, grandparents £2,500 and anybody else can give up to £1,000, all of which could make a very useful contribution to anybody's budget for a new home. These figures haven't changed for donkey's years but they are a movable feast and could come to the attention of the Chancellor at any time.

Inheritance Tax liability usually comes into effect and is payable only upon death, although with certain discretionary trusts, the liability can be immediate. However, creeping inflation has meant that many more people are now at risk of being drawn into its net. Transfers between husband and wife are exempt, so if one partner dies and their principal asset, usually their home, is worth more than the £500,000 I've mentioned, there is still no Inheritance Tax liability. However, long-term partnerships would not enjoy this exemption and therefore a couple living and owning a home together as joint tenants or indeed as tenants in common where they had left their share of the home to each other, could attract a tax liability upon the death of one of them for amounts or property in excess of the £250,000 threshold.

Even with a married couple, there is the distinct possibility that upon the death of a surviving spouse, a tax liability could occur. Although when the first one dies, the transfer between husband and wife is exempt, when the second one dies, if the value of the home exceeds the threshold, then tax is payable. That is unless during the lifetime of the first one to die, they had had the foresight to use up their individual threshold allowances by giving their part of the home to someone else, such as a child. If the amount exceeds the threshold and they die within the seven years, there may still be a liability, although there is taper relief available that reduces the rate at which the tax is charged for anyone dying after the third year.

One way of giving money that might appeal to an elderly person who has capital invested to earn interest, is for them to give you a mortgage. Anyone can provide a private mortgage, not just a bank or building society. It must, however, be clearly evidenced in writing, signed by all the parties and registered as a charge on the land. Any solicitor should be able to arrange this.

This really is a most useful approach. Suppose Aunt Lucy has £30,000 invested, currently earning her interest on which she pays tax. If she uses it to give you a £30,000 mortgage at 1% under the current mortgage rate she will get a better return (on which she will still pay tax), you will have a cheap mortgage, from an understanding source, and the money stays in the family. Aunt Lucy's will may have to be rewritten to avoid complications in the future, but this is not a difficult undertaking. If both parties are interested in Aunt Lucy living in a granny flat in the new home, a whole new range of possibilities is opened up that I shall discuss later.

Capital Gains Tax

Many self-builders achieve a 20% cost value differential by building their own home, and some do even better. Providing that the new property is your principal private residence, there is normally no tax to pay on any gain in equity. Private Residence Relief says that, 'any gain from the disposal of your home will be fully exempt, if your disposal was of some or all of a house and its grounds, which has been your principal private residence throughout the period you have owned it (ignoring the last three years of ownership), and which in total, did not exceed half a hectare' (one and a quarter acres). Relief is not available if all or part of your home has been let or used for business but that is not meant to catch out those who work from home or have a home office, such as company representatives.

There is no set time limit for having to live in the new home in order for it to qualify as your principal private residence, although the figure of 12 months is often bandied about; probably because it is this figure that appears in the legislation in regard to certain concessions. Normally, however, so long as you live in the property for at least one year, nobody will ask any awkward questions, although if you make a habit of self-building time and time again, the taxman could deem that you were trading and tax you accordingly. On the other hand, if there is a genuine need for you to move within the normally recognised 12 months, and if you didn't make a habit of it, the taxman is likely to use his discretion.

Even if you have difficulty in selling your old home once the new one is built, there is a concession available whereby both properties can be considered as exempt for CGT purposes for up to 12 months, with the taxman having discretion to extend this period for another 12 months, to a maximum of two years, so long as good reason is demonstrated. There is no facility to extend this concession period beyond the two years. If this situation is likely to occur, then it is perhaps better to retain the old house as your principal private residence until such time as it is sold, and once that's happened, the exemption will transfer to your new house. Be aware though, that any gain made on the new house, beyond the concession period and the date when the house becomes your principal private residence, could be taxable, subject to my comments below.

This concession also applies to the situation where an individual buys land on which they have a house built for use as their main residence or where an individual purchases an existing property and, before using it as their principal private residence, arranges for alterations or conversions before taking steps to dispose of their existing principal private residence. In these cases, for the purposes of exemption from Capital Gains Tax, a period of 12 months' grace is again allowed, extendable by another 12 months at the discretion of the taxman, for events that are outside the individual's control, such as the need to go to appeal. Once again there is no discretion to extend this period beyond the two years.

This is important and it could affect a great many people who buy land and, for one reason or another, take some time to get around to building on it. Let's say a couple own a paddock in a nearby village that they do nothing with for several years, and then they decide to try for planning permission. They are successful and they build themselves a new house on it and move in. From that moment, the new house becomes their principal private residence. But when

they sell it, under the concession ruling, they are liable for CGT on any gain made before the property became their main home, including the uplift in value due to the granting of planning permission.

I can recall many cases where this two-year concession has been breached for one reason or another. In truth though, I don't know of anybody who has fallen foul of this tax in this way upon subsequently selling their home. Perhaps that's because the only mechanism I can find for this all coming to light is if the seller of a house ticks the answer 'Yes' on their Tax Return Form in relation to the question, 'If you have disposed of your only or main residence, do you need the Capital Gains pages?'

It is not unusual for properties to come onto the market in tandem with a plot, formed from part of the garden. If you decide to sell off your old home and live in the existing property until such time as your new home is ready to occupy, then, so long as you are moving from one home to another in the course of the project, in normal circumstances no Capital Gains Tax should be payable. However, if you do decide to make alternative arrangements, then consideration has to be given as to how you dispose of the unwanted property and your possible involvement with CGT. If you decide to do it up and sell it off, then technically, you could be liable for capital gains on any increase in value, although you would be able to offset the costs of any refurbishment, together with the costs involved in the separation of the two properties. If you decide to let out the house, then when you eventually sell it there could also be a CGT liability and, in addition, you will be liable for Income Tax on the rental received.

But what of the situation when you own the land? If you apply for planning permission on part of your garden and then, assuming you are successful, you sell it off as a plot, then, so long as it was part of your main home and the whole was not larger than half a hectare, there will normally be no liability for CGT. If you retain the plot for yourself, build on it and move into the new home, there will, just as in the example above, not normally be a tax liability.

But, if you decide to build the new house and then sell it off, in an attempt to make the developer's profit as well as the increase in value of the land, you could be in trouble. The taxman might rule that you

Above: A solidly dependable house where the styling borrows from the period between the wars. (Custom Homes Ltd)

are trading and it is not GCT that you will be liable for, but Income Tax. Furthermore, you will be deemed to have commenced trading at the time of the application for planning permission. The land at its pre-planning value will be your capital introduction to the project and the tax you pay will include not only the normal developer's profit, but the uplift in value of the land. As if that's not bad enough, by switching to Income rather than Capital Gains Tax, the annual exemptions will not be available and you'll probably already have used up your normal allowances.

Capital gains and self-building is a very tricky area. There are some self-builders who go on to build again and again, each time living in the latest home for a year while they are building the next one. The tax inspector will only tolerate this for a limited period, after which he will claim that you are in business as a developer and will ask for a tax return to be submitted on this basis.

To return to Aunt Lucy and her gifts to you. If instead of giving you money, she gives you land or property, then there is the possibility that she could be liable for Capital Gains Tax on her gift, unless it falls within the rules for private residence relief. If the

donor pays the CGT on a gift, the payment is ignored for IHT valuation purposes. If the recipient pays the tax, it is deducted from the value transferred.

There are annual exemptions, which at the time of writing amount to £7,500 per person per year. There are a number of reliefs, including Roll-over, which allows for gains to be deferred if replacement assets are required, and Retirement relief, which is, however, gradually being phased out and will cease to apply to gains arising after 5th April 2003. Indexation allowance adjusts gains for the effects of inflation up to April 1998 by means of tables setting out multipliers that can be applied to the original acquisition costs to reduce the tax liability. Taper relief was introduced in the Finance Act 1998 to replace Indexation allowance for gains made after 5th April 1998. This reduces the amount of gain chargeable to tax by a sliding scale of percentage points according to the whole number of years the asset has been in your ownership. None of these reliefs are exclusive and one or more may apply to any gain.

Whether any or all of this applies to your circumstances, I cannot tell. The important point, in this book, which is not after all meant to be about tax but about self-building, is that before any transfers or gifts are made, professional advice should be sought as to the most tax-efficient way of going about things. But I suspect that if you're in the happy position of having to worry about these things, you are either cognisant of the dangers or able to provide for the eventualities.

I have decided that it would not be appropriate to include details of personal tax liabilities for the Republic of Ireland (Eire) and I shall confine my references within this book to those taxes that are broadly considered to be 'property' taxes, such as stamp duty and VAT.

Stamp Duty

Buying a property in any part of the United Kingdom, including land at any figure over £60,000, will involve you in the payment of stamp duty at the rate of 1% on the total sum paid and you will find this tacked on to your solicitor's bill as part of the conveyancing cost. The cut-off point is absolutely precise, which means that a plot sold at £60,000 won't attract any tax whilst a plot sold at £60,001 will attract a tax bill of £600.01! – surely a spur for negotiation. Above £250,001, the rate rises to 3% and it rises again at £500,001 to 4%, a figure that may well affect prospective self-builders in the south-east corner of the country. Stamp duty is paid on the land or property purchase only, and whatever you then spend on the house construction or renovation costs does not come into it.

In the Republic of Ireland (Eire), stamp duty is a vastly more complicated affair with differing rates according to whether you are a first time buyer or owner occupier. For first-time buyers, stamp duty is payable at the rates of: 3% from 190,501 to 254,000 Euros; 3.75% from 254,001 to 317,500 Euros; 4% from 317,501 to 381,000 Euros; 7.5% from 381,001 to 635,000 Euros; and 9% for 635,001 Euros and over. The rates for owner occupiers

are: 3% for purchases from 127,001 to 190,500 Euros; 4% from 190,501 to 254,000 Euros; 5% from 254,001 to 317,500 Euros; 6% from 317,501 to 381,000 Euros; 7.5% from 381,001 to 635,000 Euros; and 9% for 635,001 Euros and over.

As if that's not complicated enough, there are differing rates for investors and for non-residential buildings, but happily they needn't concern us here.

Value Added Tax (VAT)

Those who buy a new house from a builder or developer do not then have to pay VAT on top of their purchase price. The VAT authorities in the United Kingdom, in recognition of this fact, have made special arrangements for self-builders, and for those converting an existing structure into a dwelling or renovating former dwellings that have fallen into disuse and remained unoccupied for certain periods.

Most of the arrangements for reclaiming VAT paid out during the construction are set out in VAT Notice 719 which has the simple title, *VAT refunds for 'do-it-yourself' builders and converters*. The regulations themselves are equally simple and straightforward, and all the details are obtainable from local VAT offices,

Above: The leaflets and guidelines for the re-claim of VAT are simple to follow.

where you can get a claim pack containing leaflets and the claim forms that you will require.

The scheme allows self-builders to recover the VAT paid out during the construction of a new dwelling or the conversion of a non-residential building into a dwelling. With new build, a builder or VAT-registered subcontractor must zero-rate their services and the self-builder can recover VAT paid out on material purchases at the end of the project. With conversions, VAT has to be paid out on both the material and labour elements but is then recovered at the end of the job. A concession introduced in the 2001 budget reduces the VAT rate to 5% on all conversions. If, therefore, you are using a builder they must charge VAT at this reduced rate for both labour and materials. If you are building for yourself using subcontract labour, then those registered for VAT purposes must charge 5% which you may then recover at the end of the job together with the VAT that you have paid out at the standard rate on material purchases.

Renovation of existing dwellings does not fall within the scheme and you must therefore calculate that you will have to pay VAT at the standard rate for both labour and material elements and that this is not recoverable. However, any property that has been unoccupied for more than 10 years is considered to be a conversion and the arrangements for the recovery of VAT are as detailed above. If a former dwelling has been unoccupied for more than three years, a reduced VAT rate of 5% will apply to both labour and materials.

Additionally, certain measures have been put in place for the benefit of builders and property developers, reducing the rate of VAT to 5% for certain classes of development. These are the renovation of dwellings that have been unoccupied for three years or more; the conversion of a non-residential property into a dwelling or a number of different dwellings; the conversion of a residential property into a number of dwellings (flats); and the conversion of a dwelling into a care home (or other qualifying 'relevant residential' use); or into a house in multiple occupation (e.g. bedsit accommodation).

Although not covered by the 719 notice, it is possible to avoid paying VAT on alterations to listed buildings so long as they fall within the criteria laid down in a questionnaire included in the *Guide to VAT-free works to your listed home*, available from HM Customs and Excise. This relief is not by way of a refund and is given by allowing the builder to zero-rate his services. You cannot claim relief if you carry out the works yourself or on materials that you purchase for a builder to do the work for you.

The VAT regulations are administered by the Customs and Excise. Their simple procedures and straightforward way of doing things stem from hundreds of years of experience in clearing ships between tides and compare very favourably with the ponderous ways of the Inland Revenue, planning offices, service providers and others that the self-builder will get to know. However, their rules require that you are equally businesslike, and you should learn what is involved at an early stage.

Everything is set out quite clearly in the leaflet and it wouldn't make sense to reproduce everything said in it here, although there are some comments to make. If you are unsure about anything at all then you can and should contact your local VAT office for advice. Incidentally, they won't be listed under VAT if you're looking them up in the telephone directory; you'll find them under Customs and Excise. If you stick to the procedures, submit your claim on time with all your invoices properly listed, and answer any questions promptly, you should receive your refund in well under a month. Typically, it will pay for all the carpets and curtains in the new home.

The points to pay particular attention to are:

- If you use a package company, ask them for an itemised invoice in a form acceptable to the VAT authorities. Ensure that any last-minute extras are included. The package companies know all about doing this, but as it involves a lot of typing, they may wait to be asked.

- New buildings intended for occupation by the self-builder are covered by the scheme but if you are constructing the house with the intention to sell or let it or for some other business reason, you cannot use the scheme. That doesn't affect the self-builder's right to work from home and it doesn't affect any subsequent sale or letting of the property – it is the first use that is the governing factor.

- Extensions to existing dwellings or the creation of additional self-contained accommodation do not qualify.

- Beware paying VAT in error, as it cannot be reclaimed. VAT is payable on materials. It is not payable on labour only or supply and fix contracts for new build (apart from professional services). Nevertheless, I have seen bricklayers add VAT to their bill. They were not even VAT-registered and therefore the money would have gone into their pockets. If it had been paid then the only way of recovering it would have been to ask them nicely for its return.

You cannot reclaim the VAT on some quite unexpected materials and services. Amongst these are: architects' and surveyors' fees as well as any fees for management, consultancy, design and planning. The purchase or hire of tools and equipment (including skip hire and scaffolding) are excluded, as are fuel and transport costs and temporary fencing.

You cannot claim the VAT back on things like carpets, underlay and carpet tiles, white goods such as cookers, hobs, washing machines, refrigerators, dishwashers, etc., even if they are built in. Fitted wardrobes bought in kit form or even the basic materials if you buy them yourself are excluded from any reclaim, as are doorbells and electrically operated doors or gates! Aerials and satellite dishes cannot be included in your VAT claim. There are others but these are perhaps the most surprising.

If VAT is recoverable or there is relief available for your project within the UK, then it is recoverable at the rate paid for any purchase of materials from within the European Union (EU). Most continental builders' merchants display prices inclusive of VAT and it's therefore important that you retain the invoice and that it establishes quite clearly the rate at which VAT has been paid. You must then convert the invoice and the VAT paid to sterling at the exchange rate at the time of acquisition, so you will need to make a careful note of that on the day. Those importing materials from outside the EU will have to pay VAT at the standard rate at the port of entry. If your project is eligible for VAT recovery or relief then you will need

proof of purchase together with proof that the imported materials have been used in your project.

You make one claim only, and it must be made within three months of receiving a certificate that the building is completed. It can include VAT paid in respect of boundary walls, drives, patios, a garage, etc. If you leave this ancillary work until after you move in, then any VAT paid out after the date of your reclaim is not recoverable. Take this into account when drawing up your programme.

When you make your claim, package up all the precious invoices that you have collected so carefully, and either take them to the VAT office and get a receipt for them there and then, or send them off by registered post and make enquiries if you do not receive an acknowledgement within 14 days.

For those building in the Republic of Ireland (Eire), I'm afraid that there is no provision for the recovery of VAT. Materials are split between 'prime' materials such as bricks, blocks timber and tiles, etc., upon which VAT is paid at the rate of $12\frac{1}{2}$%, and second-fix or fitments materials, such as sanitaryware, kitchen units and paint etc., upon which the rate is 20%. Labour is subject to a rate of $12\frac{1}{2}$% with the threshold for VAT registration by the builder set at a turnover of 63,500 Euros. A builder offering a labour and materials or full build contract will add $12\frac{1}{2}$% to his total bill but he can then recover the $7\frac{1}{2}$% extra VAT paid out on some of the materials.

Insurances

For all self-builders, renovators and converters, having the right insurance policy to suit their project and your own personal circumstances is as important as any other element in the creation of their new home. However, unlike car insurance where the law requires that you arrange things before driving, or normal household insurance where the bank or building society will insist on adequate cover, this is something that you will probably have to remember to do for yourself.

It needn't be expensive and indeed to take the analogy of the car insurance it can often prove no more expensive for something that is of infinitely greater value and significantly greater importance.

Every year there is a happy band of people who are glad that they remembered to take out adequate self-build insurance when they wake up to the aftermath of floods or storms or the consequences of a visit from thieves or vandals. And every year there are an unhappy few who either took a chance or completely forgot about insurance who then have to face the consequences not only of their own losses but of those suffered by third parties. You ignore insurances at your peril!

If you're placing a single contract with a builder and you are absolutely confident that they carry all of the relevant and necessary insurances, then there's probably no need for you to take out additional cover but you do need to discuss this with them. Make sure that they're aware that you are relying on them and that they understand that your reliance is an integral part of your contract with them. On the other hand, even if you receive their assurances, can you be absolutely certain that your dependence is well founded and what will happen if your builder simply disappears or goes bust?

Leaving aside this worst-case scenario, it may still be sensible to consider taking out your own self-build insurance policy, even if there is a single contract with a properly insured builder. With things such as kitchen furniture and fittings, there is a distinct possibility that you might choose to arrange their purchase yourself. It's also possible that the suppliers might well undertake the fitting as part of their contract with you. If there's a theft or an accident on site resulting in injury to someone, you might feel that a claim on the main contractor's insurances might be justified and your builder, being a good chap, may agree with you. But the chances are that in those circumstances his insurers might turn around and disclaim all liability if the invoices and contracts were not in his name. Such a situation, which is not at all unusual, would make the saving of the relatively small outlay of an insurance premium seem very much like a false economy and there is a strong argument in favour of 'better safe than sorry'.

Of course, for those using either their own labour or through the management of subcontract labour, a self-build insurance policy is absolutely essential. It does help, however, if one understands the full nature and extent of the different parts of a policy and how they apply to your circumstances.

The first element of a self-build policy is *Public Liability Insurance,* which, most importantly, covers you for any claim made against you by a third party who suffers loss or injury as a result of your self-building operations. If you are tempted to think that this is unlikely to happen to you, consider the fact that in most years nearly a quarter of the claims can fall into this category. If the fence panels that you have just fixed are hurled into your next-door neighbours' motorcar by the wind or if the bricklayers inadvertently spill mortar or paint over the same poor vehicle, then your neighbour will have a legitimate claim against you and you need to know that you are covered. Similarly, this element of the insurance covers you against injury suffered by persons visiting your site or to anyone hurt outside the site as a direct result of your building activities. That includes persons who are trespassing on your site and you might be surprised to learn that if a child or any other person unlawfully enters your site and suffers injury then that does not absolve you from liability. The same rule applies to materials that are removed from your site, with or without authorisation, and cause an accident, injury or damage elsewhere.

Most household insurance policies have some sort of Public Liability cover attached to them covering the householder for accidents that may happen to others within the house or garden but this will almost certainly not apply to any building works, even if the new property is being constructed within the grounds.

The next important element of self-build insurance is known as *Employer's Liability* and there are those who make the mistake of not realising that this is important for the self-builder. Even though you might be persuaded that you are not directly employing someone in the sense that you will be 'stamping their cards' or collecting their PAYE contributions, you are still deemed to have a contract of employment with those whom you engage to carry out work on your site on your behalf. This is important. However many times the subcontractor and others will want to assure you that they are self-employed, when push comes to shove, if they have an accident on your site, they will turn to you for compensation. Self-employed

Above: Insurance is there to cover for many things, including storm damage such as this half-finished home in Ireland has suffered.

Right: Make sure cover is underwritten by a household name. Full details and a prospectus are in the back of this book.

DMS SERVICES LTD
Orchard House, Blyth, Workshop,
Nottinghamshire S81 8HF
Telephone: 0909 591652
Fax: 0909 591031

AXA INSURANCE

SELFBUILDERS INSURANCE POLICY
Prospectus and Proposal Form

subcontractors do not get unemployment or sickness benefits in the same way as others do and if they are laid off because of something that happens on your site then they or their solicitors or advisors may well see you and your insurance policy as a means of financial rescue. Perhaps this is best illustrated by the fact that nearly eight out of every hundred claims involve injuries or accidents on site.

The last element of a self-build policy is known as *Contractors' All-Risk Insurance* or *Contract Works Cover* and this is the element that will cover you for the more usual problems associated with theft and vandalism together with storm, flood or fire damage. Claims against this element of self-build site insurance account for well over half of all those made.

Self-build sites are not a Mecca for thieves and the incidences are perhaps scarcer than on some of the larger, more commercial sites. Nevertheless, the consequences of a visit by thieves or vandals can have dire repercussions for the self-builder out of all proportion to their level of occurrence. The favourites, as far as materials are concerned, are timber, copper piping and insulation as well as the more obvious targets of high-value kitchen units and appliances and sanitaryware. As if the loss and the subsequent disruption to the self-build programme aren't enough, the main problems revolve around the fact that when these items are stolen, little or no thought is given by the thieves to the consequential losses. If they can get the basin off the wall quickly with a hacksaw rather than by turning off the water supply and dismantling the connection then they will and to hell with the damage that the resultant flood causes.

There is very little protection against storm damage, although there are some obvious precautions that any prudent person would take. In the storms of recent memory and over the last decade, the insurance policies held by many self-builders were all that stood between them and ruin in respect of both the rebuilding of property and the damage inflicted on third parties.

The observant amongst you will notice that several times within this book, and in particular when I am urging consultation over insurance matters, I refer to DMS Services Ltd. Whilst I acknowledge the existence and the undoubted worth of many other companies, it is this company with its unrivalled track record to which I am indebted for much of the information I am able to give on this subject. A copy of the DMS AXA proposal form, reprinted at the back of this book, can be used to obtain either cover or quotations. However, I suggest that the best course of action would be to telephone them on 01909 591652 to discuss your individual situation and to obtain the best possible advice on how to proceed. They have 20 years' experience of dealing with self-builders' insurance needs and they are also able to arrange cover and give insurance advice relevant to extensions, renovations and conversions; something that is often difficult to acquire.

Always choose an insurance policy that is under-written by a household name and one that has a proven track record of meeting claims. Make sure too that you are dealing with people who can answer your questions and who understand all about the self-build market and your particular needs.

A quick look at the main insurance cover available from leading players in the market will reveal why it is necessary to evaluate carefully just which policy is the right one for you. Policies should of course provide the three elements of cover: public liability, employers' liability and contract works cover that I have outlined above. Premiums are based on the reinstatement value of the building. That is to say, what it would cost to rebuild if it were destroyed just before moving in. The value of the plot and of the completed home are irrelevant. Most self-build policies also involve a single premium until either the new home is finished or for a fixed period, whichever happens sooner. Most can usually be extended upon payment of an extra premium if necessary. The new AXA policy will offer different periods of cover and bolt on extras if and when required by the self-builder. This should make it possible to tailor your self-build policy to meet your needs and to make any necessary adjustments as your project advances.

Caravans which are used as site huts or as accommodation by the self-builder and their family can usually be added to the self-build policy. You will also need to discuss with your insurance provider whether you will need to take out cover for plant and tools. There is an excess on claims which often means that it is not economic to provide cover for small items, whilst large items of plant are often already covered if they are hired in. Unless you own or intend owning plant to a considerable value, it might be better not to insure it but to take tools or a mobile generator home at night. On the other hand, as I say in Chapter 10, if you are hiring plant then there may well be a more attractive option of paying a surcharge on the hire charge for the short periods that tools and plant are on site. Remember, you are insuring to protect yourself from the major disasters that can occur on site, not to protect your favourite set of socket spanners! In any case a £500 excess might make that notion as impracticable as it is inadvisable.

There are, as I've said, policies to give you different periods of cover, some of which can be extended. Remember that self-building usually takes longer than planned so allow a little leeway when you take out any policy; it will save you money in the end.

Self-build insurances do not give cover for personal possessions, furniture and effects so you will need to take out a normal household insurance policy as soon as possible. If you move into the new home before it's actually finished, that does nothing to invalidate your self-build policy and indeed recognition is often given to the fact that, by being on site, everything is more secure. Several policies on the market offer the opportunity to convert unused time from a self-build policy to Household Buildings Only cover. This is not always an attractive offer as the self-builder would lose his loyalty discounts with his existing insurer and still needs Household Contents cover; something that is not always easily or advantageously available on its own. Once again, take advice and talk to the people who know about these things to get the policy tailored to your own situation.

A self-build policy will cease to give cover on completion of the building works and if you are not able or intending to occupy the property, you will need to arrange *Unoccupied Property Insurance*. Do not assume that your normal householder's policy will extend to the second house.

Self-builders, renovators and converters may also come across the need for *Legal Contingency Insurance*, sometimes known and referred to as *Single Premium Indemnity Policies*. The likelihood of this necessity arising is discussed in detail in Chapters 2 and 3. But for now, suffice it to say that such policies can be suggested in a situation where there is a restrictive covenant on the land or where all or part of a title is defective. In these cases the insurance company will assess the risk and the likelihood of any challenge to your rights of ownership or access and give cover for a single premium.

Less common, but of interest nevertheless, is *Self-build Legal Protection* which gives cover for legal expenses for pursuing an action in relation to disputes arising directly from the construction or complete restoration of a policyholder's principal private residence. For a single premium you can take out cover, payable whether or not your case is successful, for up to £50,000 of legal fees, expenses and costs incurred in legal proceedings taken on your behalf against any third parties involved in your project.

With all matters concerned with insurance and health and safety, prevention is better than cure. First of all, don't advertise the availability and attractions of your site to either casual or detailed inspection. Keep all tools and materials in a locked site hut or container and make strenuous efforts to programme materials to arrive when they are required rather than before. This is particularly true of high-risk items such as roof insulation, plumbing materials and electrical fittings. Be especially careful just after the delivery of things like kitchen units and sanitaryware and bear in mind that they are much more valuable to a potential thief when they are still in their packing and therefore more readily moved and disposed of. As far as plant is concerned, the most obvious target is the cement mixer and it might be as well to consider removing one of the wheels so as to make stealing it all that more difficult. As I've said, other tools should either be taken home at night or locked up securely.

There is a need to deter trespass and that means that fencing should be considered at an early stage in the construction process. The determined and professional thief will not be put off but you will probably dissuade the casual or opportunistic ones. If electricity is on site, consider the use of proximity lighting. A 1000-watt light coming on suddenly in the dark will unnerve the most experienced interloper and more importantly it will alert neighbours and others to their unwanted presence. And that leads on to perhaps the most valuable thing that you can do and that is to make contact with your soon-to-be next-door neighbours and to leave them details of just where you can be contacted in an emergency.

If you do have losses, remember to collect all the evidence that you will require to support your insurance claim. Advise the police as soon as possible, asking for the name of the officer to whom you are making your report as this will be required to support the insurance claim. Take a whole series of photographs of any damage, and then contact the insurers with a coherent story. You will want to hear from them whether they are going to send an assessor along to visit your site, and whether you can start putting things right before he comes. The insurers can only help you if you give them appropriate information.

This can be in a phone call when you will:

- quote your policy number
- explain that it is a contractor's risk loss, and that there are no others involved, or that it is an employer's liability incident, or involves a third party
- state simply the extent of your loss (vandals have broken my patio window or someone has stolen £2,000-worth of bathroom suites)
- tell them you are taking action to make the place secure again
- ask them if they are sending an assessor
- confirm the address to which they should send the claim form.

Dealing with all of this in an efficient way will help to get you back on an even keel, although you will still be telling everyone about your new found enthusiasm for corporal punishment.

Building Warranties

We are all familiar with the fact that all new speculatively built houses are offered with a warranty scheme in place and that banks, building societies and other lending institutions will not consider offering a mortgage on such a property unless an approved scheme is in place. In similar vein, any self-builder needing to borrow money for their project will have to provide details of an approved warranty scheme on the new home if they are going to get a mortgage. Even if they are members of that happy band who don't need a mortgage, then they are strongly advised to have a warranty scheme in place, not only for their own peace of mind but to cover them for the eventuality of ever having to sell to someone who requires finance.

A warranty is designed first of all to ensure and secondly insure against faulty workmanship involved in the design and construction of your new home. It is not a substitute for the site insurance discussed above and nor does it take the place of normal householder's

insurance of the buildings and property, although to some degree, and in specific circumstances, the cover can overlap. Before exploring the options on warranties and in order to explain the important distinctions between these various covers and liabilities, let us take the simple example of a wall falling down.

If a wall blows down in a storm during the building process then the cost of repairing the damage will be covered under the 'All-risk' section of your Self-build Site Insurance. If a person working on the site is injured by the falling masonry then you will be covered under the Employer's Liability section of the self-build site insurance and if it's a member of the public then cover will be available under the Public Liability section of the same policy.

If this hypothetical wall blows down in a storm *after* the building is completed then you will seek to recover the cost of the damage from your normal householder's insurance policy and any injuries caused will similarly be covered under the Personal Accident or Public Liability sections of that policy.

If, on the other hand, the wall falls down within

Above: Insurance services in the UK and in Eire.

the warranty period because it was either wrongly designed or constructed, then cover to put things right will be available from or through the warranty scheme without you having necessarily to seek recompense from the responsible contractors. However, and this is the important point, cover and liability for injuries or other damage would have to come from the relevant sections of either your Self-build Site Insurance or your householder's insurance, whichever was in force and effective at the time.

You can see from this example why all of the principal lending institutions require a building warranty and why all serious self-builders should have a scheme of some sort in place, whatever their circumstances. In recent years the choices have expanded somewhat and indeed it's quite likely that, long before the shelf life of this book is over, even more schemes will join the ranks of those mentioned here.

The principal arrangements for building warranties are: -

- The NHBC 'Buildmark' warranty offered by the National House Building Council, which is a building industry organisation.
- The NHBC 'Solo' warranty offered by the same organisation to accepted self-builders.
- The 'Custom-Build' guarantee offered to self-builders by the Zurich Municipal Insurance Company.
- Project Builder devised by F. E. Wright with the backing of CGU.
- The Willis Scheme.
- The NHBG 'Homebond' guarantee, which is available for those building in The Republic of Ireland (Eire).
- Architect's Certification.
- Buildstore's warranty scheme.

The NHBC 'Buildmark' warranty

This is available to those self-builders who are using an NHBC registered builder in just the same way as any developer or house builder offers it to his purchasers. Without doubt, the NHBC is the organisation that, despite its many detractors, is recognised throughout the broad spectrum of the population, both lay and professional, and if we ever get back to the position of having a sticky housing market, it is this name which will achieve instant recognition with a prospective purchaser, or their advisors – a point that could well make the difference between having a sale or not. A builder who is registered with the NHBC has to pass certain basic tests of financial probity and building knowledge and, until he can demonstrate a clean track record, he is only allowed on the register as a probationer and is prohibited from advertising himself as a member.

Before any work commences on site, and in cases where there is bad ground or where there are trees on site, at least 21 days in advance of a start, the builder must apply to register the proposed dwelling and send in the appropriate fee. The NHBC will check out the drawings with care, particularly in relation to any peculiar circumstances and then, in due course, they will allocate a registration number, which the builder's customer is advised of. The self-builder will usually have to tell his bank or building society of this registration and separate documentation is issued for the attention of the 'purchaser's' solicitor (they insist on referring to you as purchaser).

As the work progresses but, in particular, at certain crucial stages before the work is irrevocably covered up, the inspector will come along to site and check the work for compliance with the regulations and accepted standards of workmanship. This is his total concern at this stage; your arrangements or relationships with the builder are not his responsibility – unless the builder dies or becomes bankrupt, in which case the NHBC will step in with limited and defined assistance. The only other time that the inspector becomes involved in the nature of your contract with a builder is when an agreement has been reached whereby the builder is only responsible for construction of the weathertight shell of the building. In this case they will require written evidence and understanding of the limitations of the work and responsibilities.

It is not generally understood, but the NHBC is principally an insurance company which undertakes to take on responsibility for the warranty for the structural shell and integrity of the building and, in so doing, requires that its registered members, the builders, take on responsibility for the other areas of the building and that they stick to those obligations on pain of being struck off the register. Even the structural warranty requires that the builder takes on full liability for the first two years so, in effect, with 'Buildmark', the NHBC is only exposed for the last eight years of its 10-year warranty, so long as the builder remains in viable business.

Brief mention should also be made here of the fact that the NHBC is an Approved Inspector, authorised to approve and inspect under the Building Regulations. This means that a registered builder can opt to have all of his Building Regulations approval and inspections carried out under the auspices of the NHBC, negating the need for a separate application to the Building Control section of the local authority.

The NHBC 'Solo' warranty

'Solo' is specifically designed for individuals building their own homes on their own land, using either subcontract labour or doing all or part of the work themselves. It notably excludes people who are not intending the home for their own or their immediate family's occupation, requiring a declaration to that effect within the original proposal form.

On application, the NHBC inspector will arrange a meeting, on site, at which he will make a full appraisal of your proposals, explain the scheme to you and discuss the complimentary copy of the NHBC Standards which will have been sent to you. There is no requirement for technical qualifications or specific knowledge of the building industry or process, but there is no doubt that the inspector will be making an assessment of your ability to carry through what you're planning. If it is decided at that meeting, or as a result of it, that you aren't going to go ahead and that you won't be proceeding further with the NHBC, then your initial payment will be refunded in full.

Essentially, the core cover that is provided is the same as for the 'Buildmark' scheme with the obvious exception that, with no builder being involved, the cover for the structural shell and integrity of the building is the sole responsibility of the NHBC for the full 10-year period. Under the Buildmark scheme the builder would also have been responsible for the finishing trades for a period of two years and, therefore,

under the 'Solo' scheme there is an optional Damage Limitation Period Cover available which will insure you for minor damage caused by latent defects for a period of six months. There is an additional premium for this extra cover and there is also a requirement that the work is carried out by *bona fide* subcontractors and that you enter into a formal contract with them requiring them to put right any faulty work within, at least, the six-month period. Once again, therefore, the NHBC are only really at risk if the subcontractor fails to honour his obligations or goes out of business.

The NHBC divide their description of their 'product', for that is what it is, into two phases. *Phase 1* covers the period during the actual building works. The inspector will come along at various stages, which are:

- *For a brick and block house:* excavations, substructure, ground floor preparation, visual drainage, walls to first floor, walls to plate height, roof framing and masonry complete, first-fix complete and, finally, completion and drains tested.

- *For a timber-framed house:* excavations, substructure, ground-floor preparation, visual drainage, timber frame erected, external leaf to first floor, first-fix complete and finally, again, completion and drains tested.

At each stage the inspector will either approve the work and issue a Stage Completion Certificate or, if the work is not up to scratch, he will require that any faulty work is put right. Then, when it's done to his satisfaction, he'll issue the certificate. The important and exclusive thing is that once a certificate is issued then all of the work up to and including that stage is covered by the NHBC and you can go ahead and use the certificate as a tool to obtain any draw down of finance.

Phase 2 is when the building is finished and the full 10-year warranty is issued covering the main structure of the building, any defect or damage to flues and chimneys, defects to the drains and damage to the roof and tiling. It's worthwhile mentioning that the NHBC also offer a service giving help with Standard Assessment Procedure (SAP) ratings (of which more later) and, in the same way as they do under the Buildmark scheme, they can also take on the responsibility for the Building Regulations' approval and inspection, on payment of extra fees as required. This last service is not available in Scotland, the Isle of Man and Northern Ireland and the entire 'Solo' scheme is not available for conversions.

The Zurich 'Custom-Build' warranty

This is the company that pioneered the idea and the actuality of self-build warranties, helping so many self-builders to achieve their dreams of a new home. In no small way, it is this scheme that enabled the self-build industry to change up a gear and it stood alone in the market for many years.

Whilst there are similarities between the Custom-Build scheme and Solo, there are also several major differences. First and foremost, the Zurich Municipal is not authorised by the government to perform the work or undertake the role of Statutory Building Control and Inspections. In practice that's not a drawback because, in any case, the Custom Build scheme works by a tie-up with the Building Control Department of the local authority. This means that the Building Inspector always visits their sites, with additional quality control inspections made by Custom-Build's own surveyors as the work progresses. A strong argument can be made for the separation of these responsibilities and, for some, the very fact that two or more sets of inspections are being made by differing bodies can give added reassurance, especially when linked to the perception that the local authority Building Inspector has little or no commercial axe to grind.

The track record built up by Custom-Build over the years is enviable and bears fruit in the many testaments by self-builders to the help and assistance given by their staff and inspectors. Although not possessing the instant recognition that the NHBC are favoured with, the Zurich Custom-Build warranty is equally acceptable to most building societies and banks; so much so, that many house builders and developers now offer a variation on the scheme, known as Zurich Newbuild.

As with any scheme, Custom-Build starts with the application form and sending it off with, in their case, a non-returnable deposit after which you'll receive their *Technical Manual and Builders' Guidance Notes*,

which is, undoubtedly, an excellent reference book in its own right. They do insist on a few more things than the NHBC currently appear to require in that they demand that the house is designed by a qualified architect (or other professional), that the work is carried out by professional contractors or tradesmen and that full Building Regulations consent is sought and obtained. There is also an additional expectation that the self-builder should have a source of technical advice, a 'professional friend'. This would obviously come in the form of the architect or the package deal company, if they were using one, but equally, the role could be filled by a suitable friend or somebody with the relevant knowledge of building. Whilst all of these requirements may, at first, seem a trifle pedantic, they are born out of years of experience and there is no reason to suppose that, as the Solo scheme progresses, they too will not adopt similar requirements.

In common with any other warranty schemes, if bad ground or unusual ground conditions are suspected or known, then they will require a copy of a site investigation, soil report and/or foundation design. At the completion of the project, a 10-year structural warranty will be issued with the option, on payment of an additional fee, of extending this to 15 years. There is also a scheme up and running for conversions and rebuilds called Custom-build Conversions Solutions where the offer of insurance is subject to an initial survey report and the cover offered is for six or 10 years.

Project Builder

Sterling, Hamilton, Wright, a medium-sized Lloyds broker with extensive insurance experience, are offering, under the name of Project Builder, a structural warranty scheme, backed by Trenwick. The scheme covers the whole of the UK and is available to self-builders whether they use a builder or subcontractors or even if they undertake the entire project on a DIY basis. You still need to have Building Regulations approval with the normal inspections carried out by the Building Inspector but, in addition, Project Builder will arrange for their own inspections to be carried out on their behalf by Carilion Specialist Services Ltd. The inspection stages are: footings prior to any concrete being poured, followed by one at pre-

plastered out but, if they deem it necessary and on difficult or special sites, they will come out and inspect at other times.

Cover is given for 10 or 12 years, depending on premium and runs from the date of the final inspection although it is not issued until the property is finished and a completion certificate has been issued.

The Willis Scheme

Usually referred to as the Forest of Dean scheme after the local authority that originated it. Names apart, though, it's the simplest of all of the schemes in that it works through the local Building Control department and relies on their approval and inspection of the building as it progresses. It came about through the foresight of one man, Joe Chetcuti who is the chief Building Control officer at the Forest of Dean District Council. He built his own home after reading an earlier version of this book and very quickly realised that there was a vast duplication of responsibility with, on some sites, each stage being inspected by up to four different surveyors or inspectors, all of whom had to be paid for in some way. He also realised that with the privatisation of the Building Control function to the

Above: Study all the leaflets for the various warranty schemes for the UK and for Eire.

NHBC, the local authorities were increasingly at a disadvantage in that builders who required a warranty would be persuaded to leave all in their hands. He felt that the Building Control departments of the local authorities had unrivalled experience and he was sure that a warranty scheme which directly utilised their inspections and powers would be successful. He got nowhere with any of the established bodies in this country and it was only when he approached a French insurance company that he managed to get people to listen to what he had to say. They, and later others, recognised that the local authorities exercised their control under Statutory powers, with the full force of the law behind them and that, in consequence, if a warranty scheme could be tied around their inspections, such a scheme could also be offered at a very competitive rate.

Full cover attachment is given from day one and provides for any defects in the design, workmanship or components of the structure of a new domestic dwelling that affects or causes physical loss, destruction or damage and/or affects or causes imminent instability to such a dwelling. Coverage automatically extends to include common parts, retaining or boundary walls and the drainage system within the perimeter of the building together with any garage or permanent outbuildings. The cover offered is 10 years, with an option to extend this to 12 years on payment of a slightly higher premium, and confidence in it is so high that it is applicable to any valid construction method and applies equally to new build, renovations and extensions. Anyone can apply, be they a builder, developer or self-builder. Not every local authority has yet signed up to the scheme but, as time goes by, more and more are doing so. In any event there is nothing to prevent it being run without the direct participation of the local authority, so long as local authority Building Control and Inspections are made.

The NHBG 'Homebond' guarantee

Available only in the Republic of Ireland (Eire). The National House Building Guarantee (NHBG) company's scheme is the Irish counterpart to the NHBC and to a large degree it mirrors what the NHBC offers with its

Right: Dormer-style roofs with differing planes, Tudor-style timbering and a brick plinth course have become the hallmark for the continuing popularity of the Potton designs.

Below: Elements of both traditional Surrey and Sussex design come together in this imposing house by Design & Materials Ltd.

- *The stage payment bond* For a period of two years from the date of registration, this will repay lost deposits or contract payments in the event of the builder's bankruptcy or liquidation, up to a maximum of 15% of the purchase price or 25,395 Euros, whichever is the lower. From the date of Final Notice, after the main structural inspection, to the completion and handover, for a maximum period of six months, this indemnity rises to 63,487 Euros, or 50% of the purchase price, whichever is the lower.

- *Two year defects warranty* This gives cover for water and smoke penetration for a period of two years following completion.

- *Ten-year structural defects warranty* This protects against major structural defects within a period of 10 years following certification of the home.

Buildmark scheme, but, as you would expect, with some significant differences. Builders have to register with the company and pass basic tests of ability and financial probity and, unlike the NHBC scheme, they are liable for any structural defects for the whole of the 10-year guarantee period, with the NHBG only stepping in, in effect, if the builder fails in his obligations.

Homebond works in three ways:

A homebuilder must first of all write to the builder, asking them to put any defect right and then if the builder fails to carry out the work, Homebond will step in and get another builder to effect the repairs, at no expense to the homeowner, so long as they fall within their cover. At present there is no scheme for those building with subcontractors. However, as this warranty scheme closely monitors and follows those available in the United Kingdom, I wouldn't be surprised if, sooner or later, they come up with something similar to Solo.

Architect's Certification

In the years before the advent of the Zurich Municipal Custom-Build scheme, if a self-builder wanted to build with subcontractors or his own labour then, unless they could persuade a friendly NHBC builder to take them under his wing and almost pretend to be building the house for them, the only other way of achieving the necessary certification to satisfy the bank or building society, was to go for what is known as Architect's Progress Certificates.

This was an entirely different procedure from Architectural Supervision but there was, and still is, endless confusion between the two, exacerbated by what appears to be a deliberate blurring of the distinctions by some of the building societies. *Architect's Progress Certificates* are where an architect comes out to the site, at recognised, agreed and specified times, for an agreed fee of anywhere between £50 and £250 and certifies that, at the time of his visit, the building has reached a particular stage in its construction and that the work appears to have been carried out in accordance with the plans and specification. It is not necessary for the architect carrying out the certification to be the same architect who was responsible for the design. Differing architects will place different emphasis on their responsibilities under this arrangement. Some will want to make as certain as they can that the work has been carried out satisfactorily and some will merely be concerned that the correct stage in the construction of the building has been reached.

Some building societies and banks leave the question of the architect's actual responsibilities and obligations open for the architect to define, whilst others try and tie down the architect to a warranty which he clearly cannot give under this scheme and which would override, completely, any legal limitation by reference to reasonable skill and care. For this reason the current advice to architects is that they do not accept the wording or documentation provided by

these institutions and that they confine their responsibilities and legal obligations to certifying that they have visited the property to inspect the progress and quality of the work to check, as far as they are reasonably able to do so on a visual inspection, that the works are being executed generally in accordance with the approved drawings and contract documents.

Architect's Supervision, on the other hand, involves the architect being responsible for every detail of the work, necessitating his visiting the site frequently and being involved in every aspect of the construction. It is relatively expensive and it is usually carried out by the same architect who has formulated the design, probably as part and parcel of his original arrangement with you.

Building societies and banks will accept Architect's Progress Certificates. They do not carry any warranty, as such, and the only way a claim can be established is for the self-builder to sue the architect who will then fall back on his Professional Indemnity Insurance. So, if you do go along this route it's a good idea to make absolutely certain that the architect carries such a policy and that the amount of cover under that policy is sufficient for your needs. The interesting fact is that these Progress Certificates and the liability of the architect extend only to the original party to the contract – that is, the self-builder. The burden of the contract is not passed to any successor in title, so that anybody buying the house from the original self-builder would not be able to pursue a claim against the architect. Perhaps the banks and building societies have drawn a blind eye to this point in the past – it has always been open for them to insist on a collateral contract but, the instances where this has been the case are few and far between.

The same, of course, goes for Architect's Supervision but it can be argued that, with this service, the chances of anything going wrong are lessened to the point of slim. If an architect has designed a property and he is also supervising its construction then he knows, 'to the last nut screw and bolt', just what goes into that house and he can not only watch out for potential problems but head them off before they even occur. It is also likely that the architect will be responsible for the total construction and will therefore be just as involved in the second fix and finishing trades as he is for the structural parts of the building.

Nevertheless, I think that if you are using Architect's Progress Certificates, it is still a good idea to couple them up with one of the other warranty schemes, even though there is probably no requirement from your lender that you should do so. If, for example, the builder goes bust then that would not necessarily be attributable to any fault or wrongdoing on the part of the architect and you might not be able to make a claim against him.

Before I leave this subject, just a word of warning about your choice of architect, should you decide to opt for Architect's Progress Certificates using a different architect from your original designer. Architects who work consistently in the self-build field, or are members of *Associated Self-build Architects (ASBA)*, are more likely to be amenable to your requirements and your aims. Others of, let's say, the more crusty persuasion might not be quite so sympathetic to your needs, might show distinct signs of sour grapes at the fact that you didn't go to them for their services in the first place and might, if you've used a package deal company, have a marked aversion to the whole concept of everything you're trying to achieve.

Buildstore's warranty scheme

At the time of writing a new warranty scheme, developed by Buildstore, is about to be launched. The scheme will provide a 10-year structural warranty and is particularly aimed at self-builders using the services of architects, architectural technologists and recog nised timber-frame and package-deal companies. Full details should be available from Buildstore's website or by reference to their regular newsletters.

Where do you live whilst it's all happening?

At exhibition after exhibition I have watched as, in the seminars, the representative from the building society has outlined the main choices of where to live whilst your new home is under construction; in a caravan on site, in rented accommodation or, to the sound of embarrassed laughter, with the in-laws. All

of which has then led to the explanation that, as far as their society is concerned, just as long as you can demonstrate that you can service the mortgage on two properties, they are quite happy for you to stay in your own home.

There is a palpable sense of relief in the room at this point but I know full well that when figures are finally worked out, for most people with a mortgage covering a large percentage of their borrowing capacity and a significant amount of the value of their existing home, there is going to be little or no choice but to sell up and move into temporary accommodation.

The introduction of 'Shorthold tenancies' breathed new life into a rental sector that, up until then, had almost ceased to exist under draconian legislation that made it nigh on impossible for landlords to be certain of recovering their property. Nowadays there is usually quite a considerable choice of furnished and unfurnished accommodation available at rents that do not differ significantly from the monthly mortgage payments that most people would be expecting to pay Of course, it does mean moving twice and it may well mean that all or part of your furniture has to go into storage. But it is a way of freeing up capital whilst continuing to live in relative comfort. A drawback can often be that you might need accommodation for longer than the six months that these tenancies usually run for and that, in turn, might mean either having to move or choosing a property that is likely to be available for the longer period.

Staying with in-laws or friends has many advantages, not least since not only is the capital in your old home released for use in your new home but you are spared the outgoing of the monthly rent. It's nearly impossible to predict or advise on this course of action as each family is different and, whilst for some it is an entirely successful arrangement, for others it is a nightmare experience. Remember that, for those you are moving in with, this is not their project, it is not the most important thing in their lives and their only motivation is to help you. Fitting two families into one home is not easy and it's important that you provide space and arrange breaks for both parties because, when the relatively short period of your build is over, you have to maintain the long

Above: Creating a design for a home in the face of planner,s insistence that it does not look domestic is an art.

Below: But as the rear elevation of this Potton home shows, it is possible

term relationships you started out with.

Living on site can have huge advantages. Being on the spot means that you always know what's happening on your site, who's been there and for how long. You are there for deliveries and, if you're working on the site, you've not got too far to travel when you're working late or just getting the odd few hours in. You're also hugely increasing the security on your site and that fact is often recognised in a consequent insurance discount. If you're building a replacement dwelling, and the existing structure is habitable, or capable of being camped out in, consider whether it's possible to position the new home, so that the existing property can remain until it's no longer needed.

It's not at all unusual for plots to come onto the market encumbered by an existing house. Whilst this can sometimes be a strain on finances because you're having to buy an element of property that you don't really want, it can also provide you with suitable accommodation right next door to your plot. If you don't need it or the finances dictate that you must sell it off as quickly as possible then remember to allocate the relevant costs of any separation and refurbishment against any gain for Capital Gains purposes. If you do live in it, then, under normal circumstances, the Revenue will consider that your double move is all part of the business of moving from one home to another.

Living in a mobile home on site is often considered the least favourable option. But this is an ill deserved reputation for, once again, there are distinct advantages in living on site and there are obvious financial incentives in the savings you can make on your monthly outgoings. It is a false economy to think in terms of buying too cheaply. For the period of your self-build, you are going to be living virtually rent and mortgage free apart from the cost of the mobile home purchase and it really doesn't make sense to make what is after all a trying time even more difficult. At the end of the project, if you look after it, it's a pound to a penny that you're going to get most of your money back, so why stint on what is always going to be a relatively modest proportion of your total budget? Don't forget services. Spending money on getting the electricity and water connected and in putting in the drains will pay off in the end as, in nearly all cases, the services can be used as the site supply and, when the new home is finished, easily rerouted. One cannot pretend that living in a mobile home on site is ever going to be an entirely pleasant experience so making it as comfortable as possible is certainly worthwhile. Oh, and by the way, it's a fair bet that you'll buy it from a self-builder and you'll sell it on to another.

Local authorities do not like caravans but, so long as in your negotiations with the planners you explain that you intend to live on site while you are building, a consent is not usually required. However, it's best not to antagonise either your neighbours or the planners, with whom you may be entering into particularly delicate negotiations and the best course of action is to consult with them at all stages. If you're planning to put the caravan on site long before you actually apply for planning permission for your new home, then you will need to get formal consent for its siting. If you do have problems with the council, remember that it will take an inordinately long time to get an order requiring you to move it or cease occupation, by which time you will hopefully be well on the way with your project.

Council Tax

The question often arises as to when you are deemed to have fully occupied the new home, as opposed to just camping out in it for security purposes. Many authorities will deem that full occupation takes place when the furniture is placed in the home. Others have inspectors who visit the home and certify that it will be capable of occupation at a given date, often some three months ahead. It is the inspector's job to assess the banding which the home will be placed in for Council Tax purposes. If you do not agree with the assessment, you may appeal against the new entry and/or the effective date. Some councils still issue completion or habitation certificates for Building Regulation purposes, which you can quote if necessary or appropriate. If you have been living in a caravan on the site and have paid Council Tax, make sure that you do not find yourself being billed twice when you move into your new home.

2. FINDING THE SITE OF YOUR NEW HOME

If you imagine for one moment that you're just going to pick up the telephone, ring up the local estate agents, wait until the details arrive and, if it's a nice day, get in the car to drive out to look at the plots and select one, you're in for a rude awakening. It doesn't happen like that. Finding land is, as I've said, the first hurdle at which most self-builders fall in the race to build their own home. It takes perseverance and luck. Perseverance in that you have to be prepared to follow all of the avenues that could lead to a possible plot, and luck that it's you and not somebody else who's there when one comes up.

Some people find it extremely easy to find land whilst others search fruitlessly for years. I have come across people complaining that they haven't even had a sniff at a plot in their area and that as far as they're concerned none have come up. Yet in many cases I not only know of plots that have recently come up in their area, but I also know those who have built on them. Each month I have a feature in *Homebuilding & Renovating* magazine where I attach myself to landless would-be self-builders and seek out and identify plots in their area. We then spend an enjoyable weekend looking at them. I come at this cold each month in a completely different part of the country and, whilst I admit that it's not as easy in the south-east, I usually manage to find not one but three plots to write about, and sometimes more.

I was speaking at the seminars at the Southern Homebuilding & Renovating Show a couple of years ago and in the audience was a chap who had self-built his home, some 10 years previously. He was obviously enthused by what he heard for on the way home that night he decided that he'd like to do it again. He took the dogs for a walk and identified three plots, one of which he subsequently bought. At the next show, he came to see me again to tell me how he was getting on with his new self-build. If I tell you that he lived in Berkshire, one of the notorious blackspots for plots, you'll probably be amazed.

If you're always missing out on plots, what are you doing wrong? Are you simply being too fussy? Are you looking for an ideal that'll never really happen? Are you looking at things as they are and not as they will be? Many plots are parts of gardens or they're covered in old sheds, tangled undergrowth and rusting cars. Many look far from appealing and a long way removed from anybody's dream plot. But you have to cut through all that. Close your eyes and imagine how things are going to be when you've finished. Somehow you've got to imagine the plot all tidied up, the house that you propose on it, the gardens all laid out neatly and the street scene enhanced by your efforts.

Are you, above all, making sure that you're in the right place at the right time? Plots don't hang about on the market for very long and if the person selling a plot can't get hold of you or you don't respond to his call about a plot, he'll simply move on to the next interested party.

Ask yourself whether you could extend your parameters. Could you go that little bit further out or one more junction down the motorway? Could you think in terms of buying an existing dilapidated house or one that just needs a bit of TLC and imagination to turn it into something really special? Could you think in terms of a conversion of an otherwise redundant building or a barn? Above all, are you being proactive in your search and are you keeping an open mind to all options?

Evaluating the plot or development opportunity and the actual process of buying it will be dealt with in the next chapter, so now let's move on to finding one. Of course there is a happy band of people who don't have to find a plot because they already own one and if you're one of them, you can skip the next section and move on to evaluating your plot and how to get planning on it. For the rest of you the really hard bit is about to begin and even the later stages of actual construction may pale into insignificance when set beside this task.

So where do you start?

Estate agents

Estate agents sell land. Most of the land that is sold goes through an agent, sometimes because the agent was instrumental in getting the Outline Consent in the first place. In any town there are two distinct types of estate agent. Firstly there are the long-established traditional agents who sell houses as part and parcel of their general business, which can include activities as diverse as furniture sales and livestock auctions. These are the types of agent who are also more likely to have a professional department and it is this department which is often used by prospective vendors to obtain planning on their land. They will be cagey about what they've got coming up, preferring to maintain the anonymity of their clients and the potential plots until they have a consent and specific instructions. But once they have those instructions they will act in the way that is best suited to their client, the vendor.

The other sort of estate agent is fairly familiar to us all. They very rarely get involved in actual applications for planning and instead simply take on properties and land at face value. They have a much more brash way of dealing with things and they won't always see the full potential in any particular property, existing, as they do, through high turnover, rather than long-term investment. They're much more likely to discuss what's up and coming and you'll come out of their offices, even if empty-handed, with a feeling of hope – a feeling which may dissipate quite quickly when nothing further happens.

You see, estate agents sell land, yes, but given half a chance they'd rather not sell it to a self-builder. Why not? Surely your money is as good as anybody else's? Well, no, it isn't actually, because if an estate agent sells that piece of land to you and you build your new home on it, then in the short-to-medium term all the agent is going to get out of it is a commission fee which barely scrapes over four figures.

Whereas, if he sells it to a builder or a developer he'll get the same commission fee for selling the land, and then in a very short time he'll get the very much larger commission for selling the new house that the builder constructs. As if that's not enough he'll have his board up at that site for a much longer time to bring in more customers and get more noticed than his rivals. Of course he's got to balance that wish with a duty to his vendor but in normal times that isn't too much of a problem for him and even if it's not normal times, the time lag between his recognition of that duty and his view of the plot as a key to other things takes a long while to sink in.

So, just putting your name on the books of an estate agent isn't going to produce too many plots. Visit them weekly. Get to know them almost on a personal basis and, even if you suspect that when they see you coming across the road to visit them every Saturday morning, they're inwardly groaning that it's you again, greet them with a cheery, 'Hi it's me again – anything fresh in on the plot front?' Sooner or later you'll be recognised as a *bona fide* purchaser and if your name's the one at the forefront of their minds on the day a plot comes in then, chances are you'll get to hear of it. Of course, if you suspect that no matter what you do and no matter how many times you go in they're always going to want to sell it to their builder clients then you're really up against it but there are things you can do. Try going in at the weekend, possibly on a Sunday, when temporary staff are on duty. Tell them you're on the books – even confirm it with them by checking your details with them whilst you're there. Ask if there's any land that's come in during the week and if they go across to the relevant cabinet and get you out some details then, even if they get told off on the Monday for showing them to you, you'll have got to hear of that plot. Above all, you'll have done nothing wrong. They were instructed to sell that land for the best price. Their duty is to the vendor and if you buy the land, what's wrong with that?

The more traditional agents will often want to sell land by auction or tender and whilst that can be a benefit to the self-builder insofar as it brings the land onto the open market, there are several drawbacks. Auctions are distinctly uneasy places for lay people,

Left: Get out and see everything. What the estate agents details describe and the reality of what you see may very well differ – to the good or to the bad.

Below left: The infill site in a village setting is undoubtedly most people's ideal but it is an increasingly rare find.

Below: The Internet-based land-finding agencies should be one of the first ports of call for those seeking a plot or development opportunity.

Bottom: There are plots listed in the backs of the self-build magazines.

who sit there nervously trying not to scratch that itch that inescapably comes up on their eyebrow whilst at the same time trying to keep track of the stream of indecipherable words coming from the rostrum. Similarly tenders, with their inherent lack of any proper legal framework, are extremely unpopular with purchasers. Both of these methods of buying land are explored in greater detail in Chapter 4.

The media

Newspapers, national, local and classified, self-build magazines and some well-known sales magazines are a good source of plots. Subscribe to the local papers in your chosen area and don't forget that there's quite a

bit of overlap, so subscribe to the papers in the adjoining areas. If you see a plot advertised, then get onto it immediately and don't wait for the weekend. If it's a private advertiser then be aware that they will be bombarded with offers from estate agents and others and that you, as a private individual, might well have to fight hard for their attention. Play up the fact that you're looking to self-build as an individual or a family. Vendors, especially those who will continue to live next door, are often apprehensive about any loss of control over what happens on the plot and you might well be able to put their minds at ease.

And, of course, newspapers work both ways in that you can advertise for a plot. You may get time-wasters; you may get a string of no-hope plots, which never would get planning consent. You may get the chap who's just fed-up with mowing his large lawn. But, you may get the humdinger of a plot. You may even get someone who's been trying to sell his plot through, would you believe it, your friendly local estate agent who hasn't been able to interest any of his builder chums but still didn't tell you about it.

The land-finding agencies

The first ports of call for many would-be self-builders are the land-finding agencies who are not only heavily featured in the magazines but have large stands at most of the major self-build exhibitions. Plotfinder.net contains lists of upwards of 4,000 plots or renovation opportunities at any one time. You can call them on their hotline, 0906 557 5400 or contact them on the Internet, www.plotfinder.net and at the time of writing, a year's subscription for five counties of your choice will cost just £35. They publish about a quarter of their database in *Housebuilding & Renovating* magazine each month but you must understand that this may have gone to print some months before and that these listings are liable to be out of date. Exactly the same pertains with the long-established family-run agency, Landbank Services Ltd. They occasionally publish lists of land for sale in the magazines but confine their main menu to their website, www.landbank.co.uk. For a fee, payable on purchase, they also operate a personal site location service. Buildstore claim almost 6,000 plots, renovation or

conversion opportunities on their books at any one time and they offer a lifetime subscription to their online service for £39. They can be accessed on www.buildstore.co.uk/plotsearch and they have a monthly mailing service available by telephoning 0870 870 9991 for those who don't have access to the Internet.

It's obviously a mammoth task to keep this data up to date but perhaps the most important information to be gleaned from the lists is which agents specifically and consistently deal in land. You can also deduce the going rates for plots in any area and their general availability and distribution. A day spent on the telephone going through the lists can often lead to far more opportunities than are listed.

Local authorities, English Partnerships (formerly the Commission for New Towns) and plot-creating companies

Local Authorities sell land. Some of them are well known for doing so and have a regular supply of plots specifically marketed for the self-builder. Ring your local authority and ask what plots they've got for sale and what plots they've got coming up. The plots they sell are highly valuable and desirable sites, which normally have most of the roads and infrastructure taken care of. Of course land doesn't grow on trees, so to speak, and as many authorities get to the end of the land bank and have sold off land that they would previously have built council housing on, the supply can begin to dry up. But, that doesn't mean that it's not worthwhile getting on to them because things do change and at any one time either a complete site can be in the offing or the odd spare parcel of land can be identified as suitable.

English Partnerships sell fully serviced plots in the new towns up and down the country but this is a diminishing resource. The notable exception is Milton Keynes where there is still a ready supply of really good plots at sensible prices, many of which are heavily oversubscribed upon release. They sell the plots by informal tender which means that a date is set by which all offers have to be received and they then accept the highest bid.

In America and the former dominions it's not at all unusual to find plot-creating agencies, and the principle is now arriving in this country. These companies seek out and purchase larger plots of land that either already have planning consent or where they perceive that there is a good chance of getting it. They then prepare a full development brief and agree it with the planning authorities, setting out the development criteria, including acceptable house types, with the result that detailed planning, so long as it's within those parameters is either unnecessary or a mere formality. Finally, having put in all the roads and services, they offer the plots for sale to private individuals. These companies often only exist for the duration of the scheme but there are names that are beginning to be established. Look out for their advertisements in the self-build magazines.

Being generally proactive, asking and looking around

Try having a haircut, or visiting the local pub. And when you've cut out all the horror stories which invariably happened to someone who knew someone, and got over trying to explain that you're not completely mad, you may come out with a few pointers which could lead you to a plot. Seek out the oldest person or the local village busybody to identify land that might lie hidden behind hedges or walls. Get some flyers printed and deliver them door to door in chosen villages or streets, making it clear that you are private individuals seeking to self-build and not developers. Put notice cards in shop windows, again making it clear that the land is for your own use and family occupation rather than as a pure profit-making venture.

If you do visit an advertised plot in a town or village, make a point of talking to local people. Ask for directions at the Post Office, even if you know exactly where the plot is. You'll be surprised at just how much the postmaster or mistress knows about, not only the plot you've come to see, but other plots or potential plots in the area. Talk to neighbours. They may be keen to put you off the plot and you might well have to read between the lines of their animosity to it being a plot in the first place. But you may also pick up bits of information and history on the plot that will stand you in good stead when you make an offer or start negotiations with the authorities. If you spot some building taking place in the area, stop off and talk to the chaps on site. From them you'll glean what the authority's attitude and requirements are, what sort of design they like and what sort of ground conditions you're likely to experience. Not only that, but once again you'll probably come away with information that could lead you to another plot or plots in the area.

Incidentally, it's sometimes well worthwhile visiting a plot that you know has already gone and doing all of the above and perhaps a little bit more. Ask the vendors if it really has been sold. Leave your details so that if anything goes wrong, they can contact you. Impress upon them your disappointment at missing out yet again and you might well find that they know of other plots in the area, some of which might not yet be on the market. They could have had to fight quite hard to get their planning consent and, in so doing, they might have made contact with others who were in the process of, or contemplating doing the same as them.

Studying the Ordnance Survey maps can show up gaps in the street scene that might not be visible on the ground but which might well be plots. They can also indicate areas where the density of housing is at variance with the norm or where it is apparent that infilling or backland development has taken place, often out of public view. As a tool they are invaluable for planning a proactive campaign of creating or identifying a plot prior to any approach to the owners. However they are, in the end, no substitute for getting out there yourself and checking whether things are the same on the ground.

Looking around villages or areas of your choice to see if there are any obvious plots can be worthwhile. Despite all the dire warnings about not buying land without the benefit of some sort of planning consent, often given by me, there are circumstances where a piece of land which does not have an express consent can still be considered as a plot. It's difficult to describe in absolute terms just how or why this can occur but in general I am referring to those obvious plots of land which have, for some reason or another, been left undeveloped whilst, all around them, similar plots have long since been built on. Now, you have to distinguish the difference here between, say, a street scene of large houses where each property has 30 metres to each boundary and another street scene where similar houses have long since had the land at the side developed, but one, for some reason or another, has been left undisturbed. It's not a certainty that it's a plot but it's a pretty good bet – one that could make it worth your while making enquiries at the Planning Department and, if you can track down a willing vendor, make it worth your while making an offer subject to contract and subject to receipt of satisfactory planning permission.

Infill plots don't just occur in towns and it's a good idea to look out for an unexplained gap in a village street. It could well have once been the village duck pond, clay or sandpit that's since been filled in. Equally it could also have been left as a gap to give access to fields at the rear when the farmer originally sold off the land on the road frontage for development. Now that machinery has brought about the enlargement of the fields the access is no longer useful or possibly even the fields themselves are now developed and this tongue of land remains, unused and unwanted, until either you happen along or someone thinks to make proper use of it.

Identifying the land is one thing but finding the owner can be another. If your enquiries at the village pub don't bring results, you could look in the Land Registry. Not all land is registered but quite a bit of it is, especially if it's changed hands in the recent past. Prior to December 1990, only registered owners or persons with their consent could inspect the register but now it is open for anyone to do so. A registered title is the legal evidence of ownership, or title to land. It includes details of the address and location, the owners and any charges, covenants and easements affecting it. The information supplied is in the form of a Property Register containing all the details in three succinct sections together with a plan upon which the land is outlined. If you find a piece of land and you want to trace its ownership, then you need to apply to the Land Registry with full details of the address and, if at all possible, a map or copy of the OS sheet, to identify it.

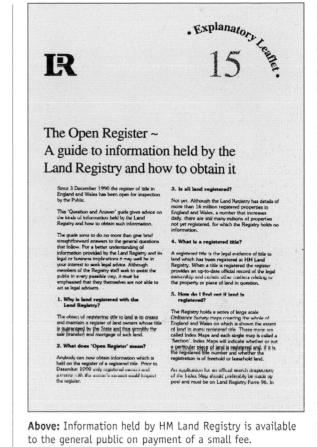

Above: Information held by HM Land Registry is available to the general public on payment of a small fee.

If you cannot identify the land in this way then you can send off for, or inspect, the Index maps held by the Registry. All registered land is marked and numbered on these Index maps and, if the plot you're interested in appears on them then you should be able to find out just who owns it. I repeat, not all land is registered, and it is the empty parcel of land that has lain fallow and unused for donkey's years that is the most likely not to have been. Nevertheless, if you're unsure of the ownership of a piece of land that's caught your eye, and local enquiries have been unsuccessful, you could apply. A modest scale of fees is payable and I would suggest that, in the first instance, you write to HM Land Registry at Lincolns Inn Fields, London WC2A 3PH, or telephone them on 020 7917 8888, asking them for their Explanatory leaflet 15.

The public utilities

These include telephone and gas companies, electricity and water boards, and Railtrack. Telephone relay stations, gas regulators, pumping stations and electricity transformers used to take up large areas of land in the middle of residential areas. In some cases the buildings used to house these things were the size of small bungalows. Nowadays, what went on in there can be accommodated in a box the size of a small chest of drawers. The land and buildings have become redundant and the planners are often more than happy to see the street scene tidied up by replacement of these anachronisms.

The drawback with these plots is that the land might well be contaminated in some way or that there might be a considerable amount of equipment and pipework to remove. Additionally, provision for access to any replacement equipment might be needed and there may be sterile zones. Try writing to the various companies, explaining what you want to do and asking if they've got any surplus and suitable land for sale. Better still, get out there and identify these things yourself and then write or call in to ask them directly about a specific property.

Railtrack own many parcels of land, not all of which are close to railway lines. They have an Estates Department that actively seeks to develop and dispose of surplus land and not so long ago I met a chap who bought a piece of land from them and has now built three houses on it, one of which he lives in.

Local authority planning departments

It is not generally understood, but the Planning Register is open for inspection by the general public and if you go to the planning office at your local authority, you can ask to see it. You may have to wait in turn for it, as many company representatives also use this source of information, but when you do get to it you will find listed all of the recent and current applications for planning permission. It's the Outline ones that are most likely to be of interest to you. Some may be under the name of your local estate agent but the chances are that he's listed as the applicant's agent and you can glean the applicant's name

from the application. A short letter to the owner might elicit a positive response. At the very least it will let the owner know that you're out there, and when the agent takes a long time to interest his builder friends or tries to tell his vendor that the market's a little slow, the owner will either be able to correct him or contact you – I've known that to happen in quite a few cases.

Of course, the owner may not want to sell, and that's more likely if it's a 'Detailed' application, where the likelihood is that the owner knows what he wants to do with the land or is planning it for himself – but not always. For the sake of a first-class stamp, it's worth a try. On the other hand, people who get planning on parts of their gardens are often awfully keen to get the money for the plot but are equally apprehensive about what might happen to it, what gets built on it, who'll be their neighbours, and what effect it'll have on their existing house. The thought of some faceless and uncaring builder sticking up something as huge as he can get it and selling it on to goodness knows who will keep them awake at night. A letter from you telling them that you are a private family, that you're very keen to live and build somewhere where you'll feel welcome and stressing that you would like your building to fit in properly, could allay some fears and bring you a plot.

Replacement dwellings – new for old

Most self-builds in the south-east corner of England, and a substantial number in other areas, are built on the site of an old dwelling that has been demolished. Sometimes local estate agents will try for ages to sell a sub-standard bungalow or house, with mortgage application after mortgage application going in, only to be rejected time and again. Nobody seems to realise that this is a building plot, not a viable building in its current form, especially the poor young couples who keep on trying to buy this cheap home. Sometimes the demolition costs can add up to a few thousand pounds, sometimes they cost a bit more, especially if the existing building contains asbestos. Sometimes, however, the demolition costs can be offset completely by the salvage value of the materials, especially if the roof tiles are local clay peg or pantiles

Right: A large percentage of self-build projects in the south-east of England are replacement dwellings. This opportunity, however, is in Scotland.

Below: Even an ugly old water tower is capable of being transformed into a modern home.

which are no longer available and therefore in high demand for extensions and renovations.

There are usually considerable savings on a green field plot. In all probability the driveway and entrance are already in. The drains and services may be connected and the garden will probably already be laid out and established, if a little overgrown. Be careful not to alert the estate agent to the possibility of this being a plot. You'd be surprised, but many times they still won't click if you ask for plots and then, as an aside, just in case there aren't any, you ask for old properties to do up. I know because I've done it myself. The last benefit, and one that I've already

referred to Chapter 1, is that the planning consent will often allow the old building to remain until the new one is complete. Now that could solve your accommodation problems for the duration of the building.

One word of caution on replacement dwellings. Many local authorities have policies whereby they will allow replacement, so long as the new home is not bigger than the original by a certain percentage. This percentage varies from authority to authority but in some cases the allowed increase in floor space is nothing whilst in others it's maybe half as much again. The *raison d'être* for this is a reluctance to see the continual erosion of small homes in favour of large ones. As a social policy that does of course have some merit but there are times when it's just plain silly. I remember a leafy road in Sussex where the large plots all had large four- and five-bedroom houses on them with swimming pools and multiple garages. In the middle of this there was a one acre plot with a 65 sq. metre bungalow on it and the authority were insisting that any replacement should not exceed its size by more than 10%. This was enshrined in their development plan and in most cases one would be on a hiding to nothing trying to overturn such a policy. But someone did. For when I drove past 18 months later, a large house, commensurate with the area, was being built.

LARGE FAMILY HOUSE
SQUEEZED ON AN IN-FILL SITE

Nottingham architects, Julian Owen Associates certainly knew how to get the very best out of this difficult site.

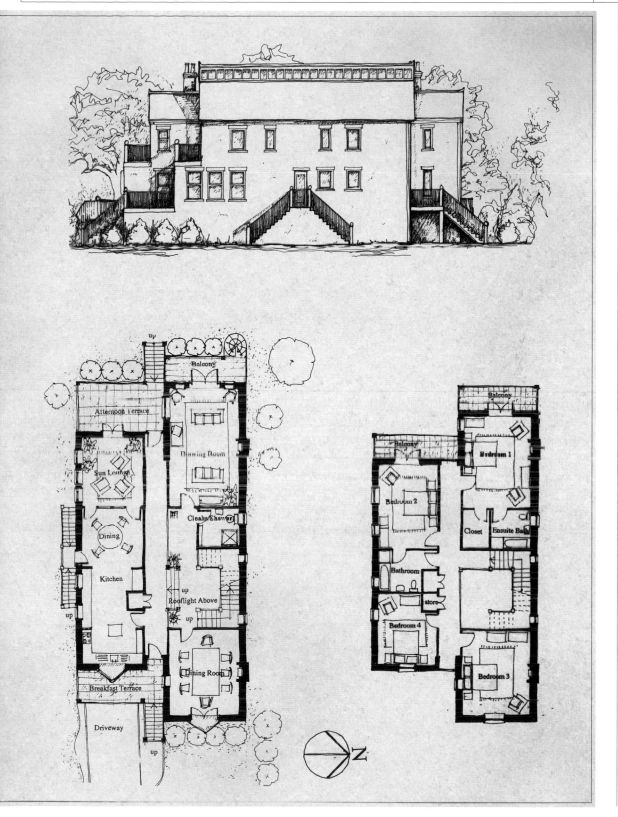

Do you already own the plot or part of it, without realising it?

Before going out bothering prospective plot owners with offers to convert their garden into your dream plot, take a close look at your own home. Is your house in a street where the density of dwellings is rising due to large gardens being divided off as plots? If not, could it be possible that you could start the trend? Maybe your garden backs onto or is side onto another road where a new access could be formed. Maybe the rear garden is so long that it's possible to create a new driveway down the side of your house and build at the bottom with very little detriment to your existing home either in amenity or financial terms? A visit to your local planning department will either confirm or deny your hopes and will cost nothing to investigate unless you decide to go for an application. Prepare the ground first though and look out for precedents that you can quote if necessary. And if you live in a semi-detached or end-of-terrace house on a corner or between blocks in a high-density location, consider whether or not there's room to extend the terrace with another similar house attached to yours.

When studying the maps one normally looks out for the obvious plot that either exists in its own right or can be subdivided from a larger property. However, it is possible to make up a plot by stitching together smaller areas of land, part of which might be a portion of your own garden. If there is a row of houses, all with relatively narrow but longer than average gardens and one of the houses is on a corner plot with access to the road, then it might be possible to join up the rear portions of several gardens to make up a plot with separate access. The trick is to devise the scheme and tie it all up with legally binding options from each of the owners, allowing you to purchase in the event of satisfactory planning permission. Beware trying to go too far without such an option as, once you've got planning consent, a single owner, maybe with land-

locked land that has no intrinsic value other than as part of your plot, could hold you to ransom. Remember that, once again, it's important to demonstrate to prospective vendors that you are a private self-builder, that the scheme can be realised with little or no detriment to their continued occupation and that it is unlikely to adversely affect their values.

Self-build clubs and associations/Internet and discussion forums

Some builders' merchants run self-build clubs where you can meet other self-builders and attend meetings and seminars to discuss self-building in general as well as trade topics and products. These clubs often run a land list in their regular newsletters and by the nature of the merchant's position in the market, they often have insight into availability that's denied others. The Association of Self-Builders (tel: 01604 493757) tries to keep their members advised of any plots that they hear of and keep a note of local authority plots.

At the moment the Internet is not a powerful force for land sales but many estate agents are getting online and it's worth keeping a check on their various

Above: Drop in and chat to other self-builders. You'll be amazed at the wealth information that you'll come away with.

sites. Of course the Internet is really a bridge between many of the recognised ways of finding land and it can contain elements of all the other categories. Discussion forums, whilst not designed to sell land, do nevertheless throw up plots from time to time, particularly where someone wants to sell off one or more plots on a multiple site that they are buying or wants someone to join with them in buying a larger site.

Self-build jungle drums

Self-build sites are often quite easy to identify by the mobile home on site and self-builders can be a surprisingly excellent source of land. Nearly all of them will have had a long hard search for a plot but 'Murphy's law' determines that, having found it, they then continue to hear of others. Maybe too, they know of plots that they had considered before they finally settled on theirs and maybe also they know of situations where other would-be self-builders have had to give up on their hopes. The jungle drums beat loud in self-build land!

Joining in with others

Sometimes self-builders have double plots or obtain planning for more than one dwelling and want to sell off the spare plots. The chances are that when they do they'll try and sell to another self-builder through the self-build media or discussion forums rather than through estate agents. Sometimes prospective self-builders will want to bid for a multiple site and will advertise for other self builders to join in with them. Buildstore have recognised this with 'Plotshare'.

In previous issues of this book the advice would have been that you consider forming a Private Self-Build Group. This still happens from time to time and I have come across situations where groups of like-minded individuals have come together to buy up things like redundant hospitals and convert them to multiple occupation, as well as other cases where new homes have been built on a community basis. But in most cases the 1988/89 crash brought an end to all that and group self-build, in many of the forms it took before those dates, is no longer really around. That's not to say that it won't be back, but it is no longer a cogent force other than where it fulfils a specific social need and comes under the auspices of community self-build.

Nevertheless, the idea of being involved with others, perhaps developing a site together, sharing work on common services and co-operating in hiring plant and employing tradesmen, can seem attractive. But in order to do so, you do have to become one body, either in the form of a limited company or a self-build group. And the financial institutions really don't want to know about private self-build groups, tending to look upon them much as the Pharaohs looked upon the plagues.

So, if a larger site comes up, it's advisable to devise some way of building on it with others, *with you all acting as individuals*. The ease or difficulty of doing this will depend on the nature of any road or drainage works and therefore the smaller the number of actual plots, the simpler the task of sorting it all out will be.

In most local authority areas three or four houses can be built with access off a private drive. The drive will not be adopted by the local authority and the home owners will have to maintain it themselves. This makes it simple for each of them to buy a plot with the usual reciprocal liabilities to be responsible for the drive and drains, which are either built by the vendor of the land, or by the purchasers sharing the costs. Private driveways with multiple use do have their drawbacks, in that it can sometimes prove difficult to get everyone to live up to and pay for their responsibilities. That's why it's important that the details are worked out and fully understood in advance. On the other hand, there is a particular benefit in being able to control just who parks on or uses a private driveway and, unlike the cost of a proper road, it's unlikely to be a major proportion of the development costs of any one plot.

If there are to be four or more homes requiring a new access, it is quite likely that the authorities will require the road and the drains under it to be constructed to highway standards, with a bond to lead to formal adoption. This costs a great deal more money and is complicated, as either a single person or a formal body of some sort has to take legal responsibility for the bond.

The actual arrangements to build any common drive, road or drains have to be made very carefully. Avoid any joint responsibility for this work; it is far preferable that it should be the responsibility of one person or body. This could be one of the self-builders but, as only approved contractors can carry out works to or abutting the highway, it is more likely to be a contractor or civil engineer. This person or firm should provide a guarantee that the work will be done, preferably as a bank bond so that if they default the bank will step in and get the work done. In return they will look for a guarantee of payment from all of the plot owners, often with the money deposited with a solicitor, or with a second charge over the plots. In this way there are mutual obligations all round that will ensure the work is done, without any one participant's special circumstances threatening the whole job.

All of which presupposes that a vendor of a site for two or more homes is willing to sell it to multiple purchasers. Ignoring situations where someone has set out to sell serviced plots, what happens when an enthusiastic would-be self-builder sees a site for three units and thinks how nice it would be to build one of them, with two other people building the others? There are two options: either the first self-builder buys the whole of the site and immediately sells off the other plots, or else all three parties persuade the vendor to sell the site in three parts. In either case all the contracts will be signed at once, either with everyone using the same firm of solicitors or else with a gaggle of solicitors sitting round the same table. The contracts should include appropriate arrangements for any shared drive or services, or else take into account any requirement for an adoptable road, in which case a separate agreement for this should be signed by all the purchasers at the same time. Either way, the first self-builder who takes the initiative in this will probably have to obtain an option of some sort to 'hold' the land while they find their fellow purchasers and sort out all the details.

The self-build industry

Many of the package-deal companies and their local representatives might know of land that is available. Quite often prospective vendors contact well-known companies asking if they have clients looking for land. Do not expect the companies to tell you about plots that other clients are contemplating buying or building on because that would be anarchic. However, clients do sometimes have to drop out or are unable to proceed for reasons that have little or nothing to do with the suitability of the plot. In those cases, if you're in touch with the staff it might be possible to 'take over' the contract and plot.

Architects and surveyors, being local, often have a far greater knowledge of the plot situation in their area and, just like the package-deal companies, there may also be a 'wastage factor' in that, from time to time clients might drop out of a project. If you as a prospective customer can impress them with your keenness, then rather than waste a lot of work, you could well be the answer to their problem.

Local builders and developers

When the housing market is buoyant, developers buy up land and form their own land bank. When the market is sluggish and sales of their houses are down they might be persuaded to offload surplus plots just to keep some sort of cashflow going. However it's always worth contacting them as they might have plots upon which they're prepared to enter into a 'Turnkey' arrangement, whereby they'll build the house to your design. It's not strictly self-building and there is unlikely to be a significant saving over buying a house 'off the peg' but it can result in what you want. Occasionally developers have plots to sell on partially finished estates. Large estates of houses need areas set aside for site huts and compounds that are required almost up to the end of a project. At times, a new and more attractive proposition can come up and the smaller developer might be persuaded to cut his losses on the old site in order to make a clean start on the new one. The beauty of these plots is that they are serviced but the drawback is that you might be limited in design expression.

Farming and rural enterprise plots

Development of agricultural land is usually only allowed if it can be proved that it is necessary for the proper maintenance and running of a viable agricultural enterprise or an approved rural industry. That doesn't mean that if you've got a couple of horses in the field you can build to be near them but if, on the other hand, you run a successful livery or riding stables with a proven track record of economic viability, you might just get consent. It's often easier to demonstrate necessity on larger farms but it is also possible to prove a need for a dwelling on smaller enterprises such as nurseries, intensive units and specialist growers. The important thing to realise is that the land and its use, rather than the house, is paramount. As such, many new enterprises are required to demonstrate that they have been running successfully for some time and that it's really necessary for someone to actually live on site before a dwelling is finally approved. That means that the applicants might have to contemplate living in a mobile home for a time and any consent that is granted might limit the occupation of the dwelling to those engaged in running the enterprise.

It's not unusual for land or property to come onto the market with an agricultural consent where, by means of a planning condition, the occupation of the dwelling is limited to someone wholly or mainly engaged in agriculture, last engaged in agriculture or the widow or widower thereof. Sometimes these drawbacks are reflected in the price but not always. Sometimes the importance of the restriction is belittled or played down and you might be told that nobody will find out and that the planning authorities aren't really bothered. Don't accept this. Although many breaches of planning permission can be authorised if, after four years, no action has been taken, breaches of conditions can be enforced for up to 10 years. In many cases, if money is being borrowed against the property, the lenders will flag up the problem and refuse to lend on it, because they know, that in the event of them having to foreclose, they would have difficulty in selling it on. But a cash purchaser will not have this safeguard. Beware buying land like this, unless you are pretty sure that you fulfil the criteria for occupation.

Change of use/conversions

The country is dotted with countless redundant and unoccupied buildings ranging from old barns to shops, factories, water towers and churches, many of which, with flair and imagination could be converted to residential use, if only the planners would allow it. The situation varies from area to area with some local authorities enthusiastically welcoming the renewal and regeneration of these buildings whilst others actually state that they'd rather see them fall down than become homes. Check out your local authority's standpoint on this one. It's often well worth making a case for a change of use or conversion. Take out an option before taking things too far so as not to see the fruits of your efforts, if successful, enjoyed by others. Remember that what the planners and conservation officers are often afraid of, is that buildings might be developed in an unsympathetic way. So, if you can demonstrate that you really want to preserve the essential aspects and historical relevance of the building, your case will be considerably strengthened.

Renovations and extensions

The land agency lists are full of renovation opportunities that vary from almost complete re-builds to properties that really just need new kitchens and bathrooms. However, unless the change envisaged is fundamental there is unlikely to be the equity gain that is available with new build. Look for the house that is really the missed opportunity; for example the 1960s house that's too small or of a design that is out of character with the local vernacular, yet enjoys an enviable plot. Rendering or cladding, new windows, modern heating systems, thermal insulation and even, at times, new roofing materials that are more in keeping, can make a huge difference to enjoyment and value. Investigate whether Permitted Development Rights apply and, if so, utilise them to the full before making any planning application where an extension's acceptability might be related to the size of the dwelling. With historic or listed buildings there may be grants available to cover part of the costs of any remedial work, and this is discussed in the next chapter.

CHANGE OF USE

There are many old barns in the country and in villages, where their original use has long since faded away. We should make use of these interesting buildings and give them a new lease of life.

Above: This barn was in the terminal stages of decay caused by decades of neglect.

Left: The owners needed the space for their business of paper conservation but it could just as easily become additional living space.

Right: It's not necessary to lose the essential character of old buildings when bringing them into the modern age.

3. ASSESSING AND UNDERSTANDING THE POTENTIAL

The sum that you can afford to pay for a suitable building or plot, and the probable size of the house that you will be able to afford to build, have been discussed in Chapter 1. The whole business of design, what the planners are likely to let you build and the various ways of getting it built, have chapters of their own later in this book. It is important that you have read them before you start plot-hunting.

There are many other things to consider and they may, or may not, have a significant effect on building costs. The considerations that are dealt with in this chapter are those which may affect whether or not the site can be developed at all, or which may detract from the value of the finished property. Remember that the fact that a piece of land is described as a building plot does not mean that it is a practicable place to build a house. It only means that the vendor has chosen the words to attract prospective purchasers. By the time this book comes out the 'Seller's pack' may well have become universal but I very much doubt that the information contained within it will have any greater significance than the bland answers to questions that any purchaser or their solicitor would normally be asking and receiving. Remember the words, and legal terminology, *caveat emptor*, meaning 'let the buyer beware'. What follows is what you must be aware of.

Start by wondering just why nobody has built there before or done something with that redundant building. Really first-class individual building plots and development opportunities have been in very short supply for the last 30 years. Why is this still a building plot? Why is this building still empty? Why did no-one do anything with it 20 years ago? There may be a simple answer. The site may have been part of the garden of a large house and only split off from it recently, or planning consent may only have been granted recently following a change in a local struc-

ture plan which has hitherto prevented any development. Or, in the case of old buildings, perhaps nobody ever thought that they could be restored to proper use. Try to find out why no-one has built on the site or developed it in some way. The reason may not preclude you from building on it, but it is something that you have to establish at an early stage.

Planning permission

There are various types of consent, and in any consideration of a plot or development opportunity, it is important to appreciate the differences between them and their relationships to each other.

- **Outline planning consent** gives permission, in principle, for the development of land. It means that some sort of building or development may take place and it is what confers the value on the plot. Outline consent does not, in itself, allow you to commence work but, rather, it allows you to move on to the next stage of the planning process. It is always given subject to conditions, the first of which is that it is valid for a period of five years from the date of its granting *but* that application must be made within a period of three years from the date of its granting, for approval of reserved matters. These reserved matters are usually the siting, design and access arrangements, which are not normally dealt with at the outline stage. There may be other conditions and, at the next stage in the planning process, these conditions will have to be satisfied.

- **Approval of reserved matters** is the next stage in the normal planning process. It is sometimes referred to as 'Detailed Permission' and it concerns itself with the actual design, siting and access arrangements for the development. In normal circumstances, it does not confer any extra value to the plot, over and above that already given to it by the outline consent. Within this application any conditions imposed by the outline consent have to be satisfied and it is possible that fresh conditions will also be imposed. An approval of reserved matters never stands alone; it is always related back to and is a part of the original outline consent. As such, and as an example, if there is a condition on the outline consent that the development is for a single-storey dwelling, and the planning officer agrees that you may, in fact, make application for a two-storey dwelling, then you cannot do so as an approval of reserved matters pursuant to the original outline consent. A fresh application will have to be made.

It is necessary to understand, however, that even though the approval of reserved matters cannot stand alone, it does not follow that it is a mere formality. Additionally, the granting of an approval of reserved matters does not preclude further applications for quite different schemes relating back to the original outline consent and the refusal of an application for approval of reserved matters does nothing to negate the original outline consent.

- **Full planning permission** is really nothing more than a rolling up together of the outline and detailed stages of an application, into one consent. It grants permission in principle and at the same time considers and approves the full details of the proposed development. As such, it lasts for a period of five years from the date of its granting and it confers value to the plot in just the same way as an outline consent would do. Where the issues of whether or not the land should be developed are not in contention and it's more a question of establishing what will be built, then a full application is wholly relevant. On the other hand, any attempt to confuse or obscure the issue of principle by making a full application, rather than an outline application, is likely to backfire.

The words *permission* and *consent* are interchangeable in all that you read here (or anywhere else) about planning matters. Planning permission says that you *may* develop land, it does not say that you *can* develop land and it confers no other rights or obligations. If you get a consent, and for physical or legal reasons that consent cannot be acted upon, then there is no liability on the local authority.

Consents for approval of reserved matters and full consents can still have conditions attached to them which have to be satisfied before any commencement of work. An example of these may be that, before any work commences on site, the approval of the local authority shall be obtained, in writing, for a landscaping and tree-planting scheme. Another common example is that, before any work commences on site, the approval of the local authority will have been sought and obtained in writing for the use of any external materials such as bricks or tiles. In these cases the approval of these items is delegated to the officers and in the latter example they may wish to see samples of the intended materials. The condition may go on to say that this approval shall be sought, notwithstanding the materials mentioned or stated on the plans, but whether or not it does, these words are implied and you cannot rely on the fact that another material was specified.

Make no mistake, these conditions and their satisfaction are vital to the continuance and viability of a planning permission. I recall the case of a chap who bought a plot of land in the Green Belt, where there is a presumption against planning. Work had already commenced on the site and he, and unfortunately his solicitor, assumed that as the building had reached oversite, the planning was therefore perpetuated. What they didn't check was whether the condition requiring the authority's approval of the external materials *before commencement of work* had been cleared. It hadn't, and the planners maintained that, due to the passage of time, the consent had lapsed. A subsequent application was then refused on the grounds that development in the Green Belt was contrary to planning policy!

There are many other conditions which can be attached to any consent and which have the effect of making it inoperable until such time as they are satisfied. Most of these will be flagged up in this chapter and in the Site Details Checklist on page 108. But beware! It is, as in the case I've outlined above, possible to commence work on a project and even to get to the stage of a practically finished dwelling without addressing a condition. However, occupation and full operation of the consent will be illegal until the formalities are sorted out.

In the normal course of events the advice must be to buy only those plots that have an express planning consent, either Outline, Detailed or Full. To every rule there must be an exception, and I have discussed this partially in Chapter 2 and will discuss it further in Chapter 5. However, for the purposes of this section of the book we will assume that you are buying a plot with planning permission. The first thing to say about planning permission is that it normally 'runs to the benefit of the land'. That means that whoever the applicant was, the consent relates to the plot and not to the applicant or the previous owner. The exceptions to this are rare and relate more to things like the siting of mobile homes for prospective farm enterprises and the occupation of an annex. In these cases the exclusivity is normally achieved by the wording on a condition on the consent.

It's surprising to some, but the number of times a plot is offered on the market on the basis of it having planning consent when the reverse is in fact true, are legion. This situation doesn't usually occur through any deliberate attempt to mislead but because of the naivety of the people selling the plot. The first thing you need to check when buying a plot with planning permission is that the consent has not lapsed. As I've said above, planning consent lasts for a period of five years from the date of the permission. If it's a Full permission then it will simply state this fact but, if it's an Outline consent, it will usually say that the consent is for a period of five years and that within a period of three years an application for Approval of Reserved Matters must be made. In effect, therefore, if your prospective plot has Outline consent and you are being offered the land more than three years after that consent was given, with no Detailed application ever having been made, then the Outline consent is out of time. What normally happens here is that either a fresh Outline application has to be made or else your prospective Detailed application has to be changed to a Full application. Either way you are at risk in that, if the policy of the local authority has changed in the intervening period, your application could fail, leaving that parcel of land with no valid consent. You can see, therefore, that it's vital that, in these circumstances, you identify the problem quickly, and only agree to purchase the plot 'subject to receipt of satisfactory planning consent'.

Land will often be offered with either a Full consent which has expired or else with the benefit of a Detailed consent which has itself expired when related back to the original outline permission. *Check the dates on all planning documents.* If the expiry date is fast approaching then the vendors could apply for an extension of time, but the chances are that they will fail to see your concern. In their minds the land has got planning and it won't occur to them that the piece of land they've thought of for so long as money in the bank could be anything other than that. Your only option is to insist on buying 'subject to receipt of satisfactory planning approval' and if they won't play ball on that, then you have three other options: you take an enormous gamble and buy the land anyway, you pull away altogether, or you consider getting an option on the land and make your own application.

It may seem strange to some people but you don't have to own a plot of land in order to make a planning application on it. In fact you don't even really need the consent of the owner and all you must do is inform them, by means of a form in the planning application documents, that you are making the application. This means that if you come across a plot where the planning is suspect, it is open to you, preferably by agreement, to make your own application in order to clarify matters. In similar vein if the plot you're interested in has no consent, but you feel that it stands a good chance of getting it, then it's open to you to make an application before you actually buy the land.

Beware, though! The owner could let you get on with all this and then, when you've sorted it all out and enhanced the value of his land by tens of thousands of pounds, he could turn around and sell it to somebody else. To avoid this, either tie things up beforehand with a formal legally binding option or, as

Above: This farmhouse in the Peal Park proclaims its history and its magic and cries out for careful restoration.

Right: A barn conversion can seem a daunting prospect and the best way of achieving useful accommodation may not always be apparent.

I've said above, buy the land subject to receipt of satisfactory planning permission, in which case, if it fails, the contract is voided.

Does the consent relate to the property on offer? Quite often you can come across the situation where a vendor gets planning permission for a part of their garden and then, when it comes to selling, decides that he really can't stomach the thought of losing a particular tree or area of garden, and he just doesn't want the new house so close to his. The plot which was outlined in red on the plan, which got planning permission and which was shown as being 18 metres wide and stopping 3 metres from their house wall, suddenly becomes 12 metres wide and a long way from their wall. The area of land is still contained within the original outlined site, but it manifestly is not the same site and it is open to the planners to rule that the consent is consequently invalid on this smaller plot. A way around this, if the smaller site is acceptable to you, is for the detailed planning applications to go in on the basis of the larger plot whilst at the same time you proceed to purchase the smaller plot. But be very careful.

Although there's nothing to stop this happening, the planners won't necessarily go along with your new home being situated to one side of the plot, as they see it, and any explanation that you're only buying a portion of the original consent will have no influence on their opinions. In like manner, vendors can often simply move the original sized plot to one side so that it either partially or wholly slips out of the original area shown on the consent. They won't see that they've done anything wrong. But planners don't see it that way. To them the area which is outside the original red line does not have the benefit of any planning consent and whilst they may be amenable to this 'new' plot being developed, nevertheless, it doesn't have consent and your application will have to be a Full one rather than an Approval of Reserved Matters. Once more, in any and all of these instances, you need to be buying 'subject to receipt of satisfactory planning permission'.

Sometimes planning is granted conditional upon something else happening. An example of this would be where planning consent is granted on a plot, or plots, conditional upon, say, an old building being demolished. You're only buying the plot and the condemned building is outside your jurisdiction. If that part of the site is sold to another party who fails to demolish the old building then, although your vendor, and/or the other purchaser, is technically in breach of contract, you might find it very difficult fully to satisfy the conditions on your consent. It probably won't come to the point of totally invalidating your planning but it could lead to some sticky moments and the exchange of more than a few letters. So, it's best to point this all out to your solicitor at an early stage, unless of course he's already picked up on it, and to make sure that some sort of timetable and undertaking is given for the work to be done. Multi-plot sites are often given planning on the condition that certain works will be undertaken to improve or create an access and it needs to be established, right at the outset, that this work will be undertaken and that it is capable of being carried out – see also access, roads and visibility splays (pages 69 and 74).

Special conditions on a planning consent can impact on whether or not the plot is suitable for your purposes in the first place. It has become common for local authorities to stipulate the maximum, and very occasionally the minimum, size that a dwelling can be. They mean what they say. If it says that the dwelling must not exceed 180 square metres plus a garage then that's what you're going to get and no more. If it says the building must be single storey, then a bungalow is all that you're going to be able to build under that consent. In some cases it may even go on to limit what is known as 'Permitted Development', disallowing the future extension of the dwelling or the occupation or conversion of the garage, without express planning consent. Before I move on I'd better, therefore, explain briefly just what this Permitted Development is, although I will be covering it in greater detail later in the book.

Within the Planning Acts there are certain classes of development that can be carried out without the need for express or specific planning consent. You may still need Building Regulations approval but you don't have to apply for planning permission to carry out certain classes of development, including extensions up to a certain size, garages where none exists, and development within the curtilage of the building. It can be varied or negated within a consent and is usually excluded in conservation areas and in sensitive planning situations.

Brief mention needs to be made about planning on neighbouring land and 'Planning Blight'. In any consideration of a plot it's necessary for you or your solicitor, or both, to investigate what planning applications have been granted or are up for consideration in the locality that could possibly affect you. If you're buying a site with a sea view and then discover that a large hotel is going to be built that will completely block that view, you'll probably want to know about it before you commit to the land. In similar vein, if a major public undertaking such as a by-pass or an airport is being mooted, then, although it might be at the stage where no formal application or plans have been formulated, it could still have a dramatic effect on the property. Indeed, the possibility of it coming to fruition could well blight your property and render it virtually unmarketable. Now, although there may well be compensation available for such blight or indeed for any diminution of value or enjoyment if the scheme is ever enacted, I wonder whether, in most circumstances, a property such as this is a suitable one to take on.

It's not at all unusual, in certain parts of the country, to come across conditions on a planning consent relating to some sort of archaeological interest. Sometimes an archaeological survey is required, either before consent is granted or before any work is commenced. These are not cheap and, if anything of particular or peculiar interest is found, there could be an almost indefinite delay on any development of the land or property.

Occasionally, development will be allowed with special foundations that allow access beneath the dwelling at some future date. Usually, however, the authorities limit their involvement to a watching brief, in which case all that needs to be done is to notify the relevant department and allow them time to come out and inspect your foundation trenches.

If the plot is in a Conservation Area, Area of Outstanding Natural Beauty, National Park or the Broads, then there may be particular planning restrictions that you will need to be aware of. Similarly, if you are planning to convert or renovate a Listed building or if your site is in what is known as a Site of Special Scientific Interest (SSSI or triple 'S' 'I'). These issues are dealt with in Chapter 5, but once again, you should make yourself aware of the implications at the evaluation stages.

Access and roads

Unless you can gain access to the plot then it's of no use to man nor beast. You must establish whether a road serves it and if so what sort of road is it? It will fall into one of the following categories and if there is any doubt, your solicitor will establish exactly which one it's in:

A private road on landowner's land
If you are fortunate enough to be building in the country on a site reached by a road in this category, then you are involved with special circumstances. You must make sure that your right of access is enshrined in any and all of the legal documentation and it will be necessary to establish just who is liable for any upkeep and just how the need for maintenance is to be established. For this you will definitely need the services of a solicitor who is used to handling this type of situation.

A private unadopted road
Access onto a private unadopted road is a different matter, and again you need a solicitor who has, or will get, relevant local experience. There are many sorts of unadopted roads, but the ones most usually found by self-builders were made in the first 40 years of the century. At that time developers often sold plots leading off a private road with no intention that it would ever be taken over, or adopted, by the local authority. This was considered to be a way of guaranteeing that the development would always be suitably exclusive in the days before the planning acts. The plots and houses built on them were often very large, although sometimes this way of doing things was used in low-cost bungalow towns known as Plotlands.

Fifty years later these unadopted roads are often in a sorry condition. Planning restraints have now largely removed the fear of unacceptable further development, and the residents owning the road would usually dearly like the authority to take it over and put it in good order. The council will not do this unless all the residents pay 'road charges', which may amount to tens of thousands of pounds for each property. As it is most unlikely that they all can (or want to) do this, the road remains unadopted with only the most urgent repair work paid for by some form of residents' association, usually only when they find the cost of filling the potholes is less than the cost of replacing their broken exhausts.

Houses on the more upmarket of these developments often have large gardens, and high land values means that they will be subdivided and sold as building plots if planning consent to do this can be obtained. The bungalows on the Plotlands also have large gardens by modern standards and they are coming up for sale as sites for a replacement dwelling. Both of these types of plot are becoming predominant, especially in the light of government antipathy towards the continued development of green-field

Above: The window in the gable end of this house hints that the loft space has either been utilised or is constructed so that it can be in the future. (Design & Materials Ltd)

sites. But there are aspects that need very careful consideration.

What are the arrangements for the ownership and maintenance of the road? What road charges are likely to be levied? (Road charges are levied on the basis of a rate per metre of road frontage and that, if you're on a corner, could be quite considerable.) Above all, what is the long-term future for property values when the 1930 vintage road in terminal decay deteriorates further? Local solicitors and estate agents will be well aware of the local politics in such a situation.

In the case of Plotlands, there is an element of them existing outside the normal confines of society. Residents who have grown up and grown old in stigmatised situations may resist changes that either highlight the eventual demise of their beloved homes or threaten to involve them in expenditure that is way beyond their means.

In the case of the estates of larger houses, the affluence of their occupants might well mean that, in the intervening period, some form of legal framework

or documentation listing each owner's rights and responsibilities will have been set down. However, there are instances where no legal ownership can be established yet, clearly, several houses enjoy joint and uninterrupted access from a road, which they all maintain to one standard or another.

The Plotlands sprang up in the immediate aftermath of the Second World War with bombed-out people moving to the countryside to construct wooden and asbestos bungalows on plots of land sold off by local farmers. The bungalows are now fast disappearing, demolished to make way for modern country homes but the roadway still remains in its old state, both legally and physically. When whole communities originally bought their individual parcels of land nobody thought that the access would be anything other than just used by them all. Nobody thought that in 50 years' time each house would have two to four cars coming and going daily and, above all, nobody thought that, one day, people would need to demonstrate legal rights of way to get to their houses.

Your solicitor will want to, nonetheless, and he may face an uphill struggle with no party having exclusive ownership and all parties unable to show collective responsibility. It doesn't mean that you can't buy the land. Quite clearly the other residents are enjoying their access and it would be in none of their interests to block up or frustrate the use of the road. The older residents probably won't see what the fuss is all about with these newcomers wanting all this legal mumbo jumbo. The simple solution, if you can't just accept things as they are, is a *single premium indemnity policy* guarding against the extremely unlikely event of a chap arriving back from Australia and claiming the road as his own, and that can be arranged quite easily by DMS Services Ltd who can be reached by telephoning 01909 591652.

Adopted roads

Adopted roads, looked after lovingly by the council, would appear to present far less trouble. However, councils make rules about anything and everything, and their roads are no exception. Their rules for roads on new housing developments are demanding and precise, with thought given to the shape of cul-de-sacs to enable a fire engine to turn around easily, etc. Arrangements for the junctions between new estate roads and highways are very carefully considered, and this is all very right and proper.

However, to the misfortune of those who buy infill plots fronting a highway, the same careful consideration is given to their own modest drive access. In general terms, the higher the category of the road – A, B, unclassified, etc. – the stricter the requirements, and whatever the classification, there will be a concern for road safety. At the very least this will involve an absolute ban on vehicles joining or leaving the road at a sharp corner or at a blind spot. More usually the requirements will also involve setting back any gate a fixed distance from the carriageway, and providing a visibility splay. The actual junction may be required to be level or at a gentle gradient for a certain distance inside your property, with a further

maximum stipulated gradient for the next few metres of your drive. It is no use saying that you and your friends drive Landrovers; the council's concern is the brakes on their dustcart. You will be expected to make sure that surface water from your drive cannot spill onto the road, and you will also have to meet specific standards for turning radii, which themselves may depend on the width of the highway at your proposed entrance.

The Highways Agency's requirements for access to a highway are absolutely crucial to every aspect of the project, and must be given very careful consideration. The fact that there is a planning consent is not enough and there are many instances of plots having a seemingly innocuous condition that 'the entrance shall be formed to the requirements of the Highways Authority', where these requirements involve 60% of the plot having to be excavated to achieve required levels. It's also no good assuming that, if the access is shown in one way on your planning, you can simply change it. If the entrance to your plot is shown on the right-hand side of the road frontage then you cannot automatically assume that it can be moved to the middle or the left hand side of the plot without attracting attention from the planners and/or the Highways Agency.

Highway requirements vary in different parts of the country, and the rules in East Anglia are obviously going to be very different from those in parts of Wales or parts of the North. If you are considering a plot with access from a highway, you must get hold of the Highways Agency's requirements at a very early stage and consider whether the development that you propose for the plot will be practicable. And bear in mind that it is most unlikely that you will be able to negotiate any meaningful relaxation of their requirements.

Ransom strips

Whatever sort of road there is, does it directly abut the property or is there a strip of land in between? If there is, either visible on the ground, or apparent in the documentation or the plans, does the plot owner have the clear right to join the two?

Ransom strips are pieces of land: narrow strips, as

little as 150mm wide in some cases, between your plot and the access, which prevent the site from being developed. They are not there by accident. Someone has arranged for them, and the purpose is either to stop anyone building on the plot at all, or to make him pay a huge sum to buy the strip. This may sound like some sort of sharp practice, but in fact it is rarely anything of the sort. What has happened is best understood by looking at the historical background.

Ransom strips are usually in place to stop anyone building on the site at all, and the story probably starts when all the land, including both the strip and the plot, were part of the garden of a house or possibly a smallholding or farm. This may have been a hundred years ago. Someone who wanted to buy part of the land for some purpose or other, but who did not intend to build on it, probably approached the landowner, knowing full well that the owner did not want anyone building there anyway, perhaps because he wanted to preserve his privacy or the view from the house.

Now, the land could have been sold with a covenant to the title to prevent anyone ever building there. However, to make it even more certain that no one could do so, it was sold with just a pedestrian access and no way of getting a vehicle to it at all. As the purchaser did not want to build on it anyway, everyone was happy with this arrangement.

A hundred years later the big house has been demolished and the site where it stood is covered with modern homes at ten to an acre. At the time when they were built, it would have been sensible for our plot to have been developed as part of the same estate, but, maybe because the owner could not be traced, the plot lay dormant. Then, possibly by inheritance, the plot passed to someone who bothered to go to look at it. It is a gap in a built-up area and as such is likely to get planning consent. The new owner applies for Outline planning permission, not knowing or not bothering to mention that their boundary does not go quite to the road, and consent is granted.

What does our plot owner do now? He can trace the owner of the ransom strip, who will probably now be the hard-hearted developers who developed the site of the big house, and ask them to sell the strip. Alternatively, he can build anyway and hope that no-one else remembers about the ransom strip. If they do the former, the owner of the ransom strip may ask for a sum approaching or exceeding one third of the value of the unencumbered plot. If they take the other course and simply annex the strip and build a house, they run the risk of being detected and ending up with a house without an access.

One way out of this problem is to sell the plot, now with planning permission, as a building plot and to let the purchaser deal with this situation. The vendors will claim that they knew nothing about the ransom strip and, in most cases, it would be nigh-on impossible to gainsay them. In every sense of the words, the unsuspecting purchaser will then have 'bought it'. You need to make sure you are not such a purchaser. There are thousands and thousands of plots like this in Great Britain, and architects and surveyors who deal regularly with one-off houses for private individuals come across them quite frequently.

A similar situation arises when land without planning permission is sold and the vendor wants to ensure that he will receive a share of the increased value if it ever gets planning permission. Once again they could do this by means of a covenant in the deeds but, just to make sure, they create a ransom strip. At the time, both parties will agree to this, but a subsequent purchaser may not be told about it.

So what can you do to avoid finding you have a ransom strip situation? First of all, your solicitor will make sure you have a good title, but as far as access is concerned he can only rely on the vendor's solicitor's reply to a standard question in his enquiries. If the vendor's solicitor has not been told of the ransom strip, he may not be able to detect it from an old deed plan to an unregistered title. The planners may also simply not know it exists.

Does this frighten you? No need. If you follow a few simple rules you can spot a ransom strip very easily.

Rule one is that whenever you buy an isolated building plot you must first ask yourself 'why has no one built here before?' The vendor may give you a good reason, which you should treat with suspicion until it is confirmed. By following this simple rule you can avoid buying plots which are village duck ponds that have been filled in, or have a war-time air-raid shelter below the ground, or suffer a horrid smell from a tannery across the valley whenever the wind is in the east – or which have a ransom strip.

Rule two is to measure every part of the boundary on the ground and compare it with the plan on the title deeds – and this means the title deeds and NOT the plan in the estate agent's particulars! Why is the plot the shape that it is? If there seems to be a mystery, go to the public library and look at the 19th-century ordnance survey maps of the area. They often provide clues as to what has happened.

Rule three is to drop in at the local pub, strike up a conversation with the local busybody and ask his opinion of your prospective purchase. You may get told the soil is full of eelworm and won't grow brassicas, or that it was once the scene of a horrible murder, or that, 'there's a ransom strip, you know'.

Finally, if you do find a ransom strip situation, remember that it may be possible to sort it all out at a practicable cost if you go about things in the right way. Do not tell the owner of the strip that he is a despicable rogue. It is unlikely that he is and in any event he may not have created the ransom strip in the first place. It is actually often better not to approach him at all, but to employ an estate agent or intermediary. And certainly do nothing at all until you have taken professional advice. In some situations insurance is available to deal with an old ransom strip or an access title problem and, once again, details of this can be obtained from DMS Services Ltd on 01909 591652.

Shared access

Because self-builders are often concerned with plots that have been carved out of a large garden, they are often involved with arrangements for shared drives. If planning consent has been given on this basis, then the existing access can continue to be used. However, if you alter it in any way, the local authority may take

the view that you are forming a new access, and will insist that it meets all of their requirements. This requires careful thought. Equally careful consideration has to be given to the arrangements which you make with the established owner of the drive for its future maintenance, for its use by vehicles delivering materials to build your new home, and for parking on it. Local authorities will usually permit up to four houses to share one private drive, beyond which they are likely to consider it to be a road and subject to all sorts of regulations. The basis on which you may be sharing a drive with three other people requires very careful consideration.

A very basic requirement is an arrangement that there is no parking of any sort under any circumstances on the shared part of the drive, especially if this would have the effect of restricting normal access. It is also very desirable that the shared length should be constructed to a very high standard, and should be properly kerbed, so that it is as indestructible as possible to avoid difficulties over sharing the cost of refurbishing it at some time in the future. And when that time arrives, if you've followed the advice given above, then hopefully you are going to be able to insist that it is resurfaced, and that your neighbours pay their share of the cost.

Shared drives have short-term advantages and long-term problems, and if there is a shared drive some building societies will restrict the percentage of the value of the property on which they will grant a mortgage. Solicitors will elaborate on their disadvantages to prospective purchasers and estate agents might well confirm that the property value could be lessened by such an arrangement. However, this is frequently the only way in which some individual plots can be developed, and they are a necessary evil.

With all of these disadvantages, you might be tempted to think that you can just alter things, and go on to create a new access to the highway without the express consent of the planners. Even if they do agree that a fresh access to the road is acceptable, then they're going to insist on that access conforming to laid-down requirements. And they may not be achievable, particularly in respect of visibility splays but also in respect of requirements for gates, turning and parking areas.

Visibility splays

These cause endless problems, which probably start with a simple condition on the planning consent that says, 'the access onto Acacia Avenue shall be formed in accordance with the requirements of the Highways Agency'. All perfectly harmless, you may think. That is, until you realise and read on that their requirements involve a visibility splay and when you get out and measure the requirements for it, the lines cross your neighbour's land.

A word, first about what a visibility splay is, so that you can understand the full implications. The wording might ask for visibility splays 5.5 metres by 120 metres east and 5.5 metres by 90 metres west. Almost certainly that means that your plot is on the southern side of an east west road with the frontage facing roughly north. The longer visibility splay will relate to the traffic approaching on your side of the road and is calculated by measuring to a point 5.5m back from the carriageway edge along the centre line of your proposed driveway. From that point you then take a line eastwards 120m until it meets the carriageway and a similar line from the same point but to the west this time, and for only 90m, until it again meets the edge of the carriageway. These are your visibility splays. Now, if everything within those two triangles is within your plot then you've nothing to worry about except for the fact that, at all times, you'll have to keep those areas clear of any obstruction higher than 1005mm, and that includes shrubs and trees.

But what if the triangles you arrive at go outside your boundaries and cross the neighbour's land? The planners aren't particularly concerned about the legalities of this. Once again, planning permission says that you *may* build on the land; it does not say that you *can*. In their eyes it's up to the developer of the land to sort out any necessary easements or covenants, and all they're concerned with is that the requirements are demonstrated. So, if you're offered a plot with such a requirement and the vendors can't demonstrate that they have secured such easements or covenants, the planning is inoperable and until such time as suitable legally binding arrangements are in place, you need to steer clear of that plot.

You could, of course, try negotiating directly with the neighbours yourself, but be prepared for a chap who either sees this as an opportunity to afford a holiday home in Spain, or is equally determined that the plot next door will never be developed, even to the point of deliberately planting tress and shrubs within the visibility splays. It all sounds pretty hopeless, doesn't it? Well it's not always that bad. In many cases the requirements are limited or even non-existent and in others you'll find that the visibility splays cross the grass verge of the highway, which is fine. The thing always to remember is to check it both on site and on plan before you move on to buying a site.

Gates

Although many modern houses don't seem to employ gates and the drive is usually open to the road, in rural and forest areas a gate is essential, if only to keep sheep and other animals from consuming your garden. Where gates are employed, there will usually be a requirement for a 45-degree splay from each side of the gate and for the gates to be set back at least 5.5 metres from the edge of the carriageway, so as to enable a motor car to pull off the road completely whilst the gates are opened. In addition, the gates must then open inwards and if the slope of the land makes this impossible then your gates will have to move even further back.

Parking and turning

In some cases there is a requirement for all cars to be able to enter the site completely and then to be able to turn and leave the site in a forward gear. This is not universal. It will obviously be necessary if the access is off a busy road but might not be required at all if the access is from a side or estate road. If the requirement does appear on the planning document then you need to make a note of it because such a requirement can take up a large amount of land and will undoubtedly affect the positioning and indeed the size of your proposed new home. Most consents contain stipulations about parking spaces, either in addition to or instead of garaging. These can often be the parts of

VISIBILITY SPLAYS

The local authority will want an access like this ...

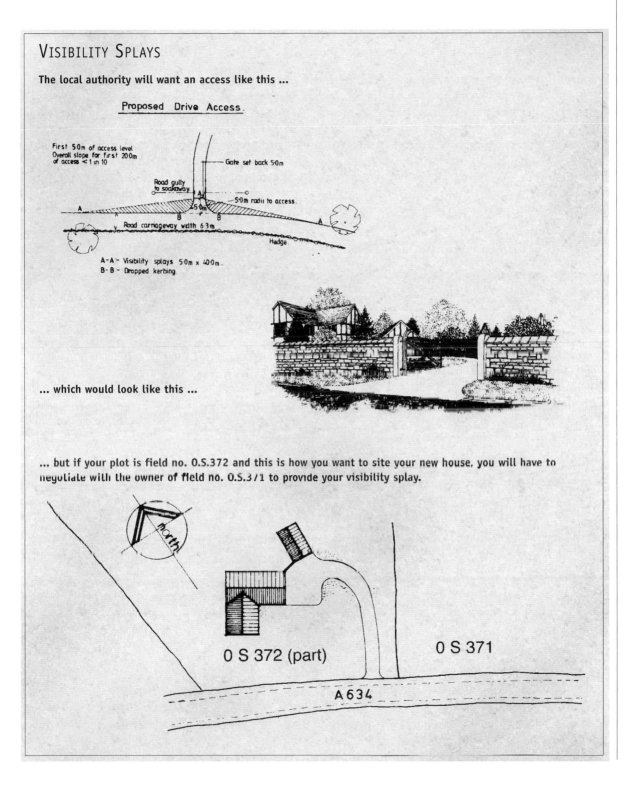

Proposed Drive Access.

First 5·0m of access level
Overall slope for first 20·0m
of access < 1 in 10

Gate set back 5·0m

Road gully to soakaway

5·0m radii to access.

Road carriageway width 6·3m

Hedge.

A-A - Visibility splays 5·0m x 40·0m.
B-B - Dropped kerbing.

... which would look like this ...

... but if your plot is field no. O.S.372 and this is how you want to site your new house, you will have to negotiate with the owner of field no. O.S.371 to provide your visibility splay.

north

O S 372 (part)

O S 371

A 634

the driveway created and taken up in the formation of the turning areas, but check the planning documents and requirements to make sure that what is being asked for is achievable.

Construction traffic

A major consideration when assessing a plot or development opportunity is just how you're going to get the materials on-site, and indeed, in many cases, considerable quantities of spoil off-site.

If you're going to have to offload materials at the bottom of an unmade lane half a mile from your plot and either manhandle or carry them to site on dumper trucks, it's going to cost time and money. If a lorry can't get to you at all and you haven't advised the suppliers, you could find yourself liable for abortive delivery charges. Trusses, for example, come on very long articulated lorries and if there are any low bridges or other obstructions, such as trees, you will need to take these into account. Ready-mixed concrete lorries are prodigiously heavy and if you crack your neighbour's drains, a local authority culvert or tear up the surface of the road, it could cost you a great deal of money.

Think also of the site itself. A concrete lorry is remarkably unstable and excess gradients or cambers on the immediate approach to your foundations could tip it over. I can tell you that the sight of one of these on its side in your footings is a daunting and very expensive experience. If you think that this is going to be a problem, arrange a dumper to take the stuff onto the site itself or hire a concrete pump. And if you feel that there's any likelihood of vehicles getting stuck in soft ground, at the very least make sure that a digger is on site to pull them out or, better still arrange for them to offload on firm ground.

Many people combine building their own home with holding down a normal nine-to-five job. Deliveries of materials such as blocks and bricks are often quoted by the day, with no particular time of arrival specified. The common solution to this problem, when it's known that the site will be empty, is to leave instructions posted on a board. But boards can blow over, kids can remove them and the lorry could arrive at an unearthly hour of the morning. Whilst not directly accusing lorry drivers of insens-

itivity, I have known them to just plonk materials down at what seems to be the most convenient place for them, without thinking that they might be blocking off the site entirely. I have even heard of loads of bricks and blocks simply being left on the pavement or highway and can recall many an evening when I had to shelve the job I was going to do and frantically remove vast piles of materials before my prospective neighbours lost all patience with me and my undertaking. Wherever possible, either arrange to be on site yourself, or pay someone to be there on your behalf; preferably a tradesman who can be getting on with something whilst they wait.

Trees

Almost everyone visualises their new house nestling into a plot surrounded by leafy trees whispering quietly in the breeze as the sun filters down to a dapple-shaded lawn. But cut to reality. Trees may complicate your plans, limit the size, the shape and the siting of your new house and make it considerably more expensive to build. There are many angles to this and they are best considered under four separate headings:

Trees and foundations

Trees can affect the foundations of houses in three ways:

- The roots may simply push into or invade the foundation brickwork and crack it.
- Roots can rot, leaving voids under the foundations when the tree is felled.
- In clay soils, when a tree is felled and no longer takes hundreds of gallons of water out of the subsoil, the ground may heave and rise by two or three inches.

All of these potential difficulties are dealt with by a combination of special foundation designs which are examined later on in this chapter (see page 81) but, in general, any foundation design to meet problems due to trees is a matter for your architect and structural engineer in combination. Your plans will not receive Building Regulation approval unless they are satisfactory and all of the relevant authorities and warranty undertakers will want to ensure that things are done properly.

One thing to watch for is a bad ground situation due to a tree having been felled before you bought the plot, often because the vendor wanted it out of the way before he advertised the land for sale. Sometimes he will have carefully filled in the hole. If the subsoil is clay the work involved in dealing with this can be considerable but any avoidance of the problem, to save money in the short term, can prove a costly and false economy.

The minimum distance between a new house and a tree depends on the tree's species, potential height and the nature of the ground. There are strict rules for this and they are, most conveniently, set out in the NHBC handbook. Whoever is designing your house and its foundations will deal with these problems, probably on the basis of, and as a result of, the soil invest-igation survey that you have almost certainly had carried out if there are mature trees present on your site. As a rule of thumb, it is unwise to build closer to a tree than four metres or one third of its mature height, whichever is the greater. On some soils this distance may be increased and with some species which are particularly harmful to buildings, such as poplar, elm and willow, the distances may be quite considerable. As I've said, I will deal with special foun-dations later.

Tree roots can also cause problems with driveways, which will be a nuisance but not specifically expensive to deal with. What is more likely is that the planners will be concerned that any driveway should not adversely affect the tree by compaction of the ground beneath them or by interference with the soil's access to air and water. Tree roots can also quite dramatically affect drains. The small young and beautiful weeping willow that you plant when you first move in may grow into a very large tree indeed; a joy to behold. But one day, the toilet may refuse to flush and you might find out that your prized tree's sustenance and vigour was gained from its roots' complete invasion of your drains!

Trees and planners
This is where the trouble starts and, without usurping

Chapter 5, on the planning scene, the subject of trees is of such importance that it needs full consideration at the evaluation stage of any project. Planners and the kind of people who serve on planning committees are fond of trees and there are three ways in which they can protect them:

- They can place a Tree Preservation Order (TPO) on an individual tree or group of trees that they think worth protecting. This prevents the felling of any tree or trees subject to the order and limits any pruning to authorised work that will not harm their health or appearance. If the authorities feel that trees are in danger, they can place a provisional TPO on them in very short order and this order remains effective for six months whilst the council considers whether or not to make it permanent.

  Removal of, or damage to a tree that is the subject of TPO can result in prosecution leading to a hefty fine plus a requirement that the tree is replaced. The exceptions to this are where specific planning consent has been granted within which the removal of the tree is specified, where the tree has to be cut down or pruned by statutory undertakers such as the water, gas and electricity boards or where the tree or trees are dead, dying or dangerous. Additionally trees on Crown land, and fruit trees grown for the commercial produc-tion of fruit are exempt from these orders, although that doesn't mean that simply putting a bucket of apples for sale outside your gate would qualify you to call your tree 'commercial'.

  You can obtain details of TPOs in your area from the local authority and, in common with most areas of planning, there is the right of appeal.

- Trees in conservation areas are subject to special protection. Any work to fell, lop or prune a tree in a conservation area requires six weeks' notice in writing to be given to the local authority. If they then consider that the tree is of importance to the area, they can issue a TPO in the normal way.

- In just the same way that planning conditions

can be used to permit the felling of a tree that would otherwise be the subject of a TPO, they can also be used to protect them. Additionally, conditions within a planning consent can require the planting of further trees and it is therefore possible for a TPO to be placed on a tree that has not yet been planted.

Any application for planning consent that involves felling trees always receives special consideration. If the trees are not subject to a TPO, you may decide to fell any tree which is in the way straight away, although due thought must be given to the possible future effect on foundations, as I have outlined above. If the removal of the tree or trees is likely to create a rumpus, you might well decide to do it very quickly and at a weekend so as to prevent a provisional TPO being issued, while you're busy sharpening your chain saw. This does happen. But you must be aware that action of this kind and the furore it might cause may have the effect of putting people's backs up and delaying or complicating any subsequent application.

If there is a TPO it might be worthwhile getting a tree specialist to make an inspection, and to provide you with a report. Hopefully he or she will write, 'the specimen is over mature and should be replaced' or at least, 'an unremarkable specimen which can be replaced without affecting the character of the local arboreal environment'. For every tree that you show on your plan to be removed you should show at least three replacement trees elsewhere in the garden, and make sure that the species are from any recommended list in the local design guide.

Sometimes this will do the trick. However, you may find that you get involved in negotiating about it with the planners, often with the suspicion that they care far more for trees than they do for people. As a last resort you can of course appeal but that could set your project back six months and it might be better to alter your plans. Whatever you do, this is one area where the guidance of someone with local experience is invaluable.

Trees and your design

A large tree or a group of trees within a hundred feet of any house or bungalow is going to enhance the appearance of the property, but must be taken into consideration at the design stage. Will part of the building be in shade at certain times of the day? What about views from key rooms? Should rooms be arranged to suit this? Above all, remember that an attractive green woodland scene in June can be a dank, dark miserable outlook in January. Big trees need their own sort of garden, bearing in mind that they affect everything growing beneath them, produce huge quantities of leaves, and usually rule out having a swimming pool. Living with trees means letting them dominate your garden and whilst you, like most people, might like that very much indeed, do not let it come as a surprise.

Many planning consents have a condition that a tree planting and landscaping scheme shall be agreed either before work commences or before occupation of the dwelling. This, just as with other conditions in the consent that I have already explored, is important and it is not something that can just be swept under the carpet and forgotten about. Of course you might feel that you are being asked to put the cart before the horse, and to an extent there is a lot of truth in this, in that it's awfully difficult to get things right at the early design stages. What looks fine on plan might, when translated into reality, be very wrong. All you can do is to specify the minimum and to try to imagine each tree and its possible effect on your future home, its outlook and enjoyment. That said, you might still come away with the impression, once again, that trees are sometimes more important to the planners than homes.

If you are planting trees for planning reasons or possibly to replace those cleared to make way for a house, keep in mind that they will be there for a century at least. If your garden is big enough to split off a building plot in the future, try not to cause problems by putting a tree in the middle of the potential plot. If you are planting a tree at the corner of your vegetable garden, make sure that it is on the north corner so that it does not shade your vegetables in the years to come. Choose the species carefully, and consider whether you want to make an investment in something really worthwhile that will grace your home and its surroundings for many years to come.

Above: Light, flooding within the house, is the guiding principle behind the design of this replacement riverside house in Surrey. (Design & Materials Ltd)

Right: Nestling into a wooded hillside in Cornwall, this house will continue to mellow. (Design & Materials Ltd)

Trees and neighbours

If your neighbour has a tree which overhangs your boundary and which will interfere with the house that you want to build, you must clear the situation with your solicitor before you commit yourself to buying the plot. In most circumstances you can cut the branches which overhang your fence, and you can cut roots that encroach on your land which will affect the foundations of the house that you want to build. But this can be a complex issue. It is particularly difficult if your activities would result in the tree becoming unsafe. Perhaps it is already unsafe? If it falls onto your house, you hope that your neighbour is properly insured or else very rich. He may be neither, and almost certainly he is unlikely to tell you, which is why you have to take out a self-builder's insurance policy to cover you until the house is built and your domestic insurance takes over. Also remember that a neighbour may choose to fell his own trees, seriously affecting your view and risking changes in the subsoil that could have a detrimental effect on your foundations. Whilst in some cases such action, especially if it involves excavation close to a boundary or your buildings, could be deemed to come under the Party Walls Act 1996, there is often, in fact, little you can do about this, short of resorting to a court injunction or other legal redress.

Everything is simpler if the trees are on the land that you want to buy, but you must still consider the implications at an early stage. First of all, your tree may fall across the boundary and damage your neighbour's property. This risk is covered by your self-builder's insurance policy while you are building and by your householder's insurance when you have finished, but the policies will require that you exercise normal prudence in this matter. This definitely includes being aware of dangerous trees and trees that present a special hazard, and doing something about it. If there is a potential problem here, you should get the tree inspected by a qualified tree surgeon who can either give you a report saying that there is no hazard, or can advise on sorting things out. If you are buying a plot with potentially dangerous trees you might be able to negotiate for such a report to be a condition of your purchase.

Neighbours can often stir up trouble with the planning authorities. Many planning applications receive objections from adjoining occupiers or from those who perceive that in some way or another, their enjoyment of and privacy within their home is going to be ruined by another dwelling. In many cases this, 'pull the ladder up Jack, I'm firmly in the dinghy', approach to any new development contains little or nothing that is of any consequence in planning terms. Except where they start to mention trees. That's when the planners often sit up and start to take notice. If you start to cut down trees on your property, it won't be the local authority who initiate action, even though they will be the ones taking it – it will be your neighbours.

Ground conditions

Ideally, you are hoping to build on good bearing ground, which will support the weight of your new house using simple and cost-effective foundations. Sadly, this is not always possible and you must be conversant with other options. Incidentally, the cost of dealing with difficult foundation situations as a proportion of the total cost of the whole house has dropped dramatically in recent years with the result that most sites can now be economically developed.

The first potential problem is that there may have been mining activities in the area and that there is consequently some danger of ground subsidence. This is normally detailed in a mining report attached to the planning consent, and at the very worst it means that you will be building on a reinforced raft instead of on orthodox strip footings. The additional cost is unlikely to be more than 5% of the total cost of the new home.

Geological problems are more complicated, and more difficult to detect. The principal hazards are that there is a spring on the land or a slip plane between two types of rock, which outcrop on the land, or that you have a pocket of greensand under the turf. Fortunately all of these hazards are normally easily detected by someone with a practised eye, and in areas where they are likely to occur you will find plenty of people to point them out to you. Another problem can occur with high water tables or badly draining ground. The usual warning is an area of grass that is unnaturally green in the summer and marshy in the winter, perhaps with indicator soft rushes or sedge. At the worst, this can involve you building on piled foundations at an additional cost of up to 20% of the building cost, but it is more likely that you will have to install a few hundred pounds-worth of land drains.

A serious foundation problem can exist if you are building on filled land. This is not always readily detectable, but if there was an old building on the site you should check whether there are cellars below the ground. Again, for hundreds of years there were brick pits in villages where the locals fired their own bricks for their homes. When this ended the pits became rubbish tips, and now they are gaps between homes that appear to make ideal building plots. So they are, provided that you understand the need for special care in designing the foundations.

Should you immediately rush to employ the services of a soil investigation engineer? Well, not immediately, although it may well come to that in the end. First, try having a chat with the local Building Inspector and tell him what you're planning to do and where. He'll have seen and inspected nearly everything in the area and, even if he wasn't directly involved with the project next door to yours, he is probably still aware of what went on. He won't only have had dealings with new properties being built, he'll also have inspected any extensions that have been built and, especially if he's from the old school, I bet there's very little he doesn't know about ground conditions in your area. If he thinks that there's a possibility of bad ground then he'll say so and in that case you really need to get hold of a soil investigation company who will come along and dig or bore some trial holes to establish just what you've got. Another thing to do is to make a beeline for the oldest inhabitant, in the pub, and ask him about the history of the plot. He may remember that the village duck pond was there or that the butcher used to use the hole in the middle to chuck the old bones in.

Should this soil investigation prove to be advisable or necessary, normally everything's fine and dandy but there are a few things you need to understand about this survey. The engineer will dig or bore holes in three, possibly four, positions on the site, evaluate the contents of each bore and come to his conclusions

and recommendations based on those trial holes. What he is telling you is what he's discovered from those holes. He's not telling you what would have been in a hole a few metres away, although from the holes he's dug he may well extrapolate and assume certain conditions. What you've got to remember is that this report, useful as it is, important as it is, is nevertheless a report based on four trial holes and the only real survey that is 100% accurate is, in the end, your actual construction work. That makes it all the more important that you get out and about and ask around, because that's the only way you're going to find out that there was an old air raid shelter in the centre of where you're going to build and in the middle of all these trial holes. And if all this fails to turn up a problem and you go on to buy the plot? Well, chances are that it's not going to be that serious anyway and you'll know you did all you could but the rest was in the lap of the gods. In the end, that's what your contingency fund is there for.

Foundations

What can seem like a foundation problem to one party can, by dint of the fact that its solution has become common practice in one area, seem like the norm to another. In certain areas of North Nottinghamshire and South Yorkshire, to build without using an edge beam raft would almost be unthinkable. Yet, if the same system of foundation were suggested on a site in Essex, there would be much scratching of heads and the price would escalate way beyond its actual cost. In similar vein, the Essex builder is probably quite used to digging trenches three metres deep and lining the sides with compressible material surrounding amounts of concrete to rival the Berlin bunker, in what the Yorkshire builder would prefer to think of as civil engineering.

Special foundations need specialist engineers to design them. The need for this and/or for special foundations should be flagged up during your initial site investigations and from asking around with local builders, neighbours and the Building Inspector. It's surprising just how many actually start work, only to discover that something different has got to happen.

If you do discover that you need the services of

any of the experts in this field then the first port of call should always be the local Building Inspectors. They won't be able to recommend anyone in particular, but they will probably be able to give you three or more names of suitable people and, by reading between the lines, you should be able to deduce which one is the most favourable. Free and very good advice is available from piling contractors but they may be seen to have an axe to grind. You'll find them in Yellow Pages. Alternatively, your architect might be able to recommend someone with whom he can work to come up with the foundation solution that will suit both your site and the design proposed. That might seem like the perfect solution, and it often is, but all of this might be happening when you are still in the process of considering the plot or property and you might not want to commit to a particular architect, practice or package-deal company at that point.

Here are some of the possible foundation solutions and the reasons behind their employment:

Reinforced strip This is a simple solution to minor problems which can occur with a normal strip founda-tion where, say, there are a couple of soft spots or there are some minor differences in bearing capacity or depths. It really just involves putting either rein-forcing bar or mesh, usually 50mm from the top and the same from the bottom, in the concrete, which is sometimes also thickened up a little. It's relatively easy but care has to be taken in the placing of the reinforcement and in keeping it in place during the pour. This should be done with little metal tripods but you will often see it wrongly done with bricks, blocks or even paving slabs.

Trenchfill In certain cases where the ground is clay and there are trees present, you may have to go for trenchfill foundations where the concrete, instead of just being at the bottom of the trench, is brought nearly all the way up to the top. It can also be used in wet or waterlogged ground or where the topsoil is unstable even though the bearing ground is fine. In these conditions it can often be the best choice as, by definition, one is out of the ground in a day and the need for bricklayers to work below ground, or the pos-sibility of a fall in, is minimised. If these latter factors

Above: Studying an earth bank or exposed subsoil can tell even an amateur a great deal about ground conditions.

Right: Why is it that it always rains when you've got trenches open? These need to get the concrete in quickly before the sides fall in even more.

Above: Complex shapes are not the vernacular in all areas and simplicity is an important design format. (Custom Homes Ltd)

create this option then there can be a saving as the trench width can sometimes be narrowed to 450mm instead of the more usual 600mm. Most often, however, the use of trenchfill is dictated by the presence of clay and trees and in these cases, as I've previewed above, they can go down to depths of around three metres.

In areas where the subsoil is heavy clay, the removal of trees can have disastrous and quite dramatic effects. Trees take huge amounts of water from the subsoil and even in the depths of winter the ground beneath a tree can be quite dry and friable to a considerable depth. When the tree is removed, the ground becomes waterlogged again and, if it's clay, it will expand, causing the problem known as 'heave'. Even if the tree is not to be removed, which, as you can appreciate, is often the worst solution to the problem, account has to be taken of the effects of the living tree on your proposed home and the possibility of it dying.

The solution in these cases is often a refinement of the trenchfill principle by the employment of a compressible material down the sides of the trench, usually just to the inside edge but sometimes to both faces. This absorbs any sideways compression with any upward, frictional pressure being relieved by a slip membrane of sometimes one, but usually two layers of thick polythene. The problems are obvious. If there is 50mm, and sometimes 100mm, of compressible material on each edge of the trench, then that trench has to be dug considerably wider to accommodate both this material and the concrete it will sandwich. Additionally it's often necessary to go down to depths of up to three metres in order to seek out ground that has a consistent moisture content or where the effects of the tree's demands are reduced. Not only does all of

SPECIAL FOUNDATIONS

Reinforced strips

A simple solution to minor prolems. If you are pouring your concrete yourself take expert advice on how to keep the mesh in position.

Trench fill

Expensive in concrete but minimal labour costs. Popular with self-builders.

Edge beam raft

Commonly used but a job for an experienced tradesman.

Piled foundation

A specialist solution to difficult problems. Consultants and piling contractors will add significantly to your costs.

Subsidence raft

In coal-mining areas the local authority will insist that you build on a raft like this, and if you still have subsidence problems you will have an automatic claim for compensation.

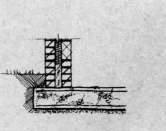

this mean that there is considerably more spoil to dispose of, but the deeper one goes, the more unstable and dangerous the foundation itself becomes. Add to that the huge amounts of concrete (sometimes up to 100 cubic metres for a single house) and the high cost of the compressible material, and you can easily see that this solution has its limits. There therefore comes a time when it's easier to go down another route.

Piled foundations In the old days the very mention of the word would strike terror into the heart of any self-builder. But things have changed quite dramatically and the rig that comes is no longer like a mobile version of the Eiffel Tower and instead, a whole range of more user-friendly mini-pile rigs have been devised. It wouldn't make sense to try to describe all of the variants but essentially they boil down to three types:

- *Driven piles* use either a shell of concrete or steel that is then filled with concrete. They are noisy and the vibration that they cause could well upset your neighbours and result in you having to replace an expensive set of antique plates that have fallen from their Welsh dresser.

- *Bored piles* are a little more friendly and mini-pile boring rigs are often mounted on a small lorry or Landrover-type vehicle which will of course need access on to the oversite area; something that needs to be considered *before* it arrives rather than afterwards.

- *Dug piles* are sometimes carried out by specialist contractors but they can just as easily be undertaken by your normal groundworker assuming he has the correct digger with the appropriate reach.

The reinforcement bars within the piles are usually, but not always, left sticking out of the top for incorporation in the ringbeam or ground-beam. It is at this point that the most recent and welcome advances have been made. One of the most difficult things after the completion of the piles, as far as the self-builder is concerned, is the ringbeam itself. If it is to be cast in situ, then not only might it need to be isolated from the ground by the compressible materials I have described under trenchfill foundations but, almost certainly, the reinforcement is more likely to be in the form of cages rather than simple mesh top and bottom. These cages have to be fabricated by specialists to a bending schedule prepared by the Engineer and their installation is a daunting task. They need to be positioned perfectly within the eventual concrete and they need to be wired up and connected to a schedule. Now, along comes the great idea of having prefabricated pile caps with similarly prefabricated ringbeams that are simply lowered into place to span between the piles, thus achieving in hours what can take days if not weeks to realise.

Incidentally, I mentioned the fact that the reinforcement is not always left sticking out of the top of the pile for incorporation into the ringbeam. This occurs when there is the possibility of lateral ground movement. Here it's possible to use wide dug piles with the narrower ground beam spanning from pile to pile, yet separated from them by a slip membrane.

Raft foundation A raft is employed where there is likely to be significant movement in the ground but the ground itself has good bearing capacity. In the coal-mining areas of the country you can see a field with a depression running across it and, as the days go by, this will move across the land. It happens when the roof is allowed to fall in as the coalface moves forward half a mile or more below ground. Any structure which is to withstand that kind of movement has to be able to float over the 'wave' whilst, at the same time, maintaining its integrity. The solution is a reinforced raft. As I've said before, in the areas where these need to be used the builders are completely familiar with them and what looks suspiciously like a swimming pool in the course of construction turns out, in the end, to be a raft foundation which shouldn't cost any more in real terms than those foundations which are considered standard in other parts of the country.

When considering special foundation situations, remember above all that you are unlikely to be alone and that others in the area will have experienced similar problems and invariably worked out the best and most cost-effective solutions. Perhaps, once again, the best place to start is at the council offices with a chat with your local Building Inspector. He'll have seen it all and I'm sure that he'll be pleased to point you in the right direction.

Radon gas

A special foundation situation in some parts of the country results from the presence of a naturally occurring radioactive gas called radon, which seeps from the ground. Radon is present everywhere in the atmosphere, and accounts for 50% of natural background radiation. (Less than 1% of background radiation comes from Sellafield or Chernobyl or any other human activity.) Modern houses with good draught proofing can build up concentrations of radon which seep up through the foundations, and in some areas this health hazard is now recognised as making a significant contribution to the statistics for deaths from lung cancer.

As a result, there are special design requirements for houses built in areas where there is a high level of radon seepage, and Building Inspectors will advise on this as a matter of course. The precautions involve making foundation slabs gas-tight, and in some areas of high risk, also providing ways for the radon to be discharged into the atmosphere. This is not complex, difficult or expensive but it has to be done. The government Radiological Protection Board has a range of free leaflets about this, and even offers test kits to indicate radon levels. You can telephone them on 01235 831600 or fax 01235 833891.

Radon has been part of everyday living for the human race since the dawn of time, and until very recently our draughty houses meant only cave dwellers were at any risk from it. Modern Building Regulations completely remove the risk, which is very small anyway, and if you build in Devon there really is very little risk that you will end up glowing in the dark.

Contaminated land

District authorities have a duty, under the Contaminated Land Regime, Part 2A of the Environment Protection Act 1990, to inspect their area for land considered to be 'contaminated land'. In consequence, landowners are also required to notify the authorities if their land is contaminated. Contaminated land is deemed to be land where the contamination is likely to affect an underground watercourse, humans, livestock or the natural environment.

The onus is therefore on a vendor to advise all interested parties of the possibility of land being contaminated and their failure to do so could result, not only in prosecution by the authorities, but the possibility of civil action for damages from an unhappy purchaser. Wherever possible, the authorities will try to enter into a dialogue with owners leading to voluntary remedial action being taken. However, they do have enforcement powers and, if all else fails, a Remediation Notice may be served requiring a landowner to take certain steps to clear up or prevent further contamination. If that fails or if the problem is so serious that the council has no alternative but to

step in and clear up the problem itself, they can do so and will seek to recover the costs of such work through the courts. Planning applications are also referred to the Environmental Protection section of the Environmental Health department of the district authority in the form of consultations, and they may make recommendations regarding the application and any remedial action they consider necessary.

All of this might seem a million miles away from most people's idea of a dream site but the fact is that as land and suitable property for conversion becomes ever more difficult to find, things like filling stations as well as previous industrial sites are being considered for housing. With a modern filling station there's usually no problem but older and pre-war stations often had concrete tanks that leaked like sieves, leaving the subsoil contaminated with hydrocarbons. At the very least, if you were to build on such a site, you could expect to have to remove the contaminated soil but, in some cases, the contamination might be considered so detrimental that no building could take place on certain parts of a site.

The names coined in recent times for sites, usually in urban areas, which have already been developed in the past but whose use has now lapsed, is 'Brownfield sites'. This conjures up visions of broken factories, contaminated land and disused waterways. In the years since the end of the Second World War, many of these sites have been left to decay in favour of the development of the 'Greenfield site'. Now, however, political pressure is being applied in an attempt to stop the wholesale destruction of the countryside and attention is being focused back onto the redevelopment and regeneration of inner city and town areas. In the main these kinds of sites are more suitable for multiple development but sometimes, and this will become increasingly common, there are single plots, which come out of their redefinement as useful land.

The problems experienced with their development are manifest but, of most interest to the individual self-builder, are probably those associated with existing foundations. That's not something that is entirely confined to an inner city site, as any who have developed an old farmyard will know. But what's more likely in the town is that these old footings may

Right: Radon gas is a problem that occurs in certain areas but it is one that is easily solvable.

well be heavily reinforced, sometimes still having the steel girders protruding from them. New foundations may have to be constructed to go below previously disturbed ground and avoid 'hard spots'. Contaminated or previously consolidated subsoils and topsoils may have to be removed and replaced entirely with fresh new earth and you will almost certainly need a full soil investigation and survey followed by an engineer's report.

Sloping sites

If you're lucky, a sloping site will come with a levels survey or contour map but if it doesn't, it's perhaps the first thing you should commission before any serious work is done on possible designs. A levels survey may, at first, appear to be an indecipherable jumble of lines and figures, but they are actually, quite easy to understand. The figures all represent a height

relative to a particular datum point, which can be the cover of a manhole or some other immovable object on or near site, but might equally be an Ordnance Survey datum point, completely removed from the plot. The figures therefore have to be read in relation to each other and if, for example, the figure on the front-left hand corner of the site reads 100.500 and the figure on the front right hand corner reads 101.500, there is a rise of one metre from left to right. Similarly, if contour lines are drawn, the figure against each one is the level along that line and you can extrapolate the relativity of any other point on your site by reference to its proximity to each line.

In parts of Wales, or in the West Riding of Yorkshire, homes are commonly built on sites with one

BUILDING ON A SLOPE

Option One
Build up above the slope. Involves suspended floors, some additional foundation costs, and the need for very careful landscaping to conceal the large area of brickwork below floor level. Will improve the view, especially from the balcony.

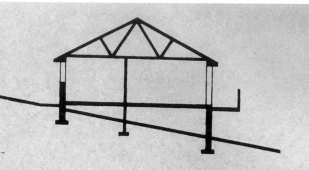

Option Two
Build into the slope. Permits a cost-effective solid floor on natural ground, but may require a retaining wall or steep garden to the rear. Excavated material will have to be carted away unless it can be used for landscaping on stand.

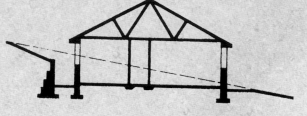

Option Three
'Cut and Fill'. This is the usual approach, combining the minimum foundation costs with the look of being built into the hillside. Care required with landscaping.

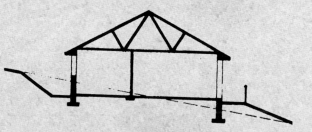

Option Four
Multi level. Garage below with living accommodation above, following the slope. Gives interesting layouts with opportunities for balconies to take advantage of views, but construction costs will be high. Inevitable steps outside and changes of level inside may limit resale potential.

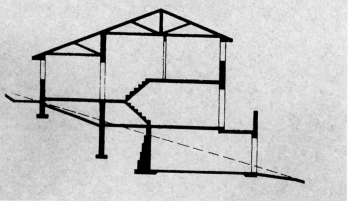

in five slopes, and local styles and the local building practices are geared to this factor. In other parts of the country any slope at all is deemed to merit special consideration. Wherever you are going to build, the first thing to do is to have a careful look at how other people choose to build on slopes in the local area, and to try to analyse the basis for the regional practice.

This may depend on the ease with which excavations can be made. If there is rock just below the surface, it will probably determine that buildings are built out from the slope because of the high cost of quarrying into it. If the subsoil is easily excavated, there are many more options. Local cottages may nestle into the hillside because in earlier centuries they had to do so to escape strong winds, which had an adverse effect on poor local building materials. This may have given the area a particular style which the planners will expect you to accept.

Wherever you build, there are two approaches to be considered. Should you arrange to remove the slope, or should you design a home to make use of the slope? If the site permits, it is invariably cheaper to excavate a level plinth for a new home, adjusting the levels and spreading the surplus soil as part of your landscaping. This involves either just digging into the slope, or else digging out part of the plinth and using the excavated material to raise the level of the other part. This is called 'cut and fill' and the sketch entitled 'Building on a slope' more than adequately illustrates it.

Digging out a level plinth is not always possible, sometimes because the site is too steep or the ground too rocky, but usually because the plot is too small to allow for the necessary changes of level. Remember that you might not be able to excavate close up to your neighbour's fence as, in law, his land is entitled to support from your land and in turn, that might mean construction of expensive retaining walls. All of which will be of enormous interest to your neighbour and will, in his view, be the cause of every ill that his property suffers from that day forward. In this case you may well have to consider a design to make use of the slope, which usually means a multi-level home.

A property of this sort is more expensive to construct than one which provides the same living accommodation on a level plinth. This may affect the eventual value, as it is generally true that while split-

level homes are exceptionally attractive and lend themselves to exciting decor, they often have a limited resale market.

New homes on sloping sites often involve special foundations. In simple terms, your designer has to make sure that the whole building will not slide down the slope. The cost of such foundations is one reason why many sloping sites have not been developed in the past, and are only now coming onto the market as rising property values make the costs acceptable.

One advantage of a sloping site is that it usually comes with an interesting view. If you are deciding whether or not to buy a plot on a hillside, remember that the view that you have from your ground level is not going to be the same view that you will enjoy through the windows of the finished house. If the outlook is very important to you, do not hesitate to take a couple of step ladders to the site and make some sort of platform that will enable you to stand at a level from which you can see the view as it would be from the windows of a finished home. You may look rather ridiculous at the time, but if the view is a key factor in making your decisions, make sure that you see what you will really be getting!

River frontages and flooding

After years of drought, with hosepipe bans seeming to become part of the pattern of summer life, we now have flooding. We're told that this too could become an annual event and it does seem clear that climate change has brought with it wildly variant and unsettled weather. In the previous edition of this book I talked about using unwanted cesspools as aquifers but now, less than three years later, the emphasis seems to have shifted in favour of flood precautions. What the floods of 2000 and 2001 have brought about is a greater awareness amongst the house-buying public and the people who insure houses. The Environment Agency has produced maps showing areas that are likely to flood. Central government is cautioning local government about the granting of planning on floodplains and there are indications that unused planning permissions in these localities will not be renewed.

The maps that the Environment Agency uses are sometimes wildly inaccurate. Nevertheless, they can

SLOPING SITE

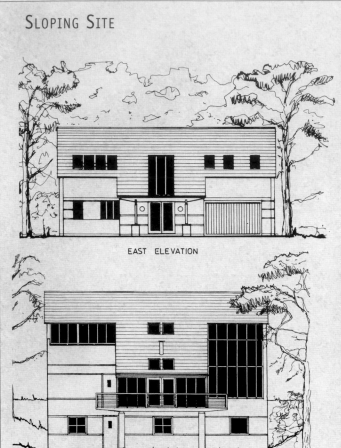

EAST ELEVATION

WEST ELEVATION

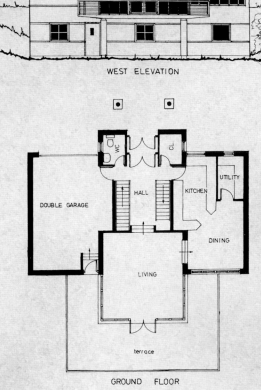

GROUND FLOOR

Nottingham-based architects Julian Owen Associates tackled the design of a new home on this site with relish.

Right: The front elevation only hints at what lies behind

Below: The living area, with its vaulted ceilings, seems almost one with the decking and garden that it overlooks on three sides.

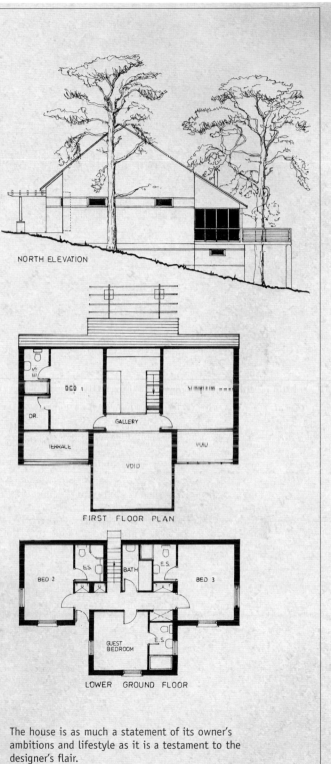

NORTH ELEVATION

FIRST FLOOR PLAN

LOWER GROUND FLOOR

The house is as much a statement of its owner's ambitions and lifestyle as it is a testament to the designer's flair.

Photographs courtesy Nigel Rigden

stop people wanting to buy houses and can severely affect the insurance premiums of those who continue to live in them. There's no doubt that there is a serious problem in some areas. Flood levels and the incidence of flooding have to be re-assessed all over the country. But for those localities where the river has been a consistent and desirable feature, there are usually solutions that have stood the test of time. In the Thames area, that solution is to build houses with a raised oversite and foundations that allow the flood-water to pass freely beneath the floor, a bit like having your house up on brick stilts or piers. It might sound dramatic but, in fact, this lower covered level often proves very useful for storing boats, canoes, and even for parking.

Plots with river frontages are always in demand, offering the prospect of interesting gardens and possibly fishing rights or even a boat house and river picnics. If you have a chance to build a riverside home you will have already considered flood levels and any special foundations requirements. But it is also impor-tant to know about the rights and obligations of a 'riparian' landowner, the name given to someone who owns a riverbank.

You may be obliged to leave an unobstructed route along the bank for Environment Agency plant and vehicles, and they may have the right to dump mud dredged from the river onto your land. You cer-tainly cannot assume that you will be able to build a boathouse or tidy up the banks without permission. On the other hand it may be a condition of your consent that the riverbank is shored up and that could involve you in some fairly expensive sheet piling. Nevertheless, if you've managed to secure a river frontage plot then you're probably not short of a bob or two and, particularly in the Thames area, you'll not have flinched from paying as much for your plot as most would only dream of their finished house being worth.

Plot details and site dimensions

Estate agents details are remarkably frothy about dimensions 'The site has a frontage of approximately 14 metres and a depth of around 45 metres', are words which might well persuade you to have a look at a plot. But when you get there, you do need much more than that to get any further forward in your assess-ment of it.

With a large overgrown plot, you may have little or no option but to consider commissioning a full survey, possibly in tandem with a levels survey. But with a small plot, there's no reason why you can't do things yourself, so long as you go about it in the right way. Start by measuring the frontage, the two sides and the rear width. Then take the measurement from the back right hand corner to the front left hand corner. When you've got that, take the measurement from the back left hand corner to the front right hand.

These last two dimensions are the triangulations. Hardly any plots are going to be perfect rectangles or even parallelograms and by using these measurements you can determine the actual shape of your potential plot. On a large piece of paper, measure out the frontage. Then, using a pair of compasses, with the point at the extreme of the left frontage, make an arc the length of the left-hand boundary. Place the point of the compasses on the extreme of the right-hand frontage and make an arc the length of the relevant triangulation measurement. Where they cross should be the proper position of the junction of the left boundary and the rear boundary. Repeat the process, in reverse, for the other boundaries. You might have to jiggle things about a bit and you might find that you need to take some measurements again, but you should, by this method, get a fairly good idea of the proper shape and dimensions of your plot.

If the boundaries are curved or uneven, use the same procedure to create a theoretical straight line shape from point to point and then measure off those straight lines to mark the actual boundaries. If the lines of measurement are interrupted by buildings, it might be necessary to leave it to a professional but you could still produce a fairly good representation by means of breaking the site up into a series of triang-ulated shapes.

Measure out the distance that any adjoining prop-erties are set back from the road, making a note of double- and single-storey projections. Measure the rear building lines as well. Although building lines as such have largely fallen into disuse and most authorities recognise that they were a bizarre invention of the recent past, where there is a definite one, it is usually necessary to conform. In any event, any building that you propose should bear a proper relation to its neighbours to prevent any excess overlooking in either direction. Make a note also of the distances that each neighbour is from the boundary, as you will be expected to conform to what is usual in the area. If possible, and especially where the boundaries are defined by hedging, try to establish who is responsible for each boundary. This might not be possible without reference to the deeds and neighbours might seize the opportunity to establish that the fence that's badly in need of repair is your responsibility whilst the hedge that is $1^1/_2$ metres thick is completely within their property and was never planted on the actual boundary!

If disputes on the boundaries seem to be in the offing, attempt to settle them before actually buying the plot, putting the onus on the vendors to establish exactly what they are entitled to sell you. Now, that's the ideal, but the fact is that these things sometimes don't crop up until the land has changed hands and the neighbour with designs on enlargement thinks that, as the new boy, you'll be an easier touch. Don't be. Get some stakes and some wire and, in consultation with your solicitor, clearly mark out the boundaries and send a letter by recorded delivery to your neighbours, telling them that you've established the boundaries and marked them out accordingly. The onus is then on your neighbour to get in touch with his solicitor to try to establish his claim on *your* land, and not vice versa. You have the initiative and, possession being nine-tenths of the law, it will be your neighbour who faces the uphill struggle.

Make a note of the north–south axis. If you're a sun-lover and the motivation for self-building is, in part, the desire for a sunroom or conservatory, this is something you'll need to know right from the start and could mean that some plots are not going to be suitable for your purposes.

Certain regions have what is known as high-exposure ratings where wind-driven rain can cause problems. In these areas you will not be allowed to use full fill cavity insulation for brick and block construction and, instead, will have to employ one of the partial fill solutions, at a slightly higher overall cost.

In areas that suffer from high exposure, the architecture has evolved to cope with it and you may have to incorporate features such as tabled verges and position the house in such a way as to minimise the wind damage. Living close to the sea can be wonderful but the effect of the wind-blown salt on your windows and joinery can be devastating. Almost certainly you'll have to shelve any ideas of painted timber or raw aluminium and even the more upmarket galvanised steel, powder-coated metal or Pvc-u joinery will need special attention and washing down on a monthly basis. Check with the local Building Control department to see if you're in one of these areas.

Drains and sewers

Any consideration of a plot must include drainage from three points of view. The first and most important is, of course, *foul drainage*, the drains which will take and dispose of the waste water from kitchens, bathrooms and toilets. Is mains drainage available and, if so, is it at the right level in the ground to enable you to connect to it by a normal gravity connection or will you have to employ a pump? Is the connection available within your plot or on the highway directly adjoining your plot and, if not, do you have the necessary easements and consents to cross other people's land in order to make the connection? If mains drainage is not available will you be able to use a septic tank or a mini treatment system? If the ground is capable of accepting percolation, will the Environment Agency and/or the local authority delegated to act on their behalf, accept such a system in that location or will they insist on a cesspool? Septic tanks are not normally acceptable in urban or built up locations.

Surface water drainage is the other form of drainage, which you will have to evaluate. This is the water that is collected by the rainwater guttering systems on your house, from its outbuildings, driveways and pathways. It all still has to be got rid of and, except in a few, ever-diminishing locations where there are combined drains, most local authorities will not allow it to discharge through the foul sewers. In some areas the local authority will insist on surface water being

Above: Sometimes the hard landscaping becomes part and parcel of the main structure. (Photograph courtesy of Robbens Systems Ltd)

connected to their surface water drainage system. In others they prohibit any private connections, even from driveways directly abutting the highway. Usually surface water drainage is discharged through gullies and pipework to a series of soakaways on the plot. These soakaways can in acceptable ground be quite simple rubble-filled holes, but in other areas where the ground is less amenable to accepting water, you might be required to construct quite elaborate soakaways from perforated concrete rings or purpose-built brickwork. It may also be necessary to conduct a percolation test for both foul- and surface-water drainage systems, of which more anon.

Land drainage is the one aspect of drainage that everybody forgets. If a site is waterlogged then it's an absolute certainty that your construction work will exacerbate the problem unless specific measures are taken to get the water away. Sometimes it's enough to lay land drains in the foundation trenches of the new home, before they're backfilled, in order to conduct the water around the house and away. At other times it may be necessary to lay individual land drains across the site to take water coming onto it from the surrounding land. What you don't want, is to live in a swamp. When looking at the plot for the first time, make a note of the kinds of vegetation. Crack willow and alder prefer damp conditions and sedge and rush growing on the land is an indicator of bad drainage.

One way of draining land quite well can be the foul drains themselves. You can't, as I've said above, directly connect any surface water or land drains to the foul drains. But the drains are, nonetheless, surrounded by clean pea shingle and the lie of that medium will follow the drains away from your site creating a form of 'French drain'.

But back to foul drainage. The best of all worlds is obviously a private foul sewer crossing your land to which you can make a gravity connection in the run of the drain. As easy is the situation where the run of the drain is in the grass verge or on unmetalled land over which you have the right to pass for a connection. More usual is the fact of the sewer being in either the footpath or the highway. Here, you're faced with an entirely different scenario. It's no use just thinking that you can gaily go along and dig holes in the Queen's highway. As with alterations to the carriageway and new access arrangements, any work in relation to new drainage connections will require various licences and consents being issued by both the highways authority and the relevant water board or sewage authority, although in most cases the local authority will act as their agents. This work can only be carried out by approved or accredited contractors and the mechanics of how it all works is discussed in Chapter 10.

If the mains drain is too far away to be reached by gravity or is at a higher level than the level of your proposed house, then the answer could well be a pumped system. A pump can be used in two ways. It can either lift the effluent from the level of one run of drains to a run at a higher level after which it can then continue as a gravity drain to the connection with the main sewer, or else it can be employed to pump the effluent all the way to the sewer connection. It involves a small holding tank which is usually fitted with twin electrically powered pumps and macerators operated by a float control. These units break up the sewage and then pump it up and along a flexible pipe to its destination. If this is to be a drain at a higher level then it normally discharges into a manhole at the start of the next run of gravity drains. Alternatively, the flexible pipe can be laid, possibly by an agricultural contractor using mole drain equipment but, more usually, by a mini digger or the narrow bucket of an ordinary digger, to the discharge point.

Some of these pumps can move the effluent for half a mile or raise the level by as much as 18 metres but the chances are that on a single dwelling or even on a small group of dwellings, nothing like this ability is needed. The pumps obviously cost money and they do need proper installation, maintenance and a power supply, but they are efficient and reliable and the costs can often be offset by the savings of having to lay a flexible pipe in soil rather than proper drains surrounded in pea shingle.

In some cases where connection to a main drain is expensive by reason of it, say, being a very busy main road, the choice of a pump to take the sewage to a different discharge point, even if an easement has to be purchased, can prove cost effective. Incidentally, as a footnote to pumps, whilst we're not talking here about surface water drainage, there are specific cases where the levels may dictate that the only way to get surface water away is to utilise a pump. In these cases a similar system is employed, but here there is no need for the macerator.

And then there is the plot where mains drainage is neither available nor achievable. The person who is selling it tells you there will be no trouble, as everyone in the area has septic tanks. This may be so, but it will be a major consideration in your development of the land, and it is important to understand clearly what is going to be involved. First of all, the good news is that all the ways of dealing with the problem are now much cheaper as a percentage of the total cost of building a home than they were a few years ago, and the current solutions are also much more effective. This is because of the use of plastics and fibreglass for the underground tanks that are involved, which have replaced the old brick ones.

All the tanks arrive as prefabricated units, which are simply dropped into place in a suitable hole and connected up. On the other hand, concern about environmental pollution means that everything to do with the discharge of sewage effluent is extremely carefully controlled and monitored. You may think that the best thing to do is to contact the Agency first of all to get their advice on what steps to take. Well, getting the various leaflets and guidelines may well be a good idea but contacting the Agency about your specific problems at too early a stage, before you've taken the best advice and allowed the professionals working on your behalf to devise a system, may not be the best plan. Far better to 'keep your powder dry' until you have the answers and can present these as an effective solution to your drainage problems as well as the Agency's concerns.

If there is an existing drainage arrangement on site – perhaps an old brick-built septic tank – which has been discharging the treated effluent for at least 20 years and is still working, it may seem an attractive option to carry on using it; one that, on paper, could save you a considerable amount of money, time and effort. On the other hand, this is a very uncertain area in the law and the Environment Agency now has the power to regulate and prevent any discharge that fails to conform to its requirements. Nevertheless, you may decide that you should use the existing system and that your drawings should show the drainage going down a pipe which is marked on the drawings 'discharge to existing septic tank'.

If the existing system is working well, and you know this for a fact, then you're doing nothing wrong. If, on the other hand, you know that, at times, the effluent flows across open ground or that there's a secret discharge to a nearby ditch or stream, then you should question whether you really want to be responsible for a local typhoid outbreak at worst, or at best, a country stream flowing grey instead of clear. Don't imagine that such activity will remain forever undetected, especially if attention is drawn to the system's existence by the presence of your new home. And don't imagine that the Environment Agency is a toothless organisation – far from it: it has tremendous powers and, once employed, the solution imposed could well prove to be far more costly that anything you would previously have envisaged.

If your plot and your proposals involve the creation of a completely new drainage system then it all comes down to three major options with a few variations and a couple of other interesting ideas. The Environment Agency, through the Building Control system, will be the final arbiters of which system you do actually employ. They will take into account the type of soil and subsoil on both your plot and the surrounding land and whether you are in the catchment area of a water supply. Almost certainly a percolation test will be required, to establish exactly what sort of system is to be employed and once more, although we're talking principally here about foul drainage, some local authorities will also require a similar test to establish what type of surface water drainage is employed.

A percolation test, which is usually carried out by the applicant or his agent with the details being given to the authorities, involves digging a hole in the ground, filling it with water and timing how long it takes for that water to go away. Obviously any old hole won't do and in general what is required is a 300mm cube with its bottom 600mm from the surface. This cube is then filled with water and allowed to soak away for 24 hours, after which it is refilled and the time taken for the water to disperse is noted. These figures are then used to calculate what system of drainage is applicable or workable on your land and the nature and quantity of any weeper drainage which will be needed. The best possible solution and the one that is likely to prove the cheapest to install, is a septic tank.

A *septic tank* is a miniature sewage works that requires no external power, involves no pumps, and houses millions of friendly bacteria which break down the sewage into sterile effluent which is discharged into the ground. Septic tanks are quite small, requiring a hole about 2 $\frac{1}{2}$ metres across and 3 metres deep, and they can cost less than £500. They are easily installed. They need to be pumped out by a small sludge tanker once or twice a year, at a cost of just under £100 a time, and all that you see of them, above ground, is the manhole, which gives access to the interior. New and innovative versions that increase aeration and speed up the bacteriological process are coming onto the market all the time. The prices are obviously higher but the principles remain essentially the same.

A septic tank relies on the fact that its final effluent will be discharged into the subsoil. That's why the percolation test is so important. If the subsoil is of an impermeable nature, such as heavy clay, or the water table is too high, then the effluent will not be able to get away and it will back up into the tank and stop the entire process.

If the ground conditions are not quite right or there is a requirement for extra refinement of the effluent because of, say, proximity to a watercourse, then the authorities may require that your septic tank discharges into a filter bed of some sort before the effluent is passed on down the weeper drains. These extra requirements for land drainage may mean that a self-builder building on a restricted plot has to seek and obtain easements allowing the installation of drains on adjoining land. In other cases, the requirements for the quality of the effluent discharge may mean that an entirely different system has to be employed, known as a mini-treatment plant.

A *mini-treatment plant* works like a septic tank insofar as it receives raw effluent and then processes it into a sterile effluent that can again be passed into the ground. Where it differs considerably is that it is electrically powered and that the quality of the effluent is often good enough to be discharged into a ditch, stream or other watercourse. In certain circumstances this can happen as a direct discharge but, more often, it is effected through either weeper drains or a filter bed of some sort. Whereas a septic tank utilises mainly anaerobic bacteria (those which live without air), the mini-treatment plant utilises both these and the aerobic bacteria (those which live in air), to break down and neutralise the sewage. This is effected by either a paddle or turbine system alternately exposing the effluent to air and water, whilst all the time passing it through towards the outlet, or by the introduction of a stream of air to the settling effluent.

The merits of each type of machine will be trumpeted by the various manufacturers but the essential factor is not how they work, but the quality of the treated effluent. The prime cost of one of these units for a single house is in the region of £3,000. In addition, they require a power source and regular maintenance. That said, they are a significant advance on the sewage disposal systems of previous generations and as we all become more and more aware of the need to restrict contamination of our ground water, rivers and streams, they have an increasingly important role to play.

I mentioned at the beginning of this section that there were some interesting variations and these have much to do with the use of reeds. Reeds can soak up and neutralise an extraordinary amount of effluent and, space permitting, a reed bed can often solve a problem with effluent quality. In some cases a septic tank can discharge, probably with the aid of a pump, onto a series of flat reed beds and in others an even more satisfactory system can be devised using floating beds of reeds growing on mats. With a series of baffles, such a system can return perfectly good water to the environment and at the same time provide a magnificent habitat for all forms of waterlife. The drawback is that most self-build plots simply don't have the space for such an enterprise.

And what if the authorities won't allow any of these solutions and all the tests prove to you and everybody else that your ground just isn't suitable? What if the plot is in a built-up area where mains drainage is either not available at all or is available but any further connections are banned until either the drains themselves have been upgraded or the local sewage treatment plant has extra capacity? Well, then you're on to the third option, the one involving a *cesspool*. A cesspool is bad news in one sense but, if that's the option that you're left with, then the best thing is to try to see it as the way forward in the development of the site of your new home. Cesspools are simply great big tanks, which hold your sewage until a vehicle comes to pump it out and take it away. The normal size of a tank for a single dwelling is 18,000 litres, and it has to be emptied quite frequently at a cost of up to £250.

A modern fibreglass cesspool will cost about £2,000 and the cost of the excavation and installation may be significant. It goes without saying that a cesspool is the solution of last choice. It also goes without saying that many of the factors which make the use of a cesspool necessary, such as waterlogged or rocky ground, are also the factors which tend to increase the cost of its installation. There may also be latent problems in that possible buyers may be put off by it and, where a cesspool is employed because the mains drains are not yet ready to accept additional burden, the planning consent may well require and demand that once the sewers have been upgraded, the house is then connected. That means that one day, maybe only a few years after the occupation of your new home, this large piece of expensive below ground equipment will become redundant. Once again, you have to look at the big picture and consider all of this as an incidental but necessary expenditure in the achievement of your new home. It does, however make sense to spend that little bit more, whilst you're building, putting in the by-pass drains and the road connection as far as the boundary.

Above: Lowering a standard septic tank into the prepared excavation.

Left: Solutions to the treatment of sewage continue to evolve with hybrids between the various methods and specialised extras for individual conditions.

Right: Chalk is usually a good medium for sub strata drainage solutions, so there must be a planning reason for this site to employ a cesspool.

Thought also needs to be given to the siting of any such tanks. Modern tankers can often pump sewage from tanks up to 60 metres away but if the route is convoluted, with your house in the way, that distance can very soon be eaten up. Balance your obvious wish to hide them at the bottom of the garden with the need to get access to them.

Grey water systems are coming onto the market whereby the less harmful wastewater from baths and wash basins can be re-cycled for use in flushing toilets. Whilst that may not seem much, there are estimates that up to one third of domestic water usage is involved in flushing the toilets. The water is of course filtered and does require chemical dosage from time to time and there is, therefore, no question of nasty

soapy water coming out of the cistern. The tanks used for grey water re-cycling are fairly small as they are constantly being topped up, whereas those used in rain water re-cycling, which can be used in the garden as well as for the toilets, have to be a lot bigger. I have my doubts that these systems, worthy as they are in terms of saving the planet, are fully cost effective for most self-builders at the moment, although it wouldn't take much of an increase in water or sewage rates to alter my view.

However, the separation and division of wastewater does lead to some interesting variations. It is sometimes possible to take grey water to a soakaway via interceptors and grease traps. It still leaves the problem of what to do with the toilet effluent and,

Above: This Aquatron system separates the grey water from the solids with the latter being composted in the large black box, ready for shovelling out for use in the garden!

around so that the water and the solids are separated. The grey water is taken to a soakaway and the solids fall into a composting bin that is shovelled out and put on the garden every so often. Not everyone's cup of tea, I admit, but interesting nonetheless, and useful in certain circumstances.

Finally, some good news. When you install a septic tank, mini-treatment plant, cesspool or some other system that negates the need to connect to the sewers, you can apply for a reduction in water and sewage rates and the savings can go towards emptying and servicing costs.

Services

Most estate agents' details state that as far as they are aware all mains services are available, but then go on to say that any prospective purchaser should satisfy themselves as to their availability. Chances are that the agents haven't even bothered to really investigate. We've already discussed drains so what we're talking about here is gas, water, telephone and electricity. You may not wish to make formal applications for all of these before you have actually bought the land, if only because you wish to avoid paying the application fees, but you should satisfy yourself that they are readily

usually, the only solution is for this to continue to go to the main sewage system. But there are other solutions, which will appeal and revolt, in unequal measures. In the main, the old-fashioned chemical toilets will not be acceptable under current regulations, but composting toilets, which have been around for some time, may be acceptable. However, I tend to think that the number of people who would relish the thought of sprinkling sawdust down the toilet after use instead of flushing it with water, is fairly small.

Of more interest for the hardy few, who by necessity or conviction cannot or will not connect to the main sewer, are the centrifugal systems. In these the toilet is flushed in the normal way and as the effluent descends the downpipe to a basement, it is whirled

available at a reasonable charge. Contact each of the suppliers and ask them for a quotation for the supply of their services together with a map of just where they are.

Following privatisation and the splitting of responsibilities, all of the service providers, including those concerned with the supply of gas, now make a charge for a new service. For an average house in a suburban street or a large village, you will need to allocate around £1,500 for the services and where the services are not close by, considerably more. If mains gas isn't available it's not the end of the world as there's always the option of Lpg (Liquid petroleum gas) or oil as the firing source. If mains electricity isn't available then things get a little more tricky. Although small modern generators have made huge efficiency strides in recent years, they are nonetheless fairly expensive to buy and maintain.

Technology, gained in part from space exploration, has come up with the option of photovoltaic cells on the roof. They are, however, frightfully expensive and at best can usually only supplement the normal power supply so they are, at their current level of development, not to be considered as true alternatives. So too with solar panels. Quite apart from the cost and the sheer ugliness of these things, they can, at best, only hope to augment other heating sources. I have heard claims of savings in fuel costs of 80%. I'm more inclined to believe that it's half as much as that in the most favourable circumstances and half as much again in most instances. The non-availability of mains water can be a problem but in some areas even that can be got around by the use of bore holes. If you're in any of these situations then you are probably thinking of building in an extremely rural location, in which case you're either a farmer or a seeker of things from another age and much of this will be old or welcome news for you.

Diverting drains and services

This book repeatedly urges anyone considering buying a building plot to find out why it has not been developed in the past. One reason may be that there is a sewer, gas line or electricity cable across the site, and that the authority which installed it took an easement

to do so from the previous owner of the land, thereby prohibiting anything being built on top of the drain or service, or within a certain distance of it. This creates what is known as a 'sterile zone' and unless the drain or service can be diverted, the plot cannot be developed. This situation is regularly exploited by self-builders because, unlike builders and developers, they often have time to arrange the diversion, and the patience to cope with the huge correspondence that is likely to be involved.

If you meet such a situation it is important to arrange an option or conditional contract on the land before you research the problem, as otherwise you may get everything sorted out only to find that the vendor puts up the price or decides to build on the land himself! The price should reflect the cost of the diversion, which can be significant, so you have to establish this before committing yourself in any way.

Make a start by obtaining a photostat of the actual easement granted to the service authority, which should be with the title deeds. If it is not in intelligible language you will have to seek the help of an expert to work out exactly what it says. If it is a very old easement, particularly a 19th-century one, you may find that there is a clause requiring the authority to move their service at their own expense if the landowner wants to build his dwelling on top of it. This is often a feature of old electricity cable easements. Do not celebrate too soon: in the 1950s the electricity boards offered sums to all the landowners who owned such rights to extinguish this part of the easement, and many of them accepted. If they did, the documentation involved may never have been with the title deeds. However, the board will not have lost their copy!

Usually you can expect to be quoted a most unreasonable sum for moving a service and it may take a lot of patience to get a quotation at all. However, once you have a quotation, it is an admission that it is technically possible to move the service and you can then start to negotiate. Try to reach the engineers concerned rather than the legal department of the services authority. The engineer may permit you to seek tenders for this work to be done from a list of approved contractors, which will probably be cheaper. It may also be possible for you to open the trench involved, lay the gravel bed and back fill after the drains, pipe or cable have been laid by the contractor. This will probably save a lot of money.

Read any quotation carefully to see that it's strictly relevant to your site. If there is an overhead line crossing your plot, and that line also crosses the line of houses on either side, the board might well seek to get the whole line buried underground, whereas all you're interested in paying for is the bit that crosses your land. Whilst that might still mean that a pole has to remain at each boundary, the costs of taking the service underground on your plot only will be significantly cheaper – unless of course you can persuade your neighbours that burying the whole thing will benefit their properties and that they really should join in with you to get it all done.

If you are successful in negotiating some arrangement for the diversion, and the arrangement to buy the land reflects the cost of the diversion, make sure that the legal arrangement with the authority refers to you or your successor in title, so that if you buy the land but have to sell it on for any reason a potential purchaser does not have to re-negotiate the whole business.

If a private drain or sewer crosses your land, probably linked to the houses on either side, this is often a cause for celebration rather than dismay – even if it crosses your plot under the planned position of your new home. You're not going to have to go to the expense of having to create a new road connection for a start. In all probability the drains are laid at 1:40 when modern drains can run at 1:60, or at a pinch 1:100, so levels are probably not going to be a problem (1:40 means that the drains fall one metre for every 40 metre run).

Your designer will probably show the drains diverted around your house with your drains connected to them. But the reality is that you would have had to build the drains anyway, and what actually happens is that you build your drains and then the other drains are diverted into yours. Usually the existing drains are allowed to continue running through the site until the last moment with your foundations built around them and then, when the diversion is made, they become redundant and can either be removed or left in the ground.

A word of warning on this point, one which does not crop up very often but is not unknown. Sometimes on a private estate the deeds allow for the use of a private drain by named houses with no provision made for the splitting off of plots and the creation of extra houses. In these cases it is often necessary to get the agreement of the other houses on the estate for the fresh connection and this is something that your solicitor needs to check out and which is really the responsibility of the vendor in the first place. On the other hand, as I've said repeatedly, vendors have a habit of failing to understand your concerns and you might find yourself having to make the running on this one. Make sure, therefore, that you do have things tied up by some sort of option or contract before you go about enhancing the value of a vendor's land. If ransoms are payable to the other occupiers then this really should come off the asking price of the plot.

Easements

This word has appeared several times in the preceding sections and it is now time to explain what it means. Easements grant a legal entitlement to the benefit of one party or owner of land, over land belonging to another party. Statutory Undertakers take out easements to enable them to cross land with, say, electricity cables or gas mains. Such services can benefit the land but they can also blight it. A high-pressure water main or sewer can sterilise land up to six metres either side of the run. Easements can also give others access or the right to pass over your land for the purposes of access to another parcel of land and their importance needs to be properly examined when you are evaluating your possible purchase.

That's the negative side. Easements can also benefit your land in granting you, say, the right to use a driveway or access or in giving you the right to connect drains or services over an adjoining piece of land. In general, they are very similar to covenants although they tend to grant specific rights of passage and use, rather than attempt to modify the way in which a particular piece of land may be used. Just like covenants, discussed below, they can be altered or modified and carry the same rights of application to the Lands Tribunal and the same warnings.

Covenants

Another legal problem which can prevent the development of a site is the existence of a restrictive covenant on the land. Covenants are clauses in a contract for the sale of land, which are binding on all future owners. They either require that something shall be done, or dictate that something shall not be done, on or with land. Such covenants may be very old indeed, and may have passed with the title to the land since the middle of the last century with the reason for their existence lost in the mists of time. The covenant that causes the most consternation is one that prohibits any development of the land. Others typically require that any property to be constructed shall be of only one storey, shall be set back a certain distance from one of the boundaries, or shall not have any windows facing in a certain direction. With modern plots it's not at all unusual to have a covenant put into the deeds by the adjoining vendor, stating that, 'no development shall take place without their prior approval of the proposals'. However, it has been maintained that the words 'such consent not to be unreasonably withheld' are implied, even if they are not actually expressed. Sometimes the house that benefited from these covenants has long since been demolished, and the original owners have died or gone away. The covenant, however, remains.

It is possible to have restrictive covenants removed but this is a job for a suitably experienced solicitor. It is an extremely lengthy business involving application to the Lands Tribunal who have discretionary powers to modify or remove covenants if they see fit. The outcome is never certain and, as with all lengthy legal procedures, the costs can escalate quite alarmingly. It is usually quicker and easier to take out indemnity insurance against the possibility of anyone claiming rights under the covenant and this is discussed in Chapter 4.

Footpaths

In rural areas a common difficulty is that there is a public footpath running over the land, possibly coming over fields from the village and joining the village street through the land where you would like to build your new home. It does not matter that the footpath is disused: if it has been gazetted and appears on the local authority's footpaths map, then it is as firmly there as if it were a public road.

It is possible to have a footpath moved, but usually only if the realignment is going to be more convenient, in every way, for those using the path. This usually means that the new alignment has to be shorter, less muddy, more easily maintained and provide a nicer view and a more pleasant walk. It is absolutely no use thinking that the footpath can be shifted to run round the edge of your site, which will not bother anyone because hardly anyone uses the path anyway. Not only are footpaths protected in law and jealously guarded by local authorities, but there are also footpath preservation associations with members who make it their business to try to make sure that they are never, ever moved. Probably the best advice on moving a particular footpath will be obtained from a local solicitor, who may know what applications to do so have been made in the past, and why they failed.

Adverse possession and unknown owners

Sometimes you'll come across a dream site but nobody knows who owns the land. Now, you could try the Land Registry but not all land is registered and the details and title deeds may be lying, gathering dust, in some solicitor's basement. Sometimes an owner may live close by but simply doesn't want anyone to know that he owns the land. Sometimes it's because an owner went abroad or was killed in the war. Other times it's because an elderly person has simply forgotten all about it.

What can you do about it? Well, very little really except ask around, take out adverts and possibly put a notice on the site, all of which may alert all the other prospective self-builders in the area to the existence of the plot; meaning that, when an owner does surface, you could find yourself in a long queue. If you live next door or are prepared to risk all, you could simply occupy the land and squat on it until you can claim squatters' rights which is more properly known as *Adverse Possession*.

If you occupy land, 'without let or hindrance' (in plain English that means without any permission from an owner, without paying any rent for the land and without an owner telling you to clear off) for a period of 12 years or more, you can register a possessory title and take out an insurance indemnity policy to cover you for the eventuality of an owner finally turning up. After a further twelve years you can register an absolute title and the land is irrevocably yours.

It sounds fantastic but it often happens and it also happens the other way around. If you buy a plot where the neighbour seems to have extended his garden to within your boundaries and you arrive one day to tell him to clear off, and thank him very much for mowing your grass, but in future he needn't bother, you might be disappointed to hear that he considers that he has established squatters' rights over your land and that he's just returned from his solicitor's, where he's registered a possessory title. It doesn't immediately establish his claim but it could mean that the whole thing goes to court and he could well win, especially if he's got photographs of his children, now aged 20 but then aged eight playing joyfully on the neatly mown lawn of your plot whilst he and his young wife sit, beaming happily, on carefully laid out garden furniture. If you visit a prospective plot and there appear to be signs of occupation, you need to move fast and inform your solicitors and/or the vendors. Any let or hindrance within the 12 years negates the adverse possession and if the owner tells him to clear off his land, preferably in writing, then for the squatter, the clock goes back to zero.

Above: Deathwatch beetle can render a piece of timber almost unrecognisable as such.

Below: Cob walling is common to many areas and in each one owes its constituent parts to the availability of local materials such as clay or chalk.

Above: The corrugated iron roof has preserved these timbers but its lightweight negates the need for common rafters.

Left: Somebody has used a cement based mortar to repair these settlement cracks and it shows. They should have matched the original lime mortar.

Neighbours

The subject of neighbours has cropped up several times so far. Neighbours are important, not only because you're going to have to live next door to them, but because they have influence on whether or what you're going to build.

Wherever possible, try to talk to the immediate and surrounding occupants of any property you're going to buy. If there has been hostility to the idea of the site being developed, it's as well to find out about it right from the start. Whether that hostility is transferred to you or whether it is confined to the original applicant depends on many factors, not least of which is that you might be the one instigating the project in the first place. Sometimes it's possible to mollify an objector. Sometimes it is impossible but at the very least you'll know what to expect and you can either modify your plans or move to head off their argument before it even gets to the notice of the planners.

I always advocate talking to anyone and everyone who could possibly know anything that might affect a site. In doing so I've discovered drains that even vendors didn't know were there and learnt things about the planning history that no amount of reading up would have taught me.

Property for conversion or renovation

There is sometimes confusion over the words 'conversion' and 'renovation'. Converting is what happens when a property or structure that was not previously a dwelling is converted to one. Renovation is where an existing or previously occupied dwelling is brought back into use or altered or modified in some way. There are, as has been discussed in Chapter 1, VAT implications.

This is not meant to be a building manual, except where I am able to give the lay person a grounding in the various disciplines for each trade likely to come across. Assessment of a conversion or renovation opportunity runs along the same lines as assessment of a greenfield plot, in that the acquisition costs, plus the building costs, taken away from the final market value, should leave a profit margin. I think it fair to warn, however, that increases in equity are often on the low side, and don't usually match up to those available with new build. Of course, it's not at all easy to predict costs on a general basis, and each individual project will have to have its costs assessed by means of a survey. A tumbledown wreck might in fact have to be practically demolished and put back up again whereas a structurally sound barn might need next to nothing doing to the main shell.

I will probably be taken to task, but many a time, when I first investigate conversion or renovation opportunities (with the exception of those where all that's needed is a bit of TLC and titivation), I apply the cost multipliers for new build as if the existing structure isn't there. In fact, crude as that may seem, my initial assessments are often correct, as benefits gained from the existing structure are usually cancelled out by increased costs due to unforeseen problems.

House renovation grants are sometimes available from your local authority to cover basic improvements such as defective walls and foundations, roofs, damp-proof courses and wiring, etc. They are discretionary and they are means-tested, which means that they are probably not available to most self-builders. In England, Historic Buildings Grants are sometimes available for listed buildings of Grades I and II that are also on the Buildings at Risk Register, compiled by English Heritage. These are discretionary with money available in one local authority and not in another, but they can provide up to 25% of the costs with a fairly low ceiling that differs from county to county. They are also means tested and, in addition, there is often a residency requirement that, for example, you have lived in the property for at least three years and that you will continue to do so for a further five. Once again this is variable. In Scotland, Building Repair grants, covering the inside as well as the outside, and Conservation Area Grants for necessary external work that will enhance or preserve the character of an area, might be available through Historic Scotland. Once again these are discretionary and means-tested. In Wales these things are handled by Cadw, which means 'keep'. Lastly, many of the government organisations are able to give lists of charities and societies prepared to give grants for specific purposes.

If you are interested in restoring or renovating old buildings, read *The House Restorer's Guide*, by Hugh

Lander, published by David and Charles. Additionally you could telephone the help and advice line of the Society for the Protection of Ancient Buildings (SPAB) on 020 7377 1644. They publish pamphlets on specific subjects to do with the restoration and maintenance of historic or ancient buildings and hold courses around the country at which you can learn the ancient crafts of building. The SPAB is consulted on Listed Building Applications affecting pre-1720 buildings.

Adjoining sites and surrounding land

In any assessment of a potential project it's important to look beyond the boundaries of the property you've come to see. As you enter the village or area, start to look at other properties. Study the architectural vernacular. Look for details that are consistent and for the types of materials, particularly walling and roofing materials that have been used or are traditional. If you are planning to build a new house or bungalow, keep a sharp eye out for recently built properties or those under construction. These will give you a pretty good indication of what is acceptable in design terms with the local authority.

Study the immediate street scene. I've already mentioned the inadvisability of trying to put a house amongst a long line of bungalows and vice versa but it goes much further than that. You, as a self-builder, will be learning all about bricks. You'll be finding out the differences between a stock brick and a sandfaced Fletton brick, a plain tile and concrete interlocking tile. You may, as a result, have definite ideas about just what you want to incorporate in your new home. But will it all be worthwhile? 'You can't make a silk purse out of a sow's ear'. If the adjoining houses are all built with relatively cheap bricks and concrete roof tiles, spending twice as much on the bricks and three times as much on plain clay roof tiles might not make a pennyworth of difference to the eventual value.

Another reason for studying the neighbouring houses is to see if they have any signs of damage. Whilst cracks in one house might well mean that it was badly built, cracks in a number of them might be an indicator of something wrong below ground.

It has to be said, but one of the most distressing factors regarding neighbouring properties is the extent

to which their appearance and general upkeep can impact on your site. I have often seen lovely plots ruined by untidy neighbours. Old rusty cars on your site you can do something about. On your neighbour's land if they think that their garden looks better with lines of disused vehicles or if their hobby is doing up old bangers, there's little or nothing you can do about it. It really brings it home to you just how much we rely on our neighbours to keep up our property values. And whilst noisy or untidy neighbours might not stay for ever, their activities will blight any project.

Wildlife

Sometimes our concerns about preserving wildlife and flora come into conflict with our wish to build a new home. It is illegal to disturb a badger set and it is also illegal to dig up or disturb some extremely rare plants. Some houses, and particularly the type of old barn that's suitable for conversion, may hold roosts of bats or provide a refuge for other protected species, such as barn owls. English Nature or the Countryside Council for Wales must be notified of any action including remedial timber treatment, renovation, demolition or extensions and they must be given time to consider and advise on the best course of action.

There is an imperative on government and authorities to identify and maintain Sites of Special Scientific Interest (SSSI's or triple 'S' 'I's). In addition there are international conventions such as The Ramsar Convention on Wetlands. These impose restrictions on the development and use of land that are often tantamount to the prohibition of any building. As such, it is very unlikely that you will be dealing with a project within their boundaries. However, if you are developing land or buildings adjoining such a site you might be subject to restrictions imposed for the benefit of, for example, nesting or roosting birds.

Values

I've already referred to the dangers of over- or under-developing a plot in Chapter 1 – something that's often referred to as the 'carrying capacity' or 'ceiling value'. This is the value of the most appropriate house or bungalow that your plot will take and the maximum that anybody would pay for anything in that street. They are determined by income levels in the general area and the expectations of anybody coming to live there. In other words, if most of the houses in your street sell for £150,000 and you want to build something a lot better, would it be attractive to somebody with £200,000 plus to spend or would a person with that amount of money want to live elsewhere?

It is vital for any self-builder to know and understand local house prices. Do this by browsing the windows of the local estate agents to see just what the type of property you're envisaging might fetch in the area. Build up a dossier of relative prices. Start with the common three-bedroom semi-detached house and work up to the larger properties so that you can get a feel for the middle ranges. There are no precise formulae for valuation. It's all comparative and when an estate agent puts a value on any property he is simply comparing it to others that he's dealt with and assessing its value relative to them.

Preliminary budget

At the start of the book we set an initial budget for the purposes of evaluating just what you'd got to spend, how much you were going to borrow and where from. Having read further, you can now set the preliminary budget(see the Site Details Checklist that follows). This may or may not be different from your first thoughts, as it will be arrived at by reference to what you have discovered in the previous chapters. It's still not the final budget by any means – there are many factors that are going to alter that, not least design, materials, the requirements of the planning authorities and, of course, your own aspirations. This is an ongoing process and it will only finish when you finally move in and add up just what it all actually cost you.

But if it starts off right, it has a better chance of finishing up right. If you have a baseline cost then when you fall in love with that kitchen that's going to cost £5,000 extra, you'll have something to add it to and a list of figures that you can hopefully scan for savings to pay for it. And if that means that you have to sit down every night for the duration of your project and relate costs to your original projections, then that's fine; for the alternative could be a nasty shock.

DEVELOPMENT POTENTIAL & MIXTURE OF MATERIALS

Barn complexes often show their own piecemeal evolution in the different walling and roofing materials that were used, subject to their availability at the time.

Right: The milking parlours and animal pens have been unused for at least ten years.

Below: Single storey sections of barns often lend themselves to ancillary accommodation or garaging, so long as they are deep enough.

Bottom: The roof is already off this large barn and the walling is being made good for a new one.

Above: Built-in timber plates can pose problems and may well need replacement with steel.

Left: Plenty of height for a second or mezzanine floor.

Site details' checklist

PLANNING

Outline planning permission?	Yes/No
Detailed/full planning permission?	Yes/No
Expiry date of planning permission?	Yes/No
Was PP gained at appeal?	Yes/No
If so was this because of local opposition or LA planning department opposition?	Yes/No
Has this died down?	Yes/No
If the land has no planning, what are the realistic chances of PP?	%
Is this the view of the planning officer?	Yes/No
Planning conditions (other than standard)?	Yes/No
Are they satisfied?	Yes/No
If no, what needs to be done?	

Are Permitted Development Rights restricted or removed?	Yes/No
Any planning on neighbouring land?	Yes/No
Any planning blight?	Yes/No
If yes, what?	

PLANNING AUTHORITY

Name of officer	
Conservation Area/AONB/National Park/ Listed buildings/SSSI or higher?	Yes/No
Archaeological interest?	Yes/No
Archaeological survey required?	Yes/No
Special foundations to facilitate future surveys required?	Yes/No
Watching brief if necessary?	Yes/No

ACCESS

PUBLIC HIGHWAY/PRIVATE ACCESS

Is there a right of access?	Yes/No
If not, what arrangements have to be made?	

Any sign of a ransom strip?	Yes/No
Does the driveway need making up?	Yes/No
Is it suitable for construction traffic?	Yes/No
If not, is there an alternative/temporary site access?	Yes/No
Visibility splays required?	Yes/No
Obtainable within site curtilage?	Yes/No
If not, are the necessary easements in place?	Yes/No
Levels right for gates/bellmouth?	Yes/No
Crossover made?	Yes/No

Pavement?	Yes/No
Grass verge?	Yes/No
Is this part of the Highway?	Yes/No

PARKING SPACE REQUIREMENTS

Turning circles/need to enter and leave in forward gear?	Yes/No

HIGHWAYS AGENCY LOCAL OFFICE
Name of officer

TREES

Are there any significant trees on site?	Yes/No
Are there any on adjoining land?	Yes/No
Location plotted?	Yes/No
Species and sizes?	Yes/No
Any tree preservation orders in force?	Yes/No
If so, on which trees?	

Any sign of trees having been removed lately?	Yes/No

GROUND CONDITIONS/SUBSOIL

What is the natural vegetation?

Any signs of sedge or rush?	Yes/No
Ground water or signs of high water table?	Yes/No
In the flowerbeds or disturbed ground, is there an indication of subsoil?	Yes/No
If yes, what do you see?	
Any trial pits dug?	Yes/No
Findings?	
Rock?	Yes/No
Streams/watercourses?	Yes/No
Radon gas precautions necessary?	Yes/No
Heavy clay?	Yes/No
With trees?	Yes/No
Any sign of local buildings employing special foundations?	Yes/No
If so, what type?	

Locals consulted?	Yes/No
Findings/rumours?	

Evidence of filled ground?	Yes/No
Any contamination?	Yes/No

Any existing foundations?   Yes/No
Local Building Control Department

Building Inspector

Any comments by him?

PHYSICAL CHARACTERISTICS/SITE DETAILS/SERVICES

Level site/slight slope/severe slope   Yes/No
Levels survey available   Yes/No
Datum point?   Yes/No

KEY DIMENSIONS
Width at building line (front)
Width at building line (back)
Triangulation measurements

OWNERSHIP OF BOUNDARIES
North
South
East
West

Sun/shade noted?   Yes/No
Exposure – none/moderate/severe
Overhead cables/powerlines?   Yes/No
If significant, are they movable?   Yes/No

DRAINS ON SITE?   Yes/No
Foul drains?   Yes/No
    Available?   Yes/No
    Location plotted?   Yes/No
        Invert
        Cover
Surface water drains?   Yes/No
    Location plotted?   Yes/No
        Invert
        Cover
Public/private
Legal right to connect?   Yes/No
Easements in place if necessary?   Yes/No
If no mains drains available, what system is
acceptable/workable?
    Cesspit
    Septic tank
    Sewage treatment plant
    Other

Environment Agency consulted and
    approvals given?   Yes/No
Is there space on site for these works or do
    you need to negotiate for it?   Yes/No

If no surface water drains available, what system
    is acceptable/workable?
    Standard soakway
    Sophisticated soakway
    Aquifer
    Stream or ditch

Any sterile zones?   Yes/No
If yes, are they plotted?   Yes/No

ELECTRICITY AVAILABLE?   Yes/No
    Overhead/underground
    Connection charge   £

GAS AVAILABLE?   Yes/No
    Connection charge   £
If not available, will you want to install an
    LPG system?   Yes/No
If so, is there space for the tank or can it go
    underground?   Yes/No
Or will you want oil?   Yes/No
If so, is there space for the tank?   Yes/No

TELEPHONE AVAILABLE?   Yes/No
    Connection charge   £

MAINS WATER AVAILABLE?   Yes/No
    Connection charge   £
If not, is a borehole possible?   Yes/No
Estimated costs
Comments

LEGAL
Rights of way established to plot's benefit?   Yes/No
Rights of way to benefit of others?   Yes/No
Covenants and easements to plot's benefit?   Yes/No
Covenants and easements to others' benefit?   Yes/No
Footpaths?   Yes/No
Any sign of adverse possession?   Yes/No
If so, how long has it been established?

Does any loss of land through adverse possession
question the viability of the plot? Yes/No
Land being sold with full title? Yes/No
All or any part of the land being sold subject to
a defective/incomplete/possessory title? Yes/No
Any protected wildlife, fauna or flora on site? Yes/No

NEIGHBOURS

Did the neighbours object to the granting of
permission? Yes/No
Is there a legacy of hostility? Yes/No
Will neighbours be able to obstruct site works? Yes/No
Is there anything you can do to resolve the situation?

ADJOINING SITES/SURROUNDING LAND

What type of buildings are in the street scene?

Are there any new dwellings in the area that give an
indication of the planners' likes and dislikes? If so,
describe.

Is there a building line? Yes/No

General characteristics of local architecture/design –
mixed/uniform?
General architectural features on nearby buildings:
Sizes
Complex/simple shapes
Brick/render/stone/black and white/hung/
timbered/other
Features, e.g. mullions/quoins/corbels/keystones/
cills/heads
Roof pitches
Roof coverings, e.g. plain tile/profiled
tile/slates/thatch/stone slate/other
Roof treatment, e.g. gabled/hipped/barn ended/tabled
verges/clipped verges
Barge boarded verge/dry verges
Soffit overhangs/soffits/exposed rafter feet/
exposed purlins
Window types, e.g. softwood painted or
stained/hardwood/upvc/metal
Glazing, e.g. clear/all bar/leaded square or diamond

Any sign of structural damage to adjoining
buildings? Yes/No
Any pollution/noise/smell/light from
neighbouring properties? Yes/No

VALUES

What are the general property values within the area?
Semi-detached house £
Bungalows 3 bedrooms £
Bungalows 4 bedrooms £
Detached houses medium 4 bedrooms £
Larger detached houses/bungalows £

What sort of property directly joins the plot?
Houses/bungalows
Detached/semi-detached
Mixed
What is the most appropriate type of dwelling for
this plot?

What is the carrying capacity (£)/ceiling value?
£

Are there things in the offing that could affect local
values (e.g. new roads, motorways, industry moving
in or out/major infrastructure works)?

METHOD OF BUILDING/PRELIMINARY BUDGET

Timber frame/brick and block/other
Builder/subcontractors/shell building plus
subcontractors/own labour
£s per sq. metre assumed £
Preliminary Building Budget £
Site costs £
Fees £
Finance costs £
Other costs £
Total costs (A) £
Value of finished house (B) £
Equity gain (B minus A) £

4. BUYING THE PROPERTY –
The legal bits

Buying land is not the same as buying other goods or services. By long-established law the purchase of land has to be evidenced in writing, and by long-established practice the legal profession has gone out of its way to make that evidencing as complicated and as obscure as possible, with its own unique vocabulary and sets of procedures. Solicitors, land agents and estate agents make their living by operating within this system and they make very little effort to explain it in any sort of plain English to their clients. If you are going to buy land then it is important that you familiarise yourself with the terminology and the procedures. It is also important that you employ professionals who know where the pitfalls are and can help you to look out for them.

When you buy a property in England, you in effect buy the land with whatever is on it at the time. The concept of land ownership goes right back to William the Conqueror who, when he stepped onto the beach at Hastings, threw his arms out wide and claimed the Kingdom for his own and for his heirs and successors. He got his feet wet, which is why the title of any coastal land extends to the median high-water mark! As time went by the Crown then parcelled out the land under various forms of tenure, which normally required payment or favours of some kind. This payment could vary from provision of goods and foodstuffs right through to the supply of soldiers for the army and wenches for ... well, for whatever they used wenches for at that time.

The basic tenet of land occupation in England and Wales stems from that early appropriation, in that all land law endeavours to ensure that land is occupied and that it serves some useful function. Great pains were always taken to make sure that land could not, in the natural course of its division and subdivision, become landlocked, for instance. As time went by the crafty got around that by the use of ransom strips and covenants, as I have already discussed, but they were always against the driving spirit of land serving a useful function.

The most important form of tenure which has come down to us through the ages is that of 'Freehold', and when you own land in this way it basically means that you hold the land free of any payment. Most land outside that still retained by the Crown is now freehold and in turn it is open for the freeholder to consider letting off all or part of their land on leasehold. There are still areas in the country where there are anachronisms such as 'Chief rents' payable to institutionalised landlords and it is still possible that land may be offered on the basis of a long leasehold or ground rent in perpetuity. Such things are now rare and in the areas where they occur, the solicitors are quite *au fait* with them, so they shouldn't cause any problems. Worthy of mention, at this point, is the forthcoming 'Commonhold' form of tenure that is being brought in for situations such as blocks of flats or properties with common rights and parts.

There are various methods of buying land and there are, as one would expect, different procedures in place within the individual parts of the United Kingdom and in the Republic of Ireland.

England and Wales

If you are buying through an estate agent, then the details might well include reference to the price. But not always, as there are three recognised and distinct ways of selling land.

Private treaty
Most land in England and Wales is sold by private treaty. This is the familiar way whereby details are prepared and the property is offered for sale at an

advertised price. Agents will try to vary this somewhat by adding words such as 'Offers in the region of' or 'Offers over' but essentially the details are 'an invitation to treat' and it is open to any interested party to make an offer on the land.

This offer is made 'subject to contract' and at this point, if the vendors are minded to accept, solicitors are instructed. The purchaser's solicitors then prepare a draft contract and a list of preliminary enquiries that they send through to the vendor's solicitors. If they wish, but there is no compulsion, the purchasers can arrange for a survey. They will also, if finance is required, make application for a mortgage and pay for the lender's survey and valuation, which they are entitled to have sight of.

In the meantime, the solicitors continue to exchange letters and enquiries and the purchaser's solicitors arrange for and receive local searches, including details held by HM Land Registry, if the land is registered, and copies of any planning permissions related to the land. When all is in place, the purchaser's solicitors will usually prepare a 'Report on Title' and arrange to discuss their findings with their client. If, as a result of these enquiries, it is decided to proceed, then each party's solicitor will arrange for their clients to sign identical contracts and will then hold them until such time as they are given instructions to 'Exchange contracts'.

This exchange of contracts, should it happen, is the first time that either party is bound to the sale and purchase and is effected by a simple telephone conversation between solicitors, noting the time and date of the exchange. Once this has happened there is no going back unless you are prepared to be in breach of contract and liable for damages. A deposit, usually 10% of the purchase price, is payable upon exchange of contracts, and each solicitor receives the copy of the contract that has been signed by the other party. This contract details the completion date, usually 21 or 28 days thereafter.

The 'Conveyance', or addition to the title deeds, noting the sale and purchase, is prepared by the vendor's solicitors and signed by the vendors. Upon the completion date, the final monies are paid over in return for the keys and the purchasers are free to take up occupation. Within three months the title must be registered and any stamp duty that is payable, which will almost certainly have been taken from the purchaser upon completion, must be paid over.

Auctions

It used to be thought that the price a property fetched in an auction room was the ultimate valuation; a proper and final demonstration of the market price. Whilst that is still true to some extent, it was always a flawed supposition because it could never take into account the individual who just had to have a property, come what may, or the failure of an auctioneer to market the property properly.

Buying land at auction is a highly legal process whereby at the fall of the hammer, the highest bidder is deemed to have accepted all of the terms and conditions of sale and to have exchanged contracts at that point, legally binding themselves to purchase and the sellers to sell. Failure to complete means that the purchaser will be charged interest at a pre-determined rate, usually 4–5% above bank rate, and that if they back out altogether, they can be sued for any re-marketing costs and any discrepancy in value.

It's not quite clear what would happen if a successful bidder got 'cold feet' in an auction room because, following the fall of the hammer, the purchaser is required to sign the contract. If they refused to do so, then although they might well be liable for misrepresentation and could be sued on the promise, it is probable that they could not actually be made to, as the law requires that any sale of land is evidenced in writing. In reality, in an auction room where others had been bidding, the chances are that the auctioneer would take a pragmatic view and re-offer the property there and then.

All of this legal framework is why most reputable auction particulars contain within their terms and conditions all or most of the questions that a proposing purchaser's solicitors would wish or need to ask, and a good few also provide copies of the searches. Nevertheless, sole reliance on these particulars is not to be recommended and if you are proposing to bid at an auction you should give your own solicitors time to study the detail and to make what enquiries they feel necessary or appropriate.

Of late, many auction details have tended to put

forward a guideline price, but experience shows that this is often wildly misleading and is often employed simply to attract interest. Most auctions are subject to a reserve price, which does not have to be advised to interested parties, and unless the bids reach that figure, the auctioneer can choose to withdraw the property. It is all too easy to get carried away in an auction room. You look across at your rival bidder and convince yourself that they are at their limit and that just one more bid will see them drop out. That is the way to come out of the room having paid far too much and it really is important that you go into an auction with a set ceiling beyond which you cannot or will not go – and stick to it!

Tenders

There are various forms of tender. Open tender, closed tender, formal and informal tender are all words that are used to describe the process but they are all variations on the theme whereby offers are solicited in writing for a property. The conditions of sale, dictated by the agents or the sellers, are the rules by which the sale will be governed.

The details for a tender often take on a similar form to auction particulars, save the fact that they normally require that all bids are received in writing by a certain date. Closer inspection, however, will reveal that in most cases, the vendors reserve the right not to accept the highest offer or indeed, any offer at all. One solicitor described the process of selling land by tender as a system whereby the estate agent gets to write his own rules. In fact, unlike an auction, where the fall of the gavel has distinct legal connotations and is binding on both parties, success by virtue of being the highest bidder in a tender does not guarantee that you'll be able to buy the property.

The problem with tenders is the lack of legal framework to an otherwise highly legal process. Sometimes the conditions of sale will require that offers are submitted together with a cheque for the deposit and go on to insist that acceptance of the tender will constitute an exchange of contracts. With no legal requirement to accept the highest offer, this really is a one way street and the system is either actually open to abuse or manipulation or, just as damagingly, the suspicion that that is the case.

Buying land by tender has been likened to entering an auction room blindfolded and with earplugs. It is hugely unpopular with purchasers because, whatever they bid, they never really know if they've missed it by £1 or obtained the land for well over the odds.

As to what to bid, that can only be arrived at by doing all of the sums but if there is any advice it is to always stick that little bit extra on to your calculations. Whilst there is no requirement that any particular offer must be accepted, if all other things are equal, the highest offer, even by a few pounds, still stands a better chance of success.

Scotland

Opponents of the process of buying land in England and Wales often point to the Scottish system, on the grounds that it would avoid costly delays and stop the incidences of gazumping and gazundering – the practice of a vendor suddenly asking for more money or a purchaser suddenly demanding a reduction in the price. The problem is that most proponents of this argument don't actually know or understand the Scottish system.

In England and Wales, all land was originally held by the Crown, before being disposed of piecemeal in the various forms of tender that have principally boiled down to 'Freehold'. In Scotland, where huge areas are still held by the Crown, land was similarly parcelled and then re-parcelled out on the basis of patronage and the 'feu' was the tenure, or form of payment that allowed continued occupation. Over time these payments in kind have largely fallen away and the feu has come to mean the larger holding from which sales of land by division and subdivision are made. 'Feu disposition' therefore means the sale or alienation of land.

Property is advertised for sale, often by solicitors who, in the main, take the place of and combine the roles occupied by estate agents and solicitors south of the border. The details they issue and the price that is quoted are really just the same as details offering land for sale by private treaty in England and Wales. If you like a property then you have to decide what price you are prepared to pay, obviously taking your lead from the figure quoted and by using comparative values.

The procedures in Scotland begin to differ from those in England and Wales when, if there are indications that your price is acceptable, you ask your solicitor to register an interest in the property. Following this, the seller's solicitors or agents should not sell to another party without telling you first. You then get a survey and valuation and, if necessary, approach your finance source, as your solicitors will not proceed further until they are satisfied that you have the full purchase monies sorted out and available.

Your solicitor then makes a written offer with an expiry date and a long list of other conditions and enquiries that the purchase is subject to. These are known as the 'missives' and they are basically the same as the conditions and preliminary enquiries that go to and fro between solicitors in England and Wales. If the other side accepts this written offer, then it is binding on both parties, unless something turns up or goes wrong in the missive negotiations.

At some point in this process, your solicitors will obtain, quite often from the seller's solicitors, the Property Enquiry Certificates, which once again are basically the same as the searches that are done south of the border. Following 'Conclusion of the Missives', the purchaser's solicitors will receive a 'Draft Disposition' and there is sometimes, but not always, a deposit required at this stage. When all is agreed between the parties, the 'Disposition' is signed and the 'Date of Entry', or completion date is agreed. With the monies paid over on the due date, the purchaser is free to take up occupation and the solicitor's last job is to register the transaction and property and pay over the stamp duty.

Northern Ireland

As you would expect, the Northern Irish system of land tenure and the buying and selling of land broadly follows that of England and Wales. There are, however, minor differences and there are elements and language that are reminiscent of the Scottish legal system.

There is no 'exchange of contracts'. An offer is made to buy land and, if accepted, when the various parties' solicitors have made all the necessary enquiries, the purchaser signs his contract and it is sent off to the vendors. When and if the vendor signs his part and returns it to the purchaser's side, a contract is deemed to be in existence. Thereafter the route to completion is virtually the same as for England and Wales with a similar legal requirement for the registration of the land and transaction, and the payment of stamp duty.

The Republic of Ireland (Eire)

Southern Ireland was, of course, once part of the United Kingdom and it is hardly surprising, therefore, that much of its legal system harks back to that time and has been retained. The system for the sale and purchase of residential and domestic land in the Republic of Ireland is substantially the same as for England and Wales, but with a couple of minor variations that are reminiscent of parts of the Scottish system. One of the first differences that a buyer from England or Wales will notice is that a booking or holding deposit of 5% is often payable with the balance of the 10% paid over on contract. Another main difference is that title is not investigated until after contract; something that bears similarity with the way the missives are conducted in Scotland. If something turns up that goes to the root of the title then the contract is voided but otherwise, if everything is as it should be, the transaction proceeds to completion in the normal way.

Solicitors

Buying and selling land is no easy matter and whatever and wherever you are buying, you do need a good solicitor. If you already have, or know, a solicitor to act for you, that is fine. Otherwise, you will probably entrust your affairs to the person whose office you contact first and it is largely true that there is little to choose between the overall competence with which different firms of solicitors will deal with the purchase. But there may be a big difference in how long they take to do the job and it is important that you impress upon whichever company you employ that 'speed is of the essence'.

Your solicitor will advise you on just how to make your offer and will want to make sure that you are not

Right: This grand house by Potton seems to sit very comfortably within and is complimented by its obviously substantial grounds.

Below: The same house but from a slightly different angle, showing the attention to detail and more of its inviting environs.

irrevocably committed before they've had a chance to examine the title properly. This normally means that you should never sign any papers or make any written offer unless it is qualified by the words 'subject to contract'. If you pay a deposit on the land then you must also make sure that your payment is made subject to contract and that the deposit is fully returnable in the event of you not proceeding. If you intend to buy at auction, effectively exchanging contracts at that point, it is crucial that your solicitors be given the chance to do all of their work beforehand.

It is also part of the solicitor's job to evaluate and verify the planning situation on the land. From reading the previous chapters, and those to come, your knowledge of planning matters could well equal or exceed that of your solicitor. However, if there are problems or inconsistencies with things such as visibility splays or planning conditions in order to make a consent operable, your solicitor will resolve them.

Along with all the documents which the solicitor receives, there will be the title deed plans. These will, in effect, form a record of plans down through time and will show the history of the plot and how it was arrived at by subdivision of larger segments of land or by addition of others. As I've warned before, there is a chance that none of them necessarily represents the site that has been pointed out to you and that possibly none of them represents the plan that the planning authorities have. Your solicitor can notice and point out any apparent discrepancies in the plans but what he can't do is verify them on the ground. You need to be able to get out there with a 30-metre tape and measure up your plot to make certain that what you are buying is the same as that which is being offered on paper. If you can't do it, or there's any doubt at all in your mind, then engage a surveyor for the purpose. Oft-times the discrepancies are immaterial but there are times when they are vital, such as with visibility splays and accesses. These things need to be sorted before, and not after, you've signed the contract.

Try to get a copy of the title deed plans that you can keep. It will come in handy for settling things like boundary disputes or arguments over repairs to fences, without expensive recourse to solicitors.

Legal options and conditional contracts

The advice for anyone buying land without express planning consent is that they should only do so, *'subject to receipt of satisfactory planning permission'*. This means that all of the normal procedures for buying the land are gone through, right up to and including the exchange of contracts but that, in the event of planning permission being refused, the contract is voided and any deposits returned. Conversely, of course, it also means that with the granting of planning consent, the contract is irrevocable and binding on both parties.

Another way of reserving land so that, in the event of a successful planning application, you can ensure that the vendor sells to you and does not retain it for his own use or sell to someone else, is to enter into a legally binding option. Normally this has to be prepared by solicitors because it is a highly legal document that must detail the length of time that the option will run for and the amount that is to be paid for it. It must also specify whether the money paid counts as part of an agreed purchase price or is additional to it.

Prospective vendors often prefer the legal option because, if the planning application fails, they normally retain the monies paid out. They might also have reservations that a conditional contract could drag on for ages whilst you try for a contentious scheme and they might, therefore, try to impose a time limit that also has the effect of voiding the contract.

The Party Walls Act 1996

This Act seeks to provide a framework for the prevention and resolution of disputes in relation to party walls, boundary walls and excavations that are close to neighbouring buildings. It requires that whenever such work is proposed, those intending to carry out the work must give the adjoining owners notice in writing. There is no penalty within the Act for non-compliance, but it recognises that if the proper notices and procedures are not followed, then legal redress or an injunction might be sought in the courts. The implication is that non-compliance would count against any offending party.

Work on existing party walls
The Act lists works that may be done to existing party walls, even though they go beyond ordinary common law rights. These include:

- Cutting into a wall to take a bearing beam or inserting a damp-proof course all the way through a party wall.
- Raising a party wall, whilst, if necessary, cutting off any projections that might prevent you from doing so.
- Demolishing and rebuilding a party wall.
- Underpinning a party wall.

- Protecting two adjoining walls by putting a flashing from the higher to the lower.

At least two months' notice in writing must be given of any intention to carry out these works and the recipient of the notice has 14 days to respond or issue a counter notice, after which a dispute is said to have arisen.

New building on the boundary line

The Act does not confer any right to build any new walls or structures that bestride or intrude upon a neighbour's land, without their prior consent. However, and this is important, where a new wall or structure is to be built up to a boundary, the Act does confer the right for the footings for that wall or structure to intrude under the neighbouring land, subject to the payment of any compensation for damage caused during the construction.

One month's notice in writing is required and, once again, if the adjoining owner responds or issues a counter notice within 14 days, a dispute is said to have arisen.

Excavations close to neighbouring buildings

You must inform an adjoining owner in writing, at least two months before the work commences, if:

- You plan to excavate or construct foundations for a new building or structure within 3 metres of a neighbouring building or structure, where the excavations will go deeper than the foundations of those structures, or
- You plan to excavate or construct foundations for a new building or structure within 6 metres of a neighbouring building or structure, where that work would cut a line drawn downwards at 45 degrees from the bottom of the neighbour's foundations.

If a dispute arises over this, or any of the other works listed above, then an independent surveyor is appointed, with their fees paid for by the person wishing to carry out the work. The surveyor will make an 'Award', setting out what work can be carried out. They will also dictate how and when the work is to be done and they will record the conditions prior to the commencement of work, so that any damages can be properly attributed and made good. Either side has 14 days to appeal to the county court but this should only be done if an owner believes that the surveyors have acted beyond their powers.

Most importantly, where work is being carried out that is expressly authorised by the Act, and where the proper procedures have been followed, the Act gives the right of entry in order to carry out those works, provided that 14 days' notice of the intention to enter is given. It is an offence for an adjoining owner to refuse entry to someone who is entitled to enter premises under the Act, if the offender knows that the Act entitles the person to be there. If the adjoining premises are vacant then a police officer must accompany the workmen, surveyor or architect, as they enter.

Undisclosed problems and final checks

By the time this book hits the shelves the 'Seller's pack' will have become universal. It may make a lot of difference, but equally, it may make very little at all. It will make it more difficult to cover up a particular fact or conveniently forget about some previously documented thing that has affected the land, but it will probably not deter the person determined to hide the truth. All vendors have to answer, through their solicitors, a list of what are known as preliminary enquiries, such as 'Do you know of anything adversely affecting the property?' The honest vendor will answer just as honestly. But proving that a less honest vendor gave the wrong answer might be frightfully difficult.

That is why, to avoid unpleasant surprises, it is so important to make the right enquiries. Just to make sure, ask yourself, one more time, 'Why hasn't this plot been built on before, or why hasn't anyone else done something with this building?' There may be a very good reason and maybe, if you've done your homework, by following the guidelines and the checklist in previous chapters, you will know what that reason is. And if not? Well, ask around just one more time, just to make sure.

Insurances and Legal Contingency Insurance

Once you've contracted on land, even though you might not have full title to it, you nevertheless have a beneficial interest in it. It is therefore possible that you could find yourself with shared liability for any mishaps that occur on the land and, on exchange, you will need to make sure that you have the necessary insurance and, in particular, Public Liability.

Defects in titles can take many forms, and many can be dealt with through special, single-payment insurance policies, known as Legal Contingency Insurance or Single Premium Indemnity Policies. As far as restrictive covenants are concerned, these policies protect the insured and their successors in title against enforcement or attempted enforcement of the covenant. It includes the costs, expenses and any damages in connection with a court action or lands tribunal action, the cost of alteration or demolition following an injunction, the loss of market value of land as a result of development being prevented and abortive capital expenditure.

Legal contingency insurance can also cover situations where title deeds are lost, where there are problems over uncertain rights of way, or possessory or incomplete titles and services indemnities where the right to use drains or other services is uncertain or unknown.

The premiums payable are assessed and evaluated according to the risk factors determined by the underwriters. It is surprising, but many solicitors seem either not to have heard of these policies, or to have forgotten about their existence. I can recall many a time when a solicitor very nearly persuaded a prospective self-builder to withdraw from a plot where the title was mildly defective or rights of way could not be proven over an access. In nearly all of these cases, when the suggestion of a single premium indemnity insurance was put back to the solicitor it was very

speedily arranged and the purchase was able to proceed, usually with the premium being paid by the vendor!

These areas of property insurance are very complicated and each proposal is evaluated separately. DMS Services Limited, who handle the standard self-builder's insurance policies are able to help. Ring them on 01909 591652.

Fees, disbursements and registration of land

Upon completion the solicitors will want to make sure that they are in funds in order to finalise the transaction and they will take their fees out of the monies they hold. For the sale and purchase of an average house and plot in the Provinces, these can be around £1,000 and it is usual for the solicitors to defray certain other costs and fees on your behalf.

These include the Stamp Duty, the rates for which are set down in the Tax section of the Finance chapter, and the estate agents fees which, for a sole agency, usually amount to $1\frac{1}{2}\%$ of the sale price. Additionally, any purchase of land or property transaction has to be registered with HM Land Registry within three months and it is therefore normal for your solicitor to arrange this and to tack the charges on to their final account, by reference to the land or property cost.

The charges for registering the land are: -

£40 for transactions up to £40,000

£60 for transactions between £40,001 and £70,000

£100 for transactions between £70,001 and £100,000

£200 for transactions between £100,001 and £200,000

£300 for transactions between £200,001 and £500,000

£500 for transactions between £500,001 and £1M

£800 for transactions in excess of £1M

5. PLANNING FOR, AND DESIGNING YOUR NEW HOME

The first thing that you need to do when thinking about the design of your new home is to examine your own motivation for self-building. Is this the culmination of a long-standing desire to create something permanent that you can be proud of and which will be there long after you are gone, or is this merely a step on the ladder to your eventual dream home? Are you doing this in order to have a home that fits your and your family's lifestyle and individual needs, or are you more interested in the possible gains in equity that are to be made? Is it about more accommodation, particularly more bedrooms, or is it about quality? Is kerb appeal and instant attraction more important than having a home that grows on you or opens up in unexpected ways when you walk through it?

For many self-builders, the making or saving of money, whilst important, is not actually the issue that has brought them to the self-build table. Nevertheless, most will be concerned to achieve the most they can for the money they can afford, or for the amount deemed suitable to spend on the project. To understand this requires a basic grasp of what makes buildings cost more or less.

The land itself is probably one of the most important factors in determining the cost of your new home, with the location of the plot being the first major design influence. Other than setting out your wish list, it does not make sense to think in too much detail about the design before the plot is chosen. Let your design evolve to suit the plot, rather than the other way around. Never go looking for a plot to suit a particular design; it is putting the cart before the horse. Planners are concerned to retain what they consider to be the local characteristics of their area as a whole, and individual parts of it in particular, and you will hear them talking about the 'local vernacular'. What they mean is the local style of building, the regional materials used, particularly on the outside and on the roof, and the features that are peculiar to their area. This is not a book on design (there's a companion book by the same authors, *The Home Plans Book*, that deals with those aspects of self-building); but it is a book that wants to make you aware of the implications of changes in design and materials.

The cheapest structure to build is always going to be the simple rectangle with gable ends. Take that simple shape and change the rendered blockwork to natural stone, and you've increased the walling costs by up to 400% and the overall costs by 10%. Change the roof tiles from concrete interlocking to plain clay tiles and you've added another 10%. Make the shape more complex or the roof more complicated, and you'll push up the costs yet again. The chances are, however, that in today's planning environment, that's exactly what the planners will want you to do. And what's the betting that that's what you want as well and that those features and characteristics are what attracted you to the area in the first place! The challenge, therefore, is to incorporate these desirable features in the most cost-effective way.

Unless you have experience of designing houses with both planning and building regulations in mind, it is certainly not a field for do-it-yourself. Virtually all who build for themselves use the services of architects, designers or package-deal companies. That is not to say, however, that in many cases the original ideas and conceptions cannot be arrived at by you and presented as the starting point for the eventual design solution. There's nothing wrong in giving the chap who's going to draw up your new home or produce drawings to convert or renovate your building, the pointers that will indeed make it *your* new home and not the product of someone else's ideals. Take a trip around the area you're going to build in *before* you talk to the designer. Photograph houses or bungalows that you like. Photograph features and details that you see on buildings, old and new, and present them to your designer at the outset. Anybody worth their salt in the self-build world won't take offence – quite the opposite. They'll probably be pleased that you've taken the trouble to illustrate your requirements in a cogent form and that you've given them a starting point.

Buy a scrapbook and stick all of your photographs in it. Make notes and cut out features and pictures from the magazines that take your fancy. In a separate section, collect illustrations of things that you don't like and at the end of the book start pasting in pictures and details that you've gleaned from advertisements and the like. Study house plan books and the brochures of package deal companies and make a note, either of particular plans that take your fancy, or of individual features. Have a look at *The Home Plans Book* that I've referred to. Maybe, just maybe, there's a design in there that completely fits the bill, in which case perhaps the best thing to do is to contact the company or practice that produced that design, with a view to doing business with them. What is more likely, though, is that you'll get design ideas from the various plans and that these will go into your scrap book to be incorporated in your eventual, and entirely individual, design.

The budget

There's that word again! No apologies, however. The budget is the most important piece of the design jigsaw. It should be the very first thing that you impress upon your designer or architect and, just to make doubly certain, it should also be the last. If the professionals you've engaged show any reluctance to talk about this aspect of your project, then I would suggest that you terminate any arrangements with them and move on to someone who will.

Present your preliminary budget to the architect or designer and then look for assurance that any design that they are about to embark on contains not just your wish list of desired features, but can be built within that budget. Do not hear what you want to hear. Beware the weak individual who is unable to shoot your hopes down in flames. Better the chap who stands up and is prepared to terminate any proposed

contract with you, on the grounds that what you want can't be achieved within your budget restraints, than the fellow who goes away and returns with a plan that you fall in love with, but can never hope to build.

So what are the factors that could seriously affect your costs? We've already discussed the topography of the land and the ground conditions and hopefully, in preparing your preliminary budget, any considerations that these factors impose have already been taken into account. The cost of the land itself might have exceeded that which you'd originally hoped for and, as was demonstrated in Chapter 1 that is going to affect the size of your new home. Size isn't everything, they say. Well it is when it comes to house-building and the bigger your new home, the more it's going to cost. Any logical thought that goes into the make-up of your new home must start by finding out the size of the building that your budget can stretch to, or the size that the planners will accept.

Building costs vary throughout the country, but they are variations on a theme and although there are hotspots, the remarkable thing is their similarity, especially when you take into account the wildly variant market values of houses from region to region. I've given you a table of probable building costs earlier on in this book but I can do no better than to point you, once again, to the Average Build Cost Guide that is constantly updated can be found at the back of *Homebuilding & Renovating* magazine. What you learn from these tables is that by far the largest swing in prices is due to the way in which the house is built.

Those building with subcontractors and a proportion of DIY can expect to make savings on build costs of close on 50% over those using a main contractor. Whereas, with the exception of Greater London, the swing between regional costs is only around 11%. Why these distortions? Well, the clue, in part, is in the figures given for Greater London where the average rise over the other areas is heading up to 20%. It's the labour costs that are inflating these figures. That's the thing that varies from region to region and goes through the roof in London and certain other cities. Material costs, on a like-for-like basis, are virtually the same wherever you're building. So the largest single saving that you can put into the cost of your new home is the amount of time that you can spend on the

Left: This sketch design from Potton is from their 'Rectory' range and is of a style that would grace any age.

Below: Modern housing does not always have to reflect 'The big house' and just as often, designs contain elements most often found in workmen's cottages, as Potton illustrate here.

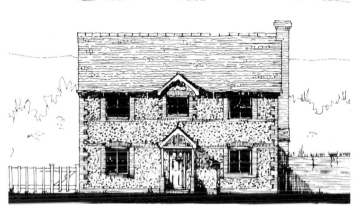

project and the degree of both management and labour that you can provide.

If you're hoping to build a 180-square-metre house and, because you feel that you'd rather not get involved in the work on site, you've decided that you're going to have to use a builder, then you've really got to cost that out at around £110,000 in the provinces. If your budget is only £90,000 then you have two choices. You can either build something smaller, at around 150 square metres, or you could opt to take on some or all of the management yourself. Building with a builder to take the project as far as the weathertight shell and then managing tradesmen and subcontractors for the second fix and fitting-out element of the house would bring the costs of your originally hoped-for house down to around £97,000; still not enough. But building by managing subcontractors and tradesmen for the whole project would bring it down to your original budget of £90,000.

Now, in truth, what would probably happen here is that there would be a compromise between size and cost. But what this must demonstrate to you is that the very foundation of design has to start with the budget and work backwards and that these fundamental principles and decisions must be discussed with your architect or designer before ever pen is put to paper.

This is not a building manual; I cannot hope to list all of the design and material influences and choices that can impact on cost. What I can hope to do, however, is to get you to think about the choices and to learn to cost things as they happen and relate those costs back to your budget so that, if necessary, you can make compensatory changes. The simple act of changing a gable to a hip could easily add £1,000 each time you do it. Changing from softwood joinery, on a 180-square-metre house, to Pvc-u could add £3,000. Stone heads and cills, *de rigueur* in some regions, could add nearly £2,000 and the choice of framed ledged and braced doors rather than pressed panelled doors could put the bill up by £1,500. All these, and many many more, are things that you'll have to learn and to weigh up and fit into your budget.

Maybe you're not prepared to compromise on the design, the size or the material choices. If so, could you look at things another way? Is it possible that you could think in terms of a design that could be built in stages or one that could evolve as finances permitted in the future? Could you cheapen the specification in some ways in order to gain more space on the understanding that at some time in the future you could, say, strip that cheap kitchen out and put a better one in place? I can't answer these questions for you.

Neither can I answer all of the questions and design considerations that follow – all I can do is to pose them, to get you to think about them and to let you seek the answers in your own aspirations, armed with the knowledge that you have gained from the remainder of this book.

What do you want it to look like, externally?

The whole reason for building your own home, rather than just nipping off and buying a house from a developer, is to get what you want, rather than something that somebody else thinks you should have. What do you want it to look like, externally? The answer to this question is often governed by the planners and the general consensus that new homes should fit in with the local vernacular. Do you want to push the boat out in design terms? Are you ready for the extra work and the costs that that could entail? Are you ready to face the fact that any radical departure from the norm might affect your chances of resale or the value of the finished home?

You'd think that most self-builders, unwilling to accept what the building industry dictates they should have, would aspire to build exciting, innovative homes. Well, you'd be wrong. It's a sad fact that most self-builders stick to convention when it comes to design, and almost all copy the houses of the developers that they purport to despise.

It's understandable, of course. Many self-builders suffer the same constraints as the developer, and if they do succeed in avoiding standardised design, it will only be with considerable effort. Many features of conformity are actually desirable, reflecting, as they do, the very best in modern living standards. But other restraints are imposed, directly or indirectly, by the planners, the dictates of finance, by fashion and by the need to ensure that a new home represents the best possible investment.

Top: Although borrowing from the past, this design is unmistakably modern. (Custom Homes Ltd)

Above: The brief for the design of this home by Design & Materials Ltd included the requirement for the gallery workroom to the upper centre of the house.

Right: A country vicarage is the obvious design influence in this Potton home.

Above. The past is always with us. It does not, however, have to be slavishly followed and modern design can make its own bold statement. (Scandia-Hus Ltd)

Could you go for freedom of expression, internally?

Happily, the planners will play no part in the internal design and you have a far wider opportunity to employ design features that suit your own lifestyle. Once more, however, the internal arrangements of most self-built homes are little different from those built by developers, with a predictable and recognised progression of associated rooms. Do you feel the need to stick to these conventional design formats? Does each area of your home have to justify its existence by reference to a particular function or could you contemplate the idea of architectural space for its own sake? Could you envisage a layout or mixture of rooms that defy the accepted wisdom, yet fit in with your own lifestyle? Do you dare to think in terms of open plan? Have you always hankered after a cathedral ceiling or are you afraid that high-vaulted rooms will require specific heating solutions if you're to maintain the same level of comfort as in other areas? Do you want a strict division between sleeping and living arrangements?

How long are you going to live in your new home?

Perhaps the first thing you need to think about, when planning the accommodation in your new home, is how long you intend to live in it. Are you planning eventually to go out of the door feet first in a wooden box or is this merely another step up the ladder on the way to your palatial Nirvana? You may think that it's going to be for ever but for many of us, five-to-seven years in one house is the most we'll manage. If you're going to be in that house for the foreseeable future then you need to think about how your lives will change over the years. If you'll only be in it for the next five years then you need to keep a weather eye on the possibility of resale and think in terms of attractiveness in general market terms rather than any peculiar or individual requirements.

Energy efficiency and conservation, and the question of just how far you go with them, depends, to a large extent, on just how long you're going to be living there. These things needn't be expensive and

they don't need to use advanced or 'wacky' technology. Often the very best results can be obtained by tried and tested methods that need only add a few pounds per square metre to your new home. Are you aware of the need to save money in the shorter as well as the longer term? Are you conscious of the fact that in later life your finances might be limited and that being saddled with high fuel costs might make your staying in the home untenable? Are your motives for energy conservation purely personal or are you trying to save the planet? Above all, are you aware that many of the energy-saving devices and technologies have very high capital costs and that you might never recover these? Have you considered which relatively cheap ideas, discussed below, could lower your running costs and pay for themselves within a reasonable timescale and certainly within the probable span of your occupation?

Energy efficiency

If energy efficiency is high on your priority list, you need to make sure that your designer fully understands this, right from the word go. Many of the factors that can make a home more energy efficient are passive ones and they start, of course, with the site that you have chosen. The orientation should, if at all possible, be south facing, plus or minus 45 degrees, ideally with shelter from prevailing winds but without shading to the house. That said, plots are fairly hard to come by, even in the best of times and, whilst this is an ideal, don't go passing up a site just because this can't be achieved.

Using the sun to heat your house saves energy and makes it more pleasant. You don't need to increase the window area but the more of them that can face south the better, although you may need external blinds to prevent over heating in the summer months. A conservatory can certainly help with the saving of energy, but in certain areas, such as Conservation Areas, Areas of Outstanding Natural Beauty and the National Parks, the planners will have a lot to say about their use and just how they look. In other areas they may be quite amenable but even then, may baulk at having them on the front of a house. Of course, some windows may always have to face north to ensure good daylight in all rooms. Any gain from any of the above is known as passive solar heating and the most important thing about it is that it is free.

A compact plan, without 'extensions', minimises the external wall area, reduces heat losses and reduces the shading of other parts of the house. A bungalow will lose more heat than a three-storey house of the same floor area. Rooms that are used most should be on the south side to take advantage of any solar gain. For rooms that are used mostly in the mornings, such as kitchens and breakfast rooms, a south-east orientation will get the best benefit from the sun. If possible, halls, landings, staircases and less frequently occupied rooms such as bathrooms and utility rooms, should go on the north side. That's the ideal, of course, but when thinking about energy conservation, all of this has to fit in with the street scene and what the planners require. Additionally, there may be other factors to take into account, such as the specific views from a window or windows. As ever, the conflicting requirements have to be brought into balance and that's the task facing you and your designers.

Energy conservation

This is the active or mechanical side of energy efficiency and one that is closely governed by the Building Regulations.

Standard Assessment Procedure or SAP is the Government's standard system for home energy rating and can be used to provide a simple but reliable indicator of the energy efficiency of a house. It estimates the space and hot water heating costs per square metre of floor area of a house (based upon such factors as its size, heating system, ventilation characteristics and standard assumptions such as occupancy and heating pattern) and converts it into a rating from 1 to 100. The higher the number, the lower the energy consumption. A SAP calculation is also a requirement under the section of the Building Regulations, dealing with Conservation of Fuel and Power, known as 'Part L', with which all new homes must comply. However, if it is your intention to build an energy-efficient home, you should regard these Regulations as an absolute minimum.

There are three basic methods of demonstrating compliance with 'Part L' and all of them have to show a SAP rating. A high SAP rating will, therefore, save a lot of effort by providing most of the information that is needed to prove compliance. SAP calculations will usually be commissioned or undertaken by your architect, designer, timber-frame manufacturer or package-deal company but a number of commercial sources will undertake them for you and many of the material suppliers and manufacturers, together with the NHBC, can provide this service.

The three methods are:

- *Elemental* This lays down maximum permissible 'U' values for walls, roofs, floors and windows. There are limits to the area of windows and doors of 22.5% of the floor area but there are options to increase this by the use of high-performance glazing. The lower the 'U' value for each element, the better. Perhaps the best illustration of all of this is to think about walls. At the time of writing the target 'U' value for walls is 0.45 but everyone expects that this will very shortly change to 0.35. A standard timber-framed open-panel walling system, using 89mm x 39mm studs, will have a 'U' value of around 0.39. If you increase the size of the studs and, by inference, the thickness of the insulation to 140mm, then the 'U' value improves to 0.29. If you were to ratchet things up even further by using the closed panel Scandinavian systems, then the 'U' values would be approaching 0.2 or slightly less.

  If you are talking in terms of brick and block, then a demonstration of just how the insulation, rather than the structure, affects 'U' value can be given by assuming a brick and block wall where the cavity is 50mm and the internal block is lightweight 125mm. If the cavity is left clear and hard plaster is used, then the 'U' value would be 0.6, which is clearly not good enough. If you changed the hard plaster to a lightweight plaster then the 'U' value would come down to 0.59 and, if you dry-lined the wall, then it would come down to 0.54. Not a lot of difference and still all outside the target 'U'

Above: The best of both worlds. Modern energy-efficient oak-framed houses with the same ambience as their 500-year-old counterparts. (Border Oak Design & Construction Ltd)

Right: Potton always realised that the interior, and in particular the inglenook fireplace was a potent selling point.

value for the walling of 0.45. However, if you insulated the cavity with full fill insulation, then the 'U' value would come down to 0.32. And by widening the cavity to 100mm with full fill insulation you would achieve a 'U' value of 0.245 with very little additional cost.

- *Target 'U' value* This allows you to calculate the average 'U' value for your design using a formula based on the outside area of your building and the floor area. So long as the average 'U' value achieves a target 'U' value, the building complies. Allowances can also be made for more efficient heating systems and for orientating the house and glazing southwards. This method is slightly more complicated than the elemental method but allows for greater flexibility in design. With both this and the elemental method, the requirements become more stringent if the SAP rating is less than 60 (a poor rating for new housing).

- *Energy rating* The principal requirement is that the design achieves a set SAP rating of between 80 and 85, depending on the floor area. So long as this score is met there are very few restrictions on the design.

SAP ratings can be a useful tool in setting targets for your design. You could, for example, set a target 10 points above the Building Regulations requirement for the Energy Rating Method. Alternatively, you could set aside a fixed amount to spend on raising the initial design specification above the Building Regulations base line. If we take an example of two houses of a similar design of 230 square metres we can compare the improved energy efficiency that is available (see opposite).

I've already illustrated how the 'U' value can be improved as far as the walling goes. It needn't stop there and I would think that if you are going to specify anything about this subject to your designer you should, perhaps, think about asking that the 'U' value for the walling approaches as close to 0.3 as possible. A loft with 200mm of insulation (100mm laid between the joists with 100mm laid across them) will have a 'U' value of 0.2. Rooms in the roof and dormer

COMPARATIVE SAP RATINGS

House 'A' (2500 sq. ft.) – built to meet the Building Regulations requirements

- *   Basic wall insulation ('U' value of 0.45)
- *   150mm loft insulation
- *   Standard double glazing (6mm air gap)
- *   Gas wall-mounted boiler serving radiators
- *   Room thermostat, programmer and thermostatic radiator valves
- *   30mm sprayed insulation on the hot water cylinder

SAP rating = 86
Annual heating and hot water cost £476 (1998/9)

House 'B' (2500 sq. ft.) – built to provide low running costs

- *   South facing orientation
- *   Good wall insulation providing a 'U' value of 0.3
- *   200mm loft insulation
- *   50mm floor insulation
- *   Double glazing with 12mm air gap and low 'e' glass
- *   Gas-condensing boiler serving radiators
- *   Room thermostat, programmer and thermostatic radiator valves
- *   70mm sprayed insulation on the hot water cylinder

SAP rating = 100
Annual heating and hot water cost £306 (1998/9)

windows need careful attention to detail but can be insulated to a high standard. If you ever intend to occupy the roof void then you might like to consider the placing of the insulation so as to provide a warm roof instead of a cold roof. With a cold roof, the insulation follows the shape of the occupied rooms below, so leaving the loft outside the insulated area. The area between the insulation and the roof structure then needs to be adequately ventilated to avoid condensation. With a warm roof, the insulation is placed between and along the route of the rafters, under the tiles. Even though the loft is not heated it therefore finds itself within the insulated envelope. Condensation is therefore unlikely, so there is not the need for ventilation.

Neither is inherently more or less efficient than the other and if, therefore, you have no plans to occupy the roof, a cold roof will be perfectly suitable and will, by virtue of the fact that the area to cover is reduced, cost less to insulate. Ground floors are much more difficult as far as heat loss calculations are concerned, as there are so many different types of floors. All of them are, however, easy to insulate during construction and a minimum of 50mm is suggested, with more if underfloor central heating is to be employed, so as to minimise heat-loss to the ground. Whether using an oversite slab or floor beams, remember to draw the proposed use and thickness of the insulation to the contractor's attention so that the floor levels and cill levels are set at the correct height to accommodate it.

The entrance and hall

The entrance hall is the window into the rest of the home. Too pokey and it gives a first impression of a cramped and often untidy space. Too big and it begs the question, 'Could this space have been better employed'?

Could it indeed have some useful function other than just as an entrance and passageway? What about all or part of the hallway becoming a dining hall or a great room? What about the idea of the hall doubling up as a sitting area? How about scrapping the idea of a hallway entirely and making the entrance through a conservatory or atrium or even directly into the living rooms, or area? Does the staircase to the upper part have to run from the hall? Could you think in terms of it being enclosed, or leading up from another room, or is the staircase itself part of the state-

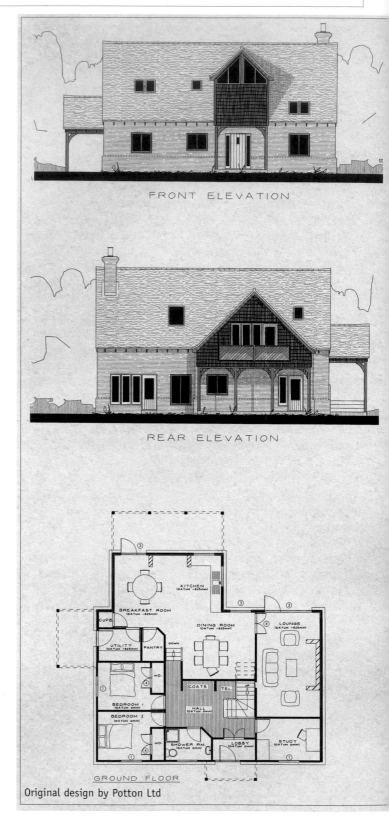

FRONT ELEVATION

REAR ELEVATION

GROUND FLOOR

Original design by Potton Ltd

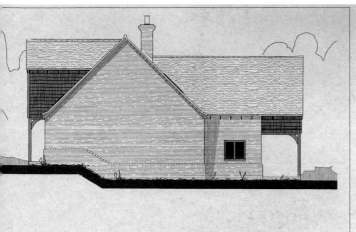

SIDE ELEVATION

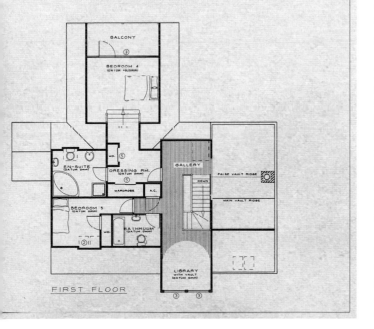

FIRST FLOOR

ment you want to make about your home?

Do you need a downstairs toilet by the front door? For general living it might make more sense to have it closer to the utility area or easily accessible from the garden. But that would mean that casual visitors and strangers would have to enter your private areas, so would that prove impracticable? Maybe there's space for both?

The lounge, living areas and family life

A large lounge, after the kitchen, is probably the biggest single selling factor in a house. The magazines illustrate and feature two extremes in their case histories, both of which happen to be very photogenic. The first type is the cosy old-fashioned one with the inglenook fireplace – all dreamy and with a feeling of solid dependability. That's the one that major package-deal companies have latched onto in order to sell the dream. The second predominant type is the open and airy living room with high vaulted ceilings, light streaming in and minimalist furnishings. What most people actually build is probably somewhere between these two.

What do you want? Are you sure you're not building a lounge around a fireplace rather than the other way around? How important is light going to be in your lounge? Will you use it in daylight hours or will it be a room to which you retreat in the evenings? Do you want the lounge to take up most of the available reception area space or would that area be better employed by dividing it up into more useable rooms?

What other rooms must the lounge adjoin? Does it have to be next to or interconnecting with any of them or could it stand alone with access only from the hall? Do you want easy access to the garden or is the thought of children traipsing mud all over your prize rug too much to bear? Do you want the conservatory opening off it or would that be more used if it came off another room? Within most lounges the fireplace is one of the most important features. Be careful, though. An inglenook fireplace looks right in a very large lounge but it can dominate a smaller one. It also looks right in houses of a certain style, particularly those that were derived from the East Anglian black and whites. It can look incongruous in a modern home. What about high or vaulted ceilings? They look lovely in the photographs, but what would it do to the heating and comfort levels?

If you do decide to split up the space, how big or how small do you think your family lounge could be before it seriously affects any resale value? What to do with the space? A snug could provide you with somewhere cosy to sit in the evenings without the need to heat up a large room. A study or a home office might, in an age when working from home is becoming ever more prevalent, almost be a necessity – but couldn't the office go elsewhere?; maybe in the attic, in the basement or even in the garage or an outbuilding? A music room or library would be nice but it'll have to be quite large if it's to house something like a grand piano. However, if that's not your instrument then it could be quite a modest affair. It'll need careful thought though, as to where it goes, what it adjoins and what's over it, if it's not to intrude on other activities within the home.

When children are young they want to play in their bedrooms and then sit with mummy and daddy in the lounge before bedtime. As they grow up, unless you can persuade them to study, they spend less time in their rooms and their tastes in music and television, and in particular, their volume levels, can cause friction. The family room was invented for this. In reality it's just a second lounge that often starts off as a playroom and then progresses to a full blown youth centre. Careful thought has to be given to its siting. If your bedroom is directly above it, you'll get no sleep. Somewhere upstairs or a long way from the kitchen, the toilet and the entrance, and you'll be woken by the nocturnal comings and goings. It might be best, perhaps, to put it in the basement or in the garage roof.

Cooking and eating

In many homes the dining room is the least used and most expensively furnished room in the house. Do you really need it? When you say that you couldn't have guests eating in the same area as the food preparation, or even adjoining and open to it, are you thinking clearly? Who do you invite to dinner? Do you really invite total strangers to dinner or are they more likely to be friends and family? Even if you do have to entertain business clients at home, do you have staff or is the person cooking the meal to be excluded from most of the party? What about an archway between the dining area and the kitchen at the very least – that way the cook could at least take some part in the general conversation.

Kitchens are one of the biggest selling points in

Above: Some kitchen designs reach back to a more utilitarian age.

Left: Others strive for the farmhouse kitchen approach with space for family eating or sitting.

Right: Whatever the style, the kitchen makes a fundamental statement about your home.

any house. Is yours the right kitchen for your house? Have you chosen from a brochure or for fashion's sake, without thinking how it will look in your home? Showroom lighting makes everything look different. Would a breakfast bar or an adjoining breakfast room become a useful and much used space?

Care also needs to be taken if you're having an Aga or Rayburn cooker, or one of their generics. Many of these need a chimney so you've got to accommodate that going through the upper floors or else position the cooker on an outside wall where it can possibly have a balanced flue. They take up a large space, they interrupt the run of modern units, they're extremely heavy and hugely expensive, yet they're loved with a passion that once even moved a poet laureate to wax lyrical. They should never be an afterthought.

Utility rooms and storage

What is the purpose of your proposed utility room? Is its use allied to that of the kitchen and, if not, does it have to connect to it? If it's really a laundry room, why cart clothes downstairs, wash them and cart them back up again? Couldn't the room go upstairs? If it's a mud room, somewhere for dirty dogs and wellies, could it just be a lobby and could it benefit, not only from a toilet, but perhaps a shower as well? Or is that going to be a great idea on paper that, in the end, just gets used as storage? If space is at a premium, how about scrapping the idea of a utility room altogether in favour of a bigger kitchen or a breakfast area?

However many advances are made with modern kitchen units and appliances, the larder still retains its affection in the housewife's mind. The trouble is that in many modern kitchens, it's expected that the units will get a clear run and there isn't always room for the larder. That's a shame because a fairly modest larder can provide the same shelf space as a lorry load of kitchen units. As it's really storage, see if it can be positioned in the utility section, so as to leave the kitchen uninterrupted. It should be positioned on a northern wall if possible with fly proof ventilation in the traditional manner, but if this proves impossible, there are electrical larder cooling units.

If you're having underfloor central heating, you're going to need some pretty big cupboards to hide all those pipes and manifolds. If you're having a central vacuum do you want that to go in a cupboard in the house or would you prefer to site it out in a garage or outbuilding? Will the linen cupboards be accessible to the communal areas or must they go in one of the bathrooms or a bedroom? Have you already got wardrobes as furniture or will you be wanting built-in wardrobes or bedroom furniture in all or some of the bedrooms?

Conservatories or sun rooms

In most cases, conservatories can be constructed under Permitted Development Rights, after the completion of the building. Good job too, because conservatories can be hugely expensive. Proprietary ones come in all shapes and sizes or can be purpose made. They can be simple, single-glazed affairs in softwood or they can be elaborate double- or triple-glazed structures in either hardwood or Pvc-u.

Which room do you want it to come off? Off the lounge is the most usual but would that fit in with your lifestyle? Might it not be better off the dining room or the family room or even the kitchen? Could it be big enough to have access to all of these rooms? What about heating? Conservatories can help to save energy by reducing heat loss through adjoining walls and by trapping heat from the sun. The savings are small but to be effective it does need to be on the south side of the building without any over-shadowing. Even high-quality conservatories should not have any permanent heating, at least not connected to the main heating system for the house, as this could lead to high fuel bills. They should also have double-glazed doors to shut them off from the main house when they are not in use.

A sun room is a different matter. That's really another room in the house, only with far more windows. Usually there is a wall up to cill height and the roof is constructed and clad in the same material as for the main roof, perhaps with roof lights as well. All of the building regulations will apply and the heating will almost certainly be part and parcel of the main house system, although it might be better to have some way of shutting it off in extremes of weather. At the very least the radiator should have its own thermostatic valve or any underfloor central heating should have its own zone and controls.

How many bedrooms do you want or need?

Whilst not wishing to preach conformity, I still feel the need to stress the importance of keeping a weather eye open for future sales. You might not want more than two or three bedrooms, and if that's what you decide, then that's fine. But do consider that a house with three large bedrooms compared against an identically sized house with four smaller ones could be at a disadvantage on value, even though its costs might be substantially the same. Could you plan for the larger rooms to be subdivided and if you sell, do you understand that it might be better for you to effect the change, rather than relying on a prospective purchaser's imagination?

What about bedroom sizes? You might well consider that as it's your house and it's you who is paying for it, your bedroom suite is going to have the lion's share of any space. On the other hand you might feel that things need to be evened out a little or you might want to head off arguments between children and make all their rooms the same size. Will you want dressing rooms? Do you need a guest suite or will one of the other main bedrooms suffice?

Bathrooms and toilets

An en-suite is considered a necessity in most larger family homes and is an important factor when it comes to resale value. Do you want it to be a shower room or a full bathroom? Many of the smaller homes that now have en-suite facilities tend to try and cram the sanitaryware into a windowless space that's not much larger than a cupboard. Would that satisfy you?

With the communal or family bathroom, do you want the toilet to be separate or would it be better to have a toilet in there as well as a completely separate one? What about en-suite accommodation for other bedrooms, or for at least one that you can then designate as a guest suite? Could the idea of one bathroom being directly accessible to and serving two bedrooms work? Have you thought through the family routines, especially in the mornings? Would doubling up the number of wash-hand basins in each bathroom help? What about hand basins in some or all of the bedrooms?

Windows and window styles

Double glazing is standard in most new homes. It reduces heat loss and offers sound insulation. Standard double glazing using a 6mm air gap gives a 'U' value of 3.3 (Remember the target for the wall was 0.3!). Increasing the air gap to 12mm and changing the glass to a low emissivity (Low 'e') glass will raise the insulation level to a 'U' value of 2.4. Changing the air gap need not cost very much extra at all but if larger air gaps are required, then the cost of the window frames might rise considerably and they may have to be purpose made. Argon filled double-glazing units and triple-glazing, standard on some of the Scandinavian systems, may also be used, but all of these will undoubtedly cost more.

The planners will have a great deal to say about the windows in your house, usually referred to as 'the fenestration'. Many people like lots of glass and don't like it interrupted by lots of transoms and mullions. Planners, on the other hand, usually hate large areas of glass and have a particular aversion to horizontal transoms, preferring windows with a more vertical emphasis and often with narrow modules. In Conservation Areas, you can almost guarantee that they will not accept Pvc-u and instead will insist on painted timber, although, after nearly four decades in the business, I've yet to fathom out precisely why.

When you're making your scrapbook, make a particular note of the type of windows in your area,

especially those that have been used on new housing of a similar ilk to the one you're planning. Departure from the normal manufacturer's ranges can be prohibitively expensive, as can the use of stone mullions, surrounds, cills and heads. Box sash windows can also be expensive although some of the manufacturers are now introducing them into their standard ranges. As for what material to choose, softwood windows are now pressure impregnated and treated so that they will last and are often guaranteed for 30 years. Hardwood windows are more expensive. I know we're always being told that they come from sustainable sources but I'm never really sure if that's true. They look best dark stained and they often don't take to paint very well. Metal or steel windows suffer from cold bridging but have the benefit that they can provide a very thin profile. As such they are often used in conjunction with stone mullions and surrounds. Make sure they are galvanised and/or powder coated. Aluminium can suffer from many of the drawbacks that steel windows have, unless there is what is known as a thermal break in the window, prohibiting the transference of cold. They are most suitable for patio doors where a combination of strength with a relatively thin profile is required. Raw aluminium is unattractive and weathers badly, and should therefore be properly powder coated or enamelled.

By the way, on the subject of patio doors. These are modern inventions and they do not trace their history or origins back to any architectural feature other than, perhaps, French doors. It just looks daft if glazing bars or leading are introduced; they should always be left clear glazed.

Pvc-u windows come in all shapes, sizes and profiles. They were meant to be the maintenance-free option but some of the cheaper ones have suffered over time with discoloration and brittleness. Avoid the cheap end of the market and opt for units where the extrusion is slower and therefore thicker, with reinforcement within the sub frames. All windows, whatever they're made of, should be washed down regularly, quite apart from normal or periodic decoration, and in sea areas, they should be thoroughly cleaned at least once a month to remove salt.

Heating your home and the hot water

The boiler, rather than the method of delivering the heat, is the most important determining factor in the energy efficiency of the home. Condensing boilers, with average efficiencies of 85%, are much better than conventional boilers, even though they do tend to cost quite a bit more. Essentially, a condensing boiler works in just the same way as an ordinary fan-flued boiler, except that it has a larger heat exchanger that absorbs more of the heat from the burner and from the flue gases. Under certain conditions, when the return water temperature is low, the flue gases condense and release latent heat back into the boiler that would otherwise be wasted. It is from this that the boiler gets its name. The gases coming out of a conventional boiler's flue are very hot, 250 degrees centigrade, but with a condensing boiler they are around 50-60 degrees centigrade so the potential for savings are obvious. The problem, as I've hinted at, is the cost of these boilers and, once again, you have to weigh up the pay-back time, particularly if you are talking about a smaller and very thermally efficient house that you do not expect to be living in for very long.

Heat pumps have recently surfaced again. The principle behind these is very like a refrigerator working in reverse. A loop of pipework, buried in the garden or a pond or stream, takes the latent heat from the outside and converts it into usable heat for the home. They are frighteningly expensive. If that changes or if there are advances in the manufacture and technology, then they might one day have a proper place in self-building. Until then, they are really only for the enthusiast or the wealthy.

The principal choice that many self-builders face is whether to have radiators or an underfloor central heating system. Underfloor heating, with its low water temperature, can combine with a condensing boiler to provide an extremely efficient system, especially if you are in the home all day. However, if your occupation is intermittent, say early mornings and evenings only, then the lack of responsiveness might be a drawback, although modern programming, with sensors to detect changes in the outside temperature is making inroads into that shortcoming. With underfloor central heating, the pipes are usually buried in a screed. It is

this that radiates the heat and provides a latent heat store and, where underfloor central heating is used on suspended timber floors, there is no doubt that some of the efficiency is lost. A tiled solid screed floor works best with underfloor heating, as do rugs instead of carpets, but most companies can compensate for this by increasing the amount of pipework.

Radiators with TRVs provide a very efficient system of delivering heat and they are inherently responsive. They cannot, however, provide such an even heat as underfloor systems, particularly in larger rooms. People get awfully worked up about the amount of wall space that they take up, but it is open to suggestion that, upstairs at least, this is really not a problem. Perhaps the best compromise therefore is to have underfloor central heating to ground and solid upper floors, and radiators with thermostatic valves to timber upper floors.

Warm air heating is efficient but fiendishly bad to live with. However well you filter it, it distributes dust and it's practically lethal for those who suffer from asthma and can cause it in others who haven't previously suffered. I know, I've been there. Electric underfloor or overhead heating cannot claim to be cost-effective or efficient due to its high capital and running costs whilst electric storage radiators, in a thermally efficient house, can be cost-effective, especially when combined with a relatively low installation or capital cost. What they cannot claim, however, is any responsive control and unless occupation is virtually constant, it is not something most self-builders would choose.

Hot-water efficiency is also governed largely by the efficiency of the boiler rather than the type of system, e.g. vented or sealed, but the more insulation you have around the hot water store (cylinder) the better and 50mm plus is a good thickness to aim for. Good controls are essential to maximise the efficiency of any heating system and they are required by the Building Regulations. Individual room control is particularly important in rooms with large south-facing windows and if your home is to have distinct areas which will be used at differing times, such as an annexe or office, then zone controls may be worth considering.

Electric showers have a fairly low flow rate and

Right: BRECSU, part of the Building Research Establishment, publish important leaflets.

Below: Although not quite as efficient as when used with a solid floor, underfloor central heating is still possible with timber first floors.

Below right: The heart of any underfloor system is the manifold and the control valves. (Robbens Systems Ltd)

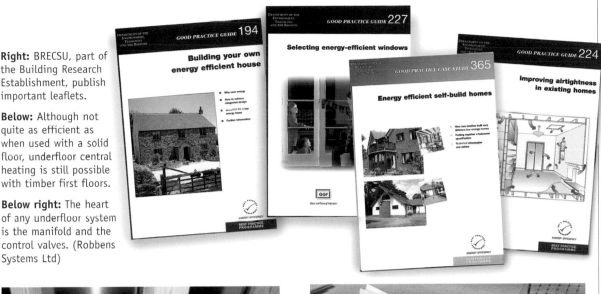

only heat the actual amount of water that is used. Nevertheless, if there is a store of hot water only a short distance away, then the cost of their purchase and installation may not be worthwhile. If you want a powerful shower, then either use a sealed hot-water system, where the hot water is delivered at mains pressure, or think of a power shower where the water is pumped. Of course these do use a lot more water and energy and they are not inexpensive.

If you want a focal fire and you want to maximise energy efficiency, then multi-fuel stoves are a very good option, especially if you are able to take advantage of a free fuel such as wood. These stoves are much more efficient than an open fire and won't give such high heat losses through the flue from increased ventilation when not in use. I repeat this information, knowing full well that the open fireplace is deeply embedded in the British psyche and that most of you will nod sagely and ignore it.

Active solar power

This is as opposed to the passive, and therefore free, solar power I have discussed above. Solar-heated hot water systems have an extremely long payback period. As the solar heat is intermittent in the United Kingdom, you would also need a back-up boiler together with a fairly large storage capacity and, in strictly economic terms, it really doesn't work out for houses. It can be cost-effective where heating is required for a swimming pool that is, after all, only used in good weather.

I have already referred to photovoltaic cells. These convert sunlight into electricity and there are times when they can even put back power into the grid. They are extremely expensive and the payback time verges on the impossible. But this, as with all technology is an ever- and fast-changing scene, and I look forward to the day when I can write an edition of this book that praises and recommends them.

Ventilation

Ventilation is important both to provide fresh air and prevent condensation. The Building Regulations require that there should be extractor fans or passive stack ventilation (PSV) in all kitchens and bathrooms. With PSV, air is drawn out of the house, without the need for electric fans, through a combination of the effect of air flowing over the roof and by the natural buoyancy of warm moist air. In order to prevent over-ventilation, humidity-controlled dampers can be fitted which need no electrical connection. Permanent ventilation must also be provided to all other rooms using trickle vents that are fitted to all windows.

Mechanical ventilation with or without heat recovery may offer benefits such as filtered air and reduced noise intrusion. The systems use fans to supply fresh air and extract stale air in a very controlled manner. The heat recovery options recover much of the heat from the extracted air and add it to the returning air using a heat exchanger so that the two air streams do not mix. Filters can be fitted to the supply air to remove dust and pollen and they can, therefore, provide very good-quality air. There is no need for trickle ventilation with such a system and this may be an important factor in reducing the noise from outside in certain locations. Mechanical ventilation will not work properly unless the house is well sealed and sealing of the house can only really be done at the construction stage, involving very close attention to detail and a close watch on workmanship. Unfortunately, open fireplaces are incompatible with these systems. The running costs are also significant and may outweigh the energy saved, so, whilst they will provide good ventilation and good-quality air, they should not generally be seen as an energy-saving or efficient feature.

Lighting

Maximising daylighting with the design and good lighting design, combined with use of low-energy compact or strip fluorescent lights will save considerable amounts on running costs. Fluorescent lamps have a much longer life than ordinary light bulbs. There are four in my house that I purchased well over 10 years ago, and they have been in almost constant daily use ever since!

Twelve-volt downlighting has become extremely popular, either as a complete replacement for other forms of lighting in certain areas or as a supplement to it. It does need a transformer that can be hidden away in a cupboard and it can save considerably on electricity. It can also be used in situations in bathrooms or saunas where mains voltage lighting would be dangerous.

Basements

In a situation where the slope of the land is going to dictate the design and that design ends up as split- or multi-level, there is the distinct possibility that you are also going to end up with one or more walls below ground level. In these cases the walls have to be treated in the same way as if they were basement walls and fully water proofed, something that is called 'tanking'.

Tanking has to be completely watertight and, with a full basement, what you are seeking to create is, in effect, a swimming pool in reverse. But this empty swimming pool is having to contend with pressures of water from outside and, as well as that, it is having to cope with ground pressures. There are many different methods of basement construction, ranging from traditional blockwork to shuttered and poured concrete and, lately, to pre-fabricated concrete sections. Most of these rely on being tanked but there is a school of thought that believes that it is impossible to tank a below-ground structure infallibly and that the right way to proceed is with a pump and sump arrangement in tandem with specialist wall and flooring panels. If you want to know more about basements, telephone the Basement Development Group on 01344 725737. Otherwise, my advice is to leave the choice of construction method to the structural engineer working with your architect. They are the ones who'll have to guarantee it and it's on their Professional Indemnity that you'll have to rely.

A basement is not naturally ventilated and the tanked walls cannot breathe. If natural light and ventilation can be achieved by high-level windows or light wells then that is always preferable. If it is to remain windowless then careful thought must be given to ventilation, especially if any activity is to take place in the basement which generates water vapour, such as with a sauna or laundry room. If the boiler is to be situated in a cellar it is important that consideration is given to its specific ventilation requirements, and now that audible gas detectors are cheaply available, they should be installed to detect any possible build-up of gas in the cellar.

In situations where the planning permission for the house sets a limit on the size, it is open to interpretation as to whether the addition of a basement would breach these requirements. The attitude of planning officers is different in every region, with some insisting that, at all times, any such habitable space is to be included and others feeling that, perhaps, so long as it does not have an effect on the overall appearance of the house, it should be allowed. If there's any doubt on this point, I suggest you denote the space as 'storage' or 'void' and occupy it later under Permitted Development Rights. Usually that'll do the trick but if the effect of a basement is to lift the house out of the ground or show windows below ground-floor level, it might be a little difficult to deny your intentions. A planning officer could then claim that either there had been a material departure from the consent, or that the effect of your future proposals was having a detrimental effect on the overall design.

Above all, what the self-builder must understand about basements, is that this accommodation is going to cost at least as much per square metre to build as the rest of the house. Do not run away with the idea that, just because you're having to dig and build foundations, somehow this space is coming for free or on the cheap. It most certainly is not!

Attics

Attic space is cheap but its use or eventual use has to be planned for in advance. You cannot simply go around cutting up ordinary trusses and you have to think ahead and use either attic trusses or a traditional purlin and spar roof construction. As with basements, the planners might, where there is a restriction on the size of the dwelling, want to consider attic space as part the allowable accommodation. Once again, if this is the case, it might be better to omit any reference to occupation of the roof space and to plan for its eventuality under Permitted Development Rights.

What will you use the attic for? Will it be additional bedrooms or bathrooms? Will it be office space, play space or a gym? If so, what are the implications for the bedrooms below? How will you get heavy office machinery or furniture up there? How will you gain access? You could, for occasional use only, put up with a pull-down loft ladder or staircase, but if you're thinking of more generalised use, you'll probably want a proper staircase. In that case you might fall foul of the Building Regulations and be required to install fire doors to all doors leading from the landing or communal area.

More often than not, the provision of attic trusses is one expense that is worthwhile. At a cost of less than £2,000 for a fairly large house it is money in the bank if you ever want to expand your home into the roof.

Contents and furniture

Make a list of your favourite furniture. Most modern furniture is designed to fit through door openings as narrow as 760mm or else be capable of disassembly. But antique furniture certainly isn't. Is the dining area going to be large enough to accommodate your dining table at its full extension and is there enough room around it for chairs and circulation? Are the ceilings going to be high enough for antique wardrobes or dressers? If your snooker table is going in the loft or the basement, make sure that the access is large enough. If it's going into a room on any upper floor, check that the floor can take the weight. Check also that there is at least two metres all around it so that there's room for the cue.

Granny flats

Any consideration about whether to include a 'granny flat' in a self-build project needs as much thought given to the possible unravelling of the situation as it does to its creation. For many the idea of bringing their parents into a loving and caring home environment, to become their built-in friend, baby- and house-sitter, is a wonderful and fulfilling dream. For others, that same thought is about as welcome as the onset of bubonic plague.

But enough of this, let's look on the positive side and consider the advantages and how the objective, once decided upon, can be achieved. First of all, the financial side. Will granny simply be passing over her share of the costs of the project as cash? Will granny be part owner of the completed establishment or will she just be coming to live in your house? What security of tenure will she have and, if it all goes wrong, how will she be able to recover her share in order to be able to house herself? All of these are questions, which may seem unpalatable or intrusive, but they are questions, nonetheless, which need answers before rather than after the event.

One way around things may be for granny to give you a private mortgage, negating or limiting your need to apply for outside finance. That way granny will retain a financial stake in the house and you will have security as long as you continue to meet the agreed repayments. Granny now has an income and that is important if you project your thinking forward to the time when she is no longer able to live with you and needs to go into a nursing home. The going rate for care in a nursing home is almost as much as the average wage. Help is available, of course, but, of late, that help has only been supplied by government upon realisation of the older person's assets down to a fairly paltry minimum. If the bulk of an older person's assets takes the form of a properly set-up mortgage, then that puts it beyond reach. The income from your repayments plus that from state and other pensions should then ensure a more comfortable placing for the later stages of your parent's life.

The important thing is to obtain sound advice from solicitors and accountants. On the death of the parent, with an arrangement such as I've described above, it is vital that any Will reflects the fact that you won't want to be turfed out of your home and that, if possible, the mortgage lapses and the deceased parent's share of the home comes to you. What can complicate this is the need to accommodate the aspirations of other siblings, who may well discount the loving care you've given your parents during the latter stages of their lives, and simply feel that you have purloined the bulk of their inheritance. Then again, what if you predecease your parents? Will they then be homeless and dispossessed or will there be provision for them to recover their equity in reasonable fashion with the minimum of upheaval? Nothing in life is for ever, and I repeat, as much care needs to go into the possible future unravelling of any financial pooling of resources as it does with its original amalgamation.

And when you've taken all of the advice and decided on your course of action, surely the planners are going to welcome your proposals with open arms? Well, not necessarily. Planners are often fearful of any suggestion that the single dwelling for which they have given consent could possibly be divided and end up, effectively, as two homes. They've been caught out before, you see, and for everyone who manages to hoodwink a planning authority into giving consent for something they didn't intend, there are countless others who are for ever blighted by that deception.

One way of alleviating the planner's fears is to demonstrate that the annexe is an integral part of the main home and to consider whether or not it needs its own entrance. Maybe the French doors from its lounge are enough? Maybe it can share access with the secondary access to the main house or even share the utility room?

Home offices

The words can cover a multitude of applications, from the company representative who sets aside a small space under the stairs, to plush suites with separate offices and toilet accommodation. The growing trend towards working from home is due, in part, to the greater use of computers and the Internet which obviate the need for a group of people working together to be in the same room and in part it's due to

Left: The work environment needs just as much consideration if it's at home as it would in a corporate office. Light, space, accessibility, storage and access to facilities all need to be planned out properly.

Below: The same room viewed from outside. The roof of the garage is often an ideal place for a home office.

the fact that many women with children now choose to work at home. In addition, companies find that they can expand into new geographical areas simply by employing representatives who are prepared to work from home, only meeting their colleagues in person at regular sales functions. It saves them the costs of office rentals and maintenance and it gives the employee a freedom and flexibility previously only enjoyed by the self employed.

The office can really go anywhere in the home if it's only ever going to be occupied or used by members of the household. However, if things start to get a little more sophisticated with staff coming in and/or clients visiting, much more careful thought has to be given as to its siting. You can't expect a secretary to have to go trooping up to your family bathroom and if your kids have left it in a mess, it's not going to impress your boss or a client. If this is the situation, you really need to be able to site the office accommodation somewhere with a separate entrance and its own dedicated toilet facilities. Maybe that could be in the utility area? Maybe it could be above or behind the garage or maybe it would be better to consider a purpose-built outbuilding?

We're talking here about working from home. What we shouldn't really be considering is running a full-blown company from home. There is a difference. If things get too big or too busy, your neighbours and the planners might well take an unhealthy interest in

the goings-on. You might be prepared to go the whole hog and apply for planning for change of use of part of your premises. In certain situations that could be successful but in a purely domestic setting, it's unlikely. In any event there's the tax angle. 'If part or all of your home has, at some time, not been used as your home; for example it, if it has been let or used for business', it will not be exempt for Capital Gains purposes under the relief that is available for your Principal Private Residence. Now none of that is supposed to catch out the writer or the company representative working from home, but if you've gone for formal planning permission, it would be frightfully difficult to argue against.

Designing for the disabled

In 1999, a new Part 'M' section of the Building Regulations came into force. The objective was to make sure that access is available and accessible, for disabled people, to the entrance storey, all habitable rooms on that storey and, most importantly, the toilet. These rules apply to all new dwellings.

Depending on the topography of the site, the access to the entrance door should be ramped, with any ramps no longer than 10 metres for gradients up to 1:15, or 5 metres for those up to 1:10. If the site has a steeper slope then steps are allowed so long as the steps have a width of no less than 900mm, the rise for each step is no greater than 150mm, and the rise between landings is no greater than 1.8 metres. In addition, if there are more than three risers, there has to be a continuous handrail on at least one side.

The threshold of the entrance door, although it can be a secondary door, should preferably be a level one with a retractable water bar, but in any event, should not exceed the 150mm.This entrance door should also have a minimum opening width of at least 775mm. In addition there are tables that set down the minimum width of internal doors in relation to the width of the corridor, dependent on whether the approach to the door is head on or not. These are designed to allow the free passage of wheelchairs.

Access to the toilet is crucial and the new regulations insist on the provision of a toilet to the main entrance storey. Whilst it is recognised that it will not always be practicable for a wheelchair to be fully accommodated within the toilet compartment, thought must be given to making that access as easy as possible. The provisions are normally satisfied if the door to the compartment opens outwards and has a clear opening in accordance with the width tables, with the washbasin positioned so that it does not impede access.

The regulations also stipulate that switches and plugs must be set at heights to assist those people whose reach is limited. In general this is in a band of between 450mm and 1200mm from the floor.

Howls of protest greeted these proposals, which many see as only the precursor of much tighter regulations to come. Already some authorities are asking designers to identify just where a lift between floors could be accommodated and many are pressing for the introduction and setting aside of such a space in all future designs. Against them are the developers, who have already seen the demise of many of their smaller two-bedroom designs and, of course, self-builders who feel that they don't want their home to conform to these stipulations. All I can say is that we are all one heartbeat away from accident or infirmity.

If you want help with the design of your new home, with particular reference to this subject, contact The Disabled Living Foundation on 020 7289 6111.

Security features

These days most windows and doors that conform to the regulations have proper locks. Couple that with double glazing and, as far as the structural components are concerned, it's probably as much as most people will want. Nevertheless, there are those for whom security is high on the agenda and for whom the building in of even greater security is an important incentive in the whole business of self-building. Proximity alarms, sensors, floodlighting; there is a wealth of equipment to satisfy even the most insecure of minds.

A feature, which can be built into a new home, is a secure cupboard, which offers protection for valuables, shotguns and the like. If this is given consideration at the design stage, it is relatively easy for an ingenious carpenter to install a hidden door to a hidden cupboard, which will escape the notice of a burglar! Those whose work involves keeping large sums of money in the house from time to time can arrange for an underfloor safe to be set in the foundation concrete, to be reached by turning back a rug or carpet in one of the ground floor rooms. This may be a condition of their special insurance.

Renovations and conversions

If building a new home from scratch means starting from a blank canvas in design terms, then renovating or converting is by no means painting by numbers. It may well be that, to a large extent, with renovations,

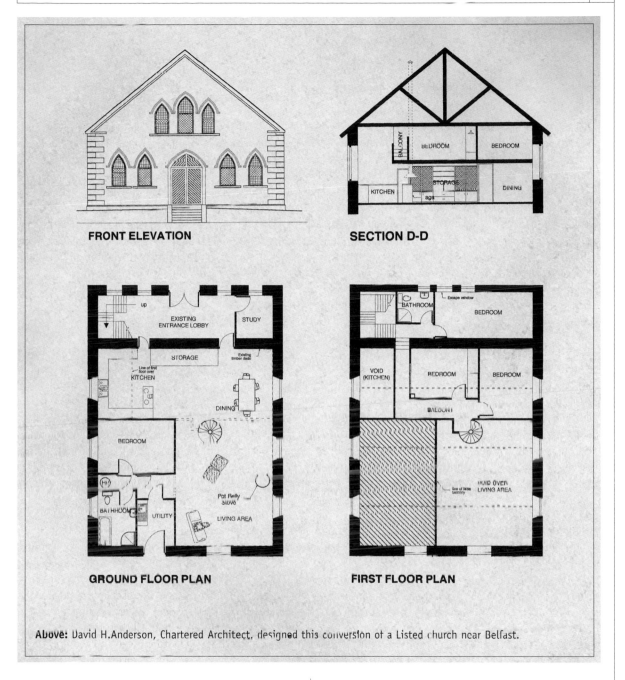

FRONT ELEVATION

SECTION D-D

GROUND FLOOR PLAN

FIRST FLOOR PLAN

Above: David H. Anderson, Chartered Architect, designed this conversion of a Listed church near Belfast.

the pattern of the accommodation is firmly set. However there's a lot you can do. In villages all over the country there are bungalows and houses that were built in the 1960s and early 70s. These stand out like sore thumbs, bearing little or no relationship to their neighbours or to any architectural vernacular. They cry out to be replaced, but that's not always economically viable, despite the complications of the VAT. Changing

their external appearance, by taking out the old landscape joinery and replacing it with more sympathetic fenestration, by rendering or otherwise changing those horrible tiled or timber-clad panels, or even by retiling the roof, should be considered as a social service. In fact, as far as most planners are concerned, it is, and a chat with them and/or the conservation officer that starts off with the premise that you want to do something to improve the street scene will go down very well.

Of course, the probability is that the accommodation might need enlarging or extending in order to bring it up to modern standards and requirements. In many village streets in sensitive areas, planners will only usually consider enlargement if it comes within the scope of Permitted Development. In Conservation Areas, the Permitted Development Rights might well have been removed. But going to them with ideas that will improve the street scene, offering them a trade-off between those and the need to extend the property, could well pay off.

Conversions obviously depend on the type of building. If it's an old water tower, a lighthouse or a pumping station, then flair and imagination, coupled with sympathy for the original structure can have quite startling results. Where it is all getting a bit predictable is with barn conversions. Perhaps it's because barns throughout the country are remarkably similar; a vast open space with a very high entrance, usually, but not always, situated in the centre of one side. As such, most barn conversions simply seem to fill in this entrance area with a vast glazed screen and then create galleried landings and upper parts that look down into a largely open plan ground floor where the only demarcation between uses is denoted by the furniture. Perhaps there's little or nothing that can be done and the fault lies with the insistence of planners that, despite the fact that the building is being con-

Above: Sometimes, even for enthusiasts, former church buildings can be a trifle too ecclesiastical-looking.

verted to a residence, it must still display its agricultural origins, at least to the outside. But if you are aware of the danger of a boring conformity, and you make your architect aware of your concerns, maybe a little more excitement could be brought into the project.

Do you need a garage?

Considered almost essential by the market, yet rarely used for the housing of motor cars. Do you want one at all and if so will you ever use it and what for? Could you think of building more house or could you envisage inclusion of the garage space within the home, on the understanding that if it ever comes to resale, it can be put back to its original purpose? Could you have a carport instead? Should the garage be attached, integral or detached? Planners feel that detached garages reflect the rural character, whilst attached and integral ones are an urban solution to the problem of what to do with the motor car.

Whatever garage you have, think carefully about its impact on the overall design of your new home. Many houses have, as their dominant architectural feature, the huge open maw of the garage doors. What to do about this and how to make them as attractive as possible has largely been left to the manufacturers, who have come up with solutions such a Tudor panelled garage doors. Well, Henry VIII didn't have a Rolls-Royce. The garage is a modern necessity that, if it has any heritage, traces its roots back to the stable or the coach house. Try, therefore to think of it in those terms, to vary its shape, the setting and above all the choice of the doors. Wherever possible, get doors to face across a plot rather than straight out to the street.

If the garage is detached or attached to the side of your new home and finances are stretched, could it be left until later? That way you could concentrate all of your monies into the home. You could even bring it up to the oversite level and treat it as a hard standing or parking. You could even, if money permitted, buy some or all of the materials at the same time as the house and store them carefully. Remember, however, that if you do buy materials after your VAT reclaim, you won't be getting the VAT back on them.

Above: In the countryside, having the garage detached from the main house, is often the preferred solution as far as the planners are concerned. It can also serve to add depth and interest to the design.

Left: An attached garage with access to the house is always popular but it can sometimes exert an overpowering influence on the design.

Below left: A carport can be the solution in some circum stances but they do need to be of a substantial construction if they are to look right.

Gardens

The garden should be an extension of the living space within the home, rather than a separate entity. Weather permitting, it should fit into the natural pro-gression between rooms. Can your access be via a sunroom or conservatory? Which rooms do you want to have direct access to the garden? Are you worried about children or dogs bringing in the dirt? In bad weather, could the garden be brought into the home by the raising of flowerbeds and planting, so that the eye is led through the window and beyond? Will access to the garden be suitable for elderly or disabled people and will the paths and patios be designed so that they too can enjoy it?

Does the house design reflect the need for direct access between the garden and the street? Carrying plants, mud and other garden materials and furniture through the house can be tedious. Of course this might not be possible. You might have a very narrow site or even a terraced property. In which case, could you access the garden through the garage? What do you want from your garden? Do you like weeding? Do you like mowing lawns and pruning shrubs? Or do you want a garden that's virtually an open-air room with easy-to-maintain surfaces and plants in pots?

In any building site there will be large amounts of spoil to get rid of, something that can prove extremely costly. Why not, therefore, consider retaining some or all of the excavated material, assuming your site's big enough? Why not use it to change the contours of the land with, perhaps, a raised shrubbery or mounded-up area giving either visual or sound privacy? Why not contain a heap of soil with a low brick wall to provide backache-free gardening?

Whilst you've got an excavator on site you could dig out a pond and pile the excavated material around it to form an attractive rockery backdrop. I'll not go into the methods of pond lining in this book, as there are plenty of other tomes specific to that subject. Much of course depends on your idea of a pond. Should it be formal in shape or containment? Should it be informal and look as natural as possible? Is it intended to house expensive Koi or is it intended as a future residence for frogs and newts? If you're going to need lighting, either under or over the water or if you're going to need pumps and filters, then think about the supply of electricity and a small shed or building to house all the equipment. Might this be possible as an underground structure beneath the rockery and, whilst you're running all this cable around, why not think of other areas in the garden that could benefit from lighting?

The thing to do is think about all of this at the design and pre-planning stages; certainly before machinery is on site and before you send away 'spoil' that you might need. Topsoil is very expensive to buy and extremely difficult to barrow around to a back garden. Stone for the rockery is horrendously expensive and having to pay for it would be all the more galling if you'd already sent loads away!

Driveways

Unless you have a very big garden indeed, the driveway is probably going to be one of the single most dominant features of your new home. I've already discussed access arrangements and the requirements of the authorities. What I'm talking about here is the driveway within the curtilage of your property. To some extent this is your business, but as you'd expect, the authorities do have some say, particularly in respect of parking and turning and the need to be able to enter and leave in forward gear. They might also, in certain circumstances, have an input on the choice of surfacing, where, for example, a tree or its roots might be affected.

In many suburban streets, there is little or no alternative to a straight driveway running between the garage doors and the road, with any associated parking or turning space leading off it to one side. The problem that this creates, quite apart from looking boring, is that there is a loss of privacy. Consider whether, if you've got the room, you could bring the entrance in on the other side of the frontage to the garage doors. That way the driveway can curve across the plot and whilst that might seem to take up more space, it will, nonetheless, afford you the opportunity of planting or banking that will give privacy to the home.

There are several choices when it comes to surfacing and once again it pays to think carefully about which you use. A pea shingle or gravel driveway is often thought of as the cheapest, easiest and quickest surface for a new driveway, which may well be true. However, it can look incongruous in a suburban street and where there are slopes there can be a problem of migration. This can be overcome by either a series of baffles or by 'sticking' the stones down with some sort of tar emulsion to a previously prepared and hard sub base. Where most pea shingle or gravel driveways go wrong is in the preparation of the sub base and the choice of edging. Any driveway is only ever going to be as good as the foundation it is laid upon and in the case of a gravel driveway that should either be hard rolled hoggin or well compacted and blinded hardcore.

Edging is important not only to look neat, but also to contain the surfacing material. It needn't always be concrete, although that's obviously best, and it can be tanalised timber. The gravel itself needs careful thought. Too often round stones are used to excessive depths that make walking or driving up it akin to trudging along Brighton beach. Choose a flat stone that is capable of compaction and lay it only in sufficient depths to give good cover.

Of course, if you ever get fed up with your gravel driveway, you'll probably find that it provides an excellent base for a Tarmac driveway. Beware the itinerant who knocks at the door telling you that they're doing a job around the corner and they've got some Tarmac left over that they can do you a good deal for. What you'll get is the heated-up scrapings from the resurfacing work down the road, and when it all comes up or fails to create a homogenous surface, they'll be long gone. Choose a company with premises and a landline rather than just a mobile number and that way your driveway can be every bit as serviceable as the Queen's highway. I question whether some of the colour choices that are available ever really look right and I have an intense dislike of coloured chippings in a rural environment, but that's really a matter of choice. Once again the sub base and the edgings are important and it's as well to insist that, before the black goes down, a good dose of weedkiller is applied.

Concrete driveways seem to have gone out of favour, at least in their traditional tamped form. Properly formed, with a good sub base and with expansion joints and bays, this can be an extremely serviceable surface that can look attractive. What seems to have taken their place, to some degree, is the imprinted and patterned concrete that purports to resemble cobbles or paving. Many people like these but what strikes me is that when they crack, they never seem to do so along the indentations, often because, in order to make them look realistic, the contractors haven't put in the necessary expansion joints.

Block pavers look right in the town but can look out of place in the country where one would, perhaps, be better advised to use proper, but much more expensive, brick pavoirs. They come in a variety of colours and, badly chosen, they do little more than imitate the petrol station forecourts that they so often grace. The costs can rival that of Tarmac and properly laid, on a good sub base with kiln-dried sand into which

they are tamped, they are virtually maintenance-free. Some like the gaps between the blocks or bricks to get mossy. Some hate it, spending endless hours scrubbing and scraping. The choice, as with all self-building, is yours but if you are after a more natural or non-intrusive surface, consider the use of grass blocks that simply blend into the lawn whilst providing a durable running surface. And, of course, although I've talked about each surfacing method in singular terms, it's open for you to think in terms of a combination of the various surfaces and textures.

Pathways and patios

The right garden path can give a special feeling to a house and garden. A winding path, moving between shrubs and raised features will gradually reveal your new home and give it an air of mystery that a straight path or an open-plan front garden can never provide.

Paths around the garden enable you and your guests to walk around when it's wet and, properly considered, can make your garden look larger than it is. On the other hand all paths need maintenance of one sort or another and if they're not properly laid they will become uneven and dangerous. Some stone flags or brick pavoirs become lethally slippery in wet weather, particularly if they're on a side of the house that doesn't get the sun so, in these situations, it might be better to consider another paving material.

The patio or terrace is the means by which we project our living arrangements from within the confines of the house, into the open air. Often it directly adjoins the house with access from one or more of the living rooms, but not necessarily. If you're after sun or perhaps even shade or a special view, then it can be divorced from the main house. But, always, thought has to be given to its primary purpose. If it's principally a feature to be admired but not regularly walked on, the gaps between the slabs can be filled with Alpine plants and dwarf walls can be set at a height where they don't impede the view, with everything arranged for visual effect. If the patio is to be used for sitting out, or for parties with lots of guests, it's important that there are no gaps to trap high heels and walls are built at a convenient height for either sitting on or at the very least, resting one's drink on.

Above: Paths and patios don't just give access to all parts of the garden in all weathers; they lend shape and form to it as well, outlining and accentuating important features.

Above: Natural clay paving from York Handmade Brick Company Ltd.

Left: A garden should be an extension to the home, another room in the open air.

The norm used to be that patios and terraces were constructed with one material or another. But I invite you to consider whether a combination of materials and textures might not give this important feature more interest. Why not have areas within a stone slabbed patio as large round pebbles set in concrete? What about mixing pavoirs or quarry tiles, on edge or flat? What about shingled areas planted with aromatic herb shrubs? How about areas of raised timber decking?

Walls, fences and hedges

Walls are a very special feature in a garden, and building a new one announces that you are seriously into landscaping. Walls also involve you in considerable expenditure. If you want to build a garden wall, it is important that you make no attempt to cut corners, as a cheap-looking wall will damage the appearance of the garden as much as an appropriate one will enhance it. If you use the wrong bricks or stone your wall will look wrong and will get worse as it weathers, while the right materials will look better and better as time goes by. Walls should give a feeling that they are part of the landscaping: they will not do this if they are inappropriate to the surroundings. In particular, this means that concrete blocks of all sorts, particularly the ornamental pierced walling blocks, should only be used in the sort of urban or seaside situation which suits them, and never as part of a rural scene.

Retaining walls are a different kettle of fish. It all depends on the height of the land that is to be retained and whether or not any buildings are to be supported, as to the type of construction but, as a rule of thumb, if you're retaining more than 1.2 metres, you need a specialist engineer to be involved in the design. As much care needs to be taken with the drainage of the retained land and the reduction of water pressure as it does with the actual strength of the wall itself. There are alternatives to building a wall, some of which, like the cages of stones you can see on British motorways, are singularly unattractive and some of which, like the cleverly designed interlocking planted blocks you see on French motorways, are much more pleasing to the eye.

Prefabricated interwoven fence panels are a flimsy and temporary solution to the immediate requirement for enclosure and privacy in a new garden. They are by no means even a medium-, let alone a long-term prospect, but if they are used in the proper place, as the backdrop for a growing hedge or a system of climbing plants then they too can serve a purpose. Heaven preserve us, however, from the waving and unsteady lines of deteriorating timber that greet us on so many estates, purporting to represent permanent boundary definitions.

There are so many other choices that I can never understand why people don't give this matter more careful thought. Post and rail fencing with its solidity, its bold statement of enclosure, coupled with uninterrupted vision, serves, with the addition of mesh at the lower level, to keep animals out. The single rail fence serves to demarcate the boundary between public pathway and grass that should not be crossed. The 2-metre-high close boarded fence serves to enclose a garden and give solid privacy at the same time whilst its cousin, the hit and miss slatted fence, gives a little of the privacy away yet provides an ideal backdrop for the climbing plants and shrubs that front it. However, if any of these were left in isolation and not combined with landscaping and planting, then they too would gradually fail in their role.

If you have an existing field hedge on a boundary to your land, you are very lucky, but it may need a great deal of work to put it in good order. First of all, check with your solicitor whether it belongs to you or your neighbour. If it is your neighbour's, or if it straddles the boundary and is jointly owned, try to impress upon him that it's important that it is maintained from both sides. If necessary, offer to nip around to his side and trim it for him. That's not altogether altruistic as a hedge that's only cut on one side will gradually become misshapen and fall over. If he won't agree, all you can do is to keep it trimmed from your side 'in accordance with good practice', but it'll never last.

Hedges undoubtedly get a bad press from time to time – even within the covers of this book, due to the fact that they are at the root of so many disputes between neighbours. It shouldn't and it needn't be so. Talking with Kent gardener, Ian Pitts, made me realise that whilst a fence is immediately socially divisive, a hedge is something that can and should bring neighbours together. It's important that things are properly thought out. There needs to be no argument about where the boundaries are, with a stake or the hedging contained within two lines of post and wire. The choice of the hedging plants themselves is also important with species being chosen for their ability to provide both privacy and beauty. But once made, and once made correctly, the choice of a hedge, over most of the cheaper forms of fencing, is likely to be something that will continue to evolve with the gardens and provide a constant topic of social intercourse and co-operation between neighbours.

A properly laid hedge is a sight to behold and it's gratifying to see that the practice is coming back. The methods of carrying out the laying of a hedge vary slightly from county to county but in the main they involve the main uprights of the hedge being almost completely cut through and then bent down and intertwined with stakes cut from the same hedge. Such a hedge becomes thicker with each season and can present a durable and stock proof enclosure, unlike its annually flailed compatriot, which becomes thinner year on year.

For those of you planting a new hedge, I can only join the howling chorus against the planting of the ubiquitous *leylandii*. Please let us consign this ghastly plant to the dustbin of history and return, once more, to the glorious mixed hedges that once graced our land. If you are going to be in your new home for a long time, think of yew or beech. Otherwise hawthorn, wild rose, maple and privet in combination will soon provide a screen, one that will complement your new home rather than surround it by a prison wall of impenetrable and poisonously dark green.

Sheds, summer houses and greenhouses

All of these, as well as garages, can often be constructed or erected at a later date under Permitted Development Rights, which are discussed in detail in Chapter 5. However you might like to include them within your initial planning permission and, that way, you'll not be using up those rights.

Under other headings, I've referred or alluded to offices, hobbies' rooms and play areas. If these are constructed as part of the house then their costs are going to be every bit as much per square metre as for any other part of the home. I invite you, therefore to consider whether these activities could best be housed in a shed or outhouse, that can cost a tenth as much.

Fuel storage tanks

In all probability this will be dealt with by your architect as part and parcel of the application for the new dwelling. However, if you're converting or renovating an existing building you may need to apply for planning permission if:

- You need to install a domestic heating oil tank, which has a capacity in excess of 3,500 litres or is more than 3 metres in height.

- The tank is to be closer to the highway than any part of the original house unless there would still be 20 metres between it and the highway.

- You want to install a new tank to store liquefied petroleum gas (Lpg) or any liquid fuel other than oil.

Huge advances have been made in the design and appearance of fuel oil tanks in recent years and it really isn't necessary to have those unsightly rusty green tanks of yesteryear. Lpg tanks too, have changed and, instead of the ugly white cylinder on your front lawn, they are now put underground where all you see is a small green plastic manhole cover, which happily merges into the lawn.

Unusual features

I've said several times that the reason most people go into self-building is so that they can have their houses just as they want them. I've also expressed my dismay that more self-builders don't push the boat out in design terms. They've led the way for the last three decades in pushing forward design to suit people rather than planners and architects, but I can't help feeling that we could all go that little bit further. That said, I have also stressed the need to think about reselling some day. Think about the impact that peculiar or unusual features may have on the resale value before you go ahead and of ways to get what you want without compromising the value of your new home.

6. MAKING THE CHOICES –
How to move forward

I do not flatter myself that this is the only book that you'll be reading about self-building and, indeed, I sincerely hope that you are looking around and asking for as much information as you can get. Discounting the late-night advice in the pub, over which one should be a trifle circumspect, there are a whole host of people out there ready and willing to give advice and the best of these will probably be other self-builders. It's like a club and, if you come across another self-builder, then I'll lay you odds that you'll be welcomed within it and that you'll go home with sheaves of information and your ears ringing with new-found knowledge. The people who work within the Industry know this and reputations and company successes are built upon its premise. Read any brochure and you'll find that it spends as much, if not more, time, relating how happy their clients are as it does explaining just what it is they do. Read any of the monthly magazines, such as *Homebuilding & Renovating* or *Build It* and you'll very quickly realise that, business as this is, industry as this is, it is predicated upon ordinary people realising their dreams.

So, the purpose of this chapter is to help you find your way through the minefield of conflicting advice, much of which has a financial axe to grind. Who do you run with? Which company should you go to and should that be a package-deal company or an architectural practice? Should you be building in timber frame or should you build in brick and block? Why does your new home have to restrict its construction to one method or another and why can't elements of each of the various methods be utilised where they are most applicable or the most likely to enable you to achieve what you want in design terms? Should you think about dumping all of the advice, all of the companies, to make your own way forward? These are the vital choices facing the self-builder who has already jumped the first hurdle of getting hold of a plot, and

they are choices which have to be made. In many ways the choices you make at this stage will colour the whole outcome of your self-build project so it's important that you understand the range of options and that you feel your way though to the eventual decision with as much information as possible.

When you've read this book, when you've read all the magazines and brochures, when you've met and talked to the people you think you might like to deal with, stand back for a moment and think. Don't be rushed; don't be pushed into anything. Make sure that you're comfortable with what's on offer. Make sure that you're comfortable with the people who are offering it. Does it sit with what you're planning? Does it feel right? If you need more information or more time, then take it and don't be hassled. Remember that to a successful company you're another client and that they don't stand or fall by your business alone. For you, however, this project is *the* project and it stands or falls by your decisions.

It is important that any professionals you engage should report back to you at specific intervals or stages. Planning a self-build project can be very worrying, and you will want to know how things are getting on. That doesn't mean that you should necessarily ring your architect or the package-deal company representative every evening, but it certainly is appropriate for him to let you know just how things are progressing on a regular basis. Keep in contact and don't be afraid to ask what's happening – after all you're the one paying for everything.

Reading the self-build literature, you could be forgiven for believing that there is a battle raging between brick and block and timber frame and that most self-builders choose the timber-framed option for their new homes. In fact, only about a quarter of self-builders chose the timber-frame route in the United Kingdom as a whole, which is substantially more than the national average for the house-building sector, where timber frame accounts for around 12% of the market (Barlow/Jackson). In Scotland, timber frame is far more prevalent, whereas in Northern Ireland brick and block is the dominant option.

How do you square this with the heavy promotion of the timber-framed option in much of what you'll read about self-building? In part, it's because of the historical fact that, until relatively recently, it was quite difficult to build a timber-framed house without using the services of a package-deal company or timber-frame manufacturer whilst at the same time there was, and is, nothing like the imperative to use a package-deal company for brick and block construction. In part, also, it's because all of the many timber-frame package-deal companies have to compete for that small section of the market that's available to them and, in order to do this, they have to keep their profiles up. That does not mean that no package-deal companies either concentrate or specialise in brick and block forms of construction, because they do, and some of them have been going strong for many years.

Despite the differing claims, most of the reputable package-deal companies do not go out of their way to promote or denigrate either main method of construction. It's generally accepted that clients can be put off by too much negative campaigning and, in any event, most of the chaps who have been in the industry for some time know that, on the whole, the advice from all sides is good. Most of them meet their competitors at exhibitions and road shows on a regular basis, staying in the same hotels, eating and drinking, sometimes to excess, with each other. The successful ones are far too busy running their businesses to waste time running down their 'friends'. Conflict, however, makes good media copy and that's where the blame for any contrived argument rests.

There is no real argument about which method is better and the reality is that both methods are equally valid. Many people, in any case, don't even know or care about the construction of their home and a significant number who have an antipathy towards timber-frame houses, occasioned by slanted media coverage, might be quite surprised to find that they live in one. Finished homes of either timber-frame or brick and block construction can, and mostly do, look exactly the same as each other. In terms of time scales I can attest from the case histories I have written up that a remarkably similar time is taken from turning the first sod to moving in. That said, for those for whom time is of the essence, then timber frame is the route to choose. Again, with costs, it's the similarity that's the startling fact and any influence either way has much more to do with the level of fitting out and the expectations brought about by the design itself, than it does with the method of construction. Bad ground or difficult foundations have the same consequences with either main method of construction, as will any requirement for expensive roof coverings or walling materials. The levels of thermal and sound insulation can vary but, again, nothing very much is unattainable with either method, if that is what your requirements are, and if they're thought out in advance. As I've said many times, informed choice is what self-building is all about and what I seek to do, in this chapter, is to explore the options rather than draw lines in the sand and form up on one side or the other.

So, let's look at some of the options and evaluate each one.

Architects

When I first came into the self-build industry, many architects had virtually thrown away their right to have any place within it, with their arrogant denial of the self-builder's right to their own expression. Indeed I often tell the story of the time I timorously suggested to one architect that perhaps a few changes might be advisable to a plan he'd drawn – and his set square embedded itself in the door, behind which I had rapidly retreated! Happily, architects like that are now slipping into a minority and the vision of the poor self-builder having to go in and see a crusty architect who demands as much respect and fear as the headmaster in his study used to, is fast receding.

In no small way, this has to do with the advent of Associated Self-build Architects (ASBA) who entered the self-build stage like a breath of fresh air in 1992. Conceived by chartered architects, Julian Owen and Adrian Spawforth, ASBA set out to show just how

Above: Natural stone and slate have been used to great effect with this Potton house, offset with surprising success by areas of render and a brick chimney.

Right: The Rectory style limits the span of the main section. Increases in accommodation are, therefore, often achieved by use of rear-facing projections.

much the profession has to offer self-builders and to instil and promote, through a like-minded membership, the principles of architects working *for* and *with* their clients in order to realise their dreams. All ASBA architects are expected to fulfil certain basic conditions and, whilst this book is not a promotion vehicle for any one group or interest, those conditions do bear publication because their criteria could be applied to any architect you may be thinking of engaging. The conditions are as follows:

1) All practices must have a registered architect taking responsibility for self-build projects. The title 'Architect' can only be used by someone who has undergone a thorough training course lasting seven years, and passed a tough set of exams that ensure a base level of knowledge and experience has been achieved.

2) The practices themselves must be members of the Royal Institute of British Architects (RIBA) or of the Scottish equivalent, the Royal Incorporation of Architects in Scotland (RIAS). Each of these organisations operates a strict code of conduct laying down rules regarding impartiality and the need to provide a professional service. Some manufacturers or suppliers do offer incentives for consultants or companies to use their services but architects must be independent in the advice they offer, or declare any vested interest. ASBA itself does carry sponsorship but the architects themselves do not receive any incentives or commissions and their practices are not under any obligation to those sponsors. All ASBA architects must offer truly independent advice to their clients.

3) ASBA architects must have no more than six professional staff. The idea behind this is that smaller practices are able to offer the flexible service that is applicable to the self-builder and to tailor their fees to suit the situation. Quite often clients will find themselves dealing directly with the partner or director who runs the business. The larger architectural practices do find it difficult to offer a personal service and, generally, are only really interested in expensive commissions that will cover their considerable overheads.

4) Architects must carry Professional Indemnity Insurance because of its great significance to the self-builder. Most banks and building societies will, in any case, insist on this before they will accept any payment or progress certificates.

5) ASBA architects also agree that they will provide an initial consultation free of charge and that they will provide as much free advice and assistance to self-builders as possible, recognising that the earlier advice is sought, the more likely the project is to succeed.

6) Finally, and perhaps most importantly, ASBA require their members to have appropriate design skills and a general commitment to one-off house design as well as an approachable, unpretentious attitude to their work and to their clients.

Well, just a quick scan through those conditions shows that these guys are a long way away from my old set-square chucking chum. Now, whilst that may sound like a promotion pack for ASBA, it isn't meant to be, however it comes across. These ideals are the ones which should distinguish the sort of architects you may wish to employ.

The key stages of building an architect-designed house using the full services right through the project from beginning to end can be described in the opposite list. Some of these points are exclusive to ASBA architects but, again, there is no reason why they have to be and your search for a suitable architect could well start with an enquiry as to how much, or how little of this they can or will provide, and for how much.

An architect's full list of services

1) *Finding a plot*. Technically, this isn't part of an architect's brief but, nevertheless, try asking a prospective architect whether they know of any land for sale in your area. Don't expect them to tell you about plots where they are already involved with another client, but there is always the possibility that they know of one where a client has had to drop out. Certainly if you do identify a plot then the architect should be called upon at the earliest possible stage to advise on its suitability.

2) *Making an offer on the plot*. We've gone into this in a fairly detailed manner in previous chapters but, nevertheless, the input of your architect may be beneficial. If the land has Outline planning consent, your architect could help you to negotiate the terms upon which you can buy, maybe subject to receipt of satisfactory detailed planning consent. If there isn't any kind of consent and you're weighing up the pros and cons of whether to do anything with the land, or whether or not planning is at all likely, then your architect may be able to advise.

3) *Site analysis*. This involves an assessment of your plot to check for hidden problems and to highlight its features. A professional can tell an awful lot about a plot just by looking at it, seeing what sort of vegetation grows on it and what sort of ground conditions are likely. If the architect feels that a more thorough site investigation is necessary, including a soil investigation, then they're almost certain to be able to put you onto the right people to carry out this work for you.

4) *Developing your brief*. The architect will want to talk to you in fairly intimate detail about what you hope to achieve and just what features you want your new home to have. The headings under which this discussion will probably progress may be: budget analysis, accommodation requirements, room-by-room analysis of your proposed occupation, and construction and materials preferences.

5) *Sketch design*. Using the brief prepared, the architect will draw up a sketch design showing the floor layouts together with elevations showing the external appearance of your new home, and any possible or suggested alternatives. This will be used to make sure that they are on the right lines to provide you with what you're looking for and at the same time to make sure that the developing house designs are likely to find favour with the planners. At this stage you should also make sure that the architect can verify that the project is capable of being completed within your budget.

6) *Purchasing the plot*. Again, this is not strictly within the province of the architect but they will want to be involved and will certainly want to assist with advice, in any way they can.

7) *Detailed design*. From the sketch design, the architect will move to the preparation of detailed plans that will be suitable for an application for planning permission. It is at this stage that the all-important issues regarding window details, brick colours, roofing tiles, driveways and a myriad of other aspects, many of which we've already explored in other chapters, are decided. For most self-builders this stage is, perhaps, the most exciting.

8) *Planning permission*. The architect will submit the planning application and prosecute it with the authorities. He will discuss any matters arising from the application with the planning officers, conservation officers and highways authorities. If any amendments are suggested or required following meetings and/or letters, then the architect will discuss these with you before agreeing to them.

9) *Building Regulations*. The architect will prepare and submit plans for Building Regulations approval. These will include any necessary structural calculations and specifications describing the basic construction of your new home, a range of health and safety standards and energy conservation issues. If any special foundation details or designs are required as the result of either the soil investigation or in consequence of the application being made, then the architect will usually arrange for these to be carried out by other professionals, on your behalf. The fees for these additional professionals will normally be charged to you direct as they are outside the architect's normal scope of activities and you will be concerned that any warranties and liabilities given will devolve directly to you.

10) *Drawings and specification for tender*. The architect will draw up a detailed specification to accompany the plans, in order to obtain tenders from suitable builders or contractors. Quotations can vary quite considerably (up to 100% in some cases!) so this is the stage at which an architect doing their job properly can save you considerable amounts of money. A properly drawn-up specification can make all the difference and easily cover an architect's fees for the entire project.

11) *Finding and appointing a contractor*. The architect will suggest suitable contractors for the tender list and when the quotations are received, and the builder is chosen, he will assist in the preparation of the contract documents.

12) *Monitoring the construction*. The architect will visit the site and make spot checks to see that the construction is being carried out in accordance with the approved and contract drawings. If any form of 'certification' is required, as discussed in detail in Chapter 1, then he will undertake this and liaise with the necessary lending institution.

13) *Snagging*. Once the building work is complete, you and your architect will inspect your new home together to check for defects. If there are any present or if work has not been completed to a satisfactory standard, your builder will be required to put this right prior to you accepting the property.

14) *Handing over and moving in*. This is what it's all been about and once your new home is completed it will be handed over in return for the final stage payment. Normally a retention of 2.5% is made out of the total tender price. This is withheld for a period of six months to ensure that the builder will put right anything that may go wrong.

I repeat that the preceding list details the full services that can be expected from an architect. You may or may not want to take advantage of all or any of this. What is important is that things start off correctly and in order to understand how that can and should happen, perhaps the best thing is to examine the areas where the relationship between client and architect is most likely to go wrong:

- *No meeting of minds.* Warning the self-builder against the architect who will insist on drawing what he thinks you should have rather than what you want, is easy. The slightly anarchic nature of most self-builders will recognise that danger immediately. More difficult to guard against, perhaps, is getting sucked into a glossy make-believe world that will spiral out of all control or relevance to your budget. The architect whose principal practice is engaged in grandiose schemes for the redevelopment of town centres and has no experience of one-off housing will never really come down to your level of costing or expectations. Either what gets drawn will be way beyond your budget or you'll be made to feel that you're somehow trying to 'do things on the cheap'. Talk to your architect and don't just hear what you want to hear. Part of being a successful self-builder is the ability to sift and assimilate information to your own advantage.

- *Lack of detail with the original brief.* The success or failure of a design is in the original brief, and the problems often occur when there is more than one architect involved and they're all afraid of giving away too much detail for fear of giving their competitors an advantage. Most architects have a fairly detailed and comprehensive checklist that they go through on the first meeting. Even so, if you've got a wish list of your own design requirements, then make certain that your architect is aware of it and that each point is discussed. Planning and design are all about compromise and some things might have to give way, but they should be lost as the result of a conscious decision rather than an oversight.

- *Rows about the budget.* Stories abound of people who've spent thousands with architects, having a house designed that could never be built within their budget. All the more incredible therefore that, in equally large measure, one can still hear of contracts between self-builders and architects where the subject of money has never even been raised! If your architect won't talk about the budget and is either not capable, or not prepared, to constantly relate it to the plans that are being drawn, don't employ him. Move on to another one who will.

- *Rows about fees.* If everything goes smoothly, the design is just what you want and it all gets built within budget, then it's highly unlikely that there'll be much of a row about fees. It's where the self-builder perceives that he has had a bad deal that rows about money abound. Certainly it can be argued that, in some cases, fees can have a disproportionate impact on an already stretched budget. 10% might sound quite reasonable but it's worthwhile extrapolating that to an actual amount. There are architects who would consider any move to negotiate fees as an attempt at vulgarity but don't let that put you off finding out just what you're letting yourself in for and what you're getting for your money.

- *Slow responses and lack of competence.* It's all too easy to imagine that you're the only client that your architect has and if that's how you feel, then perhaps in some way it's a measure of success in your relationship. However, in all probability you're not, and anything that's done for you has to been done in proper order. Even so that's no excuse for things taking an inordinately long time, particularly when it can affect planning applications or building progress, and there are times when you should expect priority. Pressure of work is one thing, but if your architect is out of his depth, you need to know, rather then let things drift on. Flair and imagination might not be translated into ability at other levels and it is important to ensure that design innovation is matched by the perhaps more pedestrian skills needed to produce working drawings and specifications.

- *Confusion over responsibilities and liabilities*. In law you cannot pass on the burden of a contract and unless there is a specific collateral arrangement, the self-builder using a design and build contractor might not have any comeback on the architect in the event of the builder ceasing to trade or behaving fraudulently. Wherever possible, insist on a direct contract with the architect and make sure that you know just what responsibilities your architect has to you.

- *Jobs for the boys*. Part of the attraction of using an architect is that they will be able to pass you on to, recommend or introduce you to other professionals you might need and to builders with whom they've worked before. But it's a double-edged sword. A strong relationship between professionals can be beneficial but they should still outsource from time to time. A long-standing relationship might get so cosy that the architect fails to check whether more competitive quotations are available. Bad ground conditions might require the input of soil investigation companies and engineers for the foundations. Complicated structures might need structural calculations. All of these have to be paid for by the self-builder, if for no other reason than to take advantage of his Professional Indemnity. However, none of them should be engaged without your prior knowledge and consent. The question also arises as to whether the average self-builder really needs the input of some professionals. Large projects will almost certainly require a full bill of quantities but if you're using a builder, your average self-build project probably doesn't.

- *Poor definition of service.* An architect's service is divided up into a number of disciplines and phases, all of which are readily understandable to those in the professions but few of which might be apparent to a self-builder. Sketch plans prepared at the earliest stages of an association, in order to establish a relationship, might not actually be capable of being built in their pre-

sented form. Drawings that might be perfectly acceptable for the obtaining of planning permission might not be sufficient for the approval of Building Regulations. Drawings that are used to obtain Building Regulations might not be suitable or detailed enough for use as constructional or working drawings. Unless an overarching fee structure is agreed, the charges for these various elements will have to be negotiated separately, particularly bearing in mind that copyright might make it difficult or impossible to split the responsibility between different practices or companies. Establish exactly just how far your relationship with an architect is to go and discuss fees for every stage.

- *Lack of, or insufficiency, of professional indemnity*. This really shouldn't happen nowadays but, where it does, it's because of a confusion over the very term 'architect' or as a result of misleading information. In order to practise in the UK, an architect has to be a member of RIBA in England or RIAS in Scotland but most importantly they have to be registered with the Architects' Registration Board (ARB). If they are not registered with that body then, although they can of course work, they cannot call themselves an architect. It is a requirement of these bodies that all practising architects carry professional indemnity insurance cover of at least £100,000, but this might not be sufficient for many self-build projects. Always check that your architect is registered and carries the correct professional indemnity. Retired architects can use 'RIBA' after their names for social reasons but nobody can practise as an architect unless registered with the ARB.

- *Rows over extras*. In any self-build project, things will change as the building progresses. If these are requests after the event by the self-builder that require fresh drawings to be prepared, then they should be prepared to pay for them at a rate that is agreed on each and every occasion. If they are required because the drawings are unclear or ambiguous, then the self-builder should certainly question whether or not they should be considered as extras. An inspecting architect, perhaps one who has not been responsible for the preparation of the principal drawings or design, might seek to enhance his take from the job by offering to prepare drawings detailing changes or explanations on queries received during his visits.

It goes without saying that you should attempt to settle any differences by amicable discussion. Having said that, it's not always that easy and things can get to the point where there's no other recourse but to bring in some outside agency to resolve the dispute.

The last resort is always the courts but that really is a last resort and it's unwise to consider it unless all other avenues have already been exhausted. The RIBA have systems in place to settle disputes and the first of these is Mediation. Here a mediator is appointed whose job it is to examine all the facts and to see if they can effect reconciliation. They usually do this by written representation and their decision is not binding on the parties unless they wish it to be. If agreement cannot be reached, then the next step up the ladder is Adjudication. This normally arises out of a contractual dispute or in consequence of the use of a JCT contract. The process varies and the adjudicator, appointed by RIBA can choose to accept either written representation or oral submissions. They may also arrange site visits and their decision must be given within 28 days. The decision of the adjudicator is binding and it can only be overturned by Arbitration or by the courts. If it is decided that the dispute has to go to arbitration then once again the arbitrator is appointed by RIBA. Effectively, this is as far as you can go under their auspices. There is no time scale for the reaching of any decision but once it is made, it is binding and can only be overturned by the courts.

Make sure that you are comfortable with the architect or practice you engage for this, probably the most important project of your life. Fortunately, architects are becoming more accessible and approachable as market pressures force them out of their offices and into the real world where the client calls the shots. Their role should be of an enabler, transforming a series of wishes and aspirations into a finished new home. That doesn't mean that they shouldn't have a meaningful input of their own but it does mean that in the end it's their client's new home and it should reflect the decisions made by you, the self-builder.

Designers

It is easy to get the idea from publications that the great majority of individual homes are built either to architects' designs, or come from the package companies. If you go to the Town Hall and ask to see the planning register you will quickly discover that the overwhelming majority of applications are made by designers who are not architects, many of them working on a part-time basis in the evenings when they have finished their other jobs. Many of them are council Building Inspectors and the like who will only design for the next door council's area, not the one that they work in. Some of them are listed in Yellow Pages, but all of them get most of their business by personal recommendation. If they have been providing this service for any length of time they are pretty good at it, although of course they might not have professional indemnity insurances. What they are very good at is gaining the confidence of clients, who happily put their trust in them.

Architectural Technicians, or Technologists as they now prefer to call themselves, have their own professional body, The British Institute of Architectural Technologists (BIAT). They publish lists of members who have achieved the approved levels of training, currently three years of supervised experience in addition to a first degree, resulting in a total of six years of training. There is a code of conduct, members are required to have professional indemnity insurance and the Institute's qualification is recognised and accepted by banks and building societies for the issuing of certificates and the release of stage payments. Architectural Technologists are not principally designers although many of them are extremely competent in this field. Their main skills revolve around the technical aspects of house design, which is why many architectural practices also have technologists working within them.

Problems arise when a person represents him/herself as an 'architect', either directly or indirectly. Only an architect who has passed all the

Left: An impressive house by Custom Homes Ltd but one where time and some soft landscaping and planting have yet to mellow the completed house.

Right: A mistake that many houses made in the 1960's and which has not been made on this Potton house, is to use the same tiles for the roof and the tile hanging.

relevant exams after a long training period is entitled to call themselves by that title and that is protected by law. Inspections during the construction period by an unqualified person are not recognised by the banks or building societies and if, therefore, you do decide to use the services of an unqualified designer, you should make absolutely certain that you have an approved warranty scheme in place, as outlined in Chapter 1. None of this is meant to denigrate the service these chaps provide but it is meant to make sure that you are aware of just what you're getting when you employ them and just how far their responsibilities and liabilities go.

The package-deal companies

In large part, the package-deal companies evolved as a response to, and in consequence of, the lack of understanding previously afforded self-builders by architects and builders' merchants. In the early Seventies there were no books such as this one, no *The Home Plans Book* and no monthly magazines devoted to the ideals and the concept of self-building. If a self-builder was brave or lucky enough to get a design done for him by an architect or designer, then when he went along to a

builders' merchants he was in for an even worse time. I can remember self-builders having to get proper printed headed paper, describing themselves as 'Private House Builders' before they could get any sort of an account and, even then, the credit limits were set so low as to render the account 'cash on delivery'.

The package-deal companies moved to fill the gap in the market, many of them starting off life as poor brethren offshoots of either timber companies or major block manufacturers. In the early days their plans, published in the form of brochures, showed houses and bungalows of mind-boggling simplicity and an utter lack of imagination. But, as the industry grew, so did the aspirations of the self-builder and, inevitably, the package-deal companies shifted their positions to give the market what it wanted. For a while, many companies held out and continued to run with the times by constantly updating their range of 'standard' designs. Inevitably, the more successful ones soon came to the conclusion that they would have to become completely flexible in their approach to design. Either the 'standards' would have to be capable of alteration or they would have to be able to accommodate 'specials'.

Design is the key, of course, and the package-deal

companies recognised that this was the bait with which they could attract their self-building clients. What the self-builder has to realise is that, although many of the package-deal companies advertise and promote themselves through their designs, in truth, their real business revolves around the supply and/or manufacture of kits and materials. They do all of this in a very highly polished and effective way, as any recipient of their literature can see and as any visitor to the exhibitions will note. The expertise they have gained over the years is apparent within the breadth of their information and there is no doubt that most, if not all of them, successfully fulfil the role of specialist designers and builders' merchants for the self-builder.

From all of this you may get the impression that the majority of self-builders now use the services of the various package-deal companies. In fact, nothing is further from the truth and there is much scratching of heads in the boardrooms of these companies as they agonise over why, and whether anything can be done about it. Perhaps the reason why only around 8% of self-builders do so (Barlow/Jackson), lies with the mental make-up of the self-builders themselves. By opting not to conform, by choosing not just to go out

and buy a developer's house, the self builder steps, quite deliberately, outside the normal pattern of behaviour. Perhaps, for the vast majority, the desire to 'do their own thing' extends to not wanting to fit in with anyone else's concepts of how things should be done and almost a determination not to seek the help of others. Perhaps a great many self-builders are also people from within the building industry itself, with skills in one or more of the trades involved and opinions which lead them down the 'go it alone' path. Be that as it may, for those who do choose to use a package deal company, there is no doubt that the comfort they get from having a 'friend' or mentor to guide them through the process is an important factor in getting them beyond the dream stage and on to the realisation of their hopes.

Interestingly, whilst many self-builders actually go on to do it all again, only a relatively small proportion choose to use the package-deal company the second and third time around, even if they have been completely happy with the service they got initially. Perhaps by then they fall into the same category and have the same opinions as the experienced self-builder who originally disdained the use of a package-deal company.

You cannot cherry-pick the design ideas of the package-deal companies and then run off and build the house without using the main part of their service. The plans in their brochures, the plans they publish in the companion book to this book, *The Home Plans Book*, and the plans they may prepare for you, are their copyright. That also extends to a design which a reasonable person would consider had been derived from one of their plans and is why you may see the words, 'or within the design concept', used in connection with their claim to copyright. If you commission a design study or feasibility study from a package-deal company and then, for any reason, you do not proceed with that company, you are almost certainly going to have to think in terms of a completely different design.

Most of the larger package-deal companies have an 'in-house' drawing office with staff architects, but others successfully employ a panel of outside architects or designers. There are arguments for and against both ways of working but, in truth, much of the competency of their drawing-office service relies on the abilities of either their field staff or the sales staff that you actually deal with. If you're dealing with a sales force who are demonstrating a chosen product and making notes of your specific and individual requirements and alterations then, in many cases, and in particular in those cases where the product can be demonstrated in the form of a show home, it is easy to get across what you're trying to achieve. There may well be an element of shoe-horning your requirements into a format but, in most cases, the compromise is well thought-out and realises everybody's ambitions. If the product, for that indeed is what it is, didn't appeal to you, then you wouldn't be there in the first place and the companies are well aware that, for some, the idea of living in a particular design can be akin to a new-found religion.

Where a completely fresh design is proposed then, whether it is drawn 'in house' or by a panel architect, the translation of your requirements depends entirely on the representative you are dealing with. These individuals are a remarkable lot, with most of them having been in the industry for many years and many of them having either come into it as a result of building their own homes or having done so since they started. In many cases they will stand between you and the architect, with the architect preparing the initial drawings on the basis of, and as a direct result of, a brief prepared by that representative. Architects and designers who work outside the package-deal companies always express amazement that such a system can work. Clients of the package-deal companies themselves are often sceptical at first and sometimes feel that they should be visiting the offices of the company or that the drawing-office staff themselves should be visiting them, not realising that in the time taken for such a person to travel to and from them, their drawings could well be done.

The amazing reality is that in the vast majority of cases, the drawings that are produced from this arm's-length way of doing things conform, almost exactly, to the client's wishes. In almost all cases this is due to the company representative's skill at interpreting what the client wants, his ability to balance that with what he knows is achievable in design terms, his knowledge of the planning criteria and his ability to translate all of that into a brief for his drawing-office staff, with whom he is likely to have an uncanny rapport. If you add to that the fact that he, as much as you, will be concerned to make sure that the project remains on budget, then you'll appreciate that he really has to draw a lot of strings together. Happily, these guys usually do just that and, in most cases, they do it jolly well.

The stages concerned with the planning and building regulations applications are also handled in two ways. Either the head office of the package-deal company makes the application with the local representative progress-chasing it, or else the local panel architect makes the application supported by the head office of the company. Once more, the suspicion is that a company based in one part of the country will not be able to properly process an application in a different part of the country. Nothing could actually be further from the truth. The package-deal companies have always set out to provide a service on a nationwide basis and their thought processes tend to consider the whole country in much the same terms as most think of their county. They are aware of regional variations in styles. They are aware of variations even within the larger regions and they have long since adapted to the provision of houses in styles that carry the local vernacular, even if, in some cases, the floor plans remain almost consistent.

Perhaps then, to the chagrin of many local architects, it is this very ability of the package-deal companies to look at architecture on a nationwide basis, that enables them to understand the local and regional variations that go to make up the delightful diversification of styles and detail. Perhaps, also, this is demonstrated in the remarkably high success rate that most companies have with planning applications, although to be fair, the more discerning and successful companies will always choose which applications they make and make sure that they control, as far as is possible, the quality of those applications.

Many of the package-deal companies specialise in timber-frame construction of some sort and their literature and advertising is concerned to extol the virtues of their own particular way of building. Not all of the companies, however, are concerned with timber frame. Some concentrate almost exclusively on brick and block construction, whilst others, recognising that the service element of their operation is of the foremost interest, do not really mind which method of construction is employed as long as there remains an element of supply.

Historically, the reason why there is such a preponderance of timber-frame companies, is that until fairly recently, the contention was that to build timber frame you would need to use a timber-frame company. This idea, promoted in earlier editions of this book, came about because of the problems that the average self-builder had in the provision of the necessary design calculations for the frames. The package-deal companies are victims of their own success in that they created a whole new genre of professionals working as timber engineers and designers who, inevitably, found their way into the freelance market. Nowadays, it is fairly easy for architects either to design a timber-framed house themselves or to draw one up and then get the relevant details and calculations checked or carried out by other professionals. This has given impetus to the 'go-it-aloners' who want to 'stickbuild', of which more later.

But back to the package-deal companies. The services they offer, whether timber framed or brick and

block, can be divided into yet more sub-categories. Some offer a design service based on standard designs. Some offer a service based on the variation or modification of standard designs within carefully defined parameters. Some offer a bespoke design service, with each house or bungalow being individually tailored to the client's and the site's dictates. Some offer a planning service whilst others will provide you with the plans so that you can prosecute your own application. Yet more do not have any design services beyond the provision of the necessary technical drawings and will provide a package deal to drawings that you provide.

All of them will be concerned to supply a recognisable package deal of materials to the specification set out in their literature and confirmed to you in their quotations. All of them, therefore, will want to ensure that you are able to put their kits or packages together and, therefore, most of them will be very concerned with helping you to obtain or evaluate labour. None of them will go so far as actually to recommend any subcontractor or builder to you but they will introduce them and then stand by to ensure that you make the correct arrangements with them. Quite obviously, a recommendation would make them a party to the contract that you make with the builders and they will want to avoid that. Nevertheless, if the package deal companies do introduce you to a builder or subcontractor, you can be pretty sure that they've vetted them in some way, in the knowledge that if things go right on site, their job is made easier. The package companies often provide advice, again with the same motives, on many other aspects of building a new home, from recommending the right people to design any special foundations that may be needed, through to helping with VAT claims. But, once again, you will find that the package-deal company will not be a party to any ensuing contract.

Of course, none of these reservations apply to the 'design and build' or 'turnkey' packages that are available, where the package-deal company is actually going to be responsible for the construction of the new house, probably also providing an NHBC warranty at the end. In essence, these companies are really building companies who have adapted their business to be able to work and promote themselves within the self-build market, sometimes on a nationwide basis, but often, in a limited regional area. They really replace the builders of old who often provided such a service in their local areas but did not have the forums to promote themselves in the professional way that is possible for their successors. Oft-times these design and build arrangements involve the self-builder in little or no work and take the project right up to completion, handover and moving in. Sometimes, however, the contract can be for the weathertight shell only and, in those cases, the self-builder becomes responsible for the fitting out and second fix trades.

The kits sold by package companies are specific to a particular house or bungalow, and the elements like the roof, walling panels, etc. have to be made weeks before they are delivered. For this reason, companies expect to be paid a substantial deposit when an order is placed, and usually require the balance of the contract sum in advance of the delivery of materials. These sums may be over half of the total cost of the new home, and self-builders are naturally concerned that this arrangement is 100% safe. Before any order is signed, the self-builder will undoubtedly have taken up references on the company or asked their bank to do so on their behalf. It is important, especially in the light of the very different services and level of service that the companies provide, that the self-builder makes absolutely sure that he understands exactly what they're getting for their money. It's also important to know just when those monies will be required and to allow for this in any cash flow projections that he makes. Most of the larger and more reputable companies are either able to offer an insurance-backed bond scheme or else operate 'client accounts' into which the monies that are, quite naturally, required in advance of delivery are placed. The money then remains in the legal ownership of the client until such time as a trustee of the account gives authority to pay it across to the company. This has advantages for the company because they can raise money against the sums in the client accounts that they operate. If you accept this arrangement, make sure you ask your solicitor or bank to check out the status of this client account, always make out cheques to the client account and not simply to the company, and if the money is going to stay in the

client account for any length of time, enquire who gets the interest. Finally, there is a legally implied assumption that the package-deal service and the goods supplied and/or manufactured will meet the requirements of the Building Regulations as well as the relevant British Standards. However, if the work is to be inspected by the NHBC or by an architect, then it is possible for there to be some variation in their requirements and in these cases, unless it is already there, when accepting the quotation of the package-deal company, you should confirm that everything should also comply with their standards. If necessary, write it on the acceptance or authorisation above your signature.

You pay for the services of a package-deal company. There is a fairly hefty mark-up on most materials and manufactured items, over and above the price that you would pay at the builders' merchants or if you went straight to a timber company that manufactured frames and trusses to order. But that would be an extremely unfair comparison, as that would exclude all of the other services that the package-deal companies provide, such as architectural services and help with labour. You don't get 'owt for nowt' in this world. If you feel that you need someone to hold your hand through all of the processes; if you feel that you have limited time to devote to your self-build and that that time would be better employed on site rather than off site chasing materials, then that's the role the package deal company fulfils. And the simple truth is that, when they are involved, they make it happen.

Package companies provide excellent services to thousands of self-builders, but in the natural way of things there are sometimes problems or disagreements. If you meet difficulties that cannot be resolved at a local level you should take pains to deal with them promptly, but in a way that demonstrates that you are a most reasonable client. Avoid writing letters in anger. If appropriate, arrange to call at the Head Office by appointment and explain the difficulty in a friendly but very firm way to someone at director level. No firm can afford to ignore a customer who has a five figure contract, and you should be treated accordingly.

Left: A substantial timber-frame house by Taylor Lane Ltd pictured just a few days after the erectors arrived on site. Once it's felted, battened and tiled it'll be all but weathertight.

Below: Schematic showing a section through a typical brick and timber wall.

Timber frame

One of the most common misconceptions is that all timber-framed houses are alike. In fact, there are many differing methods of construction which, for the sake of convenience, usually get lumped together under this heading. All the methods of building new homes, promoted by the major companies, are of equal validity and, in the end, the selection of which method you employ comes down to personal choice. The final choice will probably have much more to do with the self-builder being comfortable with the people he's dealing with, and the level and cost of service they are providing than with any construction method. Once the choice is made, it is usual for the customer to become a devotee of the construction method, and the zeal with which they defend their choice has to be seen to be believed.

The word 'traditional' has been bandied about for some time by the various competing interests. Proponents of building in brick and block claimed that theirs was the traditional way of building, in an attempt to brand timber frame as 'new' and therefore untried. The timber-frame exponents immediately hit back with the assertion that timber frame was an old and well-tested method of building, tracing its roots right back to the Middle Ages. In the end, all of them realised that they were on a hiding to nothing and,

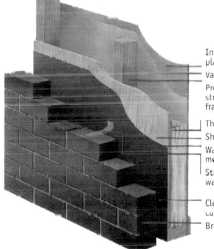

Inner lining of plasterboard
Vapour check
Preservative treated structural timber frame
Thick insulating quilt
Sheathing board
Waterproof breather membrane
Stainless steel wall tie
Clear 50mm wall cavity
Brick outer cladding

whilst the brick and block enthusiasts now prefer to describe themselves as such, the timber-frame enthusiasts prefer to promote themselves as timber and brick.

The principal method of building with timber frame is the *open panel* system and when most people describe timber frame, this is what they're talking about. It is the inner skin of a cavity wall that supports the roof and gives the building its structural strength. In a timber-framed house this is formed by panels that are usually prefabricated and then raised into position and fixed together to form a rigid structure. The panels are manufactured from softwood timber framing over which a structural sheet material, such as plywood or Sterling board, known as the sheathing, is fixed. A vapour-permeable, but waterproof, breather membrane is then fixed to the outside face of this sheathing.

Of course, it's a lot more complicated than that and if this were a technical manual I would move on to descriptions of noggins, cripple studs, headbinders, *et al*. But it's not, so I won't. The insulation which fills the space between the studs is normally put in on site, once the house is weathertight and the electrical and plumbing carcassing have been done. The wall is then finished off to the interior, and a vapour barrier and the internal boarding trap the insulation. Standard 89mm x 39mm walling panels with fibreglass insulation give a 'U' value of around 0.39. Increasing the studs and insulation to 140mm takes this down to 0.29.

Now, although most of the literature you'll pick up referring to timber and brick assumes the use of a cavity wall, there are instances where this is not so. It is possible that the outside leaf can be done away with altogether by the use of a vertical counter batten, creating a cavity, to which either expanded metal wire mesh is fixed for rendering or an external timber finish, such as shiplap boarding, can be fixed. Tile hanging can also be fixed against a single skin of timber frame. Again, the vertical batten is used to bring the horizontal battens away from the breather membrane, and the tiles are then hung from these battens in the normal way. Many of the houses from the Potton 'Heritage' range use this 'single leaf' construction and many others may use it in combination with timber and brick cavity wall construction to the ground floors. It is also worthwhile noting that, with timber and brick cavity wall construction, the cavity is always left clear and is never filled or interrupted other than by fire stops and cavity barriers which have

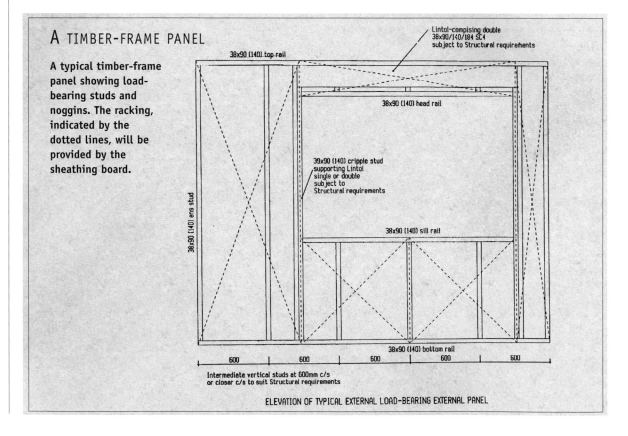

A TIMBER-FRAME PANEL

A typical timber-frame panel showing load-bearing studs and noggins. The racking, indicated by the dotted lines, will be provided by the sheathing board.

Lintol-compising double 38x90/140/184 SC4 subject to Structural requirements

38x90 (140) top rail

38x90 (140) head rail

39x90 (140) cripple stud supporting Lintol single or double subject to Structural requirements

38x90 (140) ens stud

38x90 (140) sill rail

38x90 (140) bottom rail

600 600 600 600 600

Intermediate vertical studs at 600mm c/s or closer c/s to suit Structural requirements

ELEVATION OF TYPICAL EXTERNAL LOAD-BEARING EXTERNAL PANEL

to be inserted at certain points, as required by the regulations. Custom Homes, The Self-build House Company and Potton are amongst those who use the open-panel system.

The Scandinavian timber-frame houses, whilst generically similar, utilise a slightly different form of timber framing, known as the *closed panel system,* where the panels are designed to be 'airtight'. By the very nature of the beast, this means that each panel has to be manufactured in carefully controlled factory conditions with each one being assembled, complete with the insulation and vapour barrier installed, the internal boarding fixed and all windows (usually triple glazed) and door linings fitted. The vapour barrier is installed in such a way as to create a seal not only at any abutment to an adjoining panel but also at the roof level where it is also tucked into and joined with the roof felting and boarding. Building a home that is insulated to these degrees, with achieved 'U' values for the walling of around 0.20 or less, means that thought has to be given to ventilation and it's normal for a mechanical ventilation and heat recovery system to be employed.

The arctic weather apart, there was another imperative which inspired the creation of these systems. Daylight is at a premium in northern climes and, quite simply, the more that could be done under controlled factory conditions and the less that needed to be done on site, the better. This feeds through into the ethos behind the level of fixtures and fittings included by most of the 'Hus' manufacturers and suppliers. Daylight and the need to husband as much sunlight into the house as possible is also reflected in many of the designs and layouts. In the early days of the marketing of Scandinavian houses, the designs, with their timber external cladding and 'A' frames, found little favour with planners who were conscious and protective of the 'local vernacular'. What the companies marketing these products managed to do, and to do successfully, was to combine all of the design ideals and construction imperatives of these homes with the traditions of British architecture. The principal proponents of this type of timber-framed housing are: Scandia-Hus and The Swedish House Company.

Aisle framed buildings are another form of timber-frame construction where the major loadings, instead of being borne, solely, by the walling panels, are taken by massive timber uprights supporting a skeleton frame. Potton are the major exponents of this system of building and many of their well known designs utilise it. Design apart, the essential features of these houses and, in particular, the walling panels, follow the same patterns as for the open-panel systems described above.

Structural Insulated Panels comprise two outer skins of orientated strand board sandwiching a polystyrene or polyurethane centre. As their name suggests, they can be used in structural situations for both walling and roofing where they replace the traditional stud panels and the trusses. They can either be delivered whole to the site and then have the window and door openings cut into them, or alternatively, and more usually, they are manufactured off site to specific requirements. Very few houses in the United Kingdom have actually been wholly built with these panels but they are, nevertheless, very useful in certain situations, especially where clear space is required within a roof void.

Traditional oak-framed houses are, perhaps, so unusual as to warrant consideration under a heading all of their own. Pioneered by Border Oak, although many more companies have since jumped on the bandwagon, this is 15th-century building technique brought into the modern age with a massive skeleton of heavy oak timbers forming the frame. The important difference with this system is that this frame is visible internally and externally and the building is of single-skin construction. The spaces between the oak timbers on the external walls are filled in with urethane infill panels with galvanised perimeter trims and mesh reinforcement. A sophisticated system of trims, water bars, weather seals and drainage channels then ensure that the building meets the proper standards and can deal with the worst that the British climate can provide. To sit in one of these houses is literally to go back in time. Needless to say, each one of them has to be manufactured individually and they are normally put together on a test run at the works before each part is carefully marked and shipped out to site.

Although many of the timber-frame companies will provide you with their services based on your own plans and designs, there is no doubt that, for most of

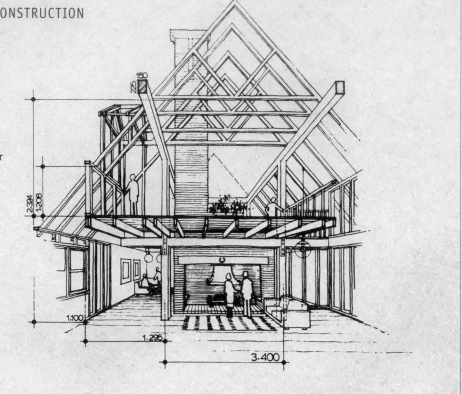

AISLE FRAME CONSTRUCTION

Pioneered in this country by Potton Ltd, this form of construction puts the loadings on the massive internal framework rather than the external studs, allowing clear space as pictured below.

them, design is the 'hook' as well as the 'bait'. However, whether or not they get involved in the preparation of the plans and the planning process itself, all of them will, if you accept their quotation, have to be involved with the preparation of the detailed and working drawings.

Developers and builders often take the timber-frame supply and arrange their own erection, but it is more usual for the self-builder to use the erection services provided by the company. The specification for the supply and erection will vary from company to company, according to the method of timber frame they employ. Some of the companies can properly be described as 'kit' suppliers in that they supply a large proportion of the component parts for the houses, including second-fix materials. Some would probably be best described as 'panel manufacturers', whilst others fall somewhere between these two stools. In many cases, but not always, the supply and fixing of windows and door frames will also be within the package-deal company's remit, as will the supply and fixing of the prefabricated roof trusses. Some comp-

anies will go on to felt and batten the roof, fix the insulation material, the vapour check and the internal plasterboard but these are usually quoted as extras.

The important thing, as ever, is that everyone, and especially you, knows just what you're getting and

OAK-FRAMED HOUSING

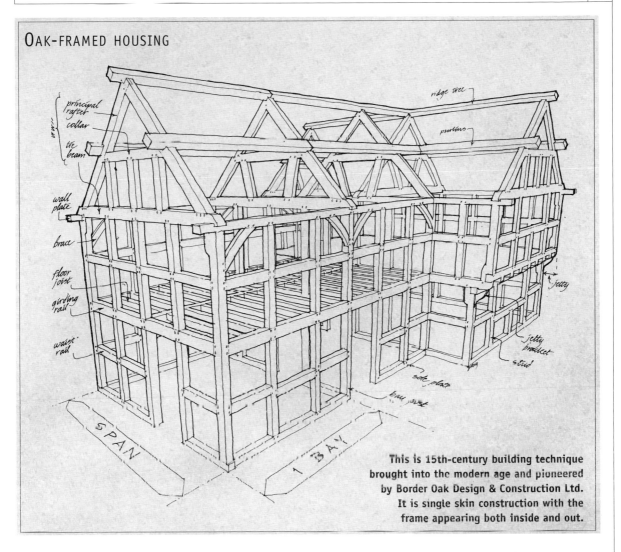

This is 15th-century building technique brought into the modern age and pioneered by Border Oak Design & Construction Ltd. It is single skin construction with the frame appearing both inside and out.

just what your contract with the timber frame company comprises. Almost certainly the external cladding will be down to you and in most cases this will take the form of an external leaf of the cavity wall, constructed in brick or stone although, in some cases, as I have previewed above, the external finish will be render or tile hanging.

I don't want this section to turn into a puff for any company in particular and the mention of any company name is a reflection of the help they have given in the preparation of this book as well as its companion volume, *The Home Plans Book*. In certain cases, it is because they offer a unique product or service. All of the major timber-frame companies working within the self-build industry, many of whom are household names, have a wealth of experience

which they can draw on to your benefit, and you'll find a list of them at the back of this book. All of them provide a slightly different service in terms of both design and specification. My task is to make you aware of the choices, as they apply. Your job is to sift through their brochures and decide which ones you feel can best help you to express and realise your dreams of a new home. The only guidance I can give is that with the current diversity of levels of service, you must make sure that you are comparing like with like.

In any consideration of timber frame, the same questions apply. Why should this book be different? It's not, except that I can answer those questions without any axe to grind and any answers given can be read in conjunction with all of the other choices which face you (see overleaf).

Frequently asked questions on timber frame

- *What's the main difference between a timber and brick house and a brick and block house?*
  Visually very little, internally as well as externally. Structurally, the inner leaf of the cavity wall is built out of prefabricated, engineer-designed and insulated panels instead of blocks.

- *Can a timber-frame house be built quicker than a brick-and-block house?*
  Yes, it can, although new large-block, thin-joint systems are coming on stream that claim to be as fast. However, the speed of the build has as much to do with the self-builder's ability to organise and finance things, both on and off site. If there's a long wait for the delivery of the frame after the groundworks, you'll lose any advantage.

- *Is a timber-frame house as strong as a brick-and-block house?*
  Yes, just as strong and just as structurally sound. Each house has the benefit of computer-aided calculations to prove that the frame will not only support the structure and the roof but that it will withstand windforce and all other exposure factors.

- *Will a timber-frame house last as long as a brick-and-block one?*
  Of course it will. Some of the oldest houses in the land are timber framed and with modern technology and precision-engineered, stress-graded timber, many of the modern houses will do as well.

- *Is a timber-frame house more susceptible to damp?*
  Not at all. All of the building practices in this country have always been concerned to prevent the ingress of damp. With a timber and brick construction the cavity, which was first invented to prevent the transference of damp, is maintained as a clear cavity, thus fulfilling its original role. Leaking pipes or incorrectly fitted flashings and trays are not peculiar to timber frame and can cause just as much damage to other methods of construction.

- *What happens about fire and in the event of a major fire how does timber frame compare?*
  Timber frame is as safe as any other form of construction with death or injury no more likely to occur. Even if the frame did catch fire, much of its integral stability would be retained.

- *What about bad workmanship on site?*
  What about it? Bad workmanship doesn't confine itself to any one method of building. However, with a large part of the construction and manufacture usually carried out under controlled factory conditions, the chances of anything going wrong are reduced. In any event, the inspectors from the Building Control departments and the warranty inspectors will watch out to make sure that everything is done properly and, as a self-builder, I bet you will as well.

- *What about hanging things like cupboards on the walls?* It isn't really a problem and in any event it's not one that's confined to timber and brick as many brick-and-block houses are now dry lined. As long as the proprietary fixings are used for normal loads such as kitchen cupboards, shelves, pictures and the like, there will be no problem. Otherwise, for very heavy bookshelves, you might need to locate the studs and fix through to them or to fix a batten on the wall.

- *Can you extend a timber-frame house?*
  Of course you can. In fact in many instances extension is even easier than with a brick and block house and not half as messy. You do obviously need to check things out with either the original frame manufacturer or with a timber engineer. But there's nothing different about that and whatever the method of construction, professional advice should be sought before anybody goes around hacking holes in a structure.

- *What levels of thermal insulation can one expect?*
  How long is a piece of string? The fact is that the sky's almost the limit and it really is down to you to evaluate your own requirements and to weigh up the competing claims from the various manufacturing companies. The thermal insulating properties of timber and brick are well known and usually exceed the regulation requirements. Timber-and-brick houses heat up very quickly and their level of insulation means that they then stay warm for longer. In addition, with no 'cold spots', they are not prone to condensation.

- *What about sound transmission?*
  Most sound from outside the house comes through the windows rather than the walls. Internal sound transmission is the biggest bugbear and there's no doubt that this is the one area where timber frame has to fight hard to beat brick and block. Internal sound transmission between rooms can be improved quite dramatically by making sure that there are no air gaps at the top or bottom of any partition. Filling the void in the wall with insulating or sound deadening material can help, as can additional layers of plasterboard. Alternatively, you could change from plasterboard to a gypsum fibreboard such as Fermacel. Sound transmission through floors can be alleviated by filling the void with mineral wool or by the use of specialist screeds.

- *Does one have to use a package-deal company or timber-frame manufacturer?*
  Not nowadays. Most timber-frame houses in the country are probably built with the aid of one of the companies, even if it's only for the manufacture of the panels, rather than the full service. Stickbuilding is, however, gaining in popularity and I'll go into that in the section entitled 'Going it alone' on page 174.

- *Will a timber frame house be as valuable as a brick-and-block house and will it be just as easy to get a mortgage or take out insurance?*
  There's no difference at all.

- *Are there environmental benefits from building timber frame?*
  Trees are the earth's lungs. They absorb and lock up carbon dioxide and they give out oxygen. Renewable forests are an undoubted benefit not only in the fight against global warming but also for their pure beauty and wildlife habitat. Thermally and energy-efficient housing means less use of non-renewable fuel sources and the effects of that go far beyond the undoubted benefit to your pocket. Although these qualities are not the sole province of timber-framed houses, they undoubtedly lead the way and their very existence has provided the spur for environmental consciousness in the housing sector.

Brick and block

Most new houses built in the United Kingdom are constructed in brick and block and, because of its universality, there is no need to defend it or extol its virtues in the same way as with timber frame. Equally, this familiarity means that many a discussion will hinge on the advisability of its use and the foolhardiness of using another system. From what you've just read above, you'll realise that these opinions are very often invalid and that brick and block is just one of the choices, rather than being the only option. Nevertheless, most people feel instinctively drawn to building in brick and block and those who do so justify their choice with as much zeal as any proponent of another method can muster.

With a modern brick-and-block, cavity-wall construction, it is the inner leaf of the cavity wall that takes the load and provides the structural stability for the house or bungalow. Whilst this block may well provide either all or part of the thermal insulation, it is more often the cavity, and the insulation that is built into it, that provides the most insulation. It wasn't always thus. When the cavity wall first started to replace the solid wall, it went on to gain full acceptance due to its undoubted ability to prevent damp from getting from the outside face of the wall across and to the inside. This remained its principal purpose for many years and, without dating myself too much, I can still remember the tooth sucking that went on when the idea of interrupting or even filling the cavity with insulation was first mooted. That the doubters were often proved right by a whole host of cowboy operators who blew all sorts of unsuitable material into cavities which had never been designed to be anything other than clear, did nothing to stop the onward march of progress and the refinement of materials and techniques into the systems we have today.

I suppose our preoccupation with the cost of heating and running our homes really began, as far as I can remember, with the Six-day War in the Middle East in June 1967. Prior to that, the words 'thermal efficiency' had no real meaning or significance for most people. In the early Sixties, many brick-and-block houses were still being built with open cavities, common-brick or breeze-block internal wall leafs and large areas of window, often single-glazed. It's not that we were any hardier in those days or that we enjoyed being cold or sitting in draughts; rather, it's the fact that heating costs were such an insignificant part of our income and expenditure.

I can still remember the 'U1' block replacing the old breeze block and I can also remember the introduction of the 'modern' idea of insulating the roof, although, to be fair, that had much more to do with the prevention of mould. The ratchet tightened inexorably from then on with the miners' strikes of the Seventies, further troubles in the Middle East in the Eighties and our twenty-first century concern over global warming. Brick-and-block construction couldn't stand still in the face of all this and it had to move with the times and the ever-increasing and tighter regulations on thermal efficiency. It's also had to answer the challenge from timber frame and there is no doubt in my mind that the high levels of thermal insulation found in modern brick-and-block houses, owe a lot to it having to keep pace with this competition. Be that as it may, the end result is that brick-and-block construction can now equal mainstream timber-frame construction in its thermal efficiency, and many houses built with this method go on to exceed the level of thermal requirements.

In much the same way as with the timber-frame heading, there are quite a few ways of going about constructing a brick and block cavity wall. Although there aren't as many companies specialising or promoting one particular method or another, there are, nevertheless, a bewildering array of different blocks to choose from and a whole host of combinations that can be used to provide you with the wall that will conform to all of the regulations. Whether you're using a package-deal company or an architect, they'll be concerned to match your aspirations with the budget and the particular or peculiar requirements of either the design or its exposure. Some blocks can cost two or even three times more than others and some of them, whilst seemingly appropriate, may not actually be suitable for your particular situation.

Perhaps one of the most common ways of building is the use of a 100mm 'Type B' insulating block as the inner leaf of the cavity with a 75mm cavity full-filled with insulation and either rendered block, brick or

Above: Note the deliberate loss of symmetry caused by the use of different window sizes on the otherwise uniform shape of the main house. This is accentuated by the bungalow section and the detached garage. (Design & Materials Ltd)

stone as the outside leaf. The two leafs of the walling are held together by special galvanised wall ties and, whilst the external leaf does not provide any load-bearing ability to the structure, it does, nevertheless, provide it with stability. That's also probably the cheapest way of constructing the wall and the 'U' values achieved are practically the same as for a standard open-panelled timber-frame wall, at around 0.38 or 0.39. However, in high exposure situations, even though modern cavity insulation materials resist damp and allow moist air to pass through them, it is often advisable, and the authorities may insist, that you maintain a clear cavity. In these cases, this is achieved by increasing the cavity very slightly to 80mm and then using a more dense insulation

material, held against the outside edge of the inside leaf by special wall ties, maintaining a 50mm cavity.

If you want to 'up' the specification even more, then there is a whole range of lightweight blocks to choose from, most of which, measured by the square metre, will cost you more to buy and most of which might prove to be more popular with your bricklayers or whoever's got to carry them up to the top lift of the scaffold. A cavity wall with an external brick, a 100mm full-filled cavity and a 100mm Tarmac Toplite block will have a 'U' value of 0.25, well below the current requirements and significantly below the cranked-up requirements that new regulations are expected to impose. Changing the full-fill cavity to a partially-filled cavity with 50mm of Celotex insulation would maintain the same 'U' value, but the extra cost would be approaching £1,000. Some of the higher insulation blocks gain much of their property by the use of a lightweight aggregate trapping air. What they gain in thermal efficiency, they can often lose in crushing strength and if there are point loadings or even heavy floor loadings, they can prove unsuitable for that situation. However, the companies have solved that problem by the introduction of special blocks with a high compressive strength together with reinforced lintel blocks. Alternatively, the simple introduction of a metal plate into the mortar bed beneath point loadings such as steel beams, in order to spread the load, will suffice.

One factor that you might like to consider is that, quite apart from the level of thermal insulation that is possible with a brick-and-block house, there is another, less well-known, but obvious benefit. When a dense material is heated up, it takes longer to cool down. In a block-built house, when the heating goes off at night, the blockwork will retain the heat for longer. By contrast, in summer, the effects of a really hot day will be delayed as warm air coming into the house gets cooled by the walls. Well, that's the theory and one that is put forward by those wishing to persuade you to use brick-and-block. It is true, of course, but if you also dry-line the house instead of using a wet plaster, the effect is largely negated.

Without a doubt the biggest innovation that's come about in the field of brick-and-block construction has been the introduction of solid first floors. Some time ago a large proportion of the claims the NHBC received related to failed ground floor oversites where either the concrete and screed had cracked or the infill had failed and the whole floor had sunk. In large part this was occurring on sites where there was a slope that made it necessary for the fill material to be greater on one side or at one end of the building than it was at the other. The solution was normally to thicken up and reinforce the oversite slab which was then cast so as to be capable of suspension. It was an expensive option with several inherent problems; and it was extremely time-consuming. Then the floor-beam manufacturers started to move in on the house-building market, having previously largely confined themselves to factories, office blocks and commercial buildings.

It very quickly became common practice for the ground floors of houses, whether timber-frame or brick-and-block, to use floor beams, and the NHBC and Building Control departments of many of the local authorities actively encouraged this, especially in situations where there was the slightest risk of differential settlement. There was resistance at first; there still is in some quarters, but gradually people began to realise that, although the costs of the flooring were slightly more than the equivalent in concrete, there were definite savings to be made in time and labour costs. A ground floor could be prepared and ready for the superstructure in under half the time taken for a consolidated, filled and concreted oversite and, moreover, the costs were a known rather than an indeterminate factor.

Before I go on I'd better just describe a floor beam and what is known as a 'beam-and-block floor'. The beams are shaped like railway lines in a 'T'section. They are laid, with the head of the 'T' downwards, from foundation wall to foundation wall, spaced one block apart. Blocks are then placed in the web between the beams to form a floor that is then brush grouted. Of late, H+H Celcon have introduced a new flooring system using lightweight aggregate with reinforcement. This not only provides an extremely thermally-efficient floor, with all of the benefits and properties of a normal beam-and-block floor, but it obviates the need for infill blocks.

It wasn't long before people started to ask, 'If we can build the ground floors like this, why can't we do the same with the upper floors?' And, of course, the floor-beam manufacturers were only too happy to oblige. One of the main selling points with brick and block had always been the sense of solidity that it gives. Imagine the disappointment of many people when, having chosen a brick-and-block form of construction with the normal timber first floors, they discovered that they were going to have studwork or lightweight partitioning for the walls upstairs. Now with a beam-and-block first floor, most, if not all of the upper-part partition walls could be in blockwork with all the advantages of sound insulation that was previously only achieved on the ground floor. There are other advantages. Solid first floors mean that transmission of sound between floors is almost eliminated and there is greater fire protection, especially where garages are integral, with rooms above them. Design & Materials, a package-deal company specialising in brick-and-block homes, say that up to 90% of their clients now chose a solid first-floor construction.

The finishing of the upper floor takes exactly the same form as it would for any of the ground floors. It can either be boarded on insulation panels as a floating floor, or it can be screeded. The provision of services can cause some scratching of heads amongst the uninitiated but, in fact, they too find their way around in much the same way as they do for the ground floors. In addition there is a built-in 'service duct' between the bottom of the infill blocks and the bottom of each floor beam and this is increased by the battens that are put in place to hold the plasterboard ceiling on the underside.

Wet plaster is a choice that is confined to brick-and-block construction and there are many devotees of this 'hard' form of finishing off the internal walls. Without a doubt there are benefits in the durability of hard plaster but there are also drawbacks in the length of time that such a finish takes to dry out and become ready for decoration. Timber-frame houses are finished off with a dry lining of plasterboard, or similar, which is then either taped and filled, or skim coated. The advantages of this system of wall finish are obvious and they will become even more obvious as the end of any self-build project approaches and the time for decorating and finally moving in gets even closer. There's no reason why brick-and-block houses can't enjoy the same benefits as their cousins by using the dry lining method. The only difference in the technique is that, instead of being fixed to the studs by nailing, the plasterboard, in a dry-lined brick-and-block house, is usually fixed by either dabs of plaster or by the fixing of battens to the walls.

Which is best, dry lining or wet plaster? Neither really. Both have their benefits and drawbacks and in the end, they cost about the same. Design & Materials report that about 80% of their clients choose dry lining. Whether that is to do with their promotion and sale of the product, or whether it is an indicator of people's preferences, I don't know, but it has to be said that in today's world of deadlines, decorating, finishing and moving in without delay becomes ever more important.

As with the timber-frame construction, certain questions constantly crop up and, as in the timber-framed section, I can answer each one without fear or favour.

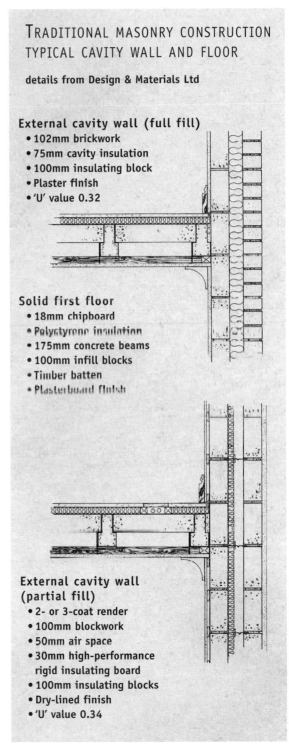

TRADITIONAL MASONRY CONSTRUCTION TYPICAL CAVITY WALL AND FLOOR

details from Design & Materials Ltd

External cavity wall (full fill)
- 102mm brickwork
- 75mm cavity insulation
- 100mm insulating block
- Plaster finish
- 'U' value 0.32

Solid first floor
- 18mm chipboard
- Polystyrene insulation
- 175mm concrete beams
- 100mm infill blocks
- Timber batten
- Plasterboard finish

External cavity wall (partial fill)
- 2- or 3-coat render
- 100mm blockwork
- 50mm air space
- 30mm high-performance rigid insulating board
- 100mm insulating blocks
- Dry-lined finish
- 'U' value 0.34

Frequently asked questions on brick and block

- *Do the foundations for a brick-and-block house have to be stronger?*
  The foundations for brick-and-block houses are almost always just the same as they are for timber-framed houses. Ground conditions are what dictate differing solutions to foundation problems although, in a very few cases, calculations can be used to prove a lighter structure which can then, for instance, find a bearing on an oversite.

- *Can the same level of thermal insulation be achieved?*
  Yes, and in fact, many of the standard methods of brick-and-block construction are equal to or better than standard timber frame in terms of 'U' values.

- *Does brick-and-block construction have better sound insulation?*
  Generally, yes, especially within the house itself. Low base notes have more power than higher frequency sounds and solid mass absorbs them more easily.

- *Will it cost more to build in brick and block?*
  Not at all. The costs experienced by most self-builders, whether they build in timber frame or brick and block, are remarkably similar, although those building in brick and block are represented in greater numbers within the group that experience very low costs. It is design, external materials and the size of a house, rather than whether it's brick and block or brick and timber, which dictate its cost.

- *Will it be easier to find labour?*
  Not easier – no different, really. Most labour knows all about building in brick and block but, as I've said, timber frame isn't that different in concept and if you use a package-deal company, they'll undoubtedly help with the introduction of builders and subcontractors who understand their system.

- *Can it be extended?*
  Yes, of course it can, but always with advice and in accordance with the regulations. No building should have holes cut into it without proper thought and consideration of the consequences.

- *Will it take longer to build?*
  There's no doubt that building in brick and block usually takes longer and that this method of construction is much more susceptible to bad, and particularly wet, weather. New large-block, thin-joint systems are coming onto the market that purport to be able to rival timber frame with their speed of erection. For most self-builders, however, the time taken from starting on site to moving in is remarkably similar, whichever construction method is chosen.

Going it alone

A self-builder, by definition, is someone who has consciously decided to step outside the norm and to do their own thing. A significant proportion will eschew any 'help' which might seem to corral them into any semblance of conformity: 60% of self-builders choose to manage the self-build on their own (Barlow/Jackson). But just how far should this quest for individuality be taken? This time, the choice has to be carefully thought out in relation to the self-builder's own abilities.

Going it alone doesn't mean that you should forgo all advice, whether given directly or indirectly. If you're a qualified architect or an extremely competent designer, then, by all means, do your own drawings and get your own planning permissions. If not, then to attempt to do so would be to enter a minefield. If you're a bricklayer, then it makes sense to do all or most of the labour on your new home, assuming you've got the time. But, if you're in your mid-fifties, have worked in an office all your life and never laid a brick, to do so would risk the success of your project and, probably your health as well.

In terms of design and the preparation of drawings, especially those for the later stages of Planning and Building Regulations, I really believe that this is best left in the hands of a professional. On the other hand, I don't see any reason why the self-builder can't be involved in the negotiations for what is, after all, his project and, as far as the 'outline' stages of planning are concerned, I believe that the private individual can often do a better job. Estate agents often charge £200 or more for 'handling' applications for 'Outline planning permission'. In fact, all that many of them do is take a photocopy of the Ordnance Survey (OS) sheet that they possess, fill in the forms that the local authority hand out, attach their client's cheque for the application fees and send it all off with, or without, a covering letter. That's all they do, apart from telling their clients the result some six to eight weeks later. In Chapter 8 you'll see that a lot more can be done to try to make sure that such an application is successful. Some of the lobbying I refer to, can only really be done by the applicant as a council taxpayer and as a potential voter. A planning officer can talk to a professional in a different way than is possible when talking directly to a member of the public. With a professional he can be quite rude or dismissive about a proposal, by hiding behind the detached relationship each of them have to both the application and the applicant. Faced with the applicant in person, or in writing, the answers given have to be couched in more conciliatory terms and any reasons for objections have to explained and expanded. Again, that's not to say that there aren't situations where a professional could be usefully employed but what I'm trying to illustrate is that it isn't always so.

Employing an architect or designer to do your plans doesn't mean that you lose control of your project. If you turn back to the section on architects you'll see that the measure of a good one is the ability to be able to translate *your* ideals, *your* requirements and *your* wishes. The same goes for anybody else or any other company. If you decide on an architect and he doesn't produce initial or sketch drawings by the second or third attempt that are to your liking, then pay him off and move on to another choice. Do not stick with something you're not comfortable with, just because you either don't want to admit you've made a mistake or in the vain hope that things will get better.

If a package-deal company is providing you with what you want, then there's no loss of sovereignty. If you're being forced into a strait-jacket that you're not comfortable with, then pull out quickly. Although this chapter is about making the choices and moving forward, that doesn't mean that, having made a decision you shouldn't proceed through the next phases without constantly enquiring whether you've chosen the right route. An initial choice to run with a package deal company may well commit you to payment for initial drawings, design studies and/or feasibility studies. When that part of their service is completed, they normally won't go any further until you've committed yourself and signed up for their full package. You do need to think carefully before going beyond those stages and I'll discuss that in the next chapter. Remember what I said earlier on, though, about not cherry picking. If you decide that you don't want to play with a package-deal company, that doesn't mean that you can run off and build the house they've designed for you – the designs remain their copyright.

All self-builders are alone to some extent whether or not they take on a mentor. The self-builder who gives the whole job over to an architect who then goes on to employ a builder still can't get away from the fact that at some stage the choices are down to him. That is, unless he's prepared to move in and only then discover that everything's just as wrong as if he'd bought a developer's house in the first place. The self-builder who uses a package-deal or timber-frame company will find themselves alone to some extent when it comes down to sourcing the materials that aren't included in the package.

If you're building in brick and block then the

choice has always been to 'paddle your own canoe' and source the materials from a builders' merchant, and that's just what the majority of self-builders do. What has changed over the last few years has been the attitude of the builders' merchants and the fact that the ordinary mortal rather than just the initiated can now expect all the help and advice necessary from them. If you're building in timber frame then, again, many of the merchants will arrange your frame purchase in just the same way as they always would have done with, say, an order for trusses. And, if you don't want to use a frame manufacturer then, as I've prefaced earlier, there's always the option of stick building.

The success of the package deal and manufacturing companies in the timber-frame industry has given rise to a whole new breed of professionals, able to provide services and advice on the design and construction of a timber-framed building. Architects can now draw on this expertise to design a timber-framed building that can be completely constructed on site. In Scotland a large proportion of buildings are now built in this way and the practice is growing in England and Wales. What are the advantages, apart from the fulfilment of a desire to go it alone? Well, flexibility, really. Flexibility of design in that even once the drawings have been done and work has started on site, design changes such as moving windows or internal walls can be accommodated subject, of course to their being structurally feasible and to the planners agreeing. Flexibility of construction.

One house I've seen in Wales used 100mm x 50mm regularised, pressure impregnated and treated timber for the external panels, which were then filled with solid insulation. The vapour barrier then went against the inside edge of this panel in the normal way but then, instead of the plasterboard, another framework of 50mm x 50mm timber was formed. All services were taken through this internal framework which was then filled with fibreglass insulation before the plasterboard was fixed to the inside face. In houses where there's only one panelled leaf, 'it can end up like a Swiss cheese', said the self-builder and occupant, and he's right. His house had a feeling of solidity I've rarely experienced.

Now, there are systems out there from package-deal companies that can emulate and, for all I know, exceed what he gained, but the point is that that self-builder achieved what he wanted from within his own resources. All of which leads me to the last of the gains in flexibility for this choice – money. Building a timber-framed house on site from lumber which is delivered from a local merchant or timber yard is never going to be as quick as if the panels were delivered already made-up for quick assembly. And that's the point, because it means that if finance is tight or, if it's not available in fairly front-loaded stages, the purchase of materials can more or less follow the progress on site, evening up the cashflow. You don't have to be anything other than a reasonable carpenter to do this but you do need to follow recognised procedures and you'll probably need help of some sort, either in a professional or a labouring capacity.

A few hardy souls are self-builders in every sense of the word, taking on all or much of the labour, as well as the management of the project. They're the true 'go it aloners' and I take my hat off to them. For most of us living in the modern world, our self-build aspirations have to fit in with a job of work and that means that we have to divide our time between what the boss would consider an extra-curricular hobby and what to us is, possibly, the biggest financial undertaking of our lives. If you're going to be crawling into work late and falling asleep at your desk, then the chances are that the job that pays for the mortgage, that pays for the house, will fall away. And when that falls away, so will your house. Most self-builders choose either to use a builder for all or part of the construction or to use subcontract labour for all or some of the trades and I'll cover that in later chapters. If you do waive the use of any other labour on site and truly go it alone, make sure that you know what you're taking on, and make sure that you keep an open enough mind to recognise when you need to seek help.

Alternative construction methods

I'm not going to cover any of these in great detail because, to a large extent, popular as they are with the media, alternatively built houses form such a tiny proportion of self-built homes that they really don't

Above: Green-oak construction, although no longer really alternative technology, does, nevertheless use methods that may be unfamiliar to some, including visiting inspectors.

Right: Picture from Beco Ltd. It may look like a giant 'Lego' set but there's a lot more to it than that.

count for much. I know that straw is a renewable and cheaply available resource. I know that old tyres should be re-cycled. Combine the two with the tyres as the damp-proof course and the bales as a tightly packed walling system that can be rendered inside and out and you've no doubt got a very useful and interesting structure. But to live in it? Not me, and if you've smelt the damp and imagined the bugs and the fire risk, you'll probably agree. I also know that log cabins, houses made from re-cycled telegraph poles and the like have their place in this world; but not in this book.

I am not a dinosaur. Within this book, I have urged self-builders to push the boat out in design terms and, in order to achieve that, I recognise the need for innovation. But looking back over my four decades in the building and property industry, I can see the many disappointments. I remember the solutions that solved the problems at the time, only to come back and haunt future occupants with problems that nobody had ever foreseen.

One method of construction that has been around fairly consistently is the use of hollow polystyrene interlocking blocks or Permanently Insulated Form-

work, as it's called. These are assembled and then filled with poured concrete and reinforcement to create an inherently sound and superbly insulated walling system. It sounds a great idea and the attractions are obvious, in that the self builder can imagine that largely he can assemble his own house. I have no doubt that this system has merit. But I can also see, and have heard of, the pitfalls. Pouring fairly liquid concrete into the top of a system of hollow blocks means that great care has to be taken to maintain consistency and avoid air pockets or any lack of adhesion; something that might well be within the capabilities of a person used to doing such work. But what about the lay self-builder? If the blocks burst, and they do from to time, then you're in awful trouble.

If you want to go for alternative technology, then please examine your reasons. If, for you, self-building is all to do with pioneering, pushing the frontiers of technology to the limits, then by all means go ahead. If it's about housing you and your family in the most cost-effective way and providing the very best in accommodation and facilities, then my advice is to stick to recognised, tried-and-tested construction methods. That doesn't mean that within those methods there won't be advances, because there always will be, and you should be aware of them, but it does mean that you should not expose your self-build to risk.

Renovation and conversion

Almost the first thing anybody will require, on deciding to embark on a renovation or conversion project, is a full survey of what's there already. This should be carried out by a competent surveyor, architect, structural engineer, or indeed a combination of more than one of these disciplines working together. They should have a thorough knowledge of basic architectural history and specialise in the restoration or conversion of old buildings.

There is always an element of having to put the cart before the horse. When a project such as this comes on the market, the value and therefore the price you are prepared to pay relies to a large extent on the soundness of the existing structure. In order to know that with any certainty, a full survey is necessary, and that's something that will cost a fair amount of money, which you might not want to spend before the property is actually yours. In essence, therefore, you need an initial estimate, from a competent and knowledgeable person, sufficient to secure the property, after which you will commission the full survey, which will, hopefully confirm the initial assumptions.

With many renovation projects, an element in bringing the building up to date will be suitable alteration of, and/or extension of the original. To envisage that you need a person with building knowledge, flair and imagination and, above all, a 'feel' for the architectural history of the building and the area. If the property to be 'done up' is in the local vernacular, possibly even Listed, then it becomes even more important that the person doing the design work and creating the specification is *au fait* with what the planners want, and what is right for the building to retain its architectural integrity. If the building is one that has little or no architectural integrity; one that is, and never was right in the street scene, then the same skills will be necessary in order to create a dwelling that does fit in with the local vernacular. You need to find the right person for this by asking around and interviewing prospective professionals in order to assess their abilities. The local authority is a good place to start for names. As well as the Building Inspector, you could also try the Planning Officers or Conservation Officers, all or some of whom will undoubtedly be able to put you on to individuals or practices who have successfully completed projects in their area.

Conversion projects, and the abilities of the professionals who specialise in them, follow similar criteria apart from the fact that, with many, there is more of a blank canvas upon which to create a new home out of something completely different. The planners might also have a pretty big input here as there is a tendency for them to want much of the original, say agricultural or industrial, heritage of the building preserved. 'I don't want it to look domestic', is not an uncommon phrase used by planning officers describing what is to be your new home!

When it comes to the building processes, the renovator or converter may use many of the same trades as are used for new building. But, whilst they might have the same description, and many of the tasks they undertake have the same name, the skills needed are significantly different. Plasterers on new dwellings spend ages trying to perfect a mirror finish and they might find it extremely difficult or even impossible to produce a genuine rough surface rather than a good one that has been subsequently distressed. For older buildings, the trades and skills in things like horsehair, sand and lime plasters are ones that are either lost or in very short supply. Carpenters, too, can have the vapours at the thought of making something out of square and bricklayers need to be able to lay bricks and stone in such a way as to emulate what's there rather than as they would do for new work. Whichever professionals or tradesmen you employ for these projects, they should be used to working on this type of building and they should be able to show a portfolio of their previous work.

Project planning – stage one

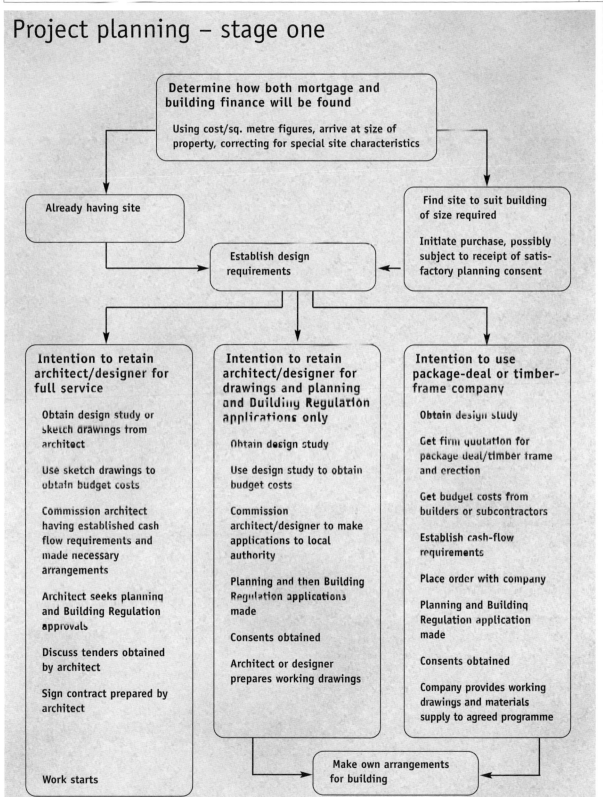

Determine how both mortgage and building finance will be found

Using cost/sq. metre figures, arrive at size of property, correcting for special site characteristics

Already having site

Find site to suit building of size required

Initiate purchase, possibly subject to receipt of satis- factory planning consent

Establish design requirements

Intention to retain architect/designer for full service

Obtain design study or sketch drawings from architect

Use sketch drawings to obtain budget costs

Commission architect having established cash flow requirements and made necessary arrangements

Architect seeks planning and Building Regulation approvals

Discuss tenders obtained by architect

Sign contract prepared by architect

Work starts

Intention to retain architect/designer for drawings and planning and Building Regulation applications only

Obtain design study

Use design study to obtain budget costs

Commission architect/designer to make applications to local authority

Planning and then Building Regulation applications made

Consents obtained

Architect or designer prepares working drawings

Intention to use package-deal or timber- frame company

Obtain design study

Get firm quotation for package deal/timber frame and erection

Get budget costs from builders or subcontractors

Establish cash-flow requirements

Place order with company

Planning and Building Regulation application made

Consents obtained

Company provides working drawings and materials supply to agreed programme

Make own arrangements for building

7. THE INITIAL DRAWINGS

Design study, initial drawings and sketch drawings are all words for the same thing, really, and all of them should lead you to an assessment of what you're aiming at, what it's likely to cost and whether it's feasible, which is why some of the package-deal companies, working within the self-build industry, expand upon things and include these drawings in what they call a 'feasibility study'.

Some architects and designers don't want to go through a design-study stage. This is because they don't want the clients to ask themselves, 'Do I want to use this architect and is he interpreting my requirements correctly?' Such an architect would far rather keep the arrangements moving gently along, until it reaches a compromise between his professional advice and the client's ideas, and he is established firmly as the client's professional agent. Maintaining this role is difficult because the client, wanting a modest house within a fixed budget, wants a clear idea of what he is going to get before he commits himself. Also, at some point in the design process, costs have to be quantified, and the decision made that the design proposed is practicable within the budget. I question whether such an architect is really suitable for the self-builder but, nevertheless, it is sometimes worthwhile trying to establish if they'll agree to carry out a design study for an agreed fee. Some won't want to play on this basis so perhaps it would be better to move elsewhere. Certainly the ASBA architects' factsheet quite clearly details a sketch design stage and although it's not always done as a formally quoted design study, the procedures they adopt do allow for a continuous evaluation of just where each project is going.

Architect's drawings

Typically, architects will probably have up to three meetings with the client before pen is even put to paper and they'll only go to the drawing board when they have fully evaluated the client's needs and requirements under all of the headings in the section on architects in the previous chapter. At any stage in this process, therefore, the architect will want to know that he is on the right lines. The self-builder will want to ensure that the drawings represent what he wants, that they are probably going to be acceptable to the planners and, most importantly, that the house can be built within his budget. If at any time one or more of these goals is not achievable, then the whole thing must stop and be re-evaluated or redrawn until it is right.

If, after several redraws, it's still wrong, then there may be no alternative but to change architects. In that case the relationship should be terminated by payment of a fee based on the work done thus far and that fee should, in all normal circumstances, reflect the level of fees charged for design studies by other companies. Of course, I'm talking here about 'worst case' and the chances are that when you went out shopping for an architect you picked him or her for their general level of abilities and the flair that they undoubtedly demonstrated to you in their portfolio. A good architect should already have asked the questions you generate. They should be as keen as you are to know that everything's on the right lines, and the drawings you get back as sketch drawings must reflect your original choice and the brief you gave. If not, then you must take steps either to bring things back into line, or sever the relationship. Stay in the driving seat. This is *your* self-build.

Package-deal design

If you're using a package-deal company for the design process, whether timber-frame or brick-and-block, then the way things proceed depends to a large extent on the choices you have made on how to arrive at the

Above: The use of two single rather than one double garage doors lessens the impact that this element has on the design. (Custom Homes Ltd)

design. Many of the companies have brochures with designs within them that can be adapted or changed to varying degrees. Most of them will be concerned that the designs that originally attracted you to their services are feasible for your circumstances. Even if a self-builder chooses a standard design from a brochure, the company will know that it may need alteration of some sort to find favour with the planners. They will also be concerned to tell you what effects any changes are going to have on their package-deal price and the total costs of the building. In some cases, therefore, it is still necessary to go through a feasibility study stage with a standard design and there may well be a charge for such a service. It is money well spent and you can use the completed study to demonstrate to yourselves, your lenders and the planners that you are on the right lines.

If you've gone to a package-deal company on the basis of having a bespoke design then, in many respects, your initial relationship with them is no different from that which you might have with an architect or designer. Once again the triumvirate of drawings, costs and acceptability comes into play – the last two depending upon the first and the first undertaken only with the last two in mind. Costs can be established in broad brush strokes and most architects or company representatives will be able to tell you right off whether or not you're on the right lines, even before the initial drawings are ready. When they are completed they'll also, probably, be able to demonstrate their faith in their own abilities by getting quotations not only for their own services but from builders and others that prove the feasibility of the project in cost terms. In planning terms, the architect or the company representative will always be keeping a weather eye open for the project to remain within the requirements of the local authority and they'll probably steer your thoughts, and the design process, to keep within those parameters.

So, back to the design itself. Almost certainly you've read diligently through Chapter 5 and just as certainly you've got a long list of requirements, a bulging scrapbook and some sketches of your own. If not, then you should get them done *before* you meet the architect or company representative so that *cont/...*

DESIGN & MATERIALS LTD

Drawings for a fairly standard house style with attached double garage showing how the addition of a few important features can enliven the design.

FRONT ELEVATION 1:100

BEDROOM 3

BATH

BEDROOM 4

GALLERY

EN-SUITE

BEDROOM 2

DRESSING AREA

MASTER BEDROOM

UPPER FLOOR PLAN

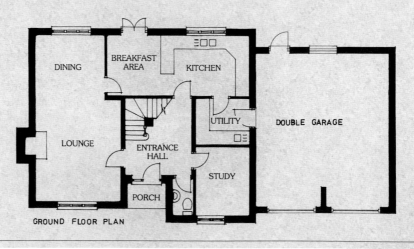

DINING

BREAKFAST AREA

KITCHEN

UTILITY

DOUBLE GARAGE

LOUNGE

ENTRANCE HALL

STUDY

PORCH

GROUND FLOOR PLAN

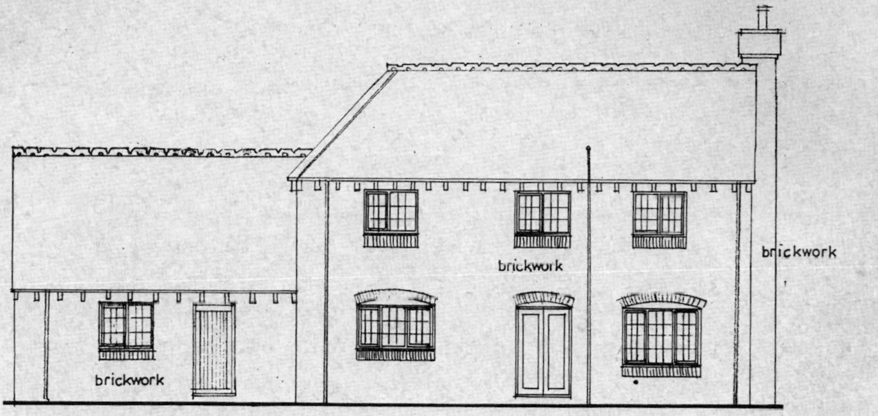

REAR ELEVATION 1:100

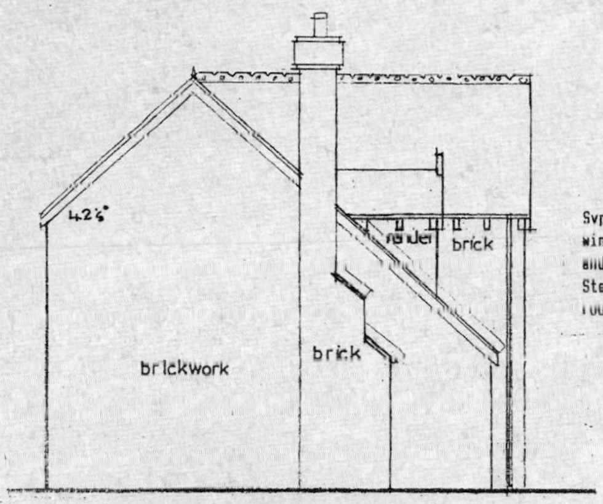

brickwork
brickwork
brickwork

SIDE ELEVATION

42½°

brickwork
brick
brick

Svp's to terminate min 900mm above openable windows and to be fitted with durable cage and weathering slate.
Stepped lead flashing and tray dpc's to all roof / chimney / wall abutments.

SIDE ELEVATION 1:100

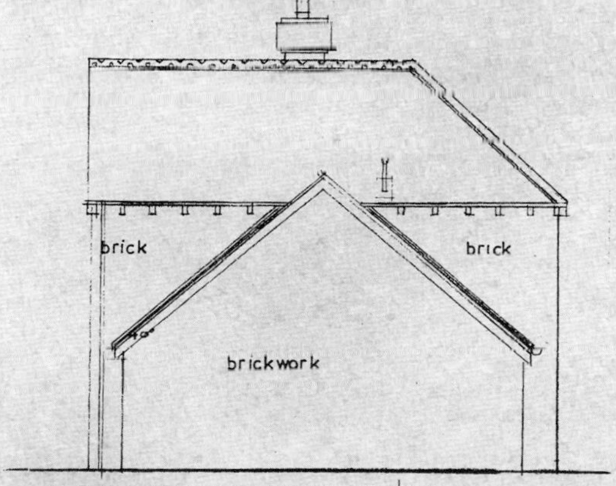

brick
brick
brickwork

42° pitch 10⅜" X 6⅝" plain clay roofing tiles, with feature panels in contrasting colour, as indicated.
Colour and type of tiles subject to approval of local authority.

Facing brickwork, colour and type subject to approval of local authority.
Feature flint panels to front elevation only.

PVC-u Casement windows, double glazed with Jacobean leaded lights

KEITH BISHOP ASSOCIATES – ARCHITECTS FROM MALVERN

An innovative and exciting design that, whilst retaining the square on all of the rooms, manages to break free from many of the constraints associated with maintaining the rectangular.

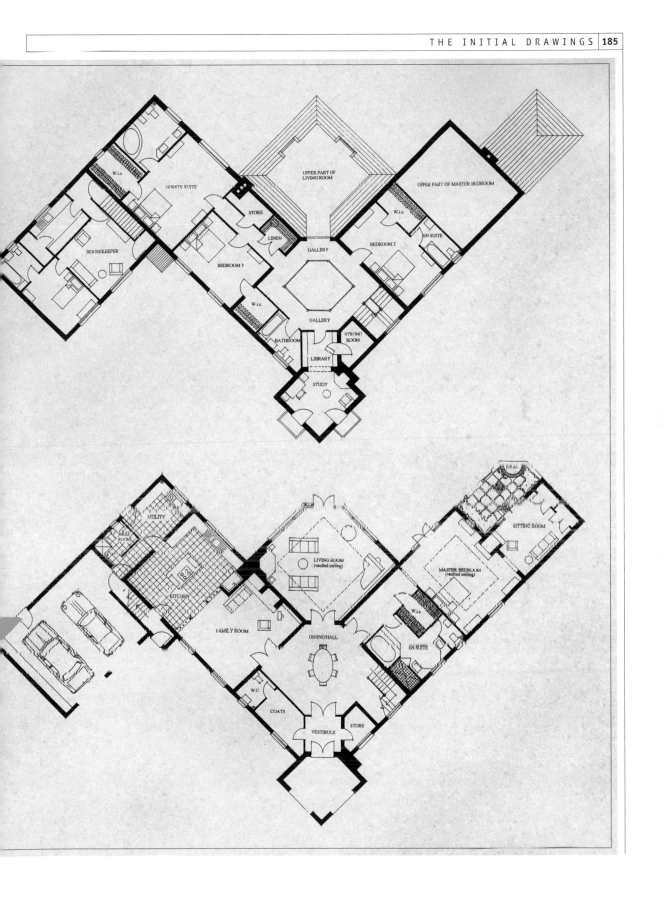

DESIGN & MATERIALS LTD

A design study for a house on a sloping site that manages to maintain an attractive façade and provides an interesting accommodation layout within some fairly tight spans.

FRONT ELEVATION

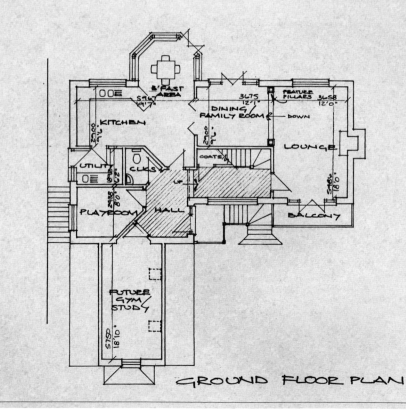

GROUND FLOOR PLAN

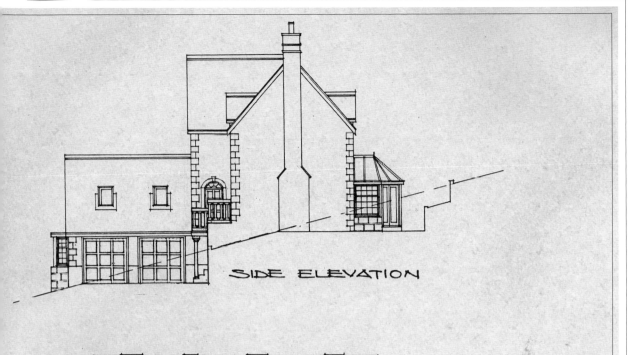

SIDE ELEVATION

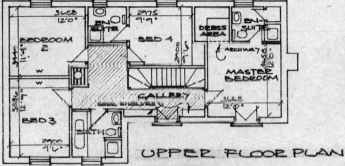

UPPER FLOOR PLAN

BEDROOM 2

EN-SUITE

BED 4

DRESS AREA

EN-SUITE

ARCHWAY

MASTER BEDROOM

GALLERY

BED 3

BATH

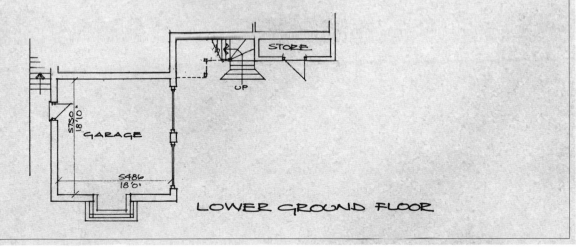

STORE

UP

GARAGE

LOWER GROUND FLOOR

JULIAN OWEN ASSOCIATES – NOTTINGHAM-BASED ARCHITECTS

A truly imaginative design based around a central lightwell and incorporating hexagonal shapes with rectangles over and to the upper floors.

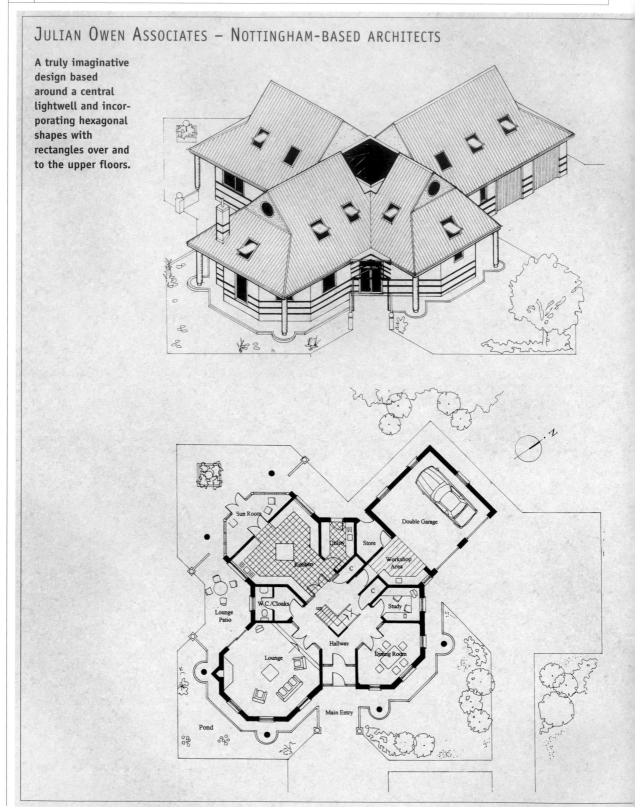

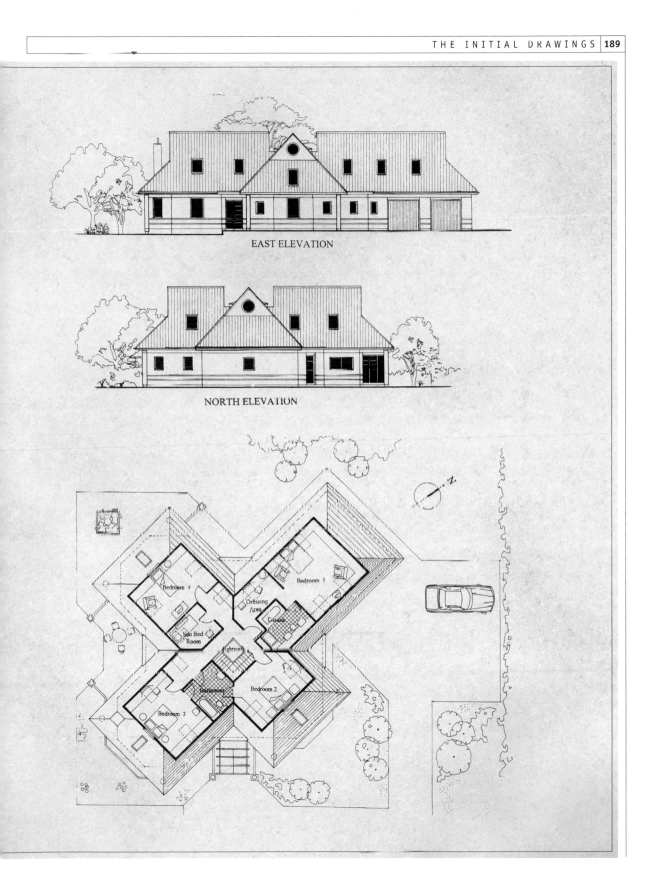

EAST ELEVATION

NORTH ELEVATION

you can make sure that the brief they depart with and the initial drawings that come back, are what you're after. Start off any meeting with a request for a general appraisal of just what they can do for you and, whilst you're probably not that interested in being 'sold to', ask just what it is that this company or practice has to offer which makes it worth choosing them above all others. A package-deal representative will be trading on the designs and the case histories within his brochure and, to be fair, they're probably the reason you've called him in the first place. An architect or designer will, in just the same way, be trading on his own track record in the form of his portfolio or else the recommendation that has brought him to your door.

The first of their questions to you should probably revolve around what you want to build and what your budget is. If the architect or representative hasn't already seen the plot then they'll want to go and inspect it before they get into a detailed discussion. Possibly they will have ideas of their own which they can sketch out with you and it's always a good idea to try to establish their thought processes and level of competence and understanding. Most of them will have fairly comprehensive checklists and question-naires to fill in with you, these having been refined over the years to make sure that when the project gets to the drawing board, all the relevant information is to hand. Your list of requirements should accompany any brief that has been prepared and there is no harm at all in showing the representative your own sketches. Don't be bashful – he won't scoff. I can assure you that however amateur the plans are, they will give him a thoroughly good guide to what you're trying to achieve. He may have seen the plot for the first time that day and then only briefly. I bet you've spent days looking at and thinking about it and you, more than anyone, will have worked out just where you want particular rooms to face, what views you want to maximise or even lose and what type of property you feel will fit. Have some paper handy so that when the chap has had a look at your plans, he can draw out his own ideas based on your plans, probably rationalising a jumble of barely connected rooms into something approaching a plan capable of construction.

'Why should we do that?' you may ask. 'Surely it's his job to come up with a design?' 'Why should we do his job for him?' This is not a Sixties' demarcation dispute, this is a self-build project and any means which serve to ensure that you get what you want in design terms are right and proper. Two parties working in isolation of each other's thought processes are unlikely to produce the best results. By comparing your ideas with the professional's input you can usually see the realisation and expansion of your plans take place before your very eyes.

When the initial or sketch drawings are completed with any alterations drawn up or noted and the costs established as far as is feasible, then it's time to stand back and evaluate what happens next. If you're happy with what's on offer and the price, then you're ready to commit yourself to the next stage with one company or practice. If not, then ask yourself just what it is that you're not happy with. Make a list and ask the people you've been dealing with to answer your questions and allay your doubts. If you're still not happy, then cut loose and take another tack with a different company or architect. Don't just let things run on – after the initial drawing stage you could well find that, if you agree to a practice or company doing more work, or going for planning, you're legally con-tracted to them. If that's not what you intended, but you've just let it happen, it'll all end in tears.

But enough of this gloom. Chances are that the feasibility stage will have demonstrated to you that you've made all the right decisions, all the right moves and that now is the time to think about the next stage of your self-build project – the planning permission.

8. THE PLANNING SCENE

I've already dealt with the important business of the evaluation and purchase of a site in Chapters 2–4. However, much of what I've said will bear repetition and expansion, and an understanding of the planning scene is an essential prerequisite for any successful self-build project. This applies as much to those who are going to leave the application in the hands of their chosen professional as it does to the self-builder who decides to handle the application himself. Even if you engage the services of a professional, you cannot divorce yourself from what follows and it is important that you and your advisors act in concert and work as a team

Planning is law. But it is law that is translated by opinion, and opinions can vary. Each local authority will interpret advice from the Department of Environment in its own way. Each planning officer will interpret his own role in the administration of the Planning Acts in his own way and a change of personnel can make a marked difference to the progress of an application. The Planning Acts are concerned with whether or not a dwelling can be built at all in a particular locality, taking into account its appearance and the way in which it will relate to its surroundings. This control is exercised by the local authority, to which an application has to be submitted to erect any new dwelling. In theory, all planning applications are considered by a committee of councillors who are advised by the council's professional planning officers but, in practice, for run-of-the-mill applications, they often just rubber-stamp the recommendations of the planners. In some local authorities, applications for Approval of Reserved Matters and non-contentious applications are not even put before the committee and, instead, the planning officers themselves have the power to determine the application using Delegated Powers handed down to them by the authority. Members of the public are entitled to appeal

to a higher body against any decision of the local authority in a planning matter.

One of the things many professionals hear when talking to their clients is that such and such a planning officer is very difficult to deal with or always reacts negatively to any application. The professional will usually listen politely but he will know the reality, which is that the planning officer, who may well be known to him, is a person who is just doing their job. Planning officers can never really win. The person who doesn't get planning for exactly what they want will feel aggrieved, and the next-door neighbour of the man who does get exactly what he wanted, may feel just as aggrieved. All planning officers can do is try to act within their powers, fairly and in as even handed a manner as their brief allows.

At meetings with planning officers, clients who are not getting their way may become extremely upset, as is evidenced by the panic buttons that you'll see in most meeting rooms. If the professional doesn't share their anger, some may even turn their resentment against their own advisor, failing to see that first, their approach won't get them very far and second (and most importantly), their architect is there in a professional capacity. As such, he has to bear in mind that he may have dealings with the planning officer on behalf of other clients and that, if he allows himself to become personally involved, he may disadvantage his other clients and jeopardise his future business. Having said that, the experienced professional will understand that, although for him this is just another job, for his client it is *the* experience of a lifetime and he is bound to be much more personally involved. It helps if each party understands everyone else's roles and viewpoints, and this book aims to assist in that understanding.

It is always the land that acquires the planning permission, not the person who applies for it. If land with planning permission is sold, the consent is available to the new owner. You don't even have to own the land in order to make an application on it and many self-builders, as we explored in previous chapters, make applications on sites which they are in the process of buying, long before they actually have legal title. It is necessary to serve notice on the owners of the land and it is advisable to tie things up with them to make sure that, if you're successful, the land doesn't get sold to someone else. This can be in the form of a legal option to purchase in the event of planning being successful or, alternatively, you can buy the land, subject to receipt of satisfactory planning permission.

Making a planning application

Planners make their recommendations in accordance with set criteria after going through set procedures. The way to obtain a planning consent quickly and easily is to ensure that it meets all the established criteria for an approval. This fact is often forgotten. A planning officer does have the discretion to make recommendations, which are at variance with planning policy, but this is unusual. The golden rule is to avoid applications which may be contentious, and to present anything unusual in a non-contentious way.

Most land is 'zoned'. That means that within the local Development Plan adopted by the Planning Authority, the land is parcelled up and allocated to specific purposes. The titles used in this allocation are probably familiar to most people with, for instance, Green Belt, referring to land where the policy is that no development shall be permitted. Land may also be designated as being for Residential, Industrial or Recreational use and other land may be zoned as White Land. This is land that, while not being designated as Green Belt, has not been zoned for any other specific purpose. Most agricultural land falls within this category. District plans will clearly show the des-

Planning
A Guide for Householders

What you need to know about the planning system

Thinking about altering or improving your home?

Putting up a building in the garden?

Building an extension?

Department of the Environment, Transport and the Regions and The National Assembly for Wales

Above: Planning offices contain records and files that are a matter of public record. The public are free to inspect them by appointment.

Left: This useful handout can be obtained from the local planning authority who may well have other helpful information and leaflets.

Right: Planning officers as well as Building Inspectors may want to come out on site, during the building process in order to check that things are being done in accordance with the plans. Whilst not strictly linked, it is often the Building Inspector who tips them off that something's wrong.

ignation of land for specific purposes and village plans will indicate the 'envelope' or boundaries within which any development is expected to take place.

None of this means that just because land falls within an area designated as being for residential use or a plot falls within the village envelope, it will necessarily get planning consent for development. It's difficult to put into words, because it relies partly on a gut feeling built up over years of practice, just why one plot of land should get planning consent whilst another most certainly will not. I say again, planning is law that, perhaps more than any other branch of the law, is interpreted by opinion. Prior to any consent or refusal, therefore, all opinions are equally valid, but some might be a trifle more valid than others. Professionals working within the planning scene have, probably, long since ceased to be surprised by the outcome of many applications and many will have stories of the plot they were certain would get planning, which didn't, and the plot they were convinced would never get planning, which did.

If you're employing a professional at this stage then their opinion might be the spur or the disincentive for you to take matters any further. On the other hand, many of you will want to make your own minds up on this issue and might like to obtain information first-hand, rather than second-hand. There may also be a slight suspicion that there are financial axes to grind if you agree to adopt a particular course of action or commission someone to do something for you, based on their advice alone.

I've talked about obvious plots left by circumstance and there are many of them in many different situations around the country. If you either own or come across such a plot, then perhaps the first thing you should do is make general enquiries at the planning office about their attitude towards that piece of land. Keep your questions on the broad theme of whether or not the piece of land would be considered as a building plot. Listen carefully to the answers and, without badgering the officer to make statements that he would rather not make, read between the lines of what they say. Now, you may think it preferable for the officer to come out to site, and in some cases it is certainly true that a visit to a site will serve to sway a wavering opinion one way or another. In most cases, however, and particularly at the first enquiry, it's likely that the officer can give an opinion by reference to plans and their own local knowledge. Phrases like, 'every application will be treated on its own merits', mean little or nothing in this context, and most planning officers will avoid using them when answering questions on the principle of whether land should be developed or not. 'We would resist such an application', or 'Such an application would run counter to the policies of this authority', are much more clear-cut and I would invite you to consider, in such circumstances, whether or not you should pursue that particular plot any further.

Of course, whether you accept such advice depends on many things, not least whether you already own the plot, but again, I invite you to consider whether a long history of planning rejections will aid your case at some future date when perhaps the authority's attitude might be slightly different. Certainly getting involved in an argument about the planning policy of the local authority is pointless. The officer will not debate the policy itself and he must, and will, confine himself to dealing with your enquiry on the basis of the implementation of that policy. Sometimes, however, the lay person will pursue the argument and may even convince themselves that the planning officer has given way and agreed with their contentions. Normally nothing is further from the truth and the reality is that the planning officer has simply extricated himself from a tricky situation by using words which seem to satisfy or partially mollify the member of the public he is faced with.

In the end, planning officers will know that, prior to any actual determination of an application, nothing they say, either verbally or in writing, is binding on the local authority, a fact that has been tested in the courts and is established in law by precedent.

Of course, the planning officer might look at your proposals and decide that an application would be acceptable or even welcome. In which case, your next question should be whether they would like to see any application made in Outline or whether they would prefer it to be a Full application. If they ask for a Full application then, in many cases, it's a pretty sure bet that, at officer level, the land is thought of in terms of being a potential plot. Beware, you are not home and dry just yet and, although rare, it is not unknown for committees to take a differing view on things. The planning officer's recommendation might also come about because they feel that it would not be possible to consider the matter in Outline, and that they therefore need more detail, in order to reflect on the issue of principle. This same procedure is also used, by means of an Article 4 direction, where they receive an Outline application, which they feel cannot be properly considered without full plans of the proposals.

If it is to be an Outline application then although you're a lot further forward than the chap who got brushed aside, you must not count your chickens before they're hatched. At this point you really need to consider whether you should be using a professional to handle the application or whether you could handle it yourself. It all depends on your own circumstances and abilities, but the chances are that if you were a complete no hoper you would not have got to this point anyway. Maybe the reason the planning officer has asked for an Outline application is that he's not really sure whether or not your particular proposal or the development of this particular plot will find favour with the planning committee. Maybe he knows that it will but, by taking it through the Outline stages of the planning process, he will then have a chance to influence the eventual outcome by the imposition of conditions. Maybe you've been advised to make this application because the planning officer felt that you weren't prepared to accept his reservations and he feels that the only way to prove them to you is for you to make an application which he hopes and believes will be turned down. Whatever the reason for arrival at this point, there is a lot that the lay person can do to ensure that the application stands the best chance of success, whether or not a professional is employed to prosecute it.

Most Outline applications are considered by committee and it is perfectly legal to lobby the members of that committee to vote on your behalf. In the first weeks of May, councillors will be asking for your support at the ballot box and, in turn, you are perfectly entitled to ask for theirs. They don't have to give it, of course, and if your request for their support is accompanied by a bottle of whisky, then you have stepped beyond the bounds of lobbying and into the realms of bribery.

When the local authority receives an application they will normally acknowledge it and give it a reference number. After this they should determine the application within a period of eight weeks unless they obtain your written consent for an extension of time.

It doesn't make sense to refuse this consent as in that case the authority may well simply determine the application by a refusal, citing a lack of time for any proper consideration. Sometimes there will be repeated applications for extension of time. This may be because they and you are still in active negotiation. But it may also be a simple failure on the part of the authority, in which case you have either the right to refuse the extension of time, bringing matters to a head, or to appeal against their failure to determine. I shall discuss that in the section on appeals but for now let us stay with the Outline application.

Assuming that all is going normally, a date will be set when your application will be considered by the committee and you and/or the professional working on your behalf should make sure that this date does not pass by without you knowing of it. Two weeks before the committee is to hear the application, contact the members of the planning committee that your local

councillor has identified as being the ones most likely to have influence, and ask them for their support. If you feel it necessary, give them a written appraisal of why you think your application has merit and, if you think it would be helpful, offer to meet them on site to discuss the application. Don't leave things any later or they won't have time to do anything and don't do it any earlier or it will not be fresh in their minds when the meeting comes up. *Do not* take things any further and *do not* badger them in any way – having made your submission, leave the rest up to them. When it comes up at committee, you'll have made sure that it will be considered by as broad a cross-section of opinion as is available and that it will not just be swept into a decision based on a single report. That is as much as you can, and should, do.

If the planning officer asks for a Full application, or if you are buying land with the benefit of an existing consent, then most of the negotiations will be concerned with the actual details of your proposed new home, rather than just the principle. In this case I earnestly believe that the application is best handled by a professional. The issues of principle are ones where the democratic process can be brought into

Above: Planning application forms may look daunting but in reality they are quite straightforward and easy to fill in and come with a list of explanations.

full play and where the lay person, by virtue of his ability to lobby, can seek to influence any outcome. An Outline application requires the minimum of drawings and may indeed only require the drawing in of a red line around the perimeter of a plot on a copy of the Ordnance Survey plan sold to you by the local authority. The merits of such an application can be argued by an articulate lay person. A Detailed application needs to be properly presented and the accompanying plans need to be sufficiently detailed and attractive in order to stand the best possible chance. Whilst I advocate consultation with the planning officers by lay people at the Outline stage, I do advise caution at the detailed stages.

Planners are anxious to influence development by advice as well as by control, and there is usually a notice at the reception desk saying just that. Unfortunately, this advice is usually a council of perfection, and it may not suit you to take it. For instance, suppose you are buying an attractive site with Outline consent. As a first stage in establishing a design it may seem sensible to call at the planning office to ask for the free advice on offer. You will be well received, will be impressed by the trouble taken to explain how the site 'needs a house of sensitive and imaginative design to do justice to its situation'. You may be shown drawings, a sketch may be drawn for you, and it is not unknown for the planning officer to drive to the site with you. This is splendid, until you realise the ideal house being described suits neither your lifestyle nor your pocket. You will wonder what the reaction is going to be to your application for the quite different house that you want, and which is the one you can afford.

The simple answer is that your application will be dealt with on its merits, and that the planning officer has an obligation to approve what he thinks acceptable, and he should not insist on what he thinks is best. However, he might well be disappointed to find that all of the advice that he gave you has been ignored, and that disappointment might well colour his thinking. From this it will be seen that a preliminary discussion with the planning officer is not to be taken lightly. As a general rule, the best person to deal with the planning office is the professional whom you employ to submit your application.

Not having face-to-face contact or negotiations with the officers themselves, in order not to compromise a future application, or cut the ground from beneath the feet of the professionals you have engaged, is one thing. Failing to take notice of the planning policy guidelines or to study the published information put out by the various planning and other agencies is quite another. These are important. When, and if, it ever comes to an appeal, the first thing an inspector will want to know is whether you have followed these guidelines and whether or not your proposals conflict with the adopted and ratified policy of the authority, as set out in the Local Development Plan.

Some will be buying a plot for which a Detailed consent has already been granted. If the consent is for just what you want then everything's fine and, so long as you've got a current Building Regulations approval, there's nothing to stop you starting work on site. If there are some minor changes that you'd like to make to the drawings then it is possible that the planners will agree to these being carried out on the basis of a 'minor amendment to the existing consent'. They will require a letter and drawings, listing and showing the amendments, but it's better to talk your ideas through with them beforehand. If they feel that they cannot accept your amendments, or if your proposals are radically different from the existing consent, then you may either have to make a fresh application for Approval of Reserved Matters, pursuant to the original Outline consent, or else make a Full application. The failure of either of these methods of application will not, of themselves, invalidate the original consents. Nevertheless, they may lapse of their own accord by virtue of being out of time, so watch out for that eventuality.

When your planning application is made you will have to pay a standard fee to the local authority and this is payable whether it refers to an Outline application, a Full application, or an application for Approval of Reserved Matters. There is no refund if the application is refused and the level of fees is reviewed at frequent intervals. At the time of writing it is £190 for a single dwelling but this is always likely to be adjusted upwards.

The consideration process of any application

Right: In certain areas, the conservatory can be built on under Permitted Development Rights but in others express permission will have to be sought.

Below: Viewed from the inside the conservatory to this Potton home provides pleasant extra living space and, if placed on the south side of the dwelling, can provide passive solar gain.

follows a general pattern in that, once the application is registered, it will be assigned to an officer who will then send out for what are known as Statutory Consultations. These are made to bodies such as the Highways Authority and the Environment Agency as well as to the local parish council. Although the planners may discuss the application within the consultation period, nothing much will be decided until they have received all of their consultations. It is better, therefore, to wait until the application has been with the local authority for about four weeks before endeavouring to enter into any meaningful discussions with the officer who has been assigned to the case. If the Parish Council approve of your plans then that's fine. If they reject them, it is not the end of the world. Parish Councils have a long history of rejecting what is put before them and there is no way of saying it other than to say that they have long since 'shot their bolt'. Statutory as their consultation is, their conclusions have little or no bearing on the decisions which the officers will reach in their recommendations, except in reinforcing an existing opinion.

When a planning application is made, letters are also sent out to neighbours and other interested parties, advising them of the application and inviting them to inspect the details of the proposals at the planning office. Anyone, not only those who have been notified, can make representation to the authorities about the application. A great many objections are invalid in planning terms but their effect is, nevertheless, to raise the profile of an application and to render it incapable of being given a delegated decision. Try to talk to your neighbours beforehand. Try to get them on your side. If possible, take their reservations on board or, at the very least, prepare the ground by explaining why you have discounted them.

The officer assigned to your case will prepare a report on your application, which will form the basis of the recommendation to the committee. If it is to be considered under 'Delegated Powers' then the same report will be submitted to the senior officer or group of officers who will determine the application. In general, the applicant is entitled to see and have a copy of the report and also to see any background papers or documents used in the preparation of the reports. If an objection is received then it is usual for any Delegated Powers to be withdrawn and for the application then to be considered by full committee. Most authorities allow members of the public to attend full committee meetings, although you are not usually allowed to talk. A few allow applicants or their agent to make a timed representation at the meeting, but not to question or interrupt their subsequent deliberations.

There is a fine line to walk at the consideration stage of any application, and your professional is the one to consult. If the application is not contentious, but the officers are, nevertheless, constantly assailed with requests to consult on it, then you may stir them into a more detailed consideration than they would have previously considered. On the other hand, if they have reservations on any part of the application and nobody goes near them, then it is possible that they will simply report their reservations to the committee and a rejection may follow for something that could have been altered. The question most professionals will ask, when telephoning after the consultation period, is the simple one, 'Can you tell me the current situation on application reference ...?' The answer will then be given in the form of a statement of just where the officer has got with the application and they will usually then go on to explain or set out any reservations or objections they may have. Hopefully, if you've followed all the rules, carefully thought out your proposals and made sure that they are non-contentious,

the officers will say that everything is all right. If not, they may go on to list changes that they would like to see and they will almost certainly then confirm this by letter.

The reservations, if any, expressed by the planning officer, may not disturb you much, in which case, your professional, having consulted you first, will quickly move to incorporate the suggestions within the plan and the application will then receive a favourable recommendation and be allowed to proceed. On the other hand, you may have doubts about some aspects of the officer's objections, in which case a meeting needs to be convened as quickly as possible. Sometimes the planners will request an input from their own architects or conservation officers and, when you attend the meeting, you and your architect may be faced with a whole group of people showing an interest in the outcome of your application and wishing to exert their influence. Whatever the attendance at the meeting, keep calm and make notes of all of the objections and requirements. If you are able to agree things at that meeting which can later be incorporated into the plans, then fine. If not, the best thing to do is simply to take away the list and discuss it privately with your advisors. If you feel that there is no compromise, then you have the right to insist that your application proceeds unaltered, but it will almost certainly proceed to a refusal. In many cases, a compromise solution can be reached that will satisfy all parties. What you have to bear in mind at all times is your objective to build a new home, and that means not only in design terms but also in budget terms. Hopefully, by reading the earlier chapters of this book, you will have anticipated any peculiar requirements for, say, external materials, and hopefully, their imposition will not come as too much of a surprise to you, and your budget will accommodate them.

Sometimes a planning officer can be persuaded that your application has merits that they had not realised. Sometimes a conservation officer can be persuaded by a series of photographs, proving that you have taken the trouble to incorporate features that are indigenous to the area. Sometimes a planning officer can see that you have followed a particular style in an area which itself has diverse styles of architecture. It all comes down to preparation and thinking about the application and proposals long before they are committed to paper and long before they finally arrive on a planning officer's desk.

What about lobbying at the Detailed stages of planning? You can try it, but it isn't nearly as effective as at the Outline stages. Local councillors may be prepared to argue with a professional planner on the question of principle, but not nearly so ready to engage them in long discussions over architectural details or merits. What you can do by lobbying is to bring about a site meeting where the committee convenes on the site. Technically, the applicant is not allowed to talk at most site meetings. In practice, when a group of disparate people have entered *your* land, they'll find it very difficult to ignore you and, in most cases I've attended, several questions have been addressed directly to the applicant or their agent. *Do* be careful to keep any answers or matters you have to raise succinct and to the point. *Don't* go off on a tirade about your application and the ills that have befallen you at the hands of the planning officer. Choose the right moment to put your point and then let the people given the power of decision come to their democratic conclusions.

Much of what I've written above has been directed at making life easy for you, the applicant, the planners and the passage of your application, by ensuring that it is, as far as is possible, non-contentious. I have to square that with my urgings in other sections of this book and within other forums, for self builders to 'push the boat out' in design terms and to think about whether they really want simply to emulate the developer's designs. If you want to do something different, then you have to take people, and especially the planners, along with you. Surprising as it may seem, it is not that difficult, and in many ways, the more 'way out' the design, the easier it can become.

Deracinated architecture, by which I mean styles taken from one region and imposed upon another, will always put the planner's backs up. New, innovative and even fantastic designs have a very different effect. A planner's job can be fairly humdrum. Day after day they are dealing with houses that look just the same or which their own brief requires that they shoehorn into conformity. Along you come with something fresh

and exciting. Now, if you can enthuse the planning officers with this design, it will represent a high point in their life as well as yours and they might get very enthusiastic about it; almost to the point of wanting to see what it really looks like when it's built.

If you are not satisfied with a decision made about a planning application, you have the right of appeal. However, it is often better to make application again, in a way which you think is more likely to be approved. If this seems a possibility, visit the planning officer and ask his advice in a straightforward way. If you do not get anywhere, only then should you consider an appeal. I shall elaborate on appeals and the appeals procedure a little later on in this chapter but, before that, a few more items need to be considered.

Designated areas

Certain areas have a special planning status and these are collectively referred to as Designated Areas. They comprise The National Parks, Areas of Outstanding Natural Beauty, Conservation Areas and The Broads. In these areas, either different planning rules apply or rights are modified in some way and I have referred to these within the various sections.

Permitted Development Rights

I've mentioned these rights several times in the book and it's perhaps time to explain just what they are and what their scope is, for they are of the utmost importance to the self-builder, the renovator and the converter.

So what are these wonderful things? Permitted Development Rights give consent for all sorts of development of land, without the need to apply for planning permission in the normal way. They are granted as part of the Planning Acts known as the General Development Orders. They are not a certainty; they can be varied or negated completely by the wording or conditions in a planning consent. They are severely restricted in National Parks, Conservation Areas, Areas of Outstanding Natural Beauty and The Broads and they can be removed or varied by the local authority serving what is known as an Article 4 direction, of which more later.

Permitted Development Rights

If your Permitted Development Rights are not impaired, then you can:

- Build an extension to an original dwelling so long as:

1) It is no bigger than 15% of the volume of the original dwelling or 70 cubic metres, whichever is the greater, up to a maximum of 110 cubic metres.

2) If it is a terraced house or is in a Conservation Area, National Park, Area of Outstanding Natural Beauty or the Broads, the volume is no greater than 10% of the original dwelling or 50 cubic metres, whichever is the greater.

3) The extension does not protrude above the original ridgeline or is more than 4 metres high or closer to the boundary than 2 metres.

4) The result of the extension does not mean that more than half of the area of land around the original house will be built upon.

5) The extension does not protrude in front of the original building line, unless that would still mean that it was at least 20 metres from the highway.

- You can carry out development within the curtilage of the building, which means that you can alter walls or rearrange rooms and occupy the roof void, subject to the limits below. However, if you live in a specially designated area, such as a Conservation Area, a National Park, an Area of Outstanding Natural Beauty or the Broads, you will need to apply for express consent for any extension to the roof or any kind of addition which would materially alter the shape of the roof. This would include roof lights or a dormer. In other areas loft conversions are allowed, so long as they do not add more than 40 cubic metres to the roof of a terraced house or 50 cubic metres to any other kind of house and the work does not increase the overall height of the roof. No planning permission is required for roof lights on any roof slope and solar panels are allowed, so long as they do not project significantly above the roof slope.

- You can construct a garage for a dwelling where none exists so long as it does not go closer to the highway than the nearest point of the original house, unless there would be at least 20 metres between it and the highway, and as long as it does not exceed 3 metres in total height or 4 metres to the ridge if it's got a pitched roof.

The PDR categories that usually concern the self-builder are listed in the above box but, in any event, it's better to check with the local planning office regarding any extension or further development that you're planning, just to make sure that you are within your rights. Building Regulation approval may also be necessary and any alterations that you make to the dwelling must not contravene the regulations or affect the stability or structural integrity of the dwelling. Incidentally, the term, 'Original dwelling' is important. It means what it says and it harks back to 1st July 1948 when the Planning Acts first came into force. For any dwelling constructed since that date, it refers to the original dwelling that was given planning permission. Any extensions undertaken since either 1st July 1948 or the original consent have the effect of soaking up the permitted development rights. In some circumstances the volume of other buildings which belong to the house, such as a garage or shed, will count against the volume allowances, even if they were built at the same time as the house or before 1st July 1948. These are where an extension comes within

- You do not need planning permission to convert an integral or attached garage into living accommodation, unless, of course, this is prevented by a condition in the original planning permission.

- You may erect a porch for a house, so long as it's at least 2 metres from the highway, it does not exceed 3 metres in height and it is no larger than three square metres.

- There is no requirement to seek planning permission for the insertion of new windows or doors, even if the effect of carrying out this work is to create an over-looking situation that would otherwise be unacceptable. This is an anomaly in the planning laws that might be addressed at some future date. You cannot carry out this work if there is, once again, a condition on the original planning, or a clause or covenant in the deeds, preventing it and, of course, you cannot carry out works of this sort to Listed Buildings, or in the specially designated areas.

- You can construct walls to the boundaries so long as they do not exceed 2 metres in height or 1 metre adjoining the highway. Hedges are not covered by these restrictions and you can plant and grow these to whatever height you wish, at present, unless there are special conditions in your planning consent or a covenant in your deeds preventing it. Moves are, however, afoot, to place restrictions on 'unfriendly', and particularly, *leylandii* hedges.

- In most cases, you can also construct sheds, greenhouses, conservatories, accommodation for pets, summerhouses, ponds, swimming pools and tennis courts, so long as they do not cover more than half of the garden and so long as any above-ground structure does not exceed the height and size restrictions listed above.

- Satellite dishes have come in for special attention. In most areas, only one dish per house is permitted, it must not protrude above the highest part of the roof and, if fixed to a chimney, it must not exceed 450mm or stick up higher than the chimney itself. In some counties, the maximum size of any dish is 900mm whilst in most others it is 700mm. In Conservation Areas, Areas of Outstanding Natural Beauty, National Parks and The Broads, the dish must not be fixed to a chimney or positioned on a roof slope that fronts a road, public footpath or a waterway.

5 metres of another building belonging to your house and where a building has been added to the property which is more than 10 cubic metres in volume and which, again, is closer than 5 metres from the house.

If you live in a Conservation Area, a National Park, an Area of Outstanding Natural Beauty or the Broads, all additional buildings which are more than 10 cubic metres in volume, wherever they are on the plot in relation to the house, are treated as extensions of the house and reduce the allowance for further extensions. In all these cases, the volume of the buildings con-

cerned are deducted from the volume limits given for the extension of your house.

Normal home maintenance, including re-roofing a house, so long as the roof profile is not altered, and external painting and decoration, unless, of course, there is a planning condition prohibiting it, is allowed. In Conservation Areas, National Parks, Areas of Outstanding Natural Beauty and The Broads you will need planning permission to alter the external appearance of a building or to clad it in stone, plastic, tile or timber, etc. but in all other areas there is no such restriction.

Phew! You can see why I suggest that before you contemplate an extension you should consult the planning officer and get a definitive ruling on whether or not you need express planning consent. And you can see why I urge that if you are planning to build a home with an eye for future extension, you carefully think out the design and the strategy you employ. If you think that the size of the building, as you envisage it eventually becoming, will put the planners off your proposals and if you and your architect feel that Permitted Development Rights are unlikely to be curtailed, then you may decide that the best course of action is to go in for the smaller dwelling with an intention to extend at a later date. If, on the other hand, you feel that the planners won't be particularly bothered about the size of the dwelling as you propose it will eventually be, but your finances dictate that you can only carry out the development in stages, then perhaps it's better to apply for the whole thing and then build in stages as finance permits.

Whichever option you adopt there are some important things that you can do to make the eventual extension easier and less intrusive. Building in the lintels for any future door or window openings and spacing the brickwork or blockwork to create straight joints ready for cutting out can save a lot of time and trouble as long as you take care to maintain the structural integrity of the walling with ties or reinforcing mesh. It's open for you to consider whether, as long as you've got the necessary consents, you put the foundations in for any future extension, thus limiting the amount of disturbance you will experience when you eventually get around to it. Foundations needn't be left open, they can be covered over and grassed or even be brought up to oversite where they can exist as a patio or parking space, until their true role can be realised.

Where a roof is to be occupied it makes no sense at all to use fink trusses which can never be altered to create living space so, instead, think about either a purlin and spar roof or an attic trussed roof. If dormer windows or roof light are going to be used, then you might not be able to put them in to start with but you can still 'cripple' the roof timbers for their eventual construction and, whilst we're on about the roof, remember to get your tradesmen to consider your future plans when installing any pipework, cable runs or insulation.

The local authority does have the power to restrict or remove some of your Permitted Development Rights by the issuing of what is known as an Article 4 direction. This is normally issued pursuant to an area being made a Conservation area or where the character of an area of acknowledged importance would be threatened by unauthorised or haphazard development. An Article 4 direction remains in force for a period of six months whilst it is being confirmed, and once confirmed it is permanent. Those affected by such a proposal have the right of appeal and, in certain circumstances, compensation may be payable for the diminution in value of a property due to its imposition. Flats and maisonettes, whilst not falling within the usual self-builder's orbit, do not have Permitted Development Rights in the same way as a house does and it is necessary to apply for planning permission to build an extension or an outbuilding such as a garage, shed or greenhouse.

Re-submissions

If you do get a refusal on your planning application, you can make a re-submission, with no additional fee payable, within 12 months of the date of the refusal. This only applies to the first refusal and not to any subsequent or serial refusals and it must be the same applicant and relate to the same site. If you choose to withdraw an application, you get another free go but it must be made within 12 months of the date of the original application.

It is always possible, and sometimes advisable, to make a fresh application in tandem with an appeal. Sometimes the local authority will delay the determination of the second application until the outcome of the appeal is known. But in other circumstances, the presence of the appeal can be a spur for them to come to a reasonable compromise, in the hope that once you have got your planning permission, you will drop the appeal that, after all, takes up a great deal of their time and resources. If both applications are successful, then you can choose which one you operate.

Highways

A new access driveway entering a class 1, 2 or 3 clas-sified road will need planning consent. This is normally dealt with at the same time as your appli-cation for the proposed dwelling and there is a duty on the planning authority to consult with the relevant highways authority, although there is no requirement for them to accept their recommendations. With class 4 or 5 roads, no planning application is necessary; the approval and the consent of the highways authority is all that is needed. Trunk roads are a completely differ-ent kettle of fish in that they come under the auspices of the Highways Agency who may well devolve their powers to other agencies or companies.

Demolition

Demolition is classed as Permitted Development, so long as the building to be demolished is not greater than 50 square metres, measured externally. If you intend to knock down an old or substandard dwelling and replace it with a new one, then you might be tempted to demolish it during the planning process, in order to save time. *Be very careful!* Once the old building is gone, there is technically nothing to replace. If the site is in Green Belt or in any situation where the planners would prefer no house to be, they could simply refuse what would be effectively a new dwelling. If you find that difficult to believe, then I have to tell you that I have seen it happen on several occasions. Never take the old building down until all the consents have been received and I believe that, in almost all cases, it is better to include the demolition in the description and the wording of your application.

If the building is Listed, you will need to apply for Listed Building Consent if you want to demolish all or part of it. If it is in a Conservation Area you will need Conservation Area Consent to demolish a building with a volume exceeding 115 cubic metres, or any part of such a building. You will also need consent to demolish a wall, gate, fence or railing over 1 metre high adjoining a highway (including a footpath or bridlepath) and over 2 metres high else-where.

Agricultural consents

These usually limit the occupation of the dwelling to someone wholly, mainly or last engaged in agriculture, or the widow or widower thereof, and they do it by imposing this as a condition on the planning consent. In certain cases, for example with a rural industry, such as stables or a riding school, the same procedures and similar conditions are used to encumber a new dwelling that is justified by the enterprise. Whilst these conditions exist in perpetuity, many local authorities will want to strengthen their hand and require the landowners to enter into a legally binding agreement giving extra force to their requirements. They may even insist that the agreement goes further and either ties the dwelling to a farm as a whole, or further encumbers an existing farm dwelling, or dwellings, which, up to then, had been free of any planning conditions. In such cases the consent will be issued subject to the preparation and execution of the agreement and until such time as the documentation is signed and sealed, no work can commence on site.

I do warn the lay person against being inveigled into buying a plot with an encumbered consent. It is not at all unusual to see plots of land offered with a few acres attached and a planning consent that contains these occupation restrictions. Quite often the prospective buyer will be told that 'Everything will be all right, as long as you keep your head down and keep a few sheep or other stock on the land'. Nothing could be further from the truth. You will effectively be in illegal occupation of the dwelling for 10 years if you're lucky and nobody tells on you; you will find it nigh-on impossible to raise money or a mortgage on the property, and the value of the finished home will be severely diminished.

However, many self-builders are farmers who either wish to create a new home for themselves on the farm or need additional housing for farm workers. Agricultural consents cut across many of the norms in planning and if you see a new house being built in a rural position outside the village envelope the chances are that it is an agricultural consent that has allowed it there. Most development plans state that 'Development in the rural area shall be resisted unless it is of proven necessity for the proper maintenance or

running of agriculture'. So before any agricultural dwelling will even be considered by the local authority, it is necessary for the applicant to prove the necessity for the new dwelling and the ongoing viability of the farm unit that will support it. A special form will have to filled in to accompany the application, listing the acreage of the farm, its usage and stocking and the number of people employed. This form will also ask what other dwellings are already on the farm and whether any have been separated from the farm or sold off.

Some local authorities will evaluate the agricultural viability in house, some will ask for an Agricultural Appraisal from a recognised authority on farming such as an Agricultural Consultancy or a Planning Consultancy specialising in agricultural matters. In all cases, it is best to provide such a report and if, in commissioning that report, it does not come down completely in your favour, it is perhaps best to delay, and to carry out any recommendations made within it before actually making any planning application. On occasion, it may be best to consider making application for the temporary siting of a mobile home on the farm until such time as financial viability can be firmly established. Local authorities will often be more amenable to this course of action and after a few years when your presence is firmly established on the farm, when your development plans are sufficiently

Above: New dwellings in the countryside are usually only allowed if it can be proved that they are necessary for agricultural or for certain rural industries.

advanced and your finances are more secure, application can be made for a permanent new home. I write this, by the way, knowing of the groans of disappointment that will follow, but as the best advice in many a circumstance.

It is open to those for whom viability is not an issue and where the Agricultural Appraisal is full-blooded in its support for the new home to consider skipping the Outline stages of the planning process and going straight to a Full application. If no development is to be allowed in the rural area, unless it is of proven necessity for the proper running and maintenance of farming, and you have proved beyond reasonable doubt that your requirement *is* necessary for the proper running and maintenance of your business, why should you bother about the issue of principle? Surely it is already established? What you need to talk about is *what* goes there, not *whether* anything goes there.

Group self-building as Village Housing

In previous editions of this book an entire chapter was devoted to group self-build. Whilst some schemes are still up and running, to a large extent this form of self-building has fallen out of favour and is now confined to social housing schemes. It is, therefore, outside the scope of this book.

There is, however, one aspect of group self-build that is applicable and relevant to this book and this chapter. Rural housing is in crisis and homelessness is increasing faster in the country areas than it is in the towns and cities. According to surveys, 27% of rural households have annual incomes of less than £7,000. Average housing prices in the south have now well and truly breached the £100,000 barrier with even entry level housing at figures way beyond the capacity of local people. Even in the rented sector, average rents have soared beyond the reach of those in housing need, fuelled by incomers and company lettings. Local authorities are struggling to contain this problem but even they are hampered by the pincer movement of their areas being attractive to incomers and housing allocations being set well below their own forecasts of need.

Village Housing was conceived in response to the government directive PPG3 Annex 'A', 'Affordable Housing for Local Needs in Rural Areas'. It is a unique way of allowing local people who are in need of housing to come together to build their own affordable homes. Crucially, it relies on being able to buy and build on land that would otherwise not be available for development, at a fraction of the cost that would normally be paid. Annex 'A' makes it clear that provision of affordable housing should be regarded as additional to the provision in the development plan for general housing demand, that local plans should *not* seek to identify sites and that the policy is one of limited exceptions. It goes on to require that where sites are released for affordable housing as an exception to normal policies of restraint, it will be essential that there are adequate safeguards to reserve the housing for local needs, both initially and on subsequent changes of occupant.

How it works is that a group of local people come together to form a self-build group. They must be people who are local to the Parish with either strong family or work ties linking them to it. In addition, they must be in housing need. This is defined as: wishing to set up home for the first time; a need to

be near to dependant relatives; being in substandard or unsuitable accommodation; or having a requirement to live close to work. The land needs to be identified, but this does not have to be within the village envelope and it can indeed be within the Green Belt, as long as it is part of and adjoining the village and is, of course, suitable for development. Normally, a small premium is payable as an incentive to the vendor but, in general, land can be bought at agricultural rates or close to them.

Initial funding of up to 40% of the costs of the scheme can be obtained from the Housing Corporation in the form of a loan that will eventually be repaid by the members taking out mortgages on the completed houses. Normally, an initial contribution of up to £1,500 is made by each member and the group has to register itself as a Self build Housing Association under the Industrial and Provident Societies Act 1965 to the National Federation of Housing Associations, adopting its rules. What this means is that the group becomes a corporate body, able to open up bank accounts, purchase land, labour and materials and negotiate overdrafts to cover any shortfalls in cashflow.

What distinguishes these self-build groups from their forebears is firstly, that there is no requirement for all of the houses to be of the same type and specification. Secondly, there is a requirement for the self-builders to enter into a legally binding agreement whereby in the event of the house being re-sold, it will be to local people in housing need at a figure, normally 20% below the full market value.

The planner's attitudes and interpretation of the requirements of the document vary from authority to authority. There is nothing in the documentation to require that affordable houses should only be in the rental sector. All it says is that there are wide variations in house prices and earnings between different areas and that this means that there can be no single national measure of what constitutes low-cost housing. Yet this is how many local authorities have chosen to interpret it. Others accept that such schemes are appropriate as long as the means are in place to make sure they remain available in perpetuity to local people at affordable prices, and quite a few have accepted them with open arms.

Listed Building Consent

There are two grades for Listed Buildings: Grade I, covering buildings of major importance, and Grade II, which comprises most of the listings that have been identified in an area as being of historical or architectural value. Listed Building Consent is required for any alterations or extensions to listed buildings, including gates, walls and fences. It is also required for any significant works, internal or external, and for the erection of any structure in excess of 10 cubic metres. There are considerable restrictions on Permitted Development Rights as detailed above and, if you carry out works that are permitted under these rights, you will still need Listed Building Consent.

Any application for permission to alter or extend a Listed Building is made to the local authority but they cannot consider the application in isolation and they must consult with what are known as Statutory Consultees, such as: English Heritage, Historic Scotland, Cadw, The Council for British Archaeology, The Ancient Monuments Society, The Society for the Protection of Ancient Buildings, The Georgian Group, The Victorian Society.

The local authority has the power to issue Repair Notices on owners who are allowing Listed buildings to deteriorate but, if the owners are unable or unwilling to carry out the necessary works and the building is unoccupied, they may carry them out themselves and charge the costs to the owners. In extreme cases, they may even consider Compulsory Purchase. There are other powers such as Closing Orders, which can prevent anybody living in a house until repairs have been carried out, and Demolition Orders, which may also require Listed Building Consent. The time limits that preclude action against certain classes of unauthorised development do not apply to Listed Buildings and the normal enforcement procedures and powers, discussed in detail below, are available.

Local authorities can issue a Building Preservation Notice if they believe that a building of merit is being endangered or if work, such as demolition, that is detrimental to the character of the building, is proposed or imminent. The building does not have to be Listed but it does have to be worthy of listing and the effect of the notice is to give the authorities six months in which to take steps to have the building Listed. A Building Preservation Notice does have to receive ratification from the Secretary of State.

Appeals

An appeal is always made against the reasons for refusal and, although other arguments can be brought into play, it is the reasons for refusal which must be concentrated upon. You can appeal against the refusal of a planning application and you can also appeal against any conditions that are imposed within a consent. In addition, you have the right of appeal against the local authority's failure to determine an application.

If there are conditions on an approval by the local authority that you feel are unfair or unreasonable, and the local authority refuse to vary or remove them, then you can appeal against the imposition of those conditions. *Beware* – the Inspector will consider the whole of the application again; he can change other conditions that you had not previously objected to, and he can impose new conditions! He can even reverse the local authority's decision altogether, although if he is thinking of doing so, you will be informed and given an opportunity to withdraw the appeal and stick with the local authority's original approval and conditions.

An appeal against a local authority's failure to determine is all well and good on paper but the reality is that most authorities, faced with such an appeal, will move to determine the application prior to the appeal being actually conducted. There is nothing to prevent a new application being made at the same time as an appeal is being entered into.

Costs are normally borne by each party, whichever method of appeal is decided upon. It is open for either party, however, to request that the other party pay their costs either in part or in whole, and the Inspector will decide the merits of such an application. He will only award costs against a party if he feels that they have acted in an unreasonable, vexatious or frivolous manner.

Before lodging an appeal, think how you can avoid it. Seek out an early meeting with the planning officer to discuss whether or not there is another way forward. At this meeting it is most important that you are not aggressive, sarcastic, or waste his time by explaining how unfair you consider the planning laws to be. You should be seen to be a most reasonable person, and take an early opportunity to say that you know he cannot commit the council in any way in his discussions with you. This will make him much more likely to be helpful, either by suggesting a way in which you can frame a further application which he may be able to support, or by giving you a clear idea of exactly what the council thinks about the issue, which is going to be useful when you are considering appeal tactics.

If the planning officer will not discuss the matter in a helpful way, do not assume he is being deliberately unfriendly. It may be that your category of application is a very hot political issue locally, and that he feels obliged to deal with you in a very formal way. If this is the case, you can at least ask him to advise you about the planning history of the area and ask for a copy of the recommendation that he made to the council in respect of your application. Of course, you should have been aware of the planning history before you made your application, but you may find to your surprise that there have been a string of previous refusals on applications made by other people, and that this was a major factor in the council's decision.

Sometimes local politics come into play in such a way that the local authority does not want to be seen to be granting consent for certain types of development even though they know they cannot sustain that argument at a higher level. It will be denied, of course, but there are cases when it appears that there is almost a deliberate policy to refuse applications, in the knowledge that their refusal will be overturned at appeal. What happens here, of course, is that when the applicant is finally successful, the local authority can turn around and claim that it was none of their doing, thus keeping on the right side of their local critics.

The council may have considered the design, siting, materials or some other feature of the proposed dwelling was inappropriate. If this is the case, it is even more important that you establish an effective relationship with the planning officer to see if you can reach an agreement on features which he will find acceptable. Try every possible means of getting approval by making further applications. A planning appeal should be your last resort, both because it effectively closes the book if it is unsuccessful, and also because it will take between five and nine months to get a decision. This time lag is usually critical to those building on their own.

What are your chances of success? Well, although many appeals are disallowed, quite a few are successful and you've probably got a 50/50 chance. It depends on so many factors. The Inspector will consider any appeal on the basis of its planning merits and any personal circumstances are unlikely to influence his decision. An important factor in any consideration is whether or not the proposal fits into the local development plan. This development plan is made up of the approved structure plan and the local plan, if there is one, together with the old-style development plan, if it is still in force. You recall that I wrote about 'zoning' earlier and that I also mentioned 'village envelopes'. The Inspector will be concerned that your proposal does not conflict with these adopted plans, or any plan which is being prepared, and he will also be concerned to see that you have followed any published advice given out by your local planning authority. If you are appealing against a refusal for a scheme which conflicts with these policies or endeavours to create development in the Green Belt, then your chances of success are fairly slim.

If your site or property is within the village envelope or within an area zoned as residential, and you can put together a reasonable case, with details of precedents, then your chances are greatly increased. Tour the area and look out for similar buildings in similar situations which have obviously recently been built. Ask about them and find out the details from the local authority planning register, relating to their approval and how they came by it. If they were granted on appeal then get a copy of the appeal documents and see if there is any argument in them which you can use in your own appeal. In every case I have been involved in, the Inspector has always taken the trouble to visit these 'precedent' sites beforehand, and has referred to them both on site and in his eventual decision.

An appeal must be made within six months of the notice of refusal and the first thing you should do is to write to the appropriate office of the planning inspectorate and obtain firstly the necessary forms and secondly, and most importantly, a copy of their excellent booklet entitled *Making your planning appeal*. From this you will discover that there are two sorts of appeal process: the written procedure and the inquiry procedure, with the latter type being subdivided into the informal hearing and the full-blown public inquiry. The booklet explains the differences between them and gives excellent general advice accompanied by flow charts showing how each type of appeal progresses.

At this point you have to decide whether you are going to handle the appeal yourself, or whether you are going to retain someone to deal with it for you. Many people do handle their own appeals, and the procedures are not difficult. The inspectors are not influenced, one way or the other, by finding they are dealing with the appellant rather than with a professional. However, the professional may be much better than you at marshalling and presenting the facts, and it is the facts on which the appeal will be determined. You should be very sure of yourself before you decide to handle your own planning appeal.

Above: The guides to planning appeals give clear and concise advice on whether and how to appeal.

If you do not do so you will have to find someone to deal with it for you, and it is important that he or she has a great deal of relevant experience of handling appeals against refusals to allow individual houses to be built on individual sites in your local area, preferably with a track record of winning! It may be difficult to find the right person, but this is something that perhaps your solicitor or architect should be able to advise you about. You should take your papers to the recommended person and ask them to quote you a fixed fee for them to handle everything for you. Beware anyone who says they want a fee just to read your papers and appraise your situation. They are probably far too high powered for your job, and are probably more used to conducting planning appeals for supermarkets.

Any full description of how to conduct a written planning appeal is beyond the scope of this book, but the key points are as follows:

An appeal is against the reasons for refusal, and starts off with your written submission explaining why these reasons are inappropriate. You do not have to set out the reasons why your application should have been granted. You must deal only with the actual reasons for refusal listed on the refusal certificate, and explain that they are unreasonable. It will require a considerable mental discipline to restrict your submission to this simple formula, but anything else you write is irrelevant. If a professional is putting this document together for you, you should ask him to let you have a look at it before he sends it off. If you are dealing with the appeal yourself, then somehow you should try to look at papers relating to other appeals. The language used is not important, nor is the quality of the typing or handwriting, but it is essential to avoid any extravagant language. Do not describe the council's decision on your application as a 'diabolical liberty': the correct phrase is that it 'failed to take all the circumstances into account'!

A copy of your opening broadside is sent to the local planning authority, which then has four weeks in which to produce its own written reply. If it does not reply within four weeks, then the appeal carries on without the council having a say. It is quite amazing how often a local authority fails to respond and relies instead upon the terms of its original rejection.

Sometimes this is because of the pressure of work. Sometimes it is because personnel have changed, or are on holiday, and sometimes it is because the local authority have nothing more to add to their original reasons for refusal. You will receive a copy of the council's written statement, and you will have two weeks during which you can submit your replies.

Following this exchange of statements there is a long pause, and then after some months you will receive a letter from the planning inspector saying that they propose to visit the site on such and such a date. The site visit is important. The local authority will be represented, and of course you will go along yourself, accompanied by any professionals working for you. You will be told that at the visit the inspector will not allow either party to make any further submissions, nor will he discuss their written submissions with them. His purpose in visiting the site is simply to see the situation on the ground, and you and your agent, and the planning officer, are simply there to answer his questions. With some inspectors this will take the form of fairly perfunctory questions like, 'Is this the brick wall you will be removing in order to create the visibility splays?' But, with others, the conversation can widen out to a quite detailed discussion of each aspect of the appeal that they identify.

The important thing to realise is that the Inspector is in the driving seat. If you try to browbeat him and launch into a detailed speech about your application and why you feel that he should support you, you will probably be harming your case. Respond to his questions quietly and get your points across within your replies. Stay close enough to the group as they walk around to be able to hear the answers given by the representative from the local authority so that, at an opportune moment, you can counter anything that you feel to be untrue. Avoid any display of enmity between yourself and any other representative and at all costs avoid any direct argument with any other party. If any other representative gets angry, remember that your very calmness contrasted with their anger is probably doing your case a lot of good. Above all, let the Inspector make the running in much the same way as you would a judge in court and defer at all times to his conducting of the appeal.

Finally, about a month after the site visit, you will receive the Inspector's findings, and these are final. If you have won, the findings act as your planning consent. If you have lost you must realise that you have come to the end of the road with that application. Only if there is a major change in the local planning situation, or if a substantially different scheme is adopted, is any further planning application likely to be successful.

The whole of this process will probably take between five and nine months. You can do nothing to hurry it up. There is a provision in legislation for the inspector to give an Advanced Notice of Decision before he issues his official finding, but this is very, very unusual.

In most cases, I believe that the written appeal is the best course of action for an application concerning a single private dwelling house. Certainly the full public enquiry, with the need for expensive barristers, is beyond the scope of most individual self-builders. On the other hand, for those who feel that they would be better able to present their case verbally, rather than in writing, the informal hearing might be their preferred choice. Anyone is free to pitch up and pitch in at such a hearing, including both supporters and objectors.

Unauthorised development and enforcement

If something is built without planning permission, and the Planning Authority does not challenge what you have done, then, after a period of four years, the unauthorised development becomes immune from enforcement procedures. Thereafter, the owner of the property can call for a Certificate of Lawful Use. It is mandatory for the local authority to issue this certificate; it confers all of the powers of a proper planning consent and it may have conditions attached to it in just the same way. The four-year rule also applies to a change of use where a building is brought into residential use. But for all other changes of use, the breach must go unnoticed and unopposed by the Planning Authority for a period of 10 years, in order for a Certificate of Lawful Use to be demanded. Breaches of conditions on a planning approval also fall under this 10-year rule. There is no time limit so far as unauthorised works to Listed buildings are concerned.

The principal way in which a planning authority will act against any breach of planning in its area is by the issuing of an Enforcement Notice. This notice details the nature of the breach and takes effect a minimum of one month after it is served, after which, if the breach of planning is not rectified, legal action may be taken. An Enforcement Notice is not served lightly. The Enforcement Officer will attempt to negotiate a settlement and/or rectification of the planning breach and, in certain circumstances, they may suggest a Retrospective Planning Application to regularise the situation.

You can appeal against an Enforcement Notice within one month of it taking effect and the appeals process follows a similar pattern to other appeals. If the appeal is lost, the inspector will detail the time limit within which the breach must be rectified and failure to abide by this can lead to legal action. If someone is carrying out development that the planning authority feels will be extremely detrimental to a building, or is harmful to the locality, they can choose to issue a Stop Notice. This requires that any activity is ceased immediately and failure to abide by this can lead to legal action being taken. Local authorities are loathe to issue these, except in exceptional circumstances, as, if the Enforcement Notice is overturned at appeal, or if it is deemed to have been legally incorrect, they may be liable to pay compensation.

Scotland, Northern Ireland and the Republic of Ireland (Eire)

Just as with the legal systems, planning laws in Scotland, Northern Ireland and indeed in the Republic of Ireland (Eire), are branches from the same tree and, in many respects, the procedures are very similar to those in England and Wales. Scotland is perhaps the most similar, with very little substantive difference in just how you go about the application and only a few minor changes in terminology.

In Northern Ireland, the local authorities have a purely consultative role in the planning process and application is made to the Planning Service of the Department of the Environment, who then have a duty to consult with them. The Planning Service issues Planning Policy Statements instead of Planning Policy Guidelines (PPG's) and any appeals are made to an Appeals Commission.

In the Republic of Ireland (Eire), a planning application is made to the local authority in very much the same way as it is in England and Wales. Importantly, you do have to have either a legal interest in the land, or the consent of the owners to make the application. You are also required to advertise your intentions in the local press and display a site notice. It is usual to apply for a Permission, which is the same as a Full planning permission in England and Wales but you can also apply for an Outline permission, which has to be followed by an Approval. This Approval basically fulfils the same role as an Approval of Reserved Matters in the United Kingdom, but with two very important differences.

A consent lasts for five years and the lifetime of the consent to build is determined by the Outline permission. You therefore need to apply for the Approval well in advance of its expiry in order to enable you to *complete* the works within its lifetime and this *includes* any necessary appeal to An Bord Pleanala (the Appeals body). Additionally, there is not the strict division between Planning and Building Regulations that exists in the United Kingdom. Applications for the detailed stages of a planning application must conform to the Building Regulations and the enquiries that the planners make in connection with any proposal include those relating to the structure and integrity of the building work. The planning permission will include a clause that all work must conform to the regulations.

A decision to grant permission, with or without conditions, is notified to the applicant and anyone else who has expressed an interest in the application. This is in the form of a Notice of Intention to Grant Planning Permission. For a period of one month following this notice, the applicant *or anyone else* may appeal to An Bord Pleanala. If no appeal is made, then one month after the original notice, the consent becomes operable and the Grant of Permission is made. Where the planning authority decide to refuse an application, the applicant has one month to appeal and the appeals body usually aims to decide appeals within four months.

9. BUILDING REGULATIONS, WORKING DRAWINGS, SPECIFICATIONS AND CONTRACTS

Planning permission is subjective and governs whether you build a new home at all and, if so, what it will look like. Building Regulations Consent, on the other hand, is objective and confines itself to the structural aspects of the build by reference to the regulations themselves. An application for approval under the Building Regulations either conforms to those regulations and is approved, or fails to conform to them and is rejected, unless, in very peculiar circumstances, such as with a thatched roof, a relaxation can be negotiated.

Building Regulations

The Building Regulations cover the structural and safety aspects of any construction and draw together a mass of other health and environmental issues. They are set out in denominated parts that deal with each aspect of building and it would not make sense for this book to examine those parts in great detail or discuss anything other than generalities. The partial exceptions to that, of course, are the references to Parts 'L' and 'M' in Chapter 5. The regulations are changed from time to time and it is the job of architects, designers and other professionals working within the industry to keep themselves up to date with those changes and to incorporate their requirements within any plans that they prepare or process. It is also their job, by inference, to make themselves as aware as possible of any impending changes to the legislation and these are usually warned of in advance by way of published discussion papers and consultations.

The Building Regulations are usually administered by the Building Control department of the local authority who have a statutory obligation to enforce them and oversee their functions within their boundaries. However, the government has also devolved the authority to inspect and certify compliance under the Building Regulations to other bodies, such as the NHBC, and in addition it is open for architects with the appropriate professional indemnity insurance to register to carry out this work. I have discussed the possible role of the NHBC in Chapter 1, so in this chapter I will confine most of my comments to the service and administration of the regulations by the local authority.

In most local authorities the Planning department and the Building Control department are situated in close proximity to each other and are usually lumped together as Technical Services. Make no mistake though, these are separate departments operating and receiving their powers through and from completely separate Acts of Parliament. Although they can, and usually do, co-operate with each other, there is no certainty of this and it is possible to fall between conflicting legislation and interpretations. Planning says you *may* build something – it does not say that you *can* build something. If you get express planning permission for something or it is implied that you have planning consent for, say, Permitted Development, then it does not absolve you from having to seek Building Regulations' approval for that development, either expressly or, by implication, due to exemption.

In like manner, if one achieves Building Regulations consent for a structure, it does not mean that you can build it without planning permission, again, either expressly or implied. A porch, for example, may be exempt from the Building Regulations in some circumstances and, in many locations, its construction could take place under the Permitted Development rights laid down by the planning laws. In a Conservation area those Permitted Development rights could be curtailed or removed and the fact that the porch could be built under a Building Regulations exemption would do nothing to change that situation. Building Regulations approval is required if you intend to carry out any of the following works:

- Erecting a new building or extending an existing building (unless it is covered by the list of exemptions below and later)

- Making structural alterations to a building, including underpinning

- In certain cases, changing its use

- Providing, extending or altering drainage facilities

- Installing a heat-producing appliance (with the exception of gas appliances installed by persons approved under the Gas Safety regulations)

- Installing cavity insulation

- Installing an unvented hot water storage system.

You do not need Building Regulations approval to:

- Install or replace electric wiring

- Replace a roof covering, as long as the same roof covering is used in the repair

- Install new sanitaryware, as long as it doesn't involve new drainage or plumbing arrangements

- Carry out repairs as long as they are of a minor nature and replace like for like.

It's as well to contact the Building Control department if you're in any doubt about whether you need to apply for Building Regulations approval.

In addition to the exclusions listed above there are common types of building work that are exempt from the regulations:

- The erection of a detached single storey building with a floor area of less than 30 square metres, as long as it does not contain any sleeping accommodation; no part of it is less than one metre from any boundary; and it is constructed of non combustible material

- The erection of any detached building not exceeding 15 square metres, as long as there is no sleeping accommodation

- The extension of a building by a ground-floor extension of a) a conservatory, porch, covered yard or covered way, or b) a carport open on at least two sides, as long as, in any of those cases, the floor area of the extension does not exceed 30 square metres. In the case of a conservatory or a wholly or partially glazed porch, the glazing has to satisfy the requirements of those parts of the Building Regulations dealing with glazing materials and protection.

At the risk of being repetitive, I must stress that you may still need planning permission for any of these works and that, if there is any doubt, you should consult the planning department of your local authority.

England and Wales

In England and Wales a Building Regulations application has to be accompanied by the necessary fees for the approval stages, after which the local authority has five weeks to process and determine the application. In practice, many applications cannot be determined within the statutory period and it has become almost commonplace for applications to be rejected several times, with each fresh, and happily free, application dealing with different points raised. Such a system, which often seems almost incredible to the lay person, would not have evolved were it not for two important points. Firstly, the legislation is worded so that it is necessary to have *made* an application for Building Regulations Approval or issued a Building Notice prior to commencement of works and secondly, the fees for the necessary inspection stages are separated and, with a Full Plans application, payable *after* the issuing of an approval.

This means that, as long as 48 hours notice in writing is given of your intention to start work on a site following an application for Building Regulations approval or the issuing of a Building Notice, then there is nothing to stop you doing so. The building does, however, still have to be inspected and approved as it proceeds and the Building Inspectors will, therefore, come along and inspect at the relevant stages. If they approve of the work, you may then carry on to the next stage in the normal way. If they do not

Right: The simplicity of the design of the Potton 'Rectory' house will also reflect in the ease of construction and conformity to the regulations.

Below: Houses with more complicated roof structures may well have to prove them by means of engineer's calcul-ations and/or need different insulation solutions.

Building Regulations approval. The essential rule is that nothing is built that fails to conform to the regulations and, if therefore, the inspector feels that the work is contrary to the regulations then, whether or not you have a formal approval, he will stop you and he has legally enforceable powers to do so. I don't think it's bandied about too much but my guess is, from personal experience, that maybe as many as 60% of new self-build dwellings commence work without having a formal Building Regulations approval.

approve or cannot sanction what you are doing, then you have to stop until either the approval is granted, or the necessary information is received that will allow them to agree to your continuing work.

Effectively, that means that, although you will be advised that by working prior to the formal approval of the plans, you are proceeding at risk, as long as you do not go beyond that which the building inspector has agreed and approved on site, you aren't really in a different position from the chap who already has

Scotland, Northern Ireland and Eire

In Scotland, where building control is referred to as The Building Warrant, the application has to be accompanied by a fee that covers both the application and the subsequent inspections. In Northern Ireland the procedures, fee structures and divisions are more or less the same as in England and Wales, except that the NHBC are not authorised to administer the regulations which must be carried out by the local authority. In the Republic of Ireland (Eire), the detailed plans submitted to the planning authorities have to conform to the Building Regulations and there is not the strict division between planning and Building Regulations that exists in the United Kingdom.

Applying for Building Regulations approval

In England and Wales, where the application and inspection fees are separated, you have to decide whether it's a good idea to make the Building Regulations application at the same time as the planning application. Obviously there is merit in the idea of having both approvals on the table as you commence work on site but some possible financial penalties are involved. With a planning application it is possible for plans to be radically or even completely altered, yet still remain under the auspices of the original application. No such sanction is given with a Building Regulations application. If the design changes, then a completely fresh Building Regulations application will have to be made, attracting an equally fresh fee. As if the fee to the local authority weren't enough, you could also find yourself having to spend considerable monies on the preparation of new detailed plans with any expensive calculations or engineer's details having to be repeated. You can see, therefore, that care needs to be taken and that a Building Regulations application should only be made when it is pretty certain that you know what you are going to be building.

Two alternative procedures are available to obtain Building Regulations approval: Deposit of Full Plans or The Building Notice.

Dealing with the second one first, if you choose this option then no detailed plans are generally required, as a far greater emphasis is placed on site inspection and supervision, although further details and/or plans may be requested during the build. The fee is the combined total of the relevant application and commencement fees, so there is no saving to be made by this method as far as local authority fees go. This procedure is really only applicable to works of a completely straightforward nature where the party carrying out the works is totally conversant with the requirements of the regulations as, without plans, there is no detailed check on the proposal before the work is carried out, and therefore, no official decision notice is issued.

The advantage is that there can be a saving in time and costs due to not having to prepare and submit detailed plans. The disadvantages are that, firstly, there is no approved plan to work to and, whilst the Inspector will try to anticipate problems, there can be delays and/or costly remedial works if any of the work fails to comply with the regulations. Secondly, building estimates may be inaccurate without the benefit of detailed plans to work to. In all the years I have been in the industry, I have no experience of any self-builder using this procedure. Whilst many self-builders proceed with the construction of their new homes without a formal Building Regulations approval having been issued, to do so without the benefit of detailed plans and full constructional details would be singularly inadvisable.

A Full Plans application has to be accompanied by plans showing the full constructional details of the proposed work. Whether or not you managed to do the plans yourself for the planning application, I earnestly believe that these plans need to be prepared by a professional. If that's you, then fine. If not, then you really need to examine your motives, swallow your 'go-it-alone' pride and engage a professional for this bit.

A FULL PLANS APPLICATION SHOULD INCLUDE:

1) The relevant application forms fully completed and the appropriate fee.
2) Detailed drawings at 1:50 scale for floor plans, 1:100 for elevations and 1:500 for site plans. These should include floor plans, typical and particular sections, elevations and site details and boundaries.
3) A full written specification which can either be noted on the plans or provided separately and then cross-referenced.

Right and overleaf: Working & construction drawings for a house. (Design & Materials Ltd)

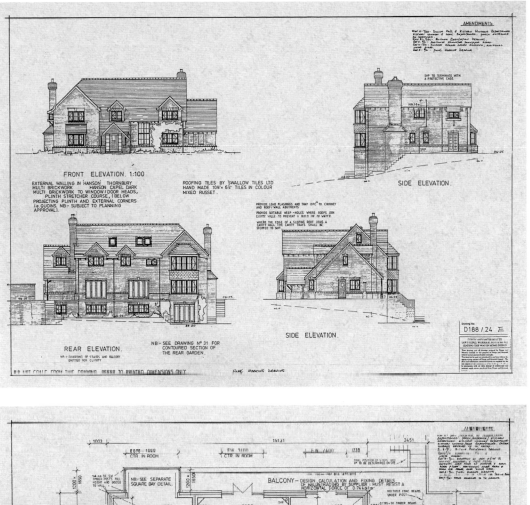

FRONT ELEVATION. 1:100

EXTERNAL WALLING IN HANSON THORNBURY MULTI BRICKWORK — HANSON CAPEL DARK MULTI BRICKWORK TO WINDOW / DOOR HEADS, PLINTH STRETCHER COURSE, I BELOW PROJECTING PLINTH AND EXTERNAL CORNERS i.e. QUOINS. NB - SUBJECT TO PLANNING APPROVAL).

ROOFING TILES BY SWALLOW TILES LTD HAND MADE 10⅝" × 6½" TILES IN COLOUR MIXED RUSSET.

SIDE ELEVATION.

REAR ELEVATION.

NB - SEE DRAWING Nº 31 FOR CONTOURED SECTION OF THE REAR GARDEN.

SIDE ELEVATION.

DO NOT SCALE FROM THIS DRAWING. REFER TO PRINTED DIMENSIONS ONLY.

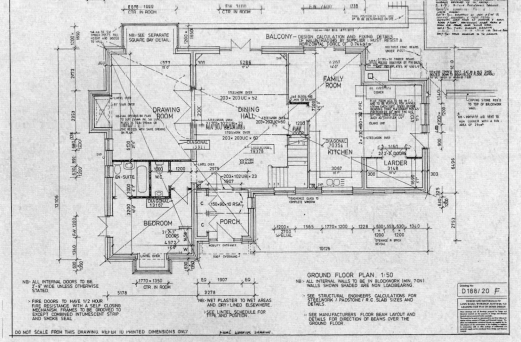

GROUND FLOOR PLAN. 1:50

NB - ALL INTERNAL WALLS TO BE IN BLOCKWORK (MIN. 7ON) WALLS SHOWN SHADED ARE NON LOADBEARING.

- SEE STRUCTURAL ENGINEERS CALCULATIONS FOR STEELWORK / PADSTONE / R.C. SLAB SIZES AND DETAILS

- SEE MANUFACTURERS FLOOR BEAM LAYOUT AND DETAILS FOR DIRECTION OF BEAMS OVER THE GROUND FLOOR.

NB - ALL INTERNAL DOORS TO BE 2'-9" WIDE UNLESS OTHERWISE STATED.

- FIRE DOORS TO HAVE 1/2 HOUR FIRE RESISTANCE WITH A SELF CLOSING MECHANISM. FRAMES TO BE GROOVED TO EXCEPT COMBINED INTUMESCENT STRIP AND SMOKE SEAL.

NB - WET PLASTER TO WET AREAS AND DRY-LINED ELSEWHERE.

- SEE LINTEL SCHEDULE FOR TYPE AND POSITION.

DO NOT SCALE FROM THIS DRAWING. REFER TO PRINTED DIMENSIONS ONLY.

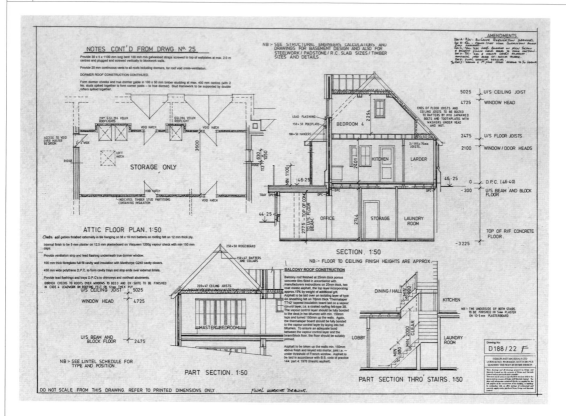

NOTES CONT'D FROM DRWG № 25

Provide 30 x 5 x 1100 mm long bent 100 mm mis galvanised straps screwed to top of wallplates at max. 2.0 m centres and plugged and screwed vertically to blockwork walls.

Provide 25 mm continuous vents to all roofs including dormers, for roof void cross-ventilation.

DORMER ROOF CONSTRUCTION CONTINUED.

Form dormer cheeks and true dormer gable in 100 x 50 mm timber studding at max. 400 mm centres (with 2 No. studs spiked together to form corner posts - to true dormer). Stud framework to be supported by double rafters spiked together.

ATTIC FLOOR PLAN. 1:50

STORAGE ONLY

Cheeks and gables finished externally in tile hanging on 38 x 19 mm battens on roofing felt on 12 mm thick ply.

Internal finish to be 5 mm plaster on 12.5 mm plasterboard on Visqueen 1200g vapour check with min 150 mm caps.

Provide ventilation strip and lead flashing underneath true dormer window.

100 mm thick fibreglass full fill cavity wall insulation with Manthorpe G240 cavity closers.

450 mm wide polythene D.P.C. to form cavity trays and stop ends over external lintels.

Provide lead flashings and trays D.P.C's to chimneys and roof/wall abutments.

DORMER CHEEKS TO ROOFS, OVER WINDOWS TO BED 3 AND EN-SUITE TO BE FINISHED IN CODE 4 LEADWORK ON ROOFING FELT ON 12mm THICK PLY

MASTER BEDROOM

NB:- SEE LINTEL SCHEDULE FOR TYPE AND POSITION.

PART SECTION. 1:50

NB:- SEE STRUCTURAL ENGINEER'S CALCULATIONS AND DRAWINGS FOR BASEMENT DESIGN AND ALSO FOR STEELWORK / PADSTONE / R.C. SLAB SIZES / TIMBER SIZES AND DETAILS.

BEDROOM 4

KITCHEN

LARDER

OFFICE

STORAGE

LAUNDRY ROOM

SECTION. 1:50

NB:- FLOOR TO CEILING FINISH HEIGHTS ARE APPROX

BALCONY ROOF CONSTRUCTION

Balcony roof finished at 25mm thick porous concrete tiles fixed in accordance with manufacturers instructions on 20mm thick, two coat mastic asphalt, the top layer incorporating approx.15% by weight of additional grit. Asphalt to be laid over an isolating layer of type 4A sheathing felt on 70mm thick 'Thermataper T142' tapered insulation board laid on a vapour control layer, i.e. a coated roofing felt-type 3B. The vapour control layer should be fully bonded to the deck in hot bitumen with min. 150mm laps and turned 150mm up the walls. Again, the thermataper board should be fully bonded to the vapour control layer by laying into hot bitumen. To ensure an adequate bond between the vapour control layer and the beam/block floor, the floor should be suitably primed.

Asphalt to be taken up the walls min. 150mm above finish and keyed into mortar joint i.e. under threshold of French window. Asphalt to be laid in accordance with B.S. code of practice 144: part 4: 1970 (mastic asphalt).

DINING / HALL

KITCHEN

LOBBY

LAUNDRY ROOM

NB:- THE UNDERSIDE OF BOTH STAIRS TO BE FINISHED IN 5 mm PLASTER ON 12·5 mm PLASTERBOARD

PART SECTION THRO' STAIRS 1:50

DO NOT SCALE FROM THIS DRAWING. REFER TO PRINTED DIMENSIONS ONLY.

FINAL WORKING DRAWING.

Drawing No:
D188 / 22 F

DESIGN AND MATERIALS LTD
LAWN ROAD, WORKSOP, NOTTS S81 9LB
LEADING THE WAY IN HOME DESIGN

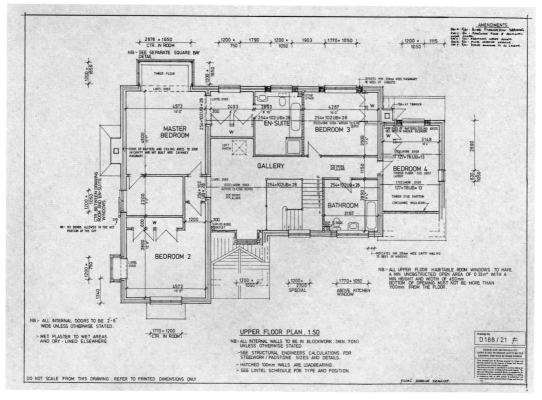

MASTER BEDROOM

NB:- SEE SEPARATE SQUARE BAY DETAIL

TIMBER FLOOR

LINTEL OVER

ENDS OF RAFTERS AND CEILING JOISTS TO STOP IN CAVITY AND NOT BUILT INTO CHIMNEY MASONRY.

EN-SUITE

STUB STACK

DENOTES MIN 328mm WIDE MASONRY TO SIDES OF GABLES

GALLERY

LOFT HATCH

SMOKE ALARM

BEDROOM 3

FOR ENDS OF RAFTERS/CEILING JOISTS SEE NOTE IN MASTER BEDROOM

BEDROOM 4
TIMBER FLOOR - SEE JOIST LAYOUT

STEELWORK OVER 127 × 76 UB × 13

TIMBER STUD PARTITION CONTAINING INSULATION

SMOKE ALARM

STEELWORK OVER WITHIN CEILING DEPTH

BATHROOM

SVP TO RIDGE OUTLET

NB:- NO BENDS ALLOWED IN THE WET PORTION OF THE SVP.

BEDROOM 2

LINTEL OVER

INDICATES MIN 328mm WIDE CAVITY WALLING TO SIDES OF WINDOWS

NB:- ALL UPPER FLOOR HABITABLE ROOM WINDOWS TO HAVE A MIN. UNOBSTRUCTED OPEN AREA OF 0.33m² WITH A MIN HEIGHT AND WIDTH OF 450mm BOTTOM OF OPENING MUST NOT BE MORE THAN 1100mm FROM THE FLOOR.

NB:- ALL INTERNAL DOORS TO BE 2'-6" WIDE UNLESS OTHERWISE STATED.

:- WET PLASTER TO WET AREAS AND DRY-LINED ELSEWHERE.

SPECIAL

ABOVE KITCHEN WINDOW

UPPER FLOOR PLAN. 1:50

NB:- ALL INTERNAL WALLS TO BE IN BLOCKWORK (MIN. 7ON) UNLESS OTHERWISE STATED.

:- SEE STRUCTURAL ENGINEERS CALCULATIONS FOR STEELWORK / PADSTONE SIZES AND DETAILS.

:- HATCHED 100mm WALLS ARE LOADBEARING

:- SEE LINTEL SCHEDULE FOR TYPE AND POSITION.

DO NOT SCALE FROM THIS DRAWING. REFER TO PRINTED DIMENSIONS ONLY.

FINAL WORKING DRAWING.

Drawing No:
D188 / 21 F

DESIGN AND MATERIALS LTD
LAWN ROAD, WORKSOP, NOTTS S81 9LB
LEADING THE WAY IN HOME DESIGN

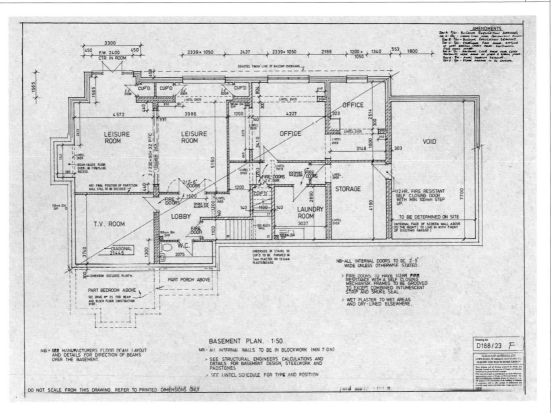

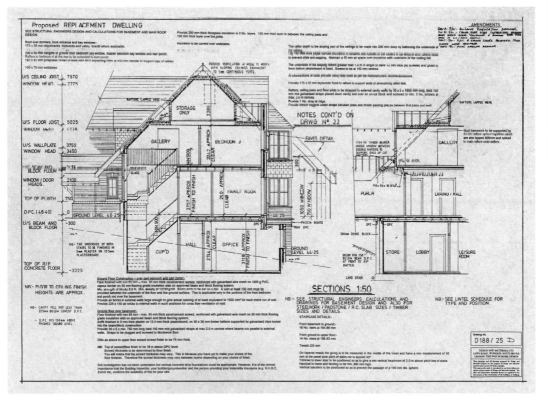

The advantages of the Full Plans application procedures are that you will then be working to set plans along set guidelines and in strict accordance, at all times, with the regulations. Many of the lenders require that a Building Regulations application is made and some, but not all, will require a formal approval before commencement of work. The disadvantage is that time needs to be allowed for the preparation of the plans, prior to application and commencement of work. In the end, both that and the cost of the preparation of the plans are, perhaps, a constant factor and, as I've said, the thought of a self-builder trying to build their own home without the benefit of detailed plans gives me the jiggers.

Amendments

When the plans are received by the Building Control department they are checked out thoroughly. If the proposals are straightforward and the work shown on the plans complies in all respects with the regulations, then an approval will be issued as soon as possible and certainly within the five-week deadline. If, for any reason, your proposals do not satisfy the regulations or there are some unclear areas or points, then the inspector will write to you inviting you to amend the plans in order to bring about compliance.

Additional details and calculations may be required and in some cases it is possible for an approval to be issued conditional upon the subsequent receipt of this information. If you're building in timber frame then the details and calculations for the timber frame itself may not actually be prepared and available until the frame is being manufactured. In these cases, as with roof trusses and steel purlins, the consent will be conditional and work may be allowed to continue up to and until these elements are reached. On the other hand, if the inspector has reason to suspect that there are conditions in the ground that will require a site/soil investigation and the design of special foundations, he will not allow work to commence until all of the details have been formulated and approved.

The detailed plans will also have to be sent to your warranty company and in most cases if there is any suspicion of bad ground or a special foundation situation, they will require exactly the same information as the Building Inspector wants and may require at least three weeks' notice of any intention to start work in those circumstances. If the NHBC is carrying out the role of inspecting and approving under the Building Regulations or if they are merely acting as your warranty company, and you are building in timber frame, they will also require an HB353B certificate to be supplied by the frame manufacturer or designer.

The Building Control department, in much the same way as the planning departments, have a statutory duty to consult with certain agencies and departments. If a proposal for a new building involves drainage and the discharge of effluent either into the subsoil or to a watercourse, then they have to consult with the Environment Agency. If the Environment Agency flag up a problem then the Building Control department will, in effect, act as their agent in enforcing their requirements and in making sure that your application is amended to take their recommendations into account. The Building Control department will also consult other agencies and departments, including and especially those dealing with fire, highways and public health.

If all of these questions, amendments and additional information cannot be answered or provided within the five-week period following the application, then a rejection notice will be issued. If you're already building at this time, then a new application will have to be made as soon as possible but if you haven't started building then you cannot do so until, and unless, either a new application is submitted or a Building Notice is issued and the requisite 48 hours' notice is given. The principle of serial applications and rejections is, for many local authorities, an established fact and a normal way of proceeding. Others state that they do not regard rejection as a particularly productive exercise and make strenuous efforts to approve Full Plans applications as quickly as possible. They are helped in that endeavour if the relevant information is provided at the application stage and if any anticipated requirements for calculations, soil and site investigations and foundation design details are available before, rather than after or approaching, their five-week deadlines. Once again attendance at the school of forward planning will pay off.

Inspections

If a formal approval has been issued it will usually be accompanied by a set of cards, each of which covers a particular stage in the construction of your new home. Even if you don't have these cards or if you are proceeding with the construction prior to the issuing of a formal approval or under a Building Notice, you are required to notify the inspector at these stages. Obviously, for things like loft conversions, the stages will be different but in general for new build they are:

- Excavations for foundations
- Foundation concrete
- Oversite
- Damp-proof course
- Foul-water drains
- Surface-water drains
- Occupation prior to completion
- Completion

You will hear stories about not having to wait for the inspector beyond a certain period and of carrying on beyond these stages if the inspector fails to turn up. Ignore them please. The stages are carefully worked out so that no important work is irrevocably covered up before it has been adequately inspected and approved. If the Building Inspector feels that you have covered up something that is wrong or that you have carried out work that is in defiance of the regulations, he has the power to order their exposure and you will bear the cost.

Apart from the obvious example of foundations and below-ground work, there is one other aspect of routine inspection that is taken very seriously and that is drains. These need to be inspected *before* they are covered up and they then need to be tested, usually involving pressure hoses and gauges. Now, you may feel that just leaving various sections or connections open will suffice, but you would be wrong and you will find that the inspector will want to see everything and that he will want to satisfy himself, in particular, that they are properly surrounded in pea gravel. In the end he has the legal right of enforcement and he has the right to issue what is known as a Stop Notice that will bring your entire site to a grinding halt until you have either rectified the incorrect work or satisfied him that the work is in order.

All of this serves to illustrate a radical difference between Planning Consent and Building Regulations approval and one that often confuses lay people. With planning permission, you have consent to build exactly what is shown on the plans and although the authorities do have some discretionary powers that I've already outlined, essentially you have consent to build *only* that which is on the approved drawings and referred to in the consent. With Building Regulations, the plans are approved as being in accordance with the regulations but, then, after the consent is issued, the inspector has the power to vary the construction. For example, if your plans show a one-metre strip foundation and your Building Regulations approval was granted on that premise but, when it comes to digging the foundations, the ground is found to be unsuitable, then the inspector can, and will, require you to change tack. He may well require you to have a soil investigation carried out or a special foundation designed by an engineer and he will require that you stop work until everything is agreed. It is no good pointing to your plans and saying that they were approved with the one-metre strip foundations. The inspector's job in assessing your application was to make sure that what was *drawn* conformed to the regulations as far as was foreseeable. On the other hand, when inspecting your building works, the inspector's job is to make sure that what is *built* conforms to the regulations. If he feels that, due to conditions experienced or evidenced on site, changes need to be made, then he has the power to require those changes.

It's at this point that self-builders can become a trifle upset at this official who's insisting on changes, delaying the job and costing them a great deal more money. In some cases the inspector can almost be seen as being in cahoots with the warranty inspector, with them both conspiring to push your project off budget. Nothing is further from the truth. If any of these officials or inspectors feel that it's necessary for changes to be made, then they are doing so in the interests of the stability and integrity of your new home and for no other reason. Their reasons and their objectives, therefore, coincide quite nicely with yours

Above: Careful choice of materials, textures and shapes give the front entrance area of this Kent house a welcoming and inviting ambience. (Scandia-Hus Ltd)

Right: A conservatory should, as in this lovely house, compliment the overall design. (Potton Ltd)

and, if you've taken note of the preceding chapters, then it's quite probable that you've already budgeted for the eventuality or allowed for its possibility within your contingency fund.

Most medieval cathedrals were built with the aid of fewer drawings than are now considered necessary for the construction of a public lavatory. Nevertheless, many of them suffered failures of some sort and in some cases these were catastrophic. In others the flying buttresses that we now admire so much, were added at a later date, or during the construction when it became apparent that the structure was about to fail. You can't go on like that and today's regulations are designed to ensure that, as far as possible, all that can be known, assessed or calculated to ensure the stability and structural integrity of your new home, is known and appreciated *before* you start work.

A properly prepared set of drawings goes a long way to making sure that there are as few queries as possible during the construction process. In some cases they are the same as for the Building Regulations application. In others they are elaborate sets of drawings, illustrating aspects of the build as wide-ranging as the foundation design through to the intricate detailing on the corbelling. Either way these are important documents and their treatment on site does not always reflect that importance. Rolled up in a back pocket or stuffed into a bucket of tools at best and left out in the rain at worst, is it any wonder it details become smudged or obliterated and things get built wrongly? Properly pinned up in the site hut or better still laminated, they will remain in pristine condition and fulfil their purpose for the whole of the build.

Specifications

Construction drawings are also used by sub-contractors to design their services. An electrician will require a drawing, which he will mark up with the wiring layout, and the plumbing and heating engineer will want drawings for the same purpose. Others will be required when the kitchen is being planned. Central heating drawings are often provided free of charge by the fuel advisory agencies, and the kitchen layouts can be obtained from various bodies; but they all start with a print of the actual construction drawing.

All setting out of construction work should be done in the units used for the design, and the converted dimensions should be used with considerable caution as they are invariably 'rounded off' and, if added together, will give rise to significant errors. Remember that room sizes on construction drawings are masonry sizes and that the finished dimensions from plaster surface to plaster surface will be about 25mm smaller. Carpet sizes will be a further 25mm smaller, allowing for the thickness of the skirting on two walls.

Revisions to drawings are normally made by altering the master drawing. When this is done the fact that the drawing has been altered should always be noted on it, and the date added. Prints of the outdated drawings should be carefully collected and destroyed to avoid confusion.

Drawings for complex and high-value projects are normally accompanied by a specification (written by an architect), and a bill of quantities (compiled by a quantity surveyor). Between them these highly technical documents describe and define every detail of the building. Many individual self-build projects confine the specification to the notations on the drawing, with or without a separate list. A full bill of quantities is sometimes relevant but in many cases is not necessary, as builders quoting will often take off their own quantities. If you are using a package-deal company or a timber-frame manufacturer or supplier, then their specification will form part and parcel of the specification for your proposed new home.

Contracts

Whenever you arrange for someone to do some building work for you, you make a contract with them. In it they undertake to do the job, and you undertake to pay them. You cannot escape it. Even if you simply say, 'Get this done, Ted, and I will see you right', you have established a contract. However, you will want to make sure that the arrangements that you make to build a new home are a good deal more specific than that!

Now there are many textbooks on the law of contract, and they are both heavy going and omit to mention that very few people arranging to build their own homes establish contracts in the way that the textbooks advise, or indeed in the way that their solicitors would advise.

Above: How a contract finishes often depends on how it starts. These contracts are simple to understand and administer.

A contract is a way of expressing an arrangement, which both parties enter into without reservations, believing that they know exactly how everything is going to happen. When they make the contract, whether verbally or in writing, they regard it simply as a convenient way of recording what they have agreed. If all goes well, everything is fine. If there are unforeseen circumstances or problems, they turn to the contract to see where they stand in the matter. If they should fall out, it is the contract that determines their legal position. The contract should thus define exactly what the parties have agreed and, if there are problems, how they are to be resolved.

The best way of establishing a formal contract that deals with all of this involves solicitors, quantity surveyors, and documents that are dozens of pages long. If you ask a solicitor what is the best way to arrange a contract or contracts to build a new house, he must recommend these involved procedures. However, such contracts will scare off most small builders and using them automatically puts you in a very special league – usually referred to as extremely expensive. For this reason only a very few of those building for themselves use them. The choice is yours. This book cannot advise you to ignore the best legal advice, but it does describe how most people arrange these affairs.

There are two very different ways of arranging for a builder to build a house for you – using an architect to establish and supervise the contract, or arranging and supervising everything yourself. If you use an architect, he will invite tenders from builders, advise you which one to accept and will draw up a suitable formal contract which he will supervise on your behalf. This is the Rolls-Royce way of doing things. The architect will charge fees of around 10% of the value of the contract, and although he or she will be concerned that you get the best value for money, he does tend to operate at the top end of the market.

If you are making a contract with a builder it is important that you do not simply accept any arrangements that he suggests, and that you settle things in a way that you are happy about. Negotiating this in an amicable way may not be easy, but you should insist on what you want, while avoiding giving the impression that you are going to be a difficult customer who should be charged extra for being a potential nuisance! The standard forms of pre-printed contract that many of the bigger builders are used to dealing with are largely unintelligible to the layman and contain all sorts of clauses which you might not want if you knew what they meant. Of far more use is the new short form of contract that has been produced by the Joint Contracts Tribunal (JCT), known as The Building Contract for a home owner/occupier. This clearly sets out the precise nature of the work to be done, the price, the terms and times of payment, the working hours and conditions and all the details to do with insurances and guarantees. It also sets out just how any disputes that arise are to be settled and most importantly, it covers things like changes to the work and specification or extras; those things that are so often responsible for arguments. It is written in plain English; at the time of writing it costs under a tenner; it is just four pages long with different coloured copies for each party and most of the items are simply covered by tick boxes!

With all of that so cheaply available you might wonder why someone would want to write their own specification. But the plain fact of the matter is that many attempt to do so and they spend hours poring over plans and books trying to list down all of the tasks they want a builder to be responsible for. A word of caution here. The tighter you attempt to draw a contract, the more likely it is that something will be left out or overlooked. If your relationship with the builder or contractor is a good one, it probably won't cause too much of a problem. But if the relationship becomes strained, a builder could point to your list and claim that the omission was never part of his remit. Many successful self-builders complete their projects with a builder on nothing more than a simple exchange of letters, referring to plans and specifications no more detailed or complicated than those prepared for the Building Regulations application, with the specification from the timber-frame or package-deal supplier attached.

Many specifications and quotations make extensive use of Prime-Cost Sums, otherwise known as PC Sums. At the stage when you are negotiating the contract you have probably not decided on the particular fixtures and fittings that you require, so a

Prime-Cost Sum is allowed for the items concerned. A PC Sum of £3,000 for the kitchen units means that the builder must allow this much for the kitchen units. If you spend less then the contract price will be reduced. If you spend more then it will be raised by the difference. Does it, however, refer to the purchase price of the units, or does it also include the cost of fitting? These things need to be specified. You will need to establish just how much is allowed for the fixing element and you will also need to understand that if you buy kitchen units cheaper because they are flat packed, there may be a corresponding increase in the fixing costs if you want the builder to be responsible for their assembly. You may also want the PC Sums of certain items to reflect the huge discounts that are available and to reflect them in your favour. Materials usually covered by PC Sums are: kitchen units, bedroom furniture, sanitaryware, fireplaces, staircases and wall and floor tiling. Somewhat confusingly, because the abbreviation is the same, provisional costs are sometimes used for things like bricks where the actual brick is known, its price is known at the time of quotation, but any shift in that price needs to be reflected in the final cost. Trades that are often covered by a PC Sum are the plumber and the electrician where the initial quotation, in the absence of detailed information, may include a PC Sum that will reflect the bare minimum needed to provide a system to comply with the regulations and the minimum standards laid down by the NHBC.

In certain cases, it may be as well to remove the items covered by the PC Sum from the builder's remit. If you do, then you do need to establish whether or not there was any profit element included in the total contract sum for these items. Should that too be removed or will the builder argue that part of it concerned the labour element or attendance upon labour? You might also like to consider whether by removing items from the builder's remit, you also remove them from his insurance liability and whether you then need to make sure that they are covered by your own policies.

Another important matter is the cost of any alterations to the agreed work, or extras. This is a potential minefield. A simple request from you that something should be fixed the other way round can involve the builder in a great deal of expensive work, and, unless it is agreed in advance, the cost can be a source of dispute. This is all covered in the JCT Building Contract for a home owner/occupier but, whether you're using that or not, the cost of all alterations and extras should be discussed and confirmed in writing before they are enacted and the specification should detail the arrangements for their agreement.

Assignment of the work is also something to watch out for. If you take on a builder because you have admired his work on another house, you probably want his same workmen to build your new home, and you do not want him to assign the contract to another builder, or to use other workmen. If this is important to you, it should be set out in the contract or in the specification. However, whilst many builders will agree not to assign the whole contract, very few would be silly enough to commit themselves to the use of particular tradesmen or subcontractors, who might well be otherwise engaged or have gone out of business.

The stages at which payment is made, the arrangements for payment, and retentions to be held for a maintenance period should also be clearly established and never, never should any payment be made other than in accordance with these arrangements. Beware any requests for a payment in advance to enable materials to be purchased at a particularly advantageous price, or any other good story. If your builder needs money in advance then it is 100:1 that he is in financial difficulties, and you are not there to bail him out. This leads to the question of what your position is if the builder fails, or dies, or just does not get on with the work. It does happen. On his part, what does he do if you disappear? All this has to be part of the contract. Finally, when you have the best contract which you consider to be appropriate to the way in which you want to go about things, for goodness sake stick to it. Be punctilious about making payments on time and generally fulfilling your part of the bargain, as to do otherwise may make things difficult if the worst happens and you have to establish your contract in law. If this is a frightening thought, then console yourself with the fact that nearly all individual builders end up by having their new home built without dispute, and retain good relationships with those who are building for them. Having the right contract is a very good beginning.

10. BUILDERS AND SUBCONTRACTORS –
Finding them, contracting with them, working with them and getting materials for them

Builders

In earlier chapters I discussed how the amount of time and money that you have available for your project influences how you build. Building with a builder who is going to take charge of the whole job and just give you a ring when it's all over can seem a very attractive option and, for those with a busy schedule, it is, more often than not, their first choice.

Money, and the desired size of your new home, may well have dictated whether the project is feasible with a builder. Those who switch from this first choice to building, either with subcontractors or a combination of them and a builder, often do so in order to save money. But these are not hard and fast rules. Builders come in all sizes, from the large contracting companies with posh offices, fleets of sign-written vans and lorries, right through to the small local chap who undertakes one or more of the trades himself, drives a second-hand pick-up and, when he can put it off no further, does his paperwork on the kitchen table.

As you'd expect, the prices have an equally large variation. Whilst the posh builder is always going to be right at the top of the price scales, the small local guy might not be too far above, and in a few cases, even below the prices you could expect for building with subcontractors. Surely therefore, if you can afford a builder, you're going to get so much more peace of mind and you're going to have to spend far less of your precious time on the project? Surely the bigger the builder, the less the hassle?

I wish it worked like that, but it doesn't. If you get the wrong builder, you can be involved with as much work, and sometimes more, as if you'd used subcontractors in the first place. If you get the right builder, then what you've got is an administrator, who'll rightly take responsibility for all of the co-ordination of labour, materials and services off your hands. What isn't always appreciated is that, in many cases, a builder is merely someone who organises subcontractors. Very few of the small-to-medium builders have many, if any, full-time employees other than themselves, on their books. Very few have their own major plant, tools or scaffolding. They hire in subcontract labour and things like diggers as they need them and their price to you is really just the addition of all the tradesmen's prices plus the costs of the materials that they are going to buy and, of course, their mark-up. That's why I often preach the value of using a combination of a builder for the weathertight shell with subcontractors for the second fix and supply-and-fix following trades.

The difficult bit of any house is to get to the roofed-in and watertight stage. For this, five separate trades have to mesh in with each other to within the day and, sometimes, within the hour. Materials, too, have to be co-ordinated to arrive so as not to clog up what is often a tight site, and building and warranty inspectors need to be pre-warned of impending stages. If ever there is thought of using a builder, rather than subcontractors, then these are the stages when they are most valuable. Once the weathertight shell is reached, then, although there is a sequence of events for the following or finishing trades, there is nothing like the imperative for them to mesh in together to quite the same degree. The plumber can go in next week. The electrician can be in there at the same time, or maybe he can go in the week after, or even the other way around.

And I question whether, in the end, the person choosing to build with a builder responsible for just the shell of the building, always has extra work to do by employing tradesmen themselves for the later stages of the building. As I've said, most builders don't carry trades on their books, particularly plumbers,

Above: The building needs to be constantly checked for square at this stage.

plasterers and electricians. If you've got a contract with a builder for the whole job, then it's a pound to a penny that the plumbing and electrical trades are covered by a PC sum. When the time comes for the plumber to be wanted on site, the builder will probably send him around to you, or arrange for you to meet him on site, so that you can tell him exactly what you want. After that, he'll get back to the builder with his actual price based on your specification and you could well find yourself at yet another meeting discussing ways in which the price can be brought down, or refinements of your specification. In all of this the builder is a bystander. Yet he is a bystander who is making a mark-up on the result of the negotia-

tions. Maybe the plumber is already known to you. Maybe he has done work for you or a friend beforehand. Maybe he was or is your principal source of information for the latest advances in plumbing technology. So just how much work have you had taken off your hands? Just how much money are you paying out to someone else, when you've all but taken over the management of this particular aspect of your project? I leave you to answer those questions.

Your architect or package-deal company is probably going to be the one either introducing you to, or helping you to find, a suitable builder. Recommendation is the key here, that and reputation. Subcontractors can move on with relative anonymity from a less than successful job but builders cannot leave their failings behind quite so easily. If you are on your own in the search for builders then most of the sources of subcontractors and practically all of the recommendations made in the section that follows on the use of subcontractors, apply with equal measure to the choice of a builder. In addition, even if you are going to use a builder and have the minimum of involvement with the various trades, I still think it is a good idea to make yourself conversant with what goes on and, as far as is possible, the general sequence of events that flow through a building project.

Always ask to see a builder's previous work and always ask to be put in touch with a previous client. I can virtually guarantee that they will have a few moans, but it is the general standard of workmanship that you are interested in, the level of commitment shown and the trustworthiness of the man or company. And if there are shortcomings that are identified by this previous client? Well, if they are serious enough then you will need to move onto the next name on your list. But if they are minor and you are tipped off about what to expect then, with the advice of your professional friend, you might still employ that builder, only with, perhaps, a few reservations which you might like to draw to the attention of the builder, in writing. Alternatively, if you are told that such and such a builder is marvellous at most things but is hopeless at one particular aspect of the build, you might like to consider removing that part of the work from his remit, in which case, as I have been pushing for you to do for the last two paragraphs, you will now need to read on about building with subcontractors.

Subcontractors

A self-builder opting to build using subcontractors effectively becomes the builder, only with one big difference. There is no contract to fall back upon. When you build with subcontract labour it is with you that the 'buck stops' and it is up to you to manage and co-ordinate the various trades, materials, plant and services. Any unforeseen factors that affect the cost or the progress on site are your responsibility. It is you who will have to sort them out, and if there are any additional costs, then it is you who will have to bear them. There are great savings to be made by opting to build with subcontractors but the reverse side of this coin is that, in turn, you have to take on the responsibilities that the builder would have undertaken, and for which he would have charged.

Management is the key, of course, and that means attention to detail and forward planning. Subcontractors price for their specific trades only and any grey areas are the responsibility of the self-builder. A tidy site where all rubbish is collected to a given point, where all materials are placed and stored correctly with due regard to their accessibility and the accessibility of other materials, is likely to be far more successful than a site that resembles the aftermath of a terrorist bomb. Of course there are degrees. I'm not suggesting for one moment that you should stand behind each tradesman in a white coat, pointing to each broken brick or picking out the odd fallen leaf or pebble from within the mortar. Such overt interference would be resented and would very quickly lead to a breakdown in relations. No, what I'm suggesting is that in the evenings, when the chaps have left site, you tidy up the old cement bags, pick up the bindings and rake the sand heap into a neat cone and cover it. That you discreetly pick up some of the better half bricks from the ground and neatly stack them beside the other loaded out bricks. There's no guarantee that they'll use them and you still may have to wince as yet another whole brick is deliberately cracked in half, but there's a chance. I often tell the story of a couple called Peter and Enid who built a lovely bungalow in the Midlands. Peter took it upon himself to tidy up the site every day and then halfway through the job he suffered a hernia (nothing to do with the self-build) and wasn't able to continue his nightly duties. The subcontractors took it upon themselves to continue his work until he was better!

Perhaps, what that serves to illustrate is that, not only does everyone appreciate a well-managed site but that the relationship between Peter and Enid and their subcontractors was particularly good. And that is another important factor to consider. These are self-employed men who, very much like the self-builder, have quite deliberately stepped outside the system. In doing so they have opted for the insecurities and uncertainties that go with their choice, in preference

Project planning – stage two

To use a builder for the whole project, a builder for the shell only with subcontractors for the finishing trades or to use subcontractors for the whole project

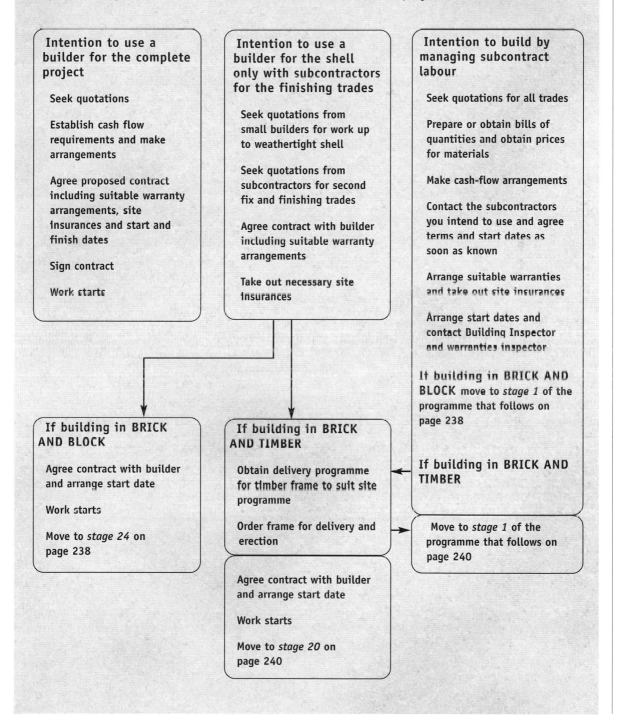

Intention to use a builder for the complete project

Seek quotations

Establish cash flow requirements and make arrangements

Agree proposed contract including suitable warranty arrangements, site insurances and start and finish dates

Sign contract

Work starts

Intention to use a builder for the shell only with subcontractors for the finishing trades

Seek quotations from small builders for work up to weathertight shell

Seek quotations from subcontractors for second fix and finishing trades

Agree contract with builder including suitable warranty arrangements

Take out necessary site insurances

Intention to build by managing subcontract labour

Seek quotations for all trades

Prepare or obtain bills of quantities and obtain prices for materials

Make cash-flow arrangements

Contact the subcontractors you intend to use and agree terms and start dates as soon as known

Arrange suitable warranties and take out site insurances

Arrange start dates and contact Building Inspector and warranties inspector

If building in BRICK AND BLOCK move to *stage 1* of the programme that follows on page 238

If building in BRICK AND BLOCK

Agree contract with builder and arrange start date

Work starts

Move to *stage 24* on page 238

If building in BRICK AND TIMBER

Obtain delivery programme for timber frame to suit site programme

Order frame for delivery and erection

Agree contract with builder and arrange start date

Work starts

Move to *stage 20* on page 240

If building in BRICK AND TIMBER

Move to *stage 1* of the programme that follows on page 240

to the relative comfort of the factory floor. Confident in their respective and individual skills, they have removed themselves from regular employment to enter the world of hire and fire, or start and finish as it is called. In effect, each and every one of them, even the one-man band, is, therefore, the representative of their own company and they need to be treated as such rather than as employees or servants. Like any small business they deserve to succeed or fail on the strength of their service and their product and it's necessary for you, the self-builder, to make sure that, as the one doing the paying, you get what you want. Some subcontractors are completely disorganised in their approach to obtaining and quoting for work and they often prove just as disorganised in their attitude to the work itself. I would suggest that you take all possible steps to avoid these fellows. Others are splendidly efficient in dealing with enquiries, giving out quotations and, as a result, the work itself. I would suggest that these are the chaps you should seek to engage.

Any builder or subcontractor is only as good as his last job but the fact is that there's no other reliable indicator. That the public perceives the whole spectrum of building trades as untrustworthy is beyond doubt, and the very reason for the rise of dot.com companies with information on builders and contractors is predicated on those fears. It is no coincidence that, when seeking the names of tradesmen, the majority supplied are plumbers and electricians. If the dodgy end of the spectrum is occupied by the constantly breaking and re-forming partnerships of the labour-only trades such as groundworkers, bricklayers and carpenters then the supply and fix trades are undoubtedly at the more stable end.

However you find your builders or subcontractors, you'll still need to make your own checks and, in the end, the decision on whether to employ them is one that you're going to have to take responsibility for. That your decision has much to do with just how you go about finding and engaging builders or subcontractors is beyond doubt. The list of headings and tips that follows is by no means mutually exclusive and many are interchangeable. Never forget to ask to see previous work. Always check that it's actually their work. Talk to previous clients and, if at all possible,

try to get some sort of financial or professional references.

By far the best way of identifying which subcontractors you should employ is by recommendation and many of the better ones don't need to advertise or look for work at all, preferring to rely on a constant stream of work that comes their way by word of mouth. Indeed many subcontractors seem almost reluctant to talk to potential new clients unless they approach them by or through some form of recommendation or third party.

Other ways of finding subcontractors or builders, come to that, are:

Other self-builders
Self-builders love to talk to other self-builders and self-build sites are a terrific source of recommendation for all sorts of things, not least labour. They'll be able to give you the names of the chaps they've used. They'll tell you how much they charged, whether they did the job properly and whether a particular tradesman is good at one section of his job, but not so good at other aspects of it. A lot of what you'll get is, of course, often going to be about price but that's not all you should look for. Good doesn't just need to mean capable of doing a good job at the right price – it also needs to mean reliable and, above all, helpful. It's no good having, arguably, the best bricklayer in the world if he turns up one Monday morning and is absent by Tuesday with a promise to come back some day. You need to know that the people you engage will dedicate themselves, in the main, to your job and that they're as interested in continuity as you are.

Now, before you run off thinking that means that, once on site, they should attend all day and every day until the job's done, that doesn't mean that there aren't times when subcontractors will be away from the site. All tradesmen have to go away at certain points in the construction, but the indicator of a reliable man is his ability to juggle the various jobs he's on, in order to maintain continuity on them all. If a bricklayer has to leave your site because he's waiting for the roof construction to be completed, then he's not going to just go home and sit and watch television. No, he's going to go and do someone else's footings for a couple of days and then, whilst the groundworkers deal with the oversite on that one, he'll come back to your job in order to do the gable ends. All of this is perfectly reasonable. Where it can go wrong, however, is if your relationship with the tradesman is on the wrong footing. If the man is unreliable in the first place, this means you haven't done your homework properly.

Architects/designers and package deal companies

One of the plus points with using a local architect or designer is that they'll be able to recommend builders and contractors who have done work for previous clients and with whom they have often formed a loose business alliance. The negative point, however, is that if this relationship has gone on for too long and got a little too cosy, the prices might have crept up quite a bit. The same can of course be true with package-deal companies but here there is a limiting factor in that the company often only really makes money when and if the property gets built. There is therefore a built-in imperative for prices to be sufficiently attractive in order to persuade or enable their clients to start work.

In all cases, the recommendation or introduction will be designed to make the company's or practice's life easier and there is therefore a built-in convergence of interest, just so long as the prices are right.

Looking for boards

Any builder or subcontractor worth his salt will be more than willing to advertise his wares. If you're stationary at the traffic lights or walking down the street, watch out for the builders' vans and jot down the numbers. Drive around your chosen area looking for builders' boards outside new properties or outside existing dwelling houses where they an extension is being built. Be careful, the boards might be quite small and they are sometimes just propped against the hedge. Whilst you might not think that a builder doing extensions would be capable of constructing a whole house, you'd probably be wrong. Extensions encompass all of the problems of house-building in microcosm. When a builder first starts work he's often that wonderful chap who's going to build the new kitchen or bathroom. When he finishes he's often just the man who mucked up the lawn. The diplomatic and

Right: The topping out, or fixing of the chimney pots, traditionally warrants a small ceremony and a drink or two. But not while you're up there.

organisational skills acquired in this field of work make whole house-building seem easy. Before contracting with the builder, however, do make sure that you get the chance to inspect the work and above all, talk to the previous clients.

Walking onto other sites

Health and safety have to be borne in mind when entering a strange site and it doesn't do to go clambering around on scaffolding talking to guys trying to do their job. Instead, try to arrive during lunch or tea breaks and talk to the people in the site hut or rest room. If you're looking for a builder, ask to speak to the site foreman or the chap in charge and then simply ask if they'd be interested in looking at your plans and giving you a quote. If you're particularly impressed with the standard of workmanship and the tidiness of the site then it's important to ask if that particular site foreman would be the one you'd get.

It's an amazing fact but of the people working on any site, a large proportion will have no clear idea of where they're going from there. If you're looking for subcontractors, you can do no better than to ask those who impress you on the site whether they would be interested in giving you a quote. If they decline, ask if they know of anybody who would be interested. However, do bear in mind the fact that it's often better to ask a tradesman for the names of disciplines working either side of them, rather than those from their own field. Tradesmen are hardly ever uncritical of others working in their own field, but a good tradesman will always want to follow another good one and they tend therefore to form loose groupings that consistently work together.

Builders' merchants and specialist merchants

A direct question at your local builders' merchants will get you names and recommendations. Remember that a builders' merchant's staff will know the chaps as well as the partnerships that form and re-form. They are also unlikely to recommend those who don't pay their bills or those who 'phoenix' leaving unpaid debts. Indirectly, hanging about in a merchant's yard could mean being able to speak to builders or to get their names from their vans. Remember too that you can judge the man or company by the van. Scruffy or badly sign-written means cheap and nasty whereas a very posh vehicle might well mean expensive. Aim at somewhere between the two.

Tool and plant-hire merchants

These are very much like builders' merchants although, as well as the financial probity, they will be able to judge their clients by the way they return the tools and plant. They're hardly likely to recommend the chap who returns the mixer full of gone-off concrete. If you're looking for a smaller builder or subcontractor, then this is a good source because the larger ones will own their own plant and won't need to use hire companies.

Yellow Pages/classified adverts

In any area the Yellow pages and the classified advertisements in local newspapers are a good source of names. As the builders and tradesmen pay for these adverts, it is possible to make some sort of a judgement based on the size and scope of the advert itself. But this should never be the sole criterion. Yellow Pages is on line with www.yell.com in association with various trade organisations, and has a Home Improvement section with an online source for locating, choosing and using a professional.

The dot.com companies

The theory is that these companies carry lists of heavily financially vetted and approved tradesmen and builders, all of whom have been inspected, passed some sort of qualifying interview and provided references from previous clients. All anyone needs to do is to log on to be presented with the names of individuals and companies, listed by their discipline and postal code. It all sounds very promising, and indeed what's already available is extremely useful. But only in part for, by their own admission, the companies have a long way to go before they are truly able to deliver what they promise and in recent months many have simply disappeared or ceased trading.

The dilemma that all of them face and which both major players left in the market, Improveline.com and HomePro.com, have had to come to terms with in their own ways, is how to create their directories. Do they fill up the lists to make them as comprehensive as possible and then check and weed out, or do they suffer a loss of credibility by having too few names because they haven't got around to doing the necessary checking? Each seems to have chosen differently in this respect.

Improveline insist on contractors having been in business for at least two years, having a low-risk credit rating and no County Court judgements against them. Although there is nominally a fee payable by contractors to get on to the list, many have not paid it. Quite a few are actually unaware that they are so listed and their names and details seem to have been lifted from other publications or sources. Contractors are given star ratings. No star means that no checks have been made. One star means basic Dun and Bradstreet checks. Two stars means that the contractors have paid the registration fee and provided more information, and three stars means that they are highly rated from customer feedback. They also have a matching service where the customer fills in a 10-page questionnaire. This is then matched with relevant contractors and the first three who show interest are put in touch with the customer.

HomePro do not insist on the two year rule and will not enter companies or contractors on their lists until they have paid the registration fee, been visited and vetted, and provided between six and 12 references from previous customers. This means that in some areas they are a little light on names. But the inclusion of the contractors and companies who were members of the Fair Trade organisation, with whom they merged in 2000, has augmented things considerably. As well as the directory, they also provide a matching service and, in recognition of the fact that many people either do not have access to computers or might prefer to talk to a human being, they have a national helpline with trained operators to guide the caller through their available services. Apart from that, the biggest single difference is in the fact that HomePro contractors are able to offer an insurance-backed guarantee of between two and 10 years.

So check these sites out for yourself but remember to read the small print and any disclaimers. Understand that you must still make your own checks in exactly the same way as you would if you gleaned the names from any other source. Above all, avoid a false sense of security, simply because they are listed in this way.

Trade associations/organisations

Scanning the membership of the trade associations, particularly those that provide some sort of insurance-backed guarantee or warranty is a useful way of obtaining names of builders and tradesmen. The NHBC, perhaps the most widely known company working in this field, makes a small charge for information over the telephone but otherwise has its membership lists on the Internet where you can browse for names in any given postal area or check whether a membership is current. They do not, however list probationers. The Federation of Master Builders, who offer their 'Masterbond' insurance-backed warranty, also publish lists of their members on the Internet.

Various other trade organisations exist, mainly to do with the plumbing and electrical trades, but also for specialist trades such as roofing, decorating and thatching. Their lists can be accessed either directly or on the Internet. Although some do profess to vet members and require that they pass certain tests as to their competence and financial probity, in many cases the lists give nothing apart from the name and addresses of current members and they cannot be an indicator of reliability or any form of recommendation. There is, for example, a statutory requirement for plumbing and heating contractors installing or carrying out any work concerning gas or gas-fired systems to be Corgi (Council for Registered Gas Installers) registered, but membership of the similar NICEIC (National Inspection Council for Electrical Installation Contractors) is purely voluntary.

Building inspectors and warranty inspectors, Highways and Environment Agency employees

Local authority and statutory bodies are not actually allowed to recommend builders or contractors. However, in their capacity as inspectors, these officials have the most intimate knowledge not only of the existence of companies, but of their performance. A question to one of them about reliable contractors will almost certainly be met with a statement to the effect that they cannot be seen to advise on this matter or to show favouritism in any way. However, further questioning will often persuade them to produce several names and it's normally possible to glean, from expression or insinuation, which ones they would give preference to.

Detailed and legally enforceable contracts are rarely made with labour-only sub-contractors, who often work simply on the basis of a verbal agreement. The best you can hope for is a quotation on a piece of headed paper. A quotation on a labour and materials basis may be quite detailed, but it will not deal with unforeseen contingencies in the way that a builder's contract does. As a result, you have to rely on finding the right man, coming to an amicable agreement with him, making sure that he does the right job, paying him only for work done, and terminating the arrangement promptly and without rancour if things are not working out.

The key word in this is amicable. Arguments between self-builders and subcontractors are rarely won by either party, as either the subcontractor will walk off the site, or else the work will proceed in an atmosphere that does not make for a good job. It is virtually impossible to enforce an arrangement made with a subcontract workman in any legal way, and you have to handle problems on a give-and-take basis. Builders have experience of this; most self-builders have not. You may feel that, in order to prevent any disagreement over what exactly is included in the sub-contractor's quotation to you, you should attempt to define and list the precise nature of his duties and obligations under the contract. Do be careful about this. If, for example, you receive a quotation from a carpenter that merely states, 'All labour for first fix, roof and second fix carpentry for new house at 19 Acacia Avenue, Anytown' then it would be almost impossible for the carpenter subsequently to turn around and claim that the fixing of the facia board and soffit was not in his remit. On the other hand, if you've attempted to list all of the carpenter's duties and, for some reason, you've forgotten to list these items, then an unreasonable carpenter, or one where the relationship with you has become strained, could well argue that he is due some extra monies.

Fortunately, there are ways in which you can take action to avoid misunderstandings and problems. Firstly, reinforce the arrangements made by giving the subcontractor a letter or a note which is either your acceptance of the written quotation if you received one or, more usually, confirms a verbal arrangement which you have made. Secondly, make sure that any acceptance is tied back to the plans and specification of the proposed building and that you have a note of the subcontractor receiving them, together with a note of the plan numbers and any dated amendments.

The business of payment is important. Labour-only sub-contractors expect to be paid promptly, and in cash. If you do not do this you are asking for trouble, and running the risk of your subcontractors going off to other work. Although you should keep a record for your own accounts of who you paid and how much you have paid them, you have no responsibility to notify the tax authorities of the payment, although a builder is obliged to do so under what are called the '714 arrangements'. This is a complicated business and its very existence gives the self-builder an edge, in that the subcontractor who works for you, as opposed to the local developer, will, if he is paid the same rates, be approximately 20% better off. This is something that is only ever obliquely referred to in the industry but it is as well for you to be aware of.

Never pay up front or too far ahead. You're a self-builder, a renovator or a converter but you are not a banker. It happens, I'm afraid. The most sensible people pay out too much too far in advance and then have to either scrape around to find someone to finish what was left or spend months trying to persuade a reluctant contractor to leave a lucrative contract to come and finish off their job. Say you have a house with two gable ends and when you get to plate height (where the roof starts), the bricklayer has to leave to let the carpenters construct the roof. If you've paid that bricklayer all but a few hundred of his total price for the job then, unless he's an extremely reliable man, there might be trouble getting him to come back. Gable ends, especially cut verges, are very time-consuming in proportion to the amount of bricks to be laid. If there's only a few hundred pounds on the job, then a less than reliable man could reason that he and his gang could earn 10 times that amount on straight work on another job. You see it all comes down to management and to making sure that you're on top of each situation and that, most importantly, you've

Construction of a Potton Home

Above: As the scaffolding comes down, the house seems as if it's being released from a cocoon.

Right: The groundwork stages, up to oversite, are virtually the same for both timber frame and brick and block.

Below: Where the big difference can come is the speed that things happen from oversite to roof on and roady for tiling; sometimes only a matter of days.

Above: At this stage the only clue that it's timber framed is in the width of the window.

chosen the right guys in the first place. A golden rule, of course, would be to say never pay any monies up front or in advance of the work but all rules need to be broken at some time and when, and if, they are broken it's down to your skill in managing people and situations. Certainly with labour-only trades, the aim should be to keep a tight rein on money going out and to try, as far as possible, to make sure that the payments schedule reflects the work done or, even better, keeps you well ahead, with an incentive left in at the end for the man to finish.

On the other hand, if a plumber on a supply-and-fix contract, having done a pretty good job for you on the carcassing, comes to you and requests a down payment towards the purchase of an expensive boiler that you have chosen and which is not available from his usual supply sources, then it's a slightly different matter. Such a request should be calmly considered. If you're completely confident in the man then, by all means go ahead but, I would suggest that a better way around such a problem would be for you to purchase the item yourself and then deduct either the cost, or the agreed PC sum, from the contract. That way title in the goods is always yours and if anything goes wrong, you're in a far stronger position. Never put yourself in the situation of effectively lending money to tradesmen, builders or anyone else for that matter, in order for them to work for you. That's the job of the banks and if they feel that they shouldn't be advancing money to someone, despite the attraction of his contract with you, then you can rest assured that they know a lot more about the fellow than you do and that they have perfectly good reasons for acting as they do.

Although the subcontractors working for you will not be employees in the strict sense, you should ensure that you have employer's liability insurances. The tiler who falls off your roof will decide that he had a 'Deemed Contract of Employment' with you before he hits the ground, or if he does not remember this, his solicitor will! Dealing with a resulting claim will be expensive whatever the outcome, and it is best left to an insurance company. Appropriate cover is part of standard self-builders' insurance policies that have been discussed in Chapter 1.

Labour-only subcontractors will expect you to provide all the plant required for the job, and to have it there on time. If there is a difficulty with this, such as a mixer breaking down, they will expect you to solve the problem at once, otherwise they will want to be paid for their wasted time or will go off to another job. The same applies to delays in delivering materials, or in arrangements to replace materials stolen from a site.

Self-builders should always employ subcontractors at fixed prices. Builders often do not, and there are complicated systems of measured work, where for example, a bricklayer is engaged at a price per thousand bricks laid. This may sound simple, but building industry practice is that some bricks at cills and reveals count as one and a half bricks, or even two bricks. Measured work rates for plastering are even more complicated. Get lots of copies of your drawings so that you can given them to prospective subcontractors, and make it quite clear that you will be employing them at a fixed price, and not in accordance with the mysterious rites of the building industry.

Avoid, at all costs, the subcontractor who wants to carry out the whole of his trade on the basis of 'daywork' or 'timework'. Many of the trades work out their prices for a job on the basis of measured rates for work and, if they're sensible, they'll qualify their quotation to you by reference to those assumptions. For example, a builder or groundworker quoting for work below ground may well quantify the depth and width of the dig, the amount of soil to be disposed of and the amount of concrete and blockwork to be used in the foundations. If, therefore, he's allowed for 10 cubic metres of concrete in the bottom of foundation trenches which are a maximum of 1.2 metres deep and he hits a soft spot where the Building Inspector wants him to increase the depth and fill up the trench with more concrete, then you could find yourself with a bill for the extra time taken to dig, the extra spoil to dispose of and the extra concrete used, over and above the specified amount. If it all ratchets up to a trenchfill foundation then the amount of concrete required could rise to two, three or many times the original. That means a very big bill for extra concrete but there may well be a corresponding saving in below-ground blockwork and, when this is quantified and compared, you will almost certainly be able to set one off against the other. You'll still come off worse, I'm afraid, but the bitter pill will be sweetened a little and, if you've read the earlier chapters carefully, you'll probably already have anticipated the problem and it won't come as too much of a shock.

Some of the trades – carpenters for one – do indeed work out their prices on the basis of the number of man hours that they will have to put into the job. For example, if a carpenter thinks that the job of constructing your roof will take two men 10 days to complete, then he'll arrive at his price for the job on the basis of 20 man days. Now, that won't necessarily be his price to you as he may well have profit to add before arriving at the quotation he wants to give you. But the principle remains – he has arrived at his price to you by reference to the time he estimates that the job will take him. When such a man gives you a fixed price quotation for the job, he is demonstrating his confidence in his own abilities both in arriving at the price in the first place and being able to achieve the targets he has set himself in the second place. These are the kind of chaps you should be playing with and, as far as those fellows who want to do the whole job on daywork are concerned, I have only one piece of advice – sup with a very long spoon.

That's not to say that there aren't times when daywork isn't right and proper. In certain instances and in certain situations, it is totally appropriate. A bricklayer who is on a price may put, at the bottom of his quotation, a rate for daywork. This may be to cover for having to stop work and put men onto unloading materials or it may be there for things like the fancy fireplace, the precise design of which you haven't yet decided on. All of this is perfectly acceptable and perfectly normal and the quoted daywork rate in these situations is the mark of a man who is thinking forward.

You'll be told by all and sundry that you've got to get at least three quotations from each trade and that anything less is laying yourself open to ruin. Balderdash is the word that springs to mind. Most builders and subcontractors in a local area are in almost constant touch with each other, either at work or in the pub. If you flood the local labour market with requests for prices then there's a chance that

none of them will bother to do the large amount of work necessary to provide you with a quotation, thinking that the odds of them getting the job are too slim. Certainly get more than one quotation, if you've got several names, but, equally certainly, if a particular tradesman is recommended by, say another self-builder, and his price comes within what you've budgeted for, why waste anybody else's time? More importantly, why risk missing the first chap's window of availability on a futile gesture?

Even if the recommended man's price is a little higher than other quotations that may not be a good enough reason to discount taking him on. Prices that you are quoted have to be related to your budget and to the big picture. A man who impresses you as someone in whom you can really have confidence may quote more than someone else, but he may be the best man for the job. A golden rule is to get a clear idea of the general level of prices for a job like yours before you start discussing the matter with any potential subcontractor. This, again, is part of learning all that you can about self-build before you actually get involved on the site.

Negotiation is a large part of management but do be very careful about trying to knock a price down. Certainly there is no reason why you can't tell a man you are considering using, that his price was a little high in comparison with others. He may then look at things again and he may well find that he has either made a mistake or some wrong assumptions. On the other hand, do be aware that if he comes down in price reluctantly, he may try to claw back the amount he perceives that he's 'lost'. He may do this by finding extras or by skimping on the job itself – either way, you may find that it would have been better to stick with his original price or to have engaged the other fellow.

The last real issue to explore before I go on to consider each of the main trades in sequence, is that of competency. Are they any good at what they do? Well, if you've arrived at the fellow by recommendation, then you already have the answer to that one but, if you found him by some other method, what do you do? The answer is you do exactly the same, only in reverse – you ask around. Ask the tradesman himself for the names of the people he last worked for and then go and visit their site and ask them what they thought of him. Chances are that he won't give you the name of the last site he was ignominiously expelled from so, if he's willing to give you the names in the first place, he's probably all right. Nevertheless, do check it out. And when you're there, don't just listen to what you're being told but use your own eyes to see for yourself.

If it's a bricklayer you're investigating, you may feel that, as a lay person, you have no powers of judgement when it comes to such an important skill. Nonsense, anybody can see if the bricks are all smudged with mortar, and if the general standard of work is untidy. Anybody can stand back and see if the perps (the vertical joints) are neatly in line and anybody can see if the beds (the horizontal joints) are straight. If it's a carpenter, then look for the joints on the skirtings and architraves. Are they finished well or are they gappy? Do the doors, and in particular pairs of doors, hang nicely with even spacing all around? The eyes in your head and the tongue in your mouth can find out a lot. Remember, a good tradesman is proud of what he does and what you've got to realise is that you're entitled to investigate all you can about someone who, after all, is going to be involved with you in probably the most important project of your life.

What follows is a brief description of the nature of each of the normal subcontract trades, together with a note on how they arrive at their prices. I have also included some warnings and specific things to look out for but I don't want you to run away with the idea that all is doom and gloom. I make these suggestions as points that can aid you in the management of your self-build site; I do not make them in order to put you off or to frighten you in any way. Indeed, your very knowledge of these things will enhance your standing with any builders or tradesmen who work on your site and will serve to assist them in doing a good job for you.

The subcontractors with whom self-builders are most likely to be involved are:

Groundworkers
Of the eight stages of inspection required by the Building Inspector, six concern the groundworker. Of the nine inspections stages listed by the NHBC, five involve the groundworker. Of all of the trades, this one, most of whose work is eventually covered up and hidden from view for ever is, without doubt, the most important. It is also the one where unforeseen problems and cost overruns can occur and much of what has been written earlier on in this book concerns itself with the anticipation of any special requirements. The chaps who undertake this trade have to be prepared to react very quickly to changing conditions and to adapt calmly to problems as they occur.

In most cases, the need for any special foundations will be flagged up at a very early stage and a subsequent soil investigation and survey will lead to a foundation design or system being adopted. In other cases, all the investigations in the world can fail to reveal a problem and it is sometimes necessary to change tack fairly rapidly and adopt a different foundation. I remember the case of a house in Harrow where there was a soil investigation that revealed that the subsoil, found in each of the three bore holes that straddled the oversite, was gravel. The recommendation was standard strip foundations 1.2 metres in depth with 600mm x 225mm of concrete.

When it came to digging the foundations for the house itself, the builders encountered a pocket of very wet clay and the foundations had to be dug to over three metres deep, shored up and pumped out prior to pouring them full of concrete. Nobody had done anything wrong. The self-builder had, very properly, commissioned a soil survey. The investigating surveyor had reported quite rightly on what he had found and the builder's quotation was based upon his recommendations. What this proved was that everybody had taken the right precautions but that, in the end, the only survey that really counts is the one that takes place when you finally dig.

Groundworkers can undertake to carry out this trade on the basis of the provision of all labour, materials and plant but it is more common for self-builders to use groundworkers working on a labour-only basis. In most cases, this labour-only basis allows for the supply of a digger but it will often exclude additional plant such as a dumper and will almost certainly exclude any lorries to dispose of spoil. The men working on the site will know where, when and whether to get any additional plant but it is important that the self-builder understands exactly what is being provided within the quotation.

It is also important to know just how the quotation has been arrived at, and on what basis. The price will be worked out by the groundworker, using a combination of measured rates and estimated time/daywork rates. You need to establish just what depths and quantities are assumed to enable you to identify when and if extras are applicable and you need to be able to establish the rates at which any extra work will be carried out. Of course, it's not always possible to anticipate every eventuality with this trade as, in some cases, changes may go beyond matters like extra dig or extra concrete and into the realms of a completely different type of foundation. In those cases you will need to stop and establish a price for the new work, almost as if you're starting again. If the changes are fundamental, then you're probably not going to lose any more time by drawing breath and establishing a new contract with the groundworkers, as the probability is that, first of all you'll have to wait whilst new details are approved by the Building and warranty inspectors and secondly, you may need to order extra materials such as reinforcement or clayboard.

Of course, if you do start off with one type of foundation and, due to unforeseen circumstances, you have to stop and change direction, then you will, I'm afraid, still have to pay for all of the abortive work that was carried out before the job had to stop.

Above: If you don't have a pump handy on site, at least identify where you can get hold of one quickly. Trenches should be dry and neatly crumbed out before concrete.

Right: The quicker you can get out of the ground the better. In bad weather or in areas with high water tables, trenchfill can be the better option.

Project planning **brick and block**

Project planning for a rectangular bungalow built in brick and block with a beam-and-block ground floor, cut verges and with the plumbers, electricians and plasterers as supply and fix trades. Plasterboard and sanitaryware from self-builder's supply.

Stage	Action	Requirements
1)	Apply for all services	
2)	Apply for building water supply	Water butt and hose
3)	Arrange insurances and warranties	
4)	Provide access, hard standing, site storage	Hardcore, site hut
5)	Strip top soil and stack for future use	Digger hire
6)	Excavate foundations, service trenches and drive and spread hardcore	Digger and hardcore
7)	**Building Inspector and warranty inspector to inspect excavations**	
8)	Pour foundation concrete	Concrete and any ancillary or reinforcing materials required
9)	**Building Inspector and warranty inspector to inspect foundation concrete**	
10)	Build foundation blockwork	Concrete blocks, wall ties, sand and cement, drainage exit lintels, cranked ventilators. Mixer
11)	Lay damp-proof course	Dpc
12)	**Building Inspector to inspect dpc**	
13)	Position floor beams and infill with blocks	Floor beams, infill blocks
14)	Brush grout beam-and-block floor	Dry sand and cement
15)	**Building Inspector and warranty inspector to inspect oversite**	
16)	Build superstructure to wallplate	Bricks, blocks, wall ties, wall insulation, door and window frames, lintels, flue liners, meter boxes. Hire and erect scaffolding
17)	Warranty inspector to inspect up to plate	
18)	Carpenter to scarf wallplate, bricklayer to bed it	Wallplate
19)	Rear end trusses as template for gable ends	Roof trusses
20)	Bricklayers to build and cut up gable ends	Bricks, blocks, wall ties, sand and cement
21)	Bricklayers to build chimney through roof	Flue liners, bricks, lead tray, sand and cement

Stage	Action	Requirements
22)	Carpenters to fix remaining trusses and finish roof, including fascias, soffits	Balance of roofing materials
23)	Tilers to felt, batten and tile roof with plumber in attendance for any flashings and to position vent pipes and lead skirts	Roof tiles, felt and batten and any ancillary fittings or fixings
24)	**Warranty inspector to inspect roof**	
25)	Decorator to decorate fascia and soffits	Decoration materials
26)	Plumber to fix guttering prior to scaffolding coming down	Rainwater goods
27)	Carpenter's first fix – door linings, window boards, tank stands, loft trap, external doors and patio doors	Carpenter first-fix materials
28)	Lay drains, services and bring into house	Drainage materials including pipes, inspection covers, pea shingle
29)	**Building Inspector and warranty inspector to inspect drains on test**	
30)	Backfill drains and service trenches	Pea shingle
31)	Glaze all windows	Glazing materials
32)	Plumbing and central heating first fix	Appropriate materials from subcontractor's or self-builder's supply
33)	Electrician's first fix	Appropriate materials from subcontractor's supply
34)	Bricklayers to build fireplace	Fireplace bricks, stone or surround
35)	Lay floating floor	Flooring grade insulation and t&g chipboard, glue
36)	Plaster out	Plasterer's materials, plasterboard
37)	**Warranty inspector to inspect first fix complete**	
38)	Plumbers second fix and water on	Subcontractor's or self-bulder's materials supply, sanitaryware, sink unit. Fit roof insulation
39)	Electrician's second fix and power on	Any special electrical fittings plus subcontractor's supply
40)	Carpenter's second fix including fitting of kitchen units	Kitchen units, internal doors and furniture, skirtings and architraves
41)	Test out and services on. Telephone installation	
42)	Decorations	All decoration materials
43)	Ceramic wall tiling	Tiles, adhesive and grout
44)	**Building and warranty inspectors' final inspection**	
45)	Clean through and arrange for Householder's insurance to take over from site insurance	

Project planning **brick and timber**

Project planning for a rectangular bungalow built in brick and timber, using a standard open-panel frame with a beam-and-block ground floor, cut verges and with the plumbers, electricians and plasterers as supply and fix trades. Plasterboard and sanitaryware from self-builder's supply.

Stage Action	Requirements
1) Apply for all services	
2) Apply for building water supply	Water butt and hose
3) Arrange insurances and warranties	
4) Provide access, hard standing, site storage	Harcore, site hut
5) Strip topsoil and stack for future use	Digger hire
6) Excavate foundations, service trenches and drive and spread hardcore	Digger, hardcore
7) **Building Inspector and warranty inspector to inspect excavations**	
8) Pour foundation concrete	Concrete and any ancillary or reinforcing materials required
9) **Building Inspector and warranty inspector to inspect foundation concrete**	
10) Build foundation blockwork	Concrete blocks, wall ties, sand and cement, drainage exit lintels, cranked ventilators. Mixer.
11) Lay damp-proof course	Dpc
12) **Building Inspector to inspect dpc**	
13) Position floor beams and infill with blocks	Floor beams, infill blocks
14) Brush grout beam-and-block floor	Dry sand and cement
15) **Building Inspector and warranty inspector to inspect oversite**	
16) Delivery and erection of timber-frame kit	Timber-frame kit. Hire and erect scaffolding.
17) **Warranty inspector to inspect timber frame erected**	
18) Bricklayers to build chimney through roof	Flue liners, bricks, lead tray, sand and cement
19) Tilers to felt, batten and tile roof with plumber in attendance for any flashings and to position vent pipes and lead skirts	Roof tiles, felt and batten and any ancillary fittings or fixings
20) Decorator to decorate fascia and soffits	Decoration materials
21) Plumber to fix guttering	Rainwater goods

Stage	Action	Requirements
22)	Bricklayers to lay bricks to elevation. Strike scaffolding	Bricks, sand and cement
23)	**Warranty inspector to inspect brick elevations complete**	
24)	Carpenter's first fix – door linings, window boards, tank stands, loft trap, external doors and patio doors	Carpenter first-fix materials
25)	Lay drains, services and bring into house	Drainage materials including pipes, inspection covers, pea shingle
26)	**Building Inspector and warranty inspector to inspect drains on test**	
27)	Backfill drains and service trenches	Pea shingle
28)	Glaze all windows	Glazing materials
29)	Plumbing and central heating first fix	Appropriate materials from subcontractor's supply
30)	Electrician's first fix	Appropriate materials from subcontractor's supply
31)	Install insulation and fix vapour barrier	Insulation and vapour barrier
32)	Tack plasterboard to walls and ceilings, and finish	Plasterboard plus plasterer's materials. Fit roof insulation
33)	Bricklayers to build fireplace	Fireplace bricks, stone or surround
34)	Lay floating floor	Flooring grade insulation and t&g chipboard, glue
35)	**Warranty inspector to inspect first fix complete**	
36)	Plumber's second fix and water on	Subcontractor's or self-bulder's materials supply, sanitaryware, sink unit
37)	Electrician's second fix and power on	Any special electrical fittings plus subcontractor's supply
38)	Carpenter's second fix, including fitting of kitchen units	Kitchen units, internal doors and furniture, skirtings and architraves
39)	Test out and services on	Telephone installation
40)	Decorations	All decoration materials
41)	Ceramic wall tiling	Tiles, adhesive and grout
42)	**Building and warranty inspectors' final inspection**	
43)	Clean through and arrange for Householder's insurance to take over from site insurance	

The groundworker's job usually stops at oversite level with the groundworker being responsible, once the blockwork foundations have been laid, for the consolidation and casting of the oversite itself. If a beam-and-block ground floor is being employed, it is sometimes the groundworker who maintains responsibility for the laying and infilling of the beams but in some cases this job can be taken on by the bricklayers. If the first or upper floors are beam and block then the self-builder needs to establish just who is going to undertake this. Whoever that is, it's normal for this to be quoted as a separate price. A beam-and-block floor is becoming recognised as the standard way of achieving the ground floor with the normal concrete oversite slipping into second place and a timber-suspended ground floor trailing well behind in third.

With a beam and block ground floor the void beneath it can be left as 'mud' so long as, first of all it doesn't come within 75mm of the bottom of the beams and secondly, any differential between the ground levels inside and outside the oversite is not greater than 600mm. On the other hand, a concrete oversite will require very careful filling and consolidation to avoid differential settlement and if there is any suspicion that the fill or the difference in depth of fill will exceed 600mm, the inspectors are, in any event, likely to require you to use floor beams.

Whichever ground floor you use, the groundworker's job will include all of the drainage for both foul and surface water and their connections. It is usual for them to bring the tails up and into the oversite in the required positions. If plastic underground piping is being used, and I would suggest that this form is best for the self-builder, then the rule is that the brown plastic pipes below ground and poking up through the oversite are the responsibility of the groundworker and the grey ones that connect to them above that level are that of the plumber.

One of the most expensive and time-consuming operations can be the removal and disposal of spoil from site. Tipping charges can be exorbitant but, on top of this, the digging process often has to stop and wait whilst lorries complete the journey to and from a tip that may be several miles away. Without loading out your site with unwanted and unusable material, it may be as well to consider what you can accommodate and, if there is going to be landscaping in the future, how much, if any, of the topsoil or subsoil may be useful for this.

Bricklayers, blocklayers and stonemasons

Although they usually get lumped together as being in the same trade there are significant differences in that a bricklayer will obviously be able to lay blocks but might not necessarily be any good at laying stone. Then again, the laying of natural stone is significantly different from the laying of reformed stone and, to complicate matters further, the laying of random coursed undressed stone is completely different from laying cut and dressed stone.

All of this stresses the importance of seeing a prospective tradesman's work before you take him on and of checking by your own observation and by reference to others he has worked for that he's the right man for the job. I won't go into the finer points of bricklaying but I would like to stress a couple of pointers that you should look out for. It's quite obvious that the laying costs of the various stones will vary according to the type of stone and, when asking for a price for stonework, a reputable tradesman will need to know exactly what material you intend to use. The very questions he asks will give you a pretty good clue about just how competent he is. With bricks, it's all too easy to assume that one brick is the same as another but, again, you'd be wrong. Sand-faced Flettons soak up mortar very quickly and can be laid just as fast, whereas some of the harder stock or engineering bricks have a very low porosity. When these are laid they do not take up the moisture in the mortar bed and, if too many are laid, they tend to 'float on the bed'. In addition, the Flettons are uniform in their size and square, whereas hand-made bricks, by their very nature, have an irregular shape. Pointing such bricks takes longer and requires much more thought and skill. Once again the mark of a good bricklayer can be the very questions he asks.

The price is usually reached by reference to measured rates for each aspect of the work after which this is normally totalled up and given as a lump-sum price. Occasionally, a bricklayer may prefer to work on the job on the basis of measured rates of, say, so many pounds per thousand bricks laid or so many pounds per square metre of blockwork laid, but this is not that common on a self-build site. A lump-sum quotation will often include a note of measured rates for additional work and I would suggest that, if it doesn't, then it's a good idea to seek out that information and agree it before the chap starts. Alternatively, there may be a daywork rate noted and, as I've explained before, that's fine for certain aspects of the work but, as a rule, totally unacceptable as the basis for the whole job.

No skilled tradesman, and particularly the bricklayer, likes to be stood over when he's working, but there are some very important things you should look out for, hopefully on the previous client's site, before the bricklayer starts on yours, but if not, then as soon as he's working for you. The neatness of the visible brickwork itself is something we've already discussed but what I'm referring to here are those aspects of the trade that soon get covered up.

Damp-proof courses are of vital importance, so much so that they, in effect, form an inspection stage all of their own. If floor beams are being used then these are often placed directly on top of the damp-proof course itself. The beams are heavy and they often have to be moved from side to side to accommodate the infill blocks. Just make sure that when this is done the damp-proof course isn't torn or rucked up. There are other damp-proof courses throughout the building that are of equal importance and it's as well to look out for them and to make sure that they're installed properly and that they're in wherever the plans call for them. These are the cavity trays and tray dpc's that trap water or moisture that may find its way into the cavity, and channel it out though weeper holes. They usually occur at an abutment of a lower roof with a cavity wall and are installed in concert with the various flashings that also occur at these points. Failure to build these in at the right height and position can result in water getting in to either the roof void or the house itself. Once installed, a careful watch needs to be taken to make sure that they are kept clear of any obstruction and, in particular, falling mortar.

Most bricklayers are labour-only and the most usual combination on self-build sites is two bricklayers served by one labourer. This is known as a two-and-one gang and on price work they will often lay between 2,000 and 3,000 bricks a day on straight runs, although that figure will drop considerably with corners, openings and fancy detailed brickwork. The only tools they usually provide are their own hand tools but, just occasionally, they may also bring their own mixer. Usually the provision of this is down to you, as is the provision of mortar boards (spot boards) and of course the sand, cement and any necessary additives. Whilst on the subject of sand, it is the one thing good bricklayers are fussy about and they may well request that it's obtained from a particular pit. This isn't because they get some sort of kick back; it's normally because they feel that that particular sand makes a better mix. If you can satisfy their whim on this one without too many hassles then it does help to start off on the right foot. And talking of starting off on the right foot, do make sure that when they all arrive on site, not only are all the materials there and ready for them but that there is a convenient water supply and hose leading to a butt placed near to the place where they'll be mixing. The first arrival of the bricklayers is always the most important and if they arrive and everything's there, ready for them, then they'll stay and get stuck in straight away.

I'll talk about scaffolding when I get to the bit about plant and machinery but it does need mentioning with regard to this trade. In the past, many a bricklaying gang undertook their own scaffold with the labourer raising the lift in slack moments when he'd made sure that the bricklayers themselves had all they needed. I don't think that that's such a good idea any more, with all the new Health and Safety legislation, and my advice is to use specialised scaffolding contractors who provide the scaffolding on a supply and erect basis. They normally guarantee to be on site within 24 hours of being notified and they normally, also, work in with the bricklayers. The scaffold they provide will conform to all of the rules and you'll know that it's safe not only for the bricklayers but for all of the following trades and for you, the self-builder. One last word about scaffolding in connection with this trade. On sloping sites it may be necessary to provide a scaffold right from ground level, known as a foot scaffold. Talk to the bricklayers about this, as if it is

Left: An increasing number of houses, whether brick and block or timber frame, now employ floor beams and blocks for the oversite.

Below: Ground floor partitions to a brick-and-block house, ready for lintels.

needed, then you may need to line up the scaffolding a couple of weeks before you would otherwise have done.

More than any other discipline, the bricklayers have to fit in with and work around other trades. They are perfectly used to this but you will need to make sure that any interweaving trades are geared up for the correct times. In all probability, the task will be made easier for you by virtue of the loose association that I have already referred to and the arrangements may well be made each night in the pub. But, don't take that for granted. Keep on asking and checking for when following or intervening trades are needed and make sure that they are notified. Continuity is a mark of a well managed site. If the bricklayers reach first-floor joists and you're having timber joists, then the carpenter needs to be on hand to cut, lay and level them up in good time for the bricklayers to carry on with the minimum of disturbance. If you're using a beam-and-block first floor and the bricklayers have quoted you for this particular job then you may need to make sure that either a digger is on site to assist with the lifting of the beams or, in some cases, you may need to organise a crane. As with all things about self-building, attendance at the school of forward planning is the key.

Carpenters and joiners

Same thing, different name, although in the south the word 'joiner' is usually associated with the making of furniture. Once again this is normally a labour-only trade with the men almost certainly providing all and any tools and machinery they need. More than any other trade, this one may need power at a time when it may not be readily available and, if you can't get a line from a friendly neighbour, you may need to hire a generator, although many of the carpenters I know have their own. Whilst on the subject of power, it is sometimes possible for a temporary supply to be brought into the meter box as it's built in. Alternatively, a temporary supply can be brought into a locked-up box, built to specifications laid down by the local board which are fairly draconian and correspondingly expensive. Incidentally, whilst many of the power tools available from hire shops are 110 volts, requiring a transformer, most of those I have seen car-

penters using (their own) work on normal voltage.

The trade of carpenter is divided into three sections: first fix, roof and second fix and many prices are given on this basis. The price is normally arrived at, not so much by measured rates, as by the carpenters themselves working out just how long each section of the job is likely to take. If your roof is to be a simple trussed roof that will take two men four days to fix, then the carpenter's price for this part of the work will be worked out on that basis. On the other hand, if your roof is a cut-and-pitch roof that is created on site and the same two men estimate that it'll take them 10 days, then the price will rise accordingly.

Although there is a rigid division between the sections within this trade and everybody on building sites knows just what jobs fit in which category, the stages do not follow on from each other in strict progression and overlap to a considerable degree. First fix is normally deemed to include the cutting and fixing of the first-floor joists, the fixing of door linings and window boards and the fixing of garage door frames. It also includes, although it has to be done at a later date, the laying of the first floor decking, the making up and erection of any stud partitioning, and the assembly and erection of the basic staircase as well as the making up and fitting of any loft traps or tank stands. But, before that second lot of work is carried out, the work to construct the roof has to be completed and then the carpenter has to wait for the roof to be covered in by the tiler.

Second fix involves the hanging of internal and external doors and patio doors, the fixing of skirting and architrave and the finishing off of things like the staircase balustrade. It does not normally include fitting of kitchen units unless this is specifically requested. It also does not normally include things like fitted bedroom furniture unless, again, this is specifically requested, although it does normally include things like built-in wardrobes. Now, before you go making a list of all of those things, let me say that what I've just written is in no way meant to be a comprehensive list of the carpenter's trade. What you do need to do is establish just what is included in any quotation, although I would repeat the warning not to try and be totally specific and, wherever possible, to leave things under their headings of first fix, second fix and roof.

Of course the design of the house will have a profound effect on the carpenter's specification, as will whether or not you're building in timber frame. If there is any internal or external boarding or cladding or if there are mock Tudor beams to be fitted after external render, then you'll have to make sure that these are included. If you're building in timber frame then, assuming you're not stickbuilding, the majority of the first fix and roof may well come under the auspices of the frame erectors and the carpenter's trade will shrink to slightly more than second fix.

The measure of a good carpenter is in the finish and if you've read the previous sections then, when you went out looking for the man to do this work, that was one of the things you especially looked out for. On the other hand, there are some other things, very like with the bricklayer, that you also need to watch out for, that may already have been covered up on the job you went to look at. If you're having a timber-first floor with joists then, almost certainly, there are places where midspan strutting is indicated on the plans and you need to make sure that this is carried out. Basically, it is needed to prevent the joists from twisting or acting independently from each other and it is provided by either proprietary struts, angled herringbone strutting using 50mm x 25mm battening or by solid-span strutting using offcuts of the joists themselves. You also need to make sure that any necessary noggins are put in between the upright studs of any stud partitioning, both to provide structural integrity and also to provide fixings for radiators, switch and electrical boxes and the like. And whilst on the subject of noggins, it's normally the carpenter's job to fix any necessary noggins to carry and support the plasterboard.

If any of the floors are to be floating floors then their laying has to be done after the plumber has carcassed but normally before the plasterer starts. The plans will give the specification but from your point of view, you need to make sure that any necessary membrane is both down and integral, that the insulation is properly laid and that the decking is glued and fixed on all edges. One other thing that you do need to check for is that the boarding or decking stops 12mm from each wall to allow for expansion. Failure to do this can result in humping up of the floor.

Roof tilers and slaters

This is normally, but not always, a labour-only trade and the only things that the men will provide are their specialist tools. Tilers will felt, batten and tile a roof and they are also responsible for any vertical tile or slate hanging with their prices arrived at by a combination of rates, according to the material to be used. It'll be up to you to make sure that everything's on site for them, including not only the roofing materials themselves, but also a decent scaffold to work off as well as facilities for them to be able to mix up any necessary mortar. If you do use a supply-and-fix contractor then they'll obviously undertake to supply as much and as many materials as are needed for the job. On the other hand, many of the specialist tiling suppliers and merchants will take your plans and provide you with a quotation for just what's needed so it's not that difficult to think in terms of using a labour-only subcontractor who may, in any event, be recommended to you.

The choice of roof covering can have a big impact on cost, not only from the perspective of the price of the materials themselves but in the knock-on costs to both labour and other aspects of the structure. Let's take a simple change from concrete interlocking roof tiles to plain concrete tiles. At first sight, to the lay person, the fact that the plain tiles are just over a third of the cost per thousand when compared to the interlocking tile may seem attractive. But, you'll need six times more tiles, so the reality is that the material cost is going to very nearly double. If you add to that the fact that there will be at least three times the amount of battening and, with all the extra loading out and fitting necessary, the labour costs will also double, you can see that this simple change has quite a profound effect. If you ratchet things up some more by the use of plain clay tiles then, although the labour content may well stay about the same, the material costs could double up yet again. And that's not where that one stops, because clay tiles absorb water far more than concrete ones, and that means that the roof structure may have to be beefed up quite considerably to take the extra weight.

And, talking of beefing up roofs, reformed slates may cost under half that of some natural slates with reformed stone-type slates priced somewhere between the two. However, the knock-on costs of the huge weight increases experienced with stone slates will mean that the overall costs of the roof will be considerably more, making this by far the most expensive roof covering.

So what do you need to watch out for when getting a price from a tiler and, once work has commenced, what do you need to keep an eye on? Well firstly, it's important that you make yourself aware of the manufacturer's recommendations regarding fixing and laying and that you equate any prices received to those requirements. The fixing and nailing requirements for a particular tile or slate may be completely different in different situations on the same house. In addition, in areas of high exposure, there will almost certainly be a requirement for extra nailing and the overlap that each tile or slate has over the one below it may need to be increased. Tiles or slates are gauged across and up a roof plane. The distance that the battens are set apart dictates the gauge of the tiles up the roof, and their lap. You do need to make sure that these spacings do not exceed the manufacturer's recommendations for your particular situation. Interlocking tiles have to be properly gauged across the roof, so as to fit and run to the verge tiles, without the need for the cutting of tiles within the roof plane. Plain tiles have to start at the verge with a tile and a half laid in each alternating course and, as the tiling is commenced from each outside edge, you need to watch out for the gauge of the tiles across the roof plane to make sure that you don't end up with silly sized cuts in the middle.

Leadwork needs to be sorted out, as there are many areas of the roof or its abutment to other parts of the structure where lead has to be employed. Sometimes leadwork comes within the plumber's remit, as with flashings, but, even here, although the plumber may make up the flashings, they may have to be fixed either by, or in conjunction with, the tiler. Sometimes, for example with soakers, where a dormer cheek abuts a roof plane, the roof tiler will take on sole responsibility. It doesn't really matter which trade carries out this work. What does matter is that somebody does it and that you establish just who that is going to be, right from the outset.

Nailing is the biggest single thing that you need to look out for. Slates of all sorts, on any roof, need nailing for every slate on every course, as they don't have the fixing lip that tiles have. Most of the reformed slates have pre-drilled holes but watch out for some of the natural slates where either there are no holes or else new ones may need drilling. Vertical tile hanging also needs every single tile to be securely nailed and in addition the battens need very secure fixings to the wall behind. On a roof plane, tiles will have a recommended nailing schedule which will ask for nailing at course intervals and will certainly specify that all verge tiles and under course tiles are nailed. To check that the tiles have been nailed correctly, stand on the scaffold and, with a length of batten, gently push up each course in a vertical line. If they have not been nailed in the correct sequence then insist on this being done. On a calm, clear and sunny day you may think that nothing is going to move these tiles but I can assure you that high winds can strip a badly nailed roof very quickly indeed. This is especially true of the leeward side of a roof plane where it is the vacuum created by the wind that, literally, sucks the tiles off the roof.

Plumbers

In the not-so-recent past, the advice was usually that the trades of plumbing and central heating were to be considered as supply and fix. To some extent that remains true today although, with the advent of so much choice and with so much more being available directly to the self-builder, more and more items are being taken out of the supply element of a plumber's price. Certainly it has long been common not to include sanitaryware in any price, as most self-builders have always preferred to buy their own, even if the fitting of it was left as part of the plumber's job. On the other hand, most self-builders were content to rely on the plumbers themselves devising a central heating system and to accept his choice of boiler and radiators. Now, with a bewildering array of different boilers, with the multiple choices between, not only differing sorts of radiators but underfloor central heating systems as well, the plumbers are finding that their

Left: Underfloor central heating pipes slotted into special metal channel clips lying either side of the joists. (Robbens Systems Ltd)

Below: The drilling or notching of joists has to be carried out in accordance with strict rules so as not to weaken the structure.

clients are not prepared to accept anything they are given. Increasingly, this means that the self-builder will want to specify his own materials and equipment and in many cases he may also want to take on responsibility for their purchase. As I've repeated time and time again, this book is not meant to be a technical journal and I don't intend, therefore, to go into the various and conflicting claims for the different systems and components, except as referred to in Chapter 5. There are, however some important points to consider in all of this.

When visiting self-build sites, the thing that has struck me is how often the self-builder finds himself way ahead of his plumber in respect of his knowledge about innovations. Sometimes this has led to problems. Sometimes the self-builder makes a choice on the basis of very good advice and adopts a system that he expects a plumber to be completely *au fait* with, only to find that, not only is the plumber quite flummoxed about what he's supposed to be doing but that the self-builder is going to have to spend a lot of time being a conduit of information between him and the manufacturers. So, when engaging a plumber, talk

to him about what you're hoping to achieve and carry him along with you in respect of the equipment you are proposing to use. If you sense any reluctance or inability to understand what you're trying to achieve, then pull away and try another subcontractor.

It'll all get better, of course. The plumbers will catch up – at least until it all changes again. Take the case of the sealed system versus the vented system that had been used in this country ever since Victorian times. From being new, cutting-edge and very daunting technology to becoming the norm took barely two years. The same goes for plastic plumbing and underfloor central heating, all of which are fast becoming the accepted ways of working, as is the, almost consequent, reversal in the role and operation of the 'familiar' hot water tank. Instead of a coil of copper tubing heating the water in the tank, which is then available for drawing off as hot water, many of the modern storage tanks reverse this process. The boiler heats the envelope of water in the tank and the cold water passing up through coils is heated by the surrounding water, to be drawn off, at the higher level, as mains pressure hot water.

In the meantime, it's important that you take your plumber along with you and that you make sure that you engage the professional who is going to be able to provide you with the system you have chosen for your new home. If you're going to use underfloor central heating or a particular boiler then, in all probability, the company supplying you with the system will also be able to recommend a plumber to do the work. I would contend that it is always better to stick with the chaps who know what they're dealing with. You may feel tempted to take a large part in the education of your local plumber and take the credit for leading him into a new technological age but take care that you don't do so at your own expense and at the expense of the good working of your new home.

If the plumber has been recommended to you by another self-builder or by the company or manufacturers of the systems you wish to employ, then the business of getting a quotation will be relatively straightforward in that you will ask for a price based on exactly what you're after. On the other hand, you may want to get prices from more than one source or you may, at the outset of your project, be unsure of just which way you will be going and what boiler or central heating system you are going to employ. In this case, it might be better to approach various registered plumbers, asking them to quote you for a standard system of domestic plumbing and central heating to NHBC and local Water Board requirements. Then, when you have all the prices in, you can choose the plumber that you feel most comfortable with and discuss with him the various options you are considering, prior to asking him to re-quote on the basis of what you actually want.

As with many trades, the plumber's is divided into first fix and second fix, with the first fix being taken up by the general carcassing and the fixing of vent and soil pipes. It's important, therefore, that the plumber is identified by at least the time the roof tiler starts, so that he can work in with him on the vent

Above: Before the power is switched on, the system will have to be checked out by a qualified electrician, using an Installation Residual Tester.

pipes as well as the leadwork to the roof that I've have already talked about. The plumber will also have to work in quite closely with the carpenter over the plumbing in of any kitchen units and with the electrician regarding power for the boilers and the earthing of any pipework. If you're using a vented system, then the carpenter will have to construct any tank stands in the roof and the plumbers will have to be on hand to put the tanks into the roof before it's closed in, otherwise they might not fit through the truss spacings.

Electricians

This is another trade that is divided into first and second fix and it is almost always a supply-and-fix trade, where the price is arrived at by reference to the time that the chap reckons the job is going to take plus the costs of the materials involved. An electrician will normally quote a fixed price for an installation shown on a drawing, or as detailed in a quotation, plus a fixed extra charge for each additional light or power outlet required. He will supply the switches and sockets (of a make and type which should be specified) but his quotation will often provide for simple batten or pendant light fittings only. As you will wish him to get the installation tested by the Electricity Board as soon as practicable, so that the mains connection can be made, he has to provide these fittings for the Board's test. Very often, however, you will be buying your own ornamental fittings, and if you can give them to him at the right time he will normally fix them free of charge in place of the pendants and battens. Do not ask for a rebate for the savings on pendants and battens – this is balanced by the cost of involvement with your own fittings, which you will have chosen for reasons which have nothing to do with ease of fixing! The electrician will also fix TV points (but not TV aerials), telephone ducting and deal with your heating thermostat and boiler wiring. He will supply and fix any immersion heater required.

Any plans that form the basis of the arrangements that you make with the subcontractor should show the position of all power points and light switches together with details of any other specialised equipment or circuits that you are employing, using clear and readily identifiable symbols. To save any argument you should make it clear that you have retained a copy of this plan and you should refer to it in any correspondence regarding your contract with the electrician. In spite of that, I would suggest that, just before the electrician starts work on site, you walk around your house, plan in hand and chalk at the ready. Imagine the rooms with the furniture in place and then check what you envisage with what you've noted on the plans. Think carefully about which way doors will open and upon which side they'll be hinged. You might well find that you want to move a few things around and, if you're going to change things, it's a lot cheaper to do it before the wiring is in place.

Plasterers

If the groundworker was the most important trade structurally, then the plasterer is, perhaps, the most important of the finishing trades as far as the look and the feeling of quality in your new home is concerned. In a way the analogy goes further, as the plastering stage is the foundation for the flair and the taste that will characterise your home. If the plastering is bad then no amount of paint and wallpaper will ever disguise this.

It is generally a supply-and-fix trade, although sometimes things like plasterboard are supplied as part of, say, a package deal. In the main that is because plaster has a limited shelf life and a decent plasterer won't want to have to try and work with material that has gone off, any more than you'll want a bad job that can, and will, be blamed on your supply. It's normal for a lump-sum price to be given for the trade and that is reached by reference to measured rates for each particular element of the work.

The two main methods of internal plastering: wet plaster and dry lining, used generally to fall either side of the timber-frame/brick-and-block divide but in recent years it has become ever more common for brick-and-block houses to use dry lining. In any event, many brick-and-block houses had stud partitioning to the upper part and they *had* to be dry-lined so it wasn't a great big step to consider it for the remaining blockwork walls. Dry lining offers far shorter drying-out times, enabling painters and decorators to work very soon after the plasterer has finished. However, wet plaster provides the harder and more durable surface that many people prefer and, for some, it has been one of the principal reasons for choosing to build in brick and block. As a self-builder the choice is, of course, yours and I'm not going to stand on either side of this line, except to say that both methods have their respective merits and, as with all the trades, there are things to watch out for.

The best way of considering them is to break the trade down into the various elements.

Walls If they're dry-lined then the plasterboard will either be fixed to the studs on timber-framed and studwork walls or, on blockwork, it will be fixed by the use of either plaster dabs or battens. If it's dabs, then care should be taken to see that there is a continuous line of dab around the edge of the board, so as to prevent cold air transmission from the wall cavity resulting in a draught and heat loss though the cavity between the plasterboard and the wall. If the walls are to be skim-coated, then the plasterboard is fixed grey side out, whilst, if they are to be taped and jointed, it needs to be cream side out. Either way, the final finish depends to a large degree on the taping and filling of the joints and the skill of the tradesman is crucial if you're going to avoid visible joints or uneven walls.

Wet plaster is sometimes referred to as render and set, where the walls are given two coats of sand and cement render with a top coat of finishing plaster. Sometimes the render coats are replaced by a specialised plaster that is then finished with a topcoat. The first coat of render may not always be necessary as its main purpose is to 'dub out' the walls and take up any unevenness in the blockwork. The second coat is the 'scratchcoat' and provides a key for the plaster finish, being scratched in a swirling pattern to facilitate this. In any method of plastering, care needs to be taken that the finish coat is sufficiently thick (3mm is the norm) and that the two applications that go to make it up are finished to a smooth surface. Where plaster fails to adhere, or where there is excessive cracking, the cause may be a number of things. One of the excuses most often heard is that the weather has been too hot or that the central heating has been turned on too soon, forcing the plaster and/or the render to dry out too quickly. Whilst either of these may be the cause, it can just as easily be caused by inadequate preparation of the background material or through the plaster coat being too thin.

Cracking of plaster with any method may be due to movement or shrinkage of the background materials and the remedy is often to wait until all movement has finished and then to cut out and fill the cracks. A point to watch for is where differing materials, such as blockwork and studwork, abut and, in these cases, the joint should be strengthened with, at the very least, scrim tape or expanded metal lathing. Fine hairline cracks like crazy paving, with the plaster coming away from the wall in sections, in large or in localised areas, may be the result of the plaster being applied when the render coat is too 'green'. If the render coat is still very wet when the finish coat is applied, then it may well shrink to a considerably greater degree than the plaster, forcing the topcoat to craze and lose adhesion.

Ceilings The average house has the ceilings either 'Artexed' or set (plastered) and, whilst Artexing, using the trade material Artex is often carried out by a completely separate trade from the plasterer, it's as well for us to consider them together for the purposes of this part of the book. If the ceilings are to be Artexed then the plasterboard is tacked cream-side down and the joints are then taped and filled prior to the application of the finish, which can be provided in all of the well-known patterns. Any coving or decorative roses need to be put up *before* the work commences and the Artexers, who normally work from the floor with long-handled applicators, will often do this job as well.

With a set ceiling, the board is tacked grey side down and then two coats of plaster are applied after all the joints have been scrim taped and filled. A board scaffold will be required to enable the plasterers to reach the ceiling by hand and, with this type of finish, decorative mouldings, roses or coving are fixed *after* the ceiling is done. Which is best? Well again it's down to choice. Artex is slightly flexible, making it eminently suitable for new buildings where shrinkage will undoubtedly occur. It cannot be allowed to get wet as it will literally wash off and will almost certainly stain and, whilst most people don't bother to paint it, you really should consider doing so, at the very least, in all wet rooms. Set ceilings provide a 'classy' finish that is, nevertheless prone to cracking, at least in the early years of a new building. However, they are easily patched up and filled and redecoration is comparatively easy.

Floors If a floor is to be screeded then this job falls to the plasterer. Apart from underfloor central heating, the most common reason for choosing a screeded floor in lieu of a floating floor is where ceramic, stone or quarry tiles are going to be used. The choice, however, does need to be made at an early stage of the construction because screed laid on the necessary floor insulation has to be at least 65mm thick. This means that in those rooms where it is to be employed, the floor beams or oversite will have to be set down in relation to other rooms which may have a floating floor. This doesn't create any real problem but you do

Above: I don't know why they're looking glum. Maybe it's just a reflective moment after finishing the dry lining, ready for decoration.

Right: The use of a self-adhesive tape when dry lining makes things much easier.

need to think about the floor coverings for each room if you are to maintain the same levels on all floors. Carpets and underlay are probably not too different, in overall thickness, from most ceramic tiles and decorative wood floorings but stone slabs are considerably thicker and you will need to take this into account when setting the sub floor levels in each room. If you're screeding a beam-and-block floor upstairs, then it's not that easy to set the beams up or down without affecting the ceiling heights on the ground floor so it's probably just as well to stick to flooring mediums of equal thickness.

Many of the underfloor central heating systems rely and work on the principle of the heating coils being buried in a screed and the various manufacturers and suppliers will have differing requirements for both its thickness and the positioning of the insulation. In some cases, the equipment may include elements of backing and insulation to be set in the screed and your plasterer may well have to work in with the heating engineer or plumber. Domestic hot water pipes may also have to run through the screed and in some areas there is a requirement that these are ducted.

Check that any floor to be screeded is clean and free from dust or mortar before any membrane or insulation is laid. In some situations the membrane goes below the insulation and in others it goes on top of it before the screed is laid. In all cases you'll need to ensure that it is laid and that, having been so, it isn't punctured or rucked up during the work. For a lasting and stable screed, the mix needs to be a dryish one, of one part of cement to three to four and a half parts of sharp sand, and the temptation to walk on the new screed should be resisted for two days. Garage floors, where a beam-and-block flooring system has been used, need to be screeded to provide the necessary structural integrity and strength. This is done by means of a screed having a minimum thickness of 50mm with reinforcement mesh set within it.

External render The rendering of the exterior is normally carried out when the scaffolding is still up, with the topcoat render finish applied as it comes down. Blockwork walling needs one undercoat in moderate conditions, with two in high-exposure situations, finished off with a topcoat to which a

Right: Floating floor insulation being cut to size for a ground floor. Note the pre-set channels for the underfloor central heating pipes and the end sections to allow the pipe to gently turn corners.

Below: Beech wood decking being laid over the pipework and insulation with a vapour membrane. (Robbens Systems Ltd)

waterproof additive can sometimes be added. Timber-framed sections will need to be wire-lathed before rendering and it's necessary to provide a ventilated cavity between the render and the sheathing. With unbacked lathing this needs to be 50mm, and with backed lathing it has to be 25mm.

All external corners, drip beading over windows and bell drips where render stops, need to be formed using purpose-made metal lathes and beading. It's not necessary to decorate external render but most people prefer to do so and there are any number of proprietary finishes on the market, all with conflicting and competing claims. Perhaps the cheapest and most commonly used is external emulsion and, with many colours, but not with white, the colour pigment can be added to the render mix itself to provide a through colour. Consistency is the watchword with all external render in terms of thickness, mix and colour.

Decorators

Many self-builders opt to carry out their own decoration and most, if not all, make a pretty good fist of it. For those who don't want to get involved, the trade can either be supply and fix or labour only with the prices worked out either on the basis of measured rates or by reference to the time the chap reckons the job is going to take. On sites you'll hear the phrase, 'If you can't make it, paint it', and certainly in the hierarchy within the building industry the painter and decorator is at the bottom. That's not a position they deserve because, firstly, the work they do is often the making or breaking of a well-finished house and secondly, quite a lot of their work involves 'snagging' or tidying up work done by the preceding trades. Preparation is two-thirds of the painter's job and that preparation includes rubbing down and filling any holes or cracks and generally making good any surface long before any paint is applied.

I'm not going to go into the differing paints and

finishes. Suffice it to say that there are many different products on the market and that you should make your choices by reading the specifications and manufacturers' claims, backed up by recommendations from both professionals and those who have experience of the product.

The tools of the trade are almost always provided by the decorators themselves, including brushes, cleaning fluids, sandpaper, fillers and hard tools but you do need to establish this fact with the subcontractors you engage. The one thing you can make sure of is that the trade is carried out in as clean an environment as possible, given that this is a building site. You remember when I mentioned grey areas? Well, this is where they all really come together. The decorator is often in the house at the same time as many of the other second-fix trades and many's the time I've seen them working away, painting things like skirtings and architraves whilst, in the same room, piles of shavings and dust are being accumulated by a carpenter hanging a door or a plumber fixing radiators to the wall. At other times I've seen a decorator trying to work around piles of rubbish that have been roughly swept to the centre of the room. I would suggest that the best thing to do in this situation is to ask the decorator to go and do something else until the other trades have finished and that you don't get him back to that room until you've arranged for all of the dust and rubbish to be cleared out. It's not the job of the carpenter making the pile of shavings to clear them up and sweep them out, any more than it is of the decorator. Whose job is it? Yes, you've guessed it, it goes with the management – and that's you.

Glaziers

In many cases, this is a specific supply-and-fix trade but at other times the work can be carried out by either one of the other subcontractors, such as the carpenter, or by the self-builders. Most aluminium and P-vcu joinery and, these days, quite a lot of the better quality timber joinery, comes pre-glazed, so what we're talking about here is the glazing of timber softwood or hardwood windows and doors.

Any price that you get for this trade will, almost certainly, have been arrived at by reference to the time that will be taken and the amount and scope of the materials that you want the tradesman to supply. Once again I'm not going to use this book to discuss the technicalities of glazing. Suffice it to say that just sticking bits of glass in the holes isn't what it's all about and that there are specific and carefully formulated procedures and recommendations that need to be followed. Modern double glazing units have to be carefully and scientifically manufactured and their fitting has to follow a precise pattern and

GOLDEN RULES

- Always try to take up references or talk to previous clients.
- Wherever possible, go by recommendation.
- Check that memberships of organisations or trade bodies are current.
- Get as many quotes as you can – but don't get hung up on the number '3' and don't miss the chap you really want.
- Don't push too hard to get them to work for you – if they don't seem interested, then they're not, they probably won't do a good job and you should move on to someone else.
- Wherever possible, insist on a warranty or insurance-backed guarantee.
- Don't become the teacher – if they don't understand what you're trying to achieve, move on to the next man.
- Make sure all site insurances are in place.
- Tie up contracts as much as possible or feasible, either by using standard forms of contract or by confirmation in writing with reference to plans and specification.
- Negotiate prices for extras before they are enacted.
- Don't be afraid to put your own interests first.

sequence about which whoever is undertaking this trade should be fully aware.

If possible, the glazing should be done off the scaffold. However, this isn't always feasible when the scaffold obstructs the windows. If you do glaze whilst trades are working above then try to make sure that some sort of protection is afforded to the units as well as to the frames and, whilst on that subject, when the units are delivered, make sure that they are properly and safely stored in accordance with the manufacturer's or supplier's recommendations. Poor treatment of the units at any stage may result in their breaking down, or in stress fractures.

Ceramic floor and wall tilers

I'm hesitant to include this as a trade in this book as most self-builders opt to do their own. Nevertheless, it is a recognised trade and whilst there are labour-only contractors out there, the most usual combination is that the suppliers will either put you onto them or include the fixing in their price.

Professionals at this trade are extremely fast in comparison to lay people and the job they do is often very much superior. If the suppliers of the tiles can get you a reasonable fixing rate then I would suggest that you earnestly consider it and when you weigh up the time it will take you, you may feel that it's worthwhile. A clean dust- and grease-free surface is the key to successful tiling, whether on floor or wall, and the quality of the grouting, and its suitability to its situation, is very important.

Health and Safety

There are various statutory requirements for those who run building sites, most of which are studiously ignored by self-builders and subcontractors alike. Provision of latrine facilities, a hut for meals, protective clothing, a first-aid box and accident register are required by the Factories Inspector who is extremely unlikely to visit your site. However, the provisions and requirements still stand and, particularly if you are employing more than five people on your site at any one time, you could find yourself running foul of what is essentially criminal rather than civil law.

The Management of Health and Safety at Work Regulations 1992 apply to everyone at work, regardless of what work it is and they require that adequate risk assessments take place regarding every aspect of work. Employers and the self-employed must identify any hazards involved with their work, the likelihood of any harm arising and the precautions that they feel are necessary. In particular, the self-employed must ensure, so far as is reasonably practicable, their own health and safety and that of other workers or members of the public. There are various methods and suggestions contained in the regulations which can be obtained from the Health and Safety Executive (HSE) but they all really boil down to a common-sense attitude to safety at work.

One thing that is glaringly absent on most self-build sites is the wearing of hard hats. Keep a few handy in your site hut and insist to all of the labour on site that they should wear them. Chances are that, whenever your back is turned or you're away from site, they still won't, but at the very least, when a tile falls off the top lift of the scaffold, if the man whose head it enters isn't wearing one, it'll be down to him. More importantly, if backed up in writing or by a notice, prominently displayed in the site hut, your insurance won't be invalidated.

The building industry has a worse safety record than coal mining. Consider what will happen if you are injured and cannot deal with the work on your self-build site. Add to this the fact that amateurs are always more likely to be injured in any situation than professionals. Perhaps this will convince you that positive safety procedures should be part of your project planning.

Employees whose misfortunes are covered by the 'Employers liability' section of the insurance are defined as:

- direct employees
- labour-only sub-contractors, whether working directly for you or working for someone to whom you have given a sub-contract
- persons hired or borrowed from another employer.

This does not include members of your family who are working for you without any charge for their services, nor does it include friends who are giving you a hand. It is a nice legal point that it does not include other self-builders who are helping you in exchange for you helping them on their own job. However, these others who may be hurt on the site are covered under your public liability section of the policy, and this includes those who are on the site in connection with some sort of business arrangement made with you (the architect making a routine inspection), those invited to the site by you (your friends and family), and trespassers on your site (the child who climbs your scaffolding while you are not there). If you have children you will have to do some very careful thinking about the extent to which you are going to let them visit the site.

Having your kids help by clearing rubbish is happy family togetherness, and a good thing. The moment one of them is hurt it becomes an irresponsible disregard of safety legislation. There is no doubt at all about this: in law they should not be there. New European safety legislation emphasises this. Unfortunately, in most family situations your children are likely to become involved with what you are doing. You will have to make your own careful decisions, decide what the rules are going to be, and see that everyone sticks to them. If you are living on the site in a caravan this will involve you deciding to fence off the caravan and family area from the building site. Remember that besides more obvious hazards, children are at risk from toxic materials on a building site. The worst of these, and certainly the one that gives most trouble, is cement. Cement dust, mixed concrete and wet mortar are very corrosive and lead to concrete burns.

As far as you personally are concerned, the self-builders' policy gives you no help at all if you are injured. For this you have to take out personal accident, death, and permanent injury insurances if you do not already have this insurance cover in some other way. This has been discussed earlier.

Valuable as these insurances are, they should not encourage you to ignore common-sense precautions. Not only is the food in a hospital unlikely to be up to the standard that you normally enjoy, your inability to manage the job while you are recovering from your injuries is going to be very expensive, and this loss is not covered by any sort of insurance. Most of the precautions you should take are common-sense matters, but please do take serious note of all of this and use the checklist 'Self-build site safety' on page 264. Site safety is an aspect of site management that is every bit as important as any other and a well-managed and tidy site is often the one that has the best safety record.

Building Control and warranty inspections

I've already mentioned this in previous chapters but it does bear repetition here just to remind you that the Building Inspectors and the inspectors from whichever warranty company you've chosen to use will need adequate notice that you have reached the various stages in the build. If there are cards, then someone needs to be responsible for them being sent in and you need to make sure that no work is progressed further than any satisfactory inspection. Remember, these inspectors, and especially the Building Inspectors, can be very good friends or very bad enemies but, if you stick to the rules and make sure that your site runs to them, they're much more likely to be the former.

Creation of a new access, alterations to the highway and connections to sewers

When a planning consent is issued, the applicant is advised to contact the Divisional Surveyor of the local County Council before any work is undertaken or planned in connection with the highway and there are information packs that will be sent out listing and detailing the procedures to be followed.

First of all, only approved and accredited contractors can carry out any works to the highway and, strictly speaking, that applies to any part of the highway, whether metalled or otherwise. There are instances, however, where other contractors can sometimes be authorised to carry out works to the unsurfaced sections of the highway, such as the grass verges, so long as they have the appropriate insurances, but I would stress that this is at the discretion of the highways authority. An approved and accredited contractor can be an individual who has passed the relevant tests and satisfied the stringent financial criteria, but it is more likely to be a firm and the local authority will be able to supply you with a list of the names of suitable companies. A Section 50 licence, under the New Roads and Street Works Act 1991, is required to open up or carry out any work to the highway and this is issued by the highways authority, which is usually the County Council to whom the authority has been devolved.

A new sewage connection, within the highway, will require not only this licence, but also consent, given under Section 106 of the Water Industry Act 1991, to make a connection to the public sewer. There is a legal right to this connection which is issued by or on behalf of the water authority, although in many cases the local authority act as their agents and application to make the new connection has to be made through them. Some authorities insist on doing this work themselves.

In areas where it has been identified that the sewer is overloaded, the local authority may adopt a policy restricting further development or connection to the sewers. On the face of it this would seem to fly in the face of the legal right to connect, but the local authorities get around that one by operating and enforcing the policy through the planning procedures.

Any works to sewers, driveways or roadways, within the curtilage of your site, can be carried out by you and your normal contractors, even if it is intended that they will be adopted when completed. Of course, the works will have to be carried out to the specification and approval of the authorities and, in certain cases it will be necessary for a bond to be taken out. Once the works stray beyond your site and onto the metalled highway, including the creation of any bell-mouth, then the work has to be put in the hands of an approved or accredited contractor. Many ground-workers will quote a self-builder for all works to the driveway and sewers within the site but make it clear that their responsibility stops at the boundary with the highway. This is all perfectly normal but it is important that the self-builder identifies the fact that there will be an additional contract, and not inconsiderable cost, for the works within the highway.

Site foremen

The idea of employing someone to specifically look after and manage a site on a day-to-day basis is a very attractive one but it's more often thought of than carried out. Nevertheless, from time to time you do come across a self-builder who has engaged a site manager or working foreman for the day-to-day supervision. Invariably, this is a retired professional, and I am usually told that they have welcomed the job to liven up their dull retirement. This has always seemed a very sensible thing to do, and if you find the right man who has spent a lifetime working for a builder or developer, he should surely be able to save you enough to cover the cost of employing him, particularly if he is paid on an informal basis.

Do be careful to pick the right person for this and beware the 'white coat' syndrome. If it's someone who's retired from the building industry then all should be well but if it's someone who used to be a factory foreman, where everyone clocked on and off, then you could find yourself with an empty site. Some of the package-deal companies have schemes whereby they introduce you to builders who will either undertake the construction as builders or will 'project manage' your new home. In effect, they look out for and engage the various tradesmen and purchase the materials for them with you paying the bills plus an agreed fee for this service. Be slightly careful of the situation where the representative of the company is then prepared, for an extra fee, to become your project manager. There could be, and usually is, a conflict of interests here. If there's a problem with the delivery or proper manufacture and erection of the package, whose side is he going to be on? Yours you might think, as you're paying him a not inconsiderable amount of money. Wrong! Almost certainly he'll side, in fact if not by admission, with the people who'll be supplying him with all of the follow-up jobs to come.

Builders' merchants

For years the builders' merchants excluded themselves, almost by design, from the self-build industry. If you were able to set up an account, the credit limits were set so low as to make it almost worthless and there was little or no help for the lay person building their own home. Then, prompted no doubt by the constant boom-to-bust cycle of the building industry, the more progressive merchants started to look around to see just how they could iron out the peaks and troughs. To a few observant souls, it became apparent that as the pointer in the building industry came to its bottom, the self-build market rose to its peak. What was the reason for this? The reason quite simply was that in times of recession the self-builder was able to obtain land that had hitherto been snapped up by the builders and developers.

As time went on, the self-build industry grew ever bigger to the point where its combined numbers far outstripped any of the major developers, at times representing almost one third of the detached houses and bungalows being built. This was major clout! But still some of the larger merchants failed to recognise the potential. Not so the smaller independents. Very quickly people realised that if they were to attract the lay person self-building, they had to provide a more user-friendly environment. No longer would it be acceptable for a chap to have to queue up at a counter, not sure of what it was he needed, only to be greeted at the end of his wait by obtuse staff making his ignorance the butt of their humour. No longer would the self-builder feel like the poor relation to the familiar builder client. Instead, they would be welcomed as the high spenders they were and given all of the assistance and knowledge that was at the disposal of the company.

Of course, what they had realised was that the merchants had always possessed the knowledge and the skills that would benefit the self-builder. What they hadn't done was to apply that knowledge so that it could be mutually beneficial. But with a little bit of retraining here and a shifting of emphasis there, it was easy to reverse years of neglect. Now the headings of the services provided read like a manual of self-building. Help in land finding. Help and specially negotiated rates for any valuation or survey of the land. Help in finding architects or designers, builders or subcontractors. And, of course, help, not only with the sourcing, obtaining and buying of materials but, most importantly, with their selection.

Before long the larger merchants jumped on the bandwagon and started to advertise and exhibit within the self-build industry. Now, most merchants will take in your plans, free of charge, and provide a quantity take off and costings. Some, but not all, have dedicated staff to deal with the self-building client and most will actively assist you in the selection, evaluation and costing of materials. Whether you use a package-deal company or not, at some stage you will also need to buy the materials that are not included in the package and it's important to establish just where you're going to go shopping for those, before you start work. The selection of the builders' merchant, or merchants should take the same form as the selection of any other company or professional you are thinking of using. Make sure that you feel comfortable with them, make sure that they appreciate just what it is you're trying to achieve and, above all, make sure that they've got the user-friendly service which you will need to rely on.

It is worth planning where you will buy materials just as soon as you are certain that you are going to build, and you should start to collect leaflets and prices as early as possible. There may seem to be obvious advantages in putting all your business through one builders' merchant or perhaps through one of the DIY superstores, but in practice most self-builders use a number of suppliers. Decisions about this depend on how much time you have to shop around and whether you live in an area where there are plenty of sources of supply. The best way to go about finding the best prices is to get to know the standard list price for the material or component concerned and then to find the salesman and ask him face to face what is his 'best price'. If this is not possible, ask him on the phone. You are unlikely to be offered very competitive terms by letter if you are only buying in one-house quantities. There are some materials that you will only order after having given very careful consideration to samples, particularly items like handmade bricks. In this case, make it quite clear that you are ordering 'as per sample' and be sure that you keep the sample safely. When you take delivery of anything that cannot be checked as it is unloaded, always give a qualified receipt on the delivery note, writing 'not checked' above your signature. This will enormously strengthen your hand in any subsequent debate about whether you got what you ordered, but remember that if there are any such problems you must deal with them immediately.

The sources of supply used by self-builders are generally as follows:

Bricks These are usually ordered through either a builders' merchant, who will have allocations, or from specialist brick merchants or manufacturers, many of whom advertise regularly in the self-build magazines. For whole houses the bricks are usually quoted at a price per thousand and you should ensure that the price you are given includes delivery to your site with a crane offload vehicle. If samples are required for yourself or, more probably, the planners, then most companies, in anticipation of an order, will arrange for these to be delivered. Builders' merchants often have extensive brick libraries and their staff can be very helpful and knowledgeable about alternatives and prices.

If you are using second-hand bricks, then you should make sure that what is delivered is the same as the sample. You should also make sure that you've got plenty of bricks and whilst the wastage factor in ordering new bricks might be 5%, with second-hand bricks this might well have to double. Remember, too, that many older bricks are in Imperial sizes and that in some localities bricks were a very peculiar size indeed.

Stone If it's reformed stone then it's ordered from similar sources to the bricks and in many respects it has all the same properties. Be careful, however, with the different ratios of the differing sized blocks that go to make up the walling and make sure that you are, in fact, getting these in the correct ratio to enable you to end up with the coursing you have chosen. It's perhaps best to put the onus for this on the suppliers by telling them quite categorically that you are relying on their expertise in this matter.

Natural stone will normally be sold direct by the quarry and it is either done so 'as dug' or as cut and dressed. If it's the former, then it's frightfully difficult to establish (as it's sold by the tonne) that you've got the right amount and you'll probably have to rely on the rough guide from the quarry as to how many metres of walling you'll get per tonne. It will all depend on the heaviness of the stone, of course, as it will with cut-and-dressed stone, although, with this, the quarry will probably be able to be much more specific about how many square metres of walling you'll get, usually between 4 and 6 per tonne.

Flint Usually bought through specialists by the drum, either knapped (split) or unknapped. One drum will usually provide about 4 square metres of walling. As this is only really used in specific localised areas, the dealers are usually well known to those in the trade or to local merchants.

Blocks The main manufacturers of walling blocks only supply through recognised merchants, although smaller local companies may deal with you direct. Prices are quoted by the square metre and, as with bricks, you will need to establish the price for delivery to your site on crane offloading vehicles. Packs are usually shrink wrapped in polythene and on the lorry they are often also on pallets. If you need to retain these pallets there is often a special charge and you will have to clear it with the depot before delivery. The pallets remain the property of the block company and they will arrange to pick them up one day, maybe with an additional charge.

Joinery These can be obtained direct from manufacturers but, with the larger companies, they are more often obtained from merchants and stockists. You'll undoubtedly want to make sure that you're getting what you want with these items and you will want to make sure that you know all about their properties, benefits and glazing arrangements. The literature from the manufacturers will tell you all about this but you will need to make sure that when they are delivered every item is checked thoroughly for damage in transit. Also, establish which items or ranges are stock items and which are made to order. A replacement or addition in the latter category can involve an awfully long wait.

Roof trusses These can be ordered direct from the manufacturers or though your builders' merchant. Don't be tempted to try to define what you're ordering: confine yourself to asking for a prefabricated roof to suit your particular drawings. That way, if there are any problems, the manufacturers will have to solve them. Sometimes the roof manufacturers will also supply the ancillary roofing materials such as facia, barge, soffit, etc. and you do need to establish this fact, even if the quantities and sizes are left up to the suppliers themselves. You will also need to establish delivery arrangements and when the trusses arrive you may need some extra labour on site to man-handle them off.

Timber Timber is priced by the cubic metre at the yard but happily this is normally translated into various prices per metre according to the sections. Most builders' merchants have their own timber yards or else there are specialist timber importers who will sell direct to the self-builder. If timber needs to be treated, then this is normally carried out in the yard for an extra cost, which may delay the delivery date. Be careful about delivery as you may get an extremely big lorry arriving with an awful lot of wood on it and no crane offload, so you may have to organise extra labour to be on site.

Roof tiles/slates Tile-company representatives will often deal directly with the self-builder, even if any eventual order is placed through a local builders' merchant. The merchants themselves will also probably have a library of roof tiles and slates, maybe attached to and part of their brick library, and their staff may be able to suggest suitable alternatives from various companies. Any order should be made on the basis of the supply of the roofing materials that the suppliers have quoted from your plans and the quantities should be left to them. It's unlikely that the quotation will fail to detail the amounts that they're supplying, so, if you're short, they may still refer you back to the quotation. But, if you can definitely establish that the fault lies with them, at least they'll then move heaven and earth to get the balance to you so as not to delay the job. You need to establish whether they will be supplying any ancillary materials and/or fixings and, in like manner to the tiles themselves, it's perhaps better to let the suppliers recommend the quantities.

Glazing Many joinery manufacturers will now supply double-glazing units to suit their windows, but some self-builders buy them separately as they find this more advantageous. If you are ordering glass, make sure that the measurements you give to the supplier are clearly marked as either 'rebate size' or 'tight-glass size'. Better still, ask the rep to come and measure up for you, and then if something doesn't fit it is his fault.

Plumbing and heating materials If you're using a supply-and-fix plumber and heating engineer then there will be very little that you need to buy for this trade. If you're using a labour-only subcontractor in part or in full then materials will be available from either specialist plumbers' merchants or from normal builders' merchants. For those who are dealing direct with specialist manufacturers or suppliers of equipment, such as underfloor central heating or special boilers, the price may be of secondary consideration to the nature of that which is being offered. Nevertheless, do try and check that you're not being taken for a ride by reference to different prices of similar equipment from other manufacturers or suppliers. With 'conventional' systems, some merchants will take your plans and give a lump-sum price for any materials.

Kitchen and utility-room units and furniture Where do you start? The offers are endless as are the ranges of differing units and equipment. 40% discounts are often only the start of what's available and in the course of my travels I've met many self-builders who bought kitchens at one third of the original price, just because they were in the right place at the right time. Keep a look out in your local paper and an extra look out for kitchen showrooms changing over their displays. Bear in mind that flair and imagination can often count more than just bunging money at something and bear in mind that the most expensive units have many of the physical characteristics of some of the cheaper ones. Try to remember, as well, that in five-to-ten years' time your kitchen may look dated and, if its cost was a reasonable rather than an excessive proportion of your budget, you could give your home a face-lift by getting a new kitchen.

Above: A fine timbered house in the traditional West-Country styling that Border Oak Design & Construction Ltd have made their own signature.

Sanitaryware Much of the same applies to this. The builders' merchants often have displays and there are specialist shops and merchants, some of which are frightfully expensive and up market. My strictures above regarding flair and imagination being more important than money apply here in equal measure. Out-of-town warehouse companies often have marvellous bargains and, if you live on the south coast, a trip to France or Belgium might be worthwhile.

Insulation materials Insulation quilt for roofs and insulation slabs for cavity walling are often best bought from specialist insulation suppliers, listed in the Yellow Pages. However, builders' merchants and some of the out-of-town DIY stores often have special offers at huge discounts.

Electrical goods If you don't use a supply-and-fix electrician then you'll probably be able to buy much of what you need at your local builders' merchant.

Alternatively there are specialist electrical outlets, some of which may not want to open an account with you and all of whom are not very sympathetic to the general public, preferring to sell within the trade. As far as light fittings and electrical goods and equipment are concerned, you could probably do no better than the out-of town stores.

Plasterboard and plastering materials Wet plastering materials and ancillary materials are best supplied by your plasterer but plasterboard is one thing that it might pay you to supply and this is available from your local builders' merchants. It may not come directly from them and it may be delivered directly to your site by the manufacturers, in which case, if you don't have a fork lift on site, you'll have to gear up some pretty strong labour to unload it and carry it into the dry.

Plant and scaffold hire

Every self-builder hires plant or equipment at some stage in building a new home, and arranging your hiring in the most effective way is an important part of your project planning.

You need to plan your tool-hire arrangements at the same time as you are deciding on suppliers and, indeed, your local builders' merchants will, in all probability, have a tool-hire department. In addition, in most larger towns, you will have a choice of tool-hire and plant-hire companies that normally have either a typed list or a glossy brochure of what's available. Give them a ring or pop in and see them and ask about their services. If a firm seems keen to have your business, they are likely to look after your requirements. If they are casual about explaining their service to you, then they are probably only interested in their established trade customers.

Much will depend on where a hire depot is situated, and a small local operation may suit you better than a plant-hire superstore. Remember that the firm you choose is going to be very important to you; take time to go to see what is on offer, and judge the reliability of both the equipment and the delivery promises that will be made. Most of the leading hire companies belong to a trade association called Hire

Association Europe. They subscribe to a national code of practice and have a common form of contract. In recent years this has done much to raise standards generally and particularly to promote safety. HAE also provides an arbitration service when required.

When you have decided on a hire company, consider how you are going to pay them. You may get a better discount as an account customer, or cash terms may be cheaper. The smaller the hire company, the more you can negotiate. Remember that they will all want deposits, and two separate forms of identification. A driving licence and a credit card are usually all that is required, although some depots that hire out expensive machines like excavators will ask you to pose for a Polaroid photo which stays with them until the machine is returned. All good fun. You may be able to use your credit card for the deposit, and usually the card voucher stays in the till and is destroyed when you return the equipment. This is really a form of 'no deposit' hire, and very useful.

It is important to remember that the plant which you hire is probably the most dangerous equipment that you will have on your site, and that a juicy accident would really set back your building programme. All HAE hirers are committed to providing proper instruction on the use of power tools, emphasising safety, and have appropriate protective clothing for sale. This instruction is very important and the standard of it varies. Some hire shops have specially trained staff responsible for this and take it very seriously indeed whilst others are perhaps a little more lax. If you feel that you need to be given additional instruction, then ask for it and, if you feel that you're not getting what you need from that company, then go and see someone else.

This leads us to the consideration of insurance for plant. Many of the hire shops or depots offer an indemnity to cover damage done to hired machinery or plant by an inexperienced operator, for an additional cost on the hire charge. This policy does not normally cover for theft from site and, if it gets stolen, you may be liable for the full cost of any replacement, unless, of course, you're covered by another policy such as your self-build insurance. If you're only going to have machinery or tools on site for, say, a day at a time, then this may still be the best way of covering things. On the other hand, the self-build insurance policies that every self-builder should have, can give cover for plant and machinery on site, whether hired, owned or borrowed, either for an extra premium, or in some cases as part and parcel of the original policy subject to various excesses. It really depends on your individual circumstances and I would suggest that the best course of action on this one is to talk to your broker.

There are two items of hired-in plant that need special consideration. The first is your mixer. Small mixers with less than 0.1 cubic metre capacity are unpopular with bricklayers and should be avoided. Larger diesel mixers are ruggedly built, and are often offered for sale very cheaply through small ads in local papers or on notice boards in builders' merchants. If you are a fair judge of used machinery it will be cheaper to buy than to hire, particularly as you should be able to sell on your mixer when you finish. Some mixers at Milton Keynes plots have been owned by dozens of self-builders and, incidentally, so have many site caravans.

Scaffolding needs thinking about carefully. It is possible to hire scaffold for erection on site and indeed there may be instances where, at the end of the job, it's necessary to hire in something like a tower scaffold for a particular task. I do not believe, however, that it's a good idea for the self-builder to attempt to provide a full scaffold for on-site erection by either himself or by one of the other tradesmen. Bricklayers will often volunteer to erect the scaffold as they go and, in the past, I have to admit that that is what I have often done. But in today's climate of awareness about health and safety in general, and the new legislation in particular, I really believe that this is not good advice. Bricklayers may well erect a scaffold that gets them through their trade but they might not really care about how the tiler is going to get on or how the plumber will get to do his flashings around the chimney, knowing that by the time those chaps are up on it, they'll be long gone. And if the

scaffolding's dangerous or illegal and one of the following trades or a member of your family falls off or through it, I'll give you one guess who's going to be liable – yes, it's you.

Reputable hire-and-erect scaffolding firms, who will come along to site and erect a proper and legal scaffold, are the answer. Most of them are fairly reliable and will usually come with just 24 hours' notice to raise, lower or extend the scaffold, working in with the other tradesmen as they go. To cover yourself even further, make sure when you engage a company that you state, in writing, that their scaffold should conform to all of the Health and Safety legislation and to best practice. Hire is normally quoted as being for a minimum period, often 10 weeks, with a weekly rate thereafter and it is normally quoted by reference to the plans. Foot scaffolds, for uneven ground or board scaffolds, for internal plastering of ceilings etc., are not usually included and, if you need these then you'll have to ask for an additional price.

One thing that you should especially watch out for is the treatment of the scaffolding by other tradesmen. Firstly, don't ever let them alter the scaffold by themselves, for that could invalidate any liabilities of the main hire and erection company and any warranties they will have given you. Next, keep an eye out for tradesmen cutting up scaffold boards or using the angle grinder you've hired in for another job to cut off the end of a putlock. It's you who will be charged for these at the end of the job, as indeed you will for the pile of fittings and clips that get buried, simply because nobody bothered to move them.

Finally, electric tools. These should always be connected through an RCD contact breaker. The hire companies have suitable plug-in units available, but they do not provide them unless you ask for them because most hirers are planning to do jobs at houses that have contact breakers in the fuse box. If your temporary site supply is not RCD protected, hire a plug-in unit.

Self-build site safety

- Get into the habit of wearing a hard hat on site and make sure that there are some spare hats in the site hut with a notice on the wall that they should be worn at all times. When accepting quotations from subcontractors, slip a little paragraph in about expecting them to wear theirs on site.

- Wear protective footwear. Wellies and boots with steel toecaps are readily available – look under 'Safety' in Yellow Pages.

- Buy two or three pairs of plastic goggles and always use them with cutting or grinding tools, etc. Encourage others on site to wear them when appropriate by hanging the spare sets up, next to the hard hats, with a suitable notice.

- Use specialist and *bona fide* scaffolding contractors only, and make sure that when you accept their quotation, you confirm that the scaffold is to be erected and maintained in accordance with all of the Health and Safety legislation and by reference to best possible practice. If scaffold boards are, quite rightly, turned back at night by the bricklayers, make sure that they are properly replaced each day and that no 'traps' are formed by the boards failing to run to a putlock.

- With conventional scaffolding, the short lengths of scaffolding that carry the boards are called putlocks. They project beyond the scaffolding at lead level and building professionals know that they are there, almost by instinct. Self-builders, however, bump into them on a regular basis. Tape some empty plastic bottles over the ends – it looks funny but is very effective.

- Whenever you hire equipment from a hire firm, ask if instruction leaflets and safety manuals are available. You may feel rather self-conscious about doing this but most hire firms will welcome your enquiry and will probably be pleased to give you the benefit of their experience. They will all have stories of the wife returning the tool that put the husband in hospital.

- Keep petrol for mixers in a locked hut, preferably in the type of can that is approved for carrying petrol in the boot of a motor car. Do not let anyone smoke in the hut where you keep the petrol. Better still, use diesel equipment.

- Professional electric power tools from a plant hire company will normally be 110 volts and equipped with the appropriate safety cut outs, etc. If you are using 230 volt DIY power tools or any other 230 volt equipment, including lighting, take the supply through an RCD contact breaker.

- If trenches for services or your foundation trenches are more than a metre deep, treat them with respect, and go by the book with shoring. If they show any tendency to collapse, deal with them from above, in company with another person. Never work in a deep trench alone.

- Packs of bricks and blocks that are crane off-loaded, with or without pallets, must always be stacked on stable ground and never piled more than two high. Take great care when cutting the bands and re-stack them by hand if packs are in any way unstable. Stop children from climbing on them and sheet them up if possible.

- Concrete burns are a self-build speciality. Bad ones can leave the bone visible and require skin grafts. Never handle concrete or mortar with your bare hands and, in particular, do not let it get down your wellies or in your shoes. If it does, then wash out the offending footwear or clothing immediately. Remember, cement burns do not hurt until after the damage is done. If you get cement dust in your eyes, flood your face under water immediately. Do not let children or animals play with or walk through wet concrete.

- Do not get involved with work on roofs unless you are used to and confident with heights. Do not take risks and never go onto a roof without the appropriate scaffolding.

- Self-builders regularly fall down stairwells. If they do not then their visitors do. Use rough timber to form a temporary balustrade until you fix the real one.

- Do not use old-fashioned wooden ladders. Always tie the ladder on at the top and if there is any danger of the feet slipping, fix a cross board at the bottom.

- Be obsessive about clearing away loose boards or noggins with a nail sticking out of them and, in case you miss one, never wear thin-soled shoes on site.

- Put together a First Aid Box containing plasters and antiseptic and fasten it on the site hut wall. You will suffer your fair share of cuts and abrasions and a poisoned finger is a nuisance.

- Watch your back when unloading heavy items or if you are handling more weight than you are used to. This also applies to digging work. The risk of straining yourself is very real. The most scrawny looking professional builders can handle heavy weights without any risk of injury. If you try it, you could put yourself out of action for a week or more.

- Watch out for machinery moving about on site and be aware that the driver might not be able to see everything behind.

- Always be careful when walking on joists. Many inexperienced people fall through joists either because they are considerably less skilful at balancing than they supposed or because the joists weren't fixed. Use scaffold boards laid across the joists and make sure that the joists are either built in firmly or held in place by battening, nailed across and to each one.

- Cover up old or new drainage manholes and pay particular attention to the backfilling or covering over of disused septic tanks and the like. If dumpers or other site vehicles are likely to go near these, then hire a metal plate rather than trusting to a sheet of ply.

11. TROUBLE SHOOTING AND PROBLEM AVOIDANCE

The whole tenet of this book has been the avoidance of problems, either by their anticipation or by their replacement with solutions. Nevertheless, problems will still crop up from time to time and, although most of them are not very serious (at least not half as serious as the man in the pub would have you believe), there are times when it's a little difficult to see the way forward. A way forward there is, however, and if you are to find that way forward then it's important to remember that when dealing with a crisis, your objective is to build the right house, within your budget and to the planned timetable. That may mean spending some of the contingency money in your budget to keep the job on schedule, or conceding a point in an argument with the council. Keeping everything moving forward is often far more important than winning a dispute over who pays for a dropped kerb or a broken double glazing unit.

Seizing the initiative is the important thing and part of that initiative is attendance at my oft-mentioned school of forward planning. So let's look at some of the possible problems under various headings, many of which have been presaged within the main text of the various chapters but all of which bear repetition.

Getting off on the right foot

When you start a self-build project its whole shape is determined by the very first decisions that you make. Are you choosing the right site? Is your solicitor really interested in working for a self-builder who wants to ask him a lot of unusual questions? Do you have the right designer working for you or the right package company? These early decisions should be made after careful consideration of all your options, and you should not just drift into them. In particular, employing the right people and firms who will be central to the whole operation is crucial. If you're not happy with how things are going at the evaluation and planning stages then stop and, if necessary, change course. Don't be hassled into making the wrong decision. If you do find out that you're going down the wrong road then, before you are legally and irrevocably committed, pull away and think again.

Site problems

Unforeseen site problems that are discovered after you have bought your site can prove a disaster. Examples include: discovering that there is a ransom strip which prevents you from having access to the site; a main drain that is not where you believed it to be; or visibility splays that cannot be achieved. These are things that you should check out *before* you sign a contract to buy the land. Remember that your solicitor will concern himself with whether your title to the land is good and solid. It is your job to make sure that you are going to be able to build on it in the way that you want.

Sometimes, despite all the precautions, despite soil investigations and surveys, the excavation of foundation trenches turns up ground conditions which have not been anticipated and which require a change of foundation design. Above ground, most building is a simple matter of a huge jigsaw going together and extras are normally either completely foreseeable or elective. Below ground, the only survey that is 100% accurate is the one that you effect when you construct your house and any contingency sum within your budget is there, first and foremost, to cover that eventuality. If it's not required, then and only then, can it be rolled forward to meet other choices.

If your excavations turn up unexpected ground conditions, then remain calm and get hold of the very best professional advice as soon as possible. Start with the Building Inspector and/or your architect and get them to put you on to a suitable engineer who'll come out to site whilst the excavations are still open. Give him time to do his tests and to come up with a solution and then, when that's prepared, make sure that you get approval from the Building Control department of the local authority and from your warranty company for what he is proposing, before you recommence work. If necessary, pay your contractors or subcontractors for the abortive work and agree a new price for the revised specification, almost as a completely new contract. They'll be as keen as you to get restarted and their price will often reflect the fact that they're on site already and all geared up to go. But don't let them jump the gun and do make sure that, when things do start again, everything is approved and that all and any of the revised materials required have been properly sourced; otherwise your site will just come to another halt.

Selling the existing home

In previous editions of this book there would have been dire warnings over the financial consequences of the existing house failing to sell in order to satisfy a mortgage commitment. The current facts are that unless you can adequately demonstrate your ability to service the mortgages on both houses, the chances are that you won't have started building without first selling the original house. If you do manage to build without having to sell the existing house, reaching the end of a self-build project and finding yourself saddled with two homes has its own problems. If you're going to occupy them both until one of them sells then you're going to have to think in terms of two Council Tax commitments and the lighting, heating, insurance and running costs of two homes. If you're going to leave one empty then you're going to have to think in terms of insurance for the unoccupied dwelling and if the one that's left empty is the one you're trying to sell, remember that empty houses never have the sales appeal of a lived-in home.

If it goes on too long, a Capital Gains Tax liability could arise. You need to add up the figures and make the decision long before it's 'stale on the market',

about what price is your cut-off or break-even price. If necessary, and if the season's all wrong, you might like to consider cutting your losses by means of a shorthold letting for six months. Don't forget that you'll have to pay tax on the income from the tenancy and don't forget that you'll probably also have to pay management fees to a letting agency.

Accidents

The building industry has a bad accident record and self-builders are even more at risk than professionals. There is a real chance that you will suffer an accident while you are building. Guard against this by learning of all the hazards, and taking common sense precautions. In particular, beware cement burns, and I write this as someone who still bears the scars of my inexperience, decades ago.

Coping with death

If you walk under a bus while you are building the new house, your estate will still have the building finance available to get the job finished. However, in order to arrange for this they will probably want £20–£30,000 of additional money to be able to employ the best builder in town to finish it quickly, perhaps so that it can be sold. If something happens to you, will this money be available in your estate? The prudent person should always take out an appropriate short-term life insurance policy, something that is unlikely to cost very much.

Domestic problems

One of the commonest reasons why work comes to a stop on a self-build site is that the couple who are building have split up. This has a disastrous effect on both the finances of the project and the enthusiasm to get the job done. These are always sad stories, and sometimes I get the impression that the self-build operation was a last ditch attempt to save a marriage that was in deep trouble anyway. If your relationship is going through a sticky patch then avoid self-build until things are better. Many is the time a self-build project has been seen, usually by one party, as the means by which, striving with common purpose, a couple can bring a shaky marriage back into line. The reality is far different and the stresses and strains that inevitably occur in any building project are the reefs upon which the marriage eventually founders.

On the other hand, many successful self-builders will tell you that building their new home gave them an opportunity to tackle something together which made them realise just what an effective team they were; that they really enjoyed working together. The self-build stories at the end of this book are adequate demonstration of that truth.

Problems with the authorities

Dealing with authority can sometimes be likened to charging, head first, at a brick wall without wearing a hard hat. Nevertheless, it is a skill which every self-builder should acquire, and there are times when you need to be able to stand back, cool off and think carefully about your objectives. Most authority is there to perform a function and that function is not usually clouded by too much sentiment. Most employees of authorities and statutory undertakers do not have very much freedom of expression in carrying out their duties and have to follow strict guidelines and procedures, laid down and adhered to with just as much zeal as tablets of stone from on high. What you need to do is to find the words to state your objectives in a way that conforms to these regulations and procedures and to do that you may, sometimes, have to put yourself in the shoes of the other man and try to look at things from his perspective.

Planning departments

For some self-builders, problems with planning departments will commence at the 'Outline' stages of planning permission and, for quite a few of them, those problems will remain insurmountable. In Chapter 5 I've discussed ways of maximising the chances of an 'Outline' application being successful. But I have also said that there are times when it pays to recognise when the end of the road has been reached and that it's then, perhaps, better to move on to another plot.

For those dealing with the planning authorities at the detailed stages there is a whole raft of other problems. Planning officers do have some leeway. But not enough to allow you to form the vanguard of precedent that will remove or destroy their authority's whole planning ethos. In any negotiation for detailed consent, a balance has to be reached between your desire for individuality and the planning officer's duty to maintain conformity with the local structure plan and design guidelines. Keeping the emphasis on the achievement of every one of your desires, however at odds with the local vernacular, can only lead to conflict and a loss of momentum on your whole self-build project. The motto has to be to steer clear of contention wherever possible or to present potentially contentious issues in as non-contentious a manner as possible. If you've got the time and the money to turn your new home into a crusade, then by all means take things to the limit but, for the average self-builder, time and money are in short supply and reasonable compromise is the order of the day.

Planning consents are fairly concise documents written in plain English on very bad-quality paper. The words on them are specific and precise, and they are meant to be read, understood, and complied with. This seems straightforward, but it is surprising how many self-builders choose to ignore the conditions of their planning consent. Those who do this may decide very lightly that there is no need to bother with what they consider to be unnecessary formalities. Then they find that they are involved in a dispute with the authority that will take a long time to resolve, and may delay all work on site until it is settled.

Building Control departments

The principal problems that the uninitiated experience with Building Control are the serial applications and rejections that characterise the way many authorities work. Some self-builders see these rejections as some sort of failing that they wrongly attribute to their architect or package-deal company. Don't let any of this worry you and, as long as the relevant procedures are adopted and adhered to, it should not cause any delay or upset in your programme.

Bad tradesmen will often portray the Building Inspector as an ogre. However, as a self-builder, you should always keep in mind that the inspector has precisely the same objectives as you in that both of you are trying to ensure that your new home is built properly and in conformance with the regulations. It is true that older and wiser Building Inspectors can appear more lenient whilst some of the younger, more eager, ones can appear to be 'going by the book'. In reality, appearances are almost always deceptive, in that the objectives are the same. If the older inspector suspects bad ground, he may throw up the query at the early stages of an application and when he comes on site he may be able to suggest a course of action or remedy. The younger one, without the background knowledge will, nevertheless, come to precisely the same conclusions as soon as he sees the excavations, so the end result is almost certain to be the same. Remember that the Building Inspector is on your side. If he thinks that, despite what your plans say, another course of action is advisable, then he is coming to that conclusion for very good reasons. Even if a suspicion of bad ground is not confirmed by subsequent exploration and investigation, the very fact that you have had it disproved is not a victory or a triumph over someone who is trying to do you down. Instead it is, and should be treated as, a worthwhile evaluation that has led you to a point of comfort in the knowledge that what you are doing is right, and that the relevant people are looking out for your interests.

Highways and environmental agencies

To a large degree the requirements of both these agencies will be dealt with by the Planning and Building Control departments. Remember that before any work can be carried out involving the highway (including creating a new access or connecting to a public sewer in the highway), a licence will be required from the highways authorities, consent will be needed to make a connection to the sewer and periods of notice will be required before the works may take place. Remember also that only accredited or approved contractors can carry out works that involve digging up or disturbing the metalled sections of the highway, including the footpath.

Where any of the agencies are involved, try to ensure that their requirements are anticipated and conformed to and try to ensure that, when making your applications, you make the Planning and/or Building Control departments aware that you have taken these factors into consideration. If you do find yourself stuck in the middle of what will be, to them, an interesting conflict of interests, then try to arrange a meeting between the sides and go to that meeting, with your professionals, in the capacity of arbitrators seeking a solution, rather than as an injured party.

Electricity, gas, water and telephone companies

For me these have always been the hardest brick walls at which I've charged headlong. All of the inflexibilities of both personnel and procedure seem to coagulate within and under their vast monolithic umbrellas. Procedure is the thing, plus timescales which, despite the dictates of your site, have to be adhered to. Make sure that you obtain the necessary quotations for supply in good time and make doubly sure that you send off any payment or order for that supply within the timescale laid down in the documentation. If the water board want six weeks' notice of your requirement for a building supply then, no matter how long and hard you shout that you need it the following day, the chances are that you'll still have to wait for the requisite period.

On the other hand, if you get into trouble and accidentally cut a main, you'll be amazed at how fast the response will be and how positive the action taken, right down to the bill for damages that will inevitably follow. If you have a suspicion that a main crosses your land then ask the relevant Board to provide you with a plan and to pinpoint the exact position. That way, if they're wrong, at least you've got a counter claim against them.

One problem that many self-builders come across is meter boxes. The electricity and gas boards provide these, and some of the ducting pipes, within their quotation for supply, but often they are not delivered. Instead, they have to be picked up at a depot by reference to an order which, yes, you've guessed it, has to be processed within certain timescales. Make sure that you've got all of this organised before your bricklayer gets to the point of needing to build them in. Although they can be cut in and fixed at a later date it's never as good a job.

Difficulties with professionals

Never lose sight of the fact that the man with the string of letters after his name is just one of the people *you* are going to employ to assist in the building of *your* new home. He may well be a very important person in his own right but, as far as the building of your new home is concerned, he is just one of many who will have an input and you are in the driving seat and must remain so. Do not let yourself be intimidated into agreeing to or going along with something that you are not comfortable with. If you are not completely happy, then stop and think carefully before going on and, if necessary (as long as you are not legally committed), pull away and look elsewhere.

Of course, if you have tied yourself into a legal contract with a professional, then you must, at some stage, have been happy with their services or you wouldn't have made the commitment. But what do you do if it all starts to go wrong half-way through the project? A bricklayer who is dismissed will, especially if he's been paid up to date, just shrug his shoulders and leave the site, leaving a few choice words ringing in your ears. A professional who has failed to live up to your expectations or even to his own promises, may not be so easy to get rid of. Any attempt at dismissal may result in a very large bill for abortive work and a writ if you do not pay very promptly. If it's a package-deal company that is failing to perform, then there may be an element of manufacture and supply to which you are undoubtedly committed. Unless, therefore, you are very sure of your ground, you may end up with a very large bill for damages, breach of contract and/or loss of profit. All of this makes it ever more necessary that you should satisfy yourself, well before the commitment stage, that you are taking the right course of action and that you're dealing with the right people.

If you do get into this situation, then the thing to do is to make sure that you do things by the book. First of all, try arranging a meeting with the company or professional with whom you are in dispute and, at that meeting, try to resolve your differences to your mutual benefit. Do not cut your nose off to spite your face. Do not imagine that your differences are irrecon-cilable or, at least, do not approach such a meeting in this frame of mind. Set down your grievances in writing, clearly and without resort to intemperate language. Commit to paper your earnest desire to find a suitable way forward and, if one can be found, take it. And if, despite all of your endeavours you feel that you have no option but to sever your relations? Well, if you do have to terminate a contract with a professional, only do so after careful consideration and in consultation with and on the advice of a solicitor who has been given the opportunity carefully to examine all of the facts and, in particular, the contract or terms of engagement.

Forgetting about insurance and warranties

How could you possibly do this after all of the exhortations and hints I've dropped throughout the text? Yet the fact is that people still do forget, or even, at times, feel that they can get away without insurance. It only takes one gale or one errant child to make a mockery of a whole self-build project, which is sufficient to blight a lifetime. Never start work on site without adequate self-build insurance and always listen to the advice from solicitors and others about single premium indemnity policies where they are deemed necessary.

Warranties need to be put in place long before work actually commences on site and certainly long before trenches are opened. If there are trees present or if bad ground is suspected, then the lead-in period of notice of commencement of works may well be extended and you will need to take this into account in your programme. I've known of self-builders building without a warranty; something that's almost impossible if a building society or bank is involved in the project. But I've also known of times when all of the bravado disappears in the realisation that a mistake has been made. It's not impossible to sell a house without a warranty, but it's certainly very difficult and it involves expensive and extensive structural surveys and complicated insurance policies.

One last thing on the subject of insurances. Don't be bashful about asking any of the people you engage for details of their insurance and indemnity policies. Ask your builder for a copy of his insurance policies even if you're playing safe by arranging one of your own. If he's going to be digging up the Queen's highway, then you need to know that he's adequately covered and if he's not then you either need to insist that he increases his cover or you engage another party to carry out that work. Ask any of the professionals for details of their indemnity policies and make sure that the amount of cover provided equals or exceeds the re-building costs of your project.

Problems with suppliers

First of all, any organisation selling goods or services on any sort of scale sometimes lets its customers down. In the building industry these problems are more prevalent due to the stop/go nature of the market, the fact that deliveries are made to a multitude of different sites, and because suppliers do not hold buffer stocks. As a result of this, most self-builders are likely to meet one or two minor irritating problems with suppliers, and a few have to cope with major problems.

If you experience problems with suppliers or products then once again it is important to keep calm and to approach things from the perspective of the big picture and your end goal – the successful completion of your new home. Try to talk directly to the sales director or the managing director of any firm or supplier that is letting you down. Present your case in a measured and reasonable fashion and endeavour, as far as possible at that meeting, to understand their problems, even if, when it is over, you decide that your best course of action is to sever the relationship. Always look at your 'worst case' losses and decide whether it would be better to walk away from a particular situation or to change suppliers altogether. Consider whether, if a product, or its delivery proves to be unreliable, there are alternatives. You may not think so but I assure you, you are wrong and, in years to come, you may have cause to welcome the changes that circumstance brought about. Initial unreliability often translates into long-term problems.

Problems with builders

In all of the chapters devoted to seeking out and engaging builders and subcontractors, I have stressed the importance of your eventual choice being made after thorough investigation and considerable personal enquiry and inspection. However, no builder is any better than his last job and many things can happen to make a previously good builder perform in an unreliable or uncharacteristic manner. Family breakdowns, ill health and money problems can all affect a builder's performance and it's important that you not only get to the bottom of what's wrong but, having done so, you take action to ensure that your site doesn't suffer. You're not a marriage guidance counsellor, you're not a doctor and you're certainly not a banker, at least in respect of your new home. What you are is a self-builder and you must not lose sight of the fact.

The tell-tale signs are not always bad workmanship, at least not in the immediately visible form. Normally you'll notice long periods when nothing seems to happen or when there are long waits for follow-on trades to arrive on site. You may be told that the plumber is busy elsewhere and that he'll be along in a few days. You may be told that the tilers are all geared up but that there's a delay on the delivery. All of this might be perfectly true but, in equal measure, these excuses may be symptomatic of something going wrong.

Maybe the state of the man's mind means that he's lost the will or the ability to organise the follow-on trades whilst he's trying to save a marriage. Maybe the plumber won't come or the merchants won't deliver the tiles because they haven't been paid for the work and the materials they provided on the builder's previous job. Maybe a clue to that could be your builder's request for an advance payment; something that you should resist at all costs. If you can, talk to the plumber directly, and ask him what the problem is, or go along to the merchants and ask them to confirm when the tiles are going to arrive. Strictly, they're not at liberty to discuss the builder's status, but by finding out exactly what the situation is regarding the tiles for your new home, you may well be able to draw some pretty firm conclusions. Perhaps, also, the merchants themselves might start pumping you for information about what exactly is going on and they might even have been told that your failure to pay on time is the reason they haven't been paid!

Stick to the contract. Only pay as and when a stage is reached and then only when you, your architect and/or the Building and warranties inspectors have approved the work. Watch out for corner cutting. A builder in trouble may try to skimp on important things and, in extreme cases I have witnessed, will even do things that are deliberately meant to deceive. I shall never forget the garage floor that was neatly screeded with a sand and cement mix. The only trouble was, there was no concrete beneath and the first car driven onto it fell through! Don't panic, something like that is very rare.

That is the value of the contract, whether it's a long and complicated one or a simple exchange of letters. Either way, the most important things it needs to contain are the price, the stages at which payment will be made and the express or implied requirement that all work must be carried out in a proper and workmanlike manner to the satisfaction of the Building and warranty inspectors and/or your architect. If you reach a point where the contract has to be terminated, you should be advised by your solicitor about what to do at every stage. In this case, your concern will be to move from the bad contractor to a new one as soon as possible, with as little disruption and delay as possible. All situations like this are different, but you will probably want to engage a quantity surveyor to give you a report on the work done and the value of materials lying on site. If there is any question of bad workmanship an independent architect's report may be required and if the NHBC or Zurich are involved, remember that they must be consulted.

If your builder goes bust

Perhaps the most worrying thing that can happen to a self-builder is that the person building the whole house for you goes bust, or they simply disappear, or tell you that they are facing bankruptcy and cannot continue with the work on your new home. What do you do?

Well, that will depend on the nature of your arrangements with the builder, your formal contract with him and whether or not that involves either an

Above: All those mortar snots mean that trouble is brewing for this wall.

Right: No proper cavity closure and snots bridging the cavity!

Pictures from Forest of Dean D.C. Building Control department.

NHBC Buildmark or a Zurich 'Newbuild' warranty (not Custombuild). Your final situation will depend on this, but in either event you must take the following immediate action, without any delay, and ignoring remonstrations by others.

1) Secure the site by changing all locks. It is not unusual for a builder's employees and subcontractors to try to recoup their losses by helping themselves to *his* valuables on the site, which will be *your* building materials or fixtures. They will convince themselves that they are entitled to do this. So may builders' merchants and other suppliers to whom the builder owes money, and they may arrive with a lorry waving delivery notes saying that ownership of materials supplied does not pass to purchasers until they are paid for. These vultures are trespassing on your site, and although the law is on their side in many respects, they cannot enter your site without your permission. Simply say, 'This is my site. The builder supplied these materials to me, and your problem is one for the liquidator. Go away.' Wire off the entrance to the site and put up a notice saying something like: – *Materials on this site are the property of Joe Self-builder, and of no other person. Any attempt at repossession against the debts of others will be treated as theft.* It may even be worthwhile moving materials elsewhere or engaging a watchman for a week.

2) Next, advise the local police of the situation. They will not help you in an argument with a repossessor, but they will be concerned to prevent a breach of the peace or a criminal trespass. Their interest may also deter the opportunist thief who notices that work has stopped.

3) Finally, consider the insurance situation. If theft, fire, vandalism, etc., were covered by the builder's insurances, and you can get details of these insurances from him, check out with the company concerned that cover still exists on the site and for how long it will be in force. The answer will usually be 'no'. If so, you must arrange your own insurance by phone in the next 10 minutes and I would suggest a call to the

experts, DMS Sevices Ltd. 01909 591652.

4) Having safeguarded your property on your site, you must move on to safeguard your legal position. Take whatever contract documents you have to your solicitor and ask him to send an appropriate notice to the builder advising him that by going bust he has voided the contract, and spelling out where he stands. Your solicitor should get off this letter by recorded delivery the same day.

If there is an NHBC Buildmark warranty in place or if the property was registered under the Zurich Newbuild scheme then you do need to get in touch with their local inspectors as quickly as possible and you will be delighted to hear that there is a considerable amount of help that they can give you.

First of all, the NHBC Buildmark scheme. If you are buying speculatively, something that is outside the scope of this book, but which may, in some cases, form the basis of your contract with a builder, such as when the builder was also the vendor of the land, then, if the builder has not started work, the NHBC will refund any amount you have paid as a deposit, up to £10,000 or, if greater, 10% of the value of the home. If, on the other hand, the builder has already started work under a contractual arrangement and he then fails to complete the job because of his insolvency or fraud, then the NHBC will provide some very important help.

They will either:

1) Pay you the amount above the *value of the home* which is needed to complete the home, substantially in accordance with the NHBC's requirements, together with, where appropriate, the cost of putting right any *defect or damage*, or:

2) They will reimburse you any amount you have paid to the *builder* for the *home* under a legal obligation but cannot recover from him, or:

3) Instead of either of the above, they may also, at their option, arrange for the work to be carried out.

Sounds good and it is, although there are special conditions, the first of which is that the NHBC will only be liable for what was in the original contract; they will not be liable for any extras that were subsequently arranged. In addition, if you have retained any part of the contract price, the NHBC will be entitled to deduct that from the sums it would pay out or, if it is the NHBC that arranges to complete the work, they will require you to pay them the amount of monies that you still owed under the original contract.

The maximum liability of the NHBC for all of this is £10,000 or, if greater, 10% of the *value of the home*. Let's put all of this into plain English by reference to a theoretical example. Let's say you have a contract with a builder to build your new home for a price of £100,000 and when you've paid out the sum of £60,000 the chap goes bust and does a runner. You've got £40,000 left in the kitty. You need to find another builder to take over the job but the best price you can get is for £60,000 as all of the builders know that, firstly, the first builder has taken a large part of the profit element with him, secondly you're in a bind, and thirdly they need to make allowances for any hidden problems that the first builder may have left. On the face of it, you're £20,000 out of pocket. But the NHBC will reimburse you this money, as long as it doesn't exceed 10% of the *value of the new home*. So, if the house is going to be worth £200,000 you're all right but, if the house was only ever going to be worth £175,000 then the most you'll get from the NHBC is £17,500. And that's another reason and another lesson which relates back to the earlier chapters where I talked about the carrying capacity of the land and warned you to be careful about not overdeveloping a plot in terms of its value.

With Zurich Newbuild, if it's a speculative sale and purchase, they will reimburse up to 10% loss of deposit in the event of the builder's bankruptcy or fraud. On the other hand, they take a very different view from the NHBC when it comes to the business of a contract with a builder for a self-build project, in that they believe that, if the builder in our example above goes bust and the subsequent builders want more to finish than is left on the job, this indicates that either the first builder's price was low or that you've paid too far ahead of the work done. They,

therefore, maintain that they're not in business to finance a bargain and equally, that they are not in business to bail out foolhardy behaviour. On the face of it this seems fairly harsh, but the truth and total fairness are probably halfway between these two attitudes. In any event, Zurich do say that they are perfectly prepared to consider giving a quotation to cover for a builder's possible bankruptcy and that they will base the premium on their knowledge of the builder and any financial checks they may make on him.

All of this goes to reinforce the oft given advice never to pay monies up front and never to give advances on payments before the relevant stages have been reached and approved. It is also worthwhile mentioning that, despite the assistance mentioned above, it does not absolve you from a duty of care and any one of these policies will refuse to pay out if it can be proved that you have acted recklessly, improperly or without due regard to proper procedure.

Sometimes, while all of this is going on, there will be siren voices from the builder, urging you to come to some new sort of financial arrangement with him or another company he owns, to finish the house. Unless there are very special circumstances, I suggest you avoid these proposals, which, in any event, if they involve payment of any money technically owed by you to the bankrupt company or builder, may put you on the wrong side of the fence as far as the Official Receiver is concerned. Sometimes it's technically possible to make money out of this whole situation where, for example, the builder goes bust just before a stage payment is due. In this case, whatever you do, do not pay any of the monies to the builder. He has failed and any money that you do owe him is properly due to the liquidator who will use it to pay off, firstly preferential creditors such as the Inland Revenue and the VAT authorities and, secondly the major creditors. When your liquidator claims money from you, ask your solicitor or accountant to enter a counter claim to include all your losses, including the additional cost of a contract with another builder, and even compensation for your distress and wasted time, etc., etc. The counter claim will be larger than the liquidator's claim. You will not get any money, but it will be set against the liquidator's claim.

The other voices you will hear, of course, are those of the subcontractors and it's open for you to consider whether you can come to some arrangement with them whereby they will work directly for you up to the completion of the house. Be aware that they may not have been paid for the preceding parts of their work. That must not bother you. You may have rightly paid the builder for those stages and the fact that he has not passed the money on is not your fault. Even if this is not technically true, the subcontractors have no contract with you – their contract is with the builder. Make it quite clear that, up until the time of the builder going bust, you have paid him for the work and that any shortfall that the subcontractors have is between them and the builder and/or the receivers. All you're prepared to do is consider employing them, at a fixed price, for the remainder of the work to be done.

I said that it was 'technically' possible to make money out of this situation and the reason I said that is that, if you're going to make a claim under the NHBC scheme, if you've withheld all or part of a stage payment that has been reached in whole or in part, then the monies withheld will be counted in the NHBC's calculations of your claim. That's why it might, in some circumstances, be better, especially if the builder goes down just before a big stage payment, to consider whether a claim would be your best option, or even necessary. Of course, if the reason why you used a builder rather than subcontractors in the first place was that you had neither the time nor the inclination to build all or part of your new home on a self-managed basis, then these last suggestions are going to be of absolutely no interest to you.

Problems with subcontractors

Prevention is always better than cure and if you've followed all the earlier advice about choosing a subcontractor and about talking to previous clients of his, then it's unlikely that you've engaged a bad one. On the other hand, the same maxim that 'a man's only as good as his last job' applies and there are times when a chap's personal or financial affairs can affect his work. This is where the skill of management comes into play. By self-managing your project you stand to

make considerable savings compared with the fellow who employed a builder. Part of that saving is made up by the management responsibility that you have taken on and, sometimes, that management responsibility means that you may have to dispense with the services of a tradesman altogether or refuse to pay until and unless work is put right. All of this may seem daunting but it is part and parcel of what you have taken on and if you feel that you are going to be incapable of dealing with these situations, then I suggest you question your chosen method of building.

Horrendous as it may seem at the time, there is little likelihood that bad workmanship by one subcontractor will scupper your whole project, although it might set it back a bit whilst you either have the work put right or seek other tradesmen. Keep a watch out for workmanship and make sure that it's up to the standard you picked the man for. If you're in any doubt about what he's doing then consult with your architect or the Building Inspector and get them to let you know whether everything's all right. If, despite your very best endeavours you and your advisors feel that the chap isn't any good after all, then move quickly to terminate your arrangement with him and, once you've decided that this is the thing to do, never change your mind. Do not bother about the other chap's feelings: any bad subcontractor has been finished lots of times before. Pay him in full for the work that he has done, and do not deduct the cost of putting right any defective work; your choice of subcontractor or lack of supervision was at fault, and you will have to pay for your mistake. It is what the contingency item in the budget is for.

Depending on others

Never let a self-build project depend on others. If Grandma is going to let you have the last £10,000 of your finances, she should hand it over before work starts. If your uncle offers the stone slates on his derelict barn for you to use on your new home, then make sure they are removed from the roof and stacked before work starts. If a neighbour has agreed to let you have an easement to connect your drain into his septic tank, then get it signed at the same time that you sign the contract to buy the land.

Final Checklist

- ☐ Start off with the budget

- ☐ Tailor the project to your financial abilities and not the other way around

- ☐ Take out the right insurances and warranties

- ☐ Read all you can. Get the magazines and study the articles and, in particular, the advertisements

- ☐ Cost out any proposals fully

- ☐ Explore every avenue to find the right project

- ☐ Always have a contingency fund

- ☐ Follow the earlier site checklist and don't leave anything out, hoping for the best

- ☐ Choose the right solicitors

- ☐ If possible, have a professional mentor or friend

- ☐ Design your new home to fit the plot or the project, and not the other way around

- ☐ Always check things on the ground

- ☐ Evaluate every aspect of your lifestyle when arriving at your design wish list

- ☐ Make sure that the brief you give your architect and designer includes that wish list

- ☐ Make sure that your architect or designer is aware of your budget and that what they produce is designed to accord with it

- ☐ Never hear what you want to hear

- ☐ Carefully consider all your options. If you're not completely happy then stop, draw breath and think things through again

- ☐ Consider whether there are more cost-effective options available that will not detract from your enjoyment of your new home

- ☐ If you feel you're going down the wrong route, stop and change tack

- ☐ Learn about planning and understand that it is all about compromise

- ☐ Learn the sequences and timings of the building process

- ☐ Talk to other self-builders. They will be able to give advice on land, professionals, local authority attitudes, labour and materials

- ❏ Never lose sight of your goal – to build a new home – even if that means that you have to trim some of your ideas

- ❏ Keep on working out the finances and stay on budget

- ❏ Never pay in advance for work

- ❏ If you pay a deposit for materials, make sure that you have a record of your payment

- ❏ Wherever possible, pay monies into a dedicated client's account or establish the existence of an insurance-backed bond

- ❏ Be aware that most extras in self-build projects are elective

- ❏ Balance extra expenditure against savings in other areas to stay on budget

- ❏ Never jump the gun. Get all consents and authorisations in place before commencing work

- ❏ Don't underestimate the costs of services

- ❏ Judge the effect on you and your family's lives before taking on any self build, renovation or conversion project

- ❏ Carefully consider your living arrangements while you are building. The more comfortable you can make them, the less stressful the project will be

- ❏ Don't let your job or career suffer because of your project – it is what is paying for it

- ❏ Keep the neighbours on side as far as possible

- ❏ Never bite off more than you can chew. Know your own limitations

- ❏ Avoid false economies

- ❏ Agree all changes or extras in writing

- ❏ Never leave old or superseded drawings around. Collect them up and destroy them

- ❏ Never put too much trust in individuals with whom you have only a fleeting relationship

- ❏ Always be prepared to admit that you have made the wrong choice and, if you have, move decisively to put things right

- ❏ Plan for all eventualities

- ❏ Aim to finish within budget

Make sure that all key elements in your proposals are always properly tied up before you enter into financial commitments and remember that Grandma, your uncle and your neighbour could all conceivably be in the same car crash and that their executors might not be very sympathetic to your case – or they could just change their minds.

Problems with neighbours

Almost all neighbours of a plot will have objected to its being granted planning permission in the first place and, even if they're the vendors, they'll be happy to take your money but less than happy at the prospect of you actually building on the land. Try your best to get the neighbours on your side. You may not always manage to do so but in the end you, and hopefully they, will have to realise that you're all going have to live near each other.

Deliveries are the one thing that upsets neighbours and, I'm afraid, quite rightly so. Firstly, if the plot is on a narrow lane and the block lorry arrives in the morning, then he'll put his feet down and proceed with unloading, seemingly oblivious to the queue of angry commuters who realise that they're going to miss their train. If you're not there or the space to put the blocks is not obvious or clearly marked out, or if there's not room on the site, he'll have no compunction about stacking them on the road or the footpath and you'll have to spend the rest of the day, when you do arrive on site, moving them.

I recall one site where the lorry driver arrived at a site and decided that the best place to put the blocks was on the side of the plot in front of the garage doors. Not only that but the best way of getting them there was to park on next door's drive! The problem was that next door's drive hadn't actually been designed or constructed to take the weight of a fully laden block lorry and it collapsed. Try, as far as possible, to ascertain when deliveries are going to be made and make sure that, if you can't be on site, somebody else is. If you know that work or deliveries are going to block off the road at a certain time, then take the trouble to inform your neighbours and to warn them that they may need to park their cars up the street. They'll never be too happy about it but at least you've done your best. And if the complaints are about noise or smoke, then do something about it. Maybe a diesel mixer could be swapped for an electric one. Maybe the radios could be turned down a little or at the very least tuned in and maybe fires could either be stopped altogether or limited to reasonable hours with the old tyres sent to the tip instead of turning the whole sky black.

Remember, above all, that this is not just any old building site, it's the site of your new home and, as such, the neighbours are going to be an important factor in your enjoyment of it. A short letter to each one apologising in advance for any inconvenience, a visit to those most affected and, perhaps, a few bunches of flowers wouldn't go amiss.

Pragmatism

Once you have started to build a new house it is important to get it finished on time, otherwise the interest charges on the building finance will get out of hand. If you do become involved in a dispute with others, settle it quickly so that the whole project is not held up. This may involve making a pragmatic decision to let others get away with things, even though you are convinced they are wrong. If you agree to a neighbour's version of where a boundary post should be put, or pay a few pounds more than agreed for materials or services, it may be the right decision if it saves time and keeps up the momentum of the whole job. Don't be a soft touch but, in equal measure, don't cut off your nose to spite your face.

12. SELF-BUILD STORIES

With a book that has a shelf life as long as this one has, it is tempting not to include actual self-build stories and instead, to point the reader towards the case histories in the monthly magazines that are packed with detailed costs and up-to-date product details. I do know, however, from talking to self-builders, that they love to read and hear about others who have done or are doing the same thing, and I know that many readers would be disappointed if there were no self-build stories in this book.

The self-build stories that follow are, quite deliberately, not written in the context of how one brick was placed upon another or how such and such a timber frame was erected. And, apart from a demonstration of the costs in relation to the market value, there is very little other information as far as prices are concerned. Whether, by the time you read this book, there will have been significant changes in property values does nothing to devalue the ratios of cost to price that these figures illustrate and the undoubted achievements of the self-builders featured. I have demonstrated the principles within this book but the detail will have to be checked out by you, with reference to the costs and values pertaining at the time of your project.

What these stories do seek to show is the human aspect of self-building, renovation and conversion and what I hope they give you is the knowledge that these people who have fulfilled the dream of creating their own homes are ordinary mortals like you. They come from all walks of life and from all age groups. I can assure you that they are all real people and I look forward to the time when your project can be included in a future edition of this book.

A Grade II Listed farmhouse in Surrey

Despite an extremely successful career in show business, John Revell always hankered to get back to his roots in the building industry and in particular, carpentry. 'Whenever I got the chance, I'd be working with wood', he explains, 'and really, once we'd done all we could with our lovely Edwardian home, there was little left but to move on. A friend tipped us off about this one, telling us that it was an old Georgian farmhouse. However, when we got here we could see that it was a lot older than that. It was liveable but it needed a lot doing to it.'

What he and his wife Debbie had found was a medieval farmhouse, Grade II Listed, in 3 ½ acres of beautifully landscaped gardens with magnificent views, a swimming pool, tennis courts and outbuildings. It had been done up in the past with various extensions, one of which, at right angles to the main house, had obviously once been the garage, but was now divided into two bedrooms with a study cum office above. 'The trouble was', John remembers, 'that nothing had really been done in sympathy with what was after all a lovely old brick and timbered building. The bricks were all wrong. There was a flat-roofed dormer, of all things, and behind the house, between it and the road, there was this common brickwork cowbarn with a corrugated asbestos roof that almost eclipsed the view of the house from the road. Yet it had the makings of a beautiful home. The older part of the house had obviously once been single-storey with massive oak trusses that would have divided any upper part into three sections. At some stage in the not-too-distant past, somebody had, rather boldly, cut these trusses and introduced steel purlins and posts that transposed the loads down to the end walls and a central post in the large lounge area, via a new oak beam. That had given them a passageway upstairs and the ability to provide four bedrooms and a bathroom.'

The first thing John and Debbie tackled was the old garage area. The linkage had to be demolished or re-faced with suitable bricks and they took the opportunity to extend it in order to create an entrance porchway, which John built himself in 16th-century French oak, leading into a utility area with a huge walk-in linen cupboard and toilet facilities. The two bedrooms were then to become the new kitchen with the upper part, including that over the extension, becoming a guest suite. 'Unfortunately, or fortunately, whichever way you look at it, there is no way that this guest bedroom can ever be connected to the other bedroom accommodation above the main house,' John points out, 'so the staircase runs up from the new entrance area, making it more or less self-contained.'

But back to the kitchen. The 'L' shape that the original extension created, seemed to John and Debbie to present them with the opportunity to open all the major living rooms, in both the old and the new sections, onto a patio arrangement that would receive full sun for much of the day. Bay windows and some decidedly creaky old French doors in the old section would have to be replaced anyway, so why not have new ones made for the new kitchen at the same time? 'I wanted to be able to open up the whole wall of the kitchen onto the patio', John explains. 'That means that the French doors have to hinge on each other but when they're open you can now walk either through the house or across the patio to any part of it. We didn't want a fitted kitchen so we chose this purpose-made furniture where each unit is painted in a different colour with the paintwork distressed to make them look original.

'We also have different work surfaces, one in teak for the sink area, one in polished granite for the cooking area and around the Aga, and one in maple for the island and preparation unit. The huge beam across the centre of the room is green French oak. It's there to hide a steel beam and I routed it out so that it fits over it and it is supported on each end by new piers. Even so it weighed $1\frac{1}{2}$ tons and it took six men

to lift it into place. The flooring is second-phase French limestone, which, with its pastel shades and uneven texture, gives the room a warm and mellow feeling.

'I made the framed ledged and braced doors myself. I like to keep to traditional fittings but I also like the juxtaposition of old and new. I like the contrast. It's a bold statement of intention, to mix old oak, rough limestone, Italian stainless steel light fittings and halogen downlighters.'

And it is this contrast between ancient and modern that is the hallmark of this lovely home. In the guest suite above the kitchen, a new pitched-roof dormer has replaced the old flat-roofed one. New oak beams have been put in place in the ceiling. A bed has been built off a plinth and head carved in iroco by John. The floors are random oak strip, the whole having a traditional feel. Yet, smack in the middle of the room is a roll-top bath on iroco feet and through an opening is a wash stand and bowl in polished concrete and a tiled shower cubicle that a whole family could fit in with jets, power sprays and a central gully in the floor. Press buttons on the bed and you can call up 200 DVDs and 200 CDs from the central music system and jukebox with eight separate zones, and controls in each room. Look above and you'll see low voltage halogen lights. In the corner, as there is throughout the house, there's an alarm. Not just any alarm but one that works as a microphone that detects sounds or movement and analyses it so that one movement or sound will be ignored but, if repeated, allows a central control company to listen in and record what's being said and done. They then notify the police and only when they are in position do the alarms go off.

'The heating is something I'm proud of,' says John. 'We put the boiler in the outhouse with a large heat-store in the utility area. All of the new sections of the house now have underfloor central heating but the older sections have Walney cast-iron radiators. I love them. They're almost items of furniture in their own right and we've painted most of them with Hammerite. As we've put new oak or elm floors in everywhere, we were able to run the pipework underneath. It's all Hep20 which means that there are no joints and we could go where we wanted. We've brought the upstands up in copper and there are traps to give access to those fittings. The house has five temperature-controlled zones and intelligent controls make sure that there is always hot water and that every room is at the right temperature.'

In the large lounge the contrast between old and new is apparent once more with Bang Olufsen tower speakers set in the inglenook fireplace, and knarled old beams side by side with Italian stainless steel lighting and minimalist Italian furniture. 'We had to consult the Conservation and Planning Officers regarding every stage of the refurbishment of this listed building,' John recalls. 'We discussed bricks with them. They agreed that we should use single-glazed windows in the rear wall of the kitchen as they looked right, and the Building Inspector thankfully concurred. They agreed with us that the old cow-barn should be clad in timber and that the roof should be seamless aluminium so that we now have that as a huge garage and store plus a studio for Debbie. We took their advice on lime mortar mixes. They wouldn't allow us to make some of the flat roofs into pitched roofs but that doesn't harm us and, instead, is a useful space to hide the satellite dishes and aerials. And they wanted us to retain the old oak staircase from the lounge to the upper part of the main house where we've now got three bedrooms, a large family bathroom and a shower room. I reckon that staircase was put in during the Fifties so is of no inherent or architectural value. But you've got to let them win on some things and, after all, we've got most of what we want here.'

John and Debbie bought the house for just over £1 million. They've spent £280,000 on it, including £25,000 on plumbing and sanitaryware alone, and it's now worth a cool £1.7 million. And as if that's not enough, John made a television series chronicling the refurbishment of their home that went out on the Discovery channel, who've now commissioned similar programmes from him and his new production company. 'The house that John built' has therefore successfully combined John's two, quite different careers and we can all look forward to more of his obvious enthusiasm for building and refurbishment on our screens.

A barn conversion in Sussex

'It's all her idea. She drives it,' says Philip to anyone who asks about their barn conversion in the middle of the Sussex countryside. 'She's the one who arranges these things and to a large extent, she's the major part of the labour force.'

The 'she' is Pauline, Philip's wife and what she's 'arranged' in the past has been a series of houses that they've bought, done up and then sold off at a profit. They haven't lived in them; they've lived in the same five-bedroom Victorian house for much of the time, but now, with the children finally off their hands, they are going to move into this project. 'I've always wanted to do a barn,' Pauline explains, 'and then this one came up. It's not that big but it's in an eighth of an acre, including an old stockyard and the site of a barn that blew down in the gales of '87. What we love, though is that it's on the edge of the South Downs Way, just up the lane there through the trees where it opens up, and you should see the view!'

They bought the barn for £137,000 and they will have spent a total of around £60,000 on it, boosting its value to about £250,000. It's not a big barn by most standards but what is attractive is that it doesn't follow the usual format and the home that they've managed to create has an individuality about it. There are two bedrooms on the ground floor and a further one up in the roof space with a gallery overlooking the living area where the lounge enjoys a vaulted ceiling and French doors opening onto the walled patio garden area. The principal construction of the main barn is stone and brick walling under a peg-tiled roof and both Pauline and Philip were concerned with energy efficiency within and from this old building.

'We tried very hard to get the best 'U' values,' Pauline explains. 'We decided that we'd use a builder for the main structure and the refurbishment of the walls, some of which had bowed a little. He waterproof-rendered the inside of the walls and then we fixed 28mm Celutex insulation sheets vertically, held against the wall with battens, against which

Above: John and Debbie were always concerned to preserve the essential character of their listed farmhouse. They worked with the local conservation officer and despite extensive alterations, extensions and modernisation, the end result is probably truer to the original than when they first saw it.

Left: Natural limestone flooring, solid oak beams and kitchen furniture instead of units.

Right: To gain access to the more or less self-contained guest suite, John had to design and build a very special staircase.

Above: Pauline and Philip stand proudly outside what will be the front of their new home.

Left: Pauline did most of the plastering herself as she wanted it to look old without looking deliberately distressed and most tradesmen found that concept difficult to grasp.

Right: Insulation to the walls and to the roof was very important to Pauline and Philip and they made sure that there were no gaps or cold spots.

we've tacked the plasterboard. In the roof and on the sloping ceilings, we've got 70mm Celutex on top of the rafters with a vapour barrier before the plasterboard, which we painted before we fixed it so that there was not so much cutting into the exposed beams. It was hard work, painting all that board beforehand on what was, to all intents and purposes, an exposed site, but it was well worth it in the end and we did the same with the floor boards for the first floor.'

Pauline did the plastering herself. 'I hadn't intended to. The builder started off doing it but he couldn't get the finish I wanted. I'm not blaming him. All his training and experience has led to the production of a mirror finish and that's just not what I wanted and what the two of us felt was right for an old building. He tried to do it rough but there's a big difference between proper rustic plasterwork and smooth plaster that's just been distressed. When he tried, all we got was swirling trowel marks. I wanted it rough but not abrasive, with all the natural knocks and blemishes that you'd expect with an old barn.'

'It helps that she is a potter,' Philip interjects. 'Yes,' Pauline agrees, 'I suppose that the ability to manage something squishy and wet, getting the consistency right and not dropping it on the floor, was what I brought to this work. Also the confidence that you get when you learn how to centre clay on a wheel ... that and the knowledge that if I didn't get it right I could always scrape it off and start again. I used Carlite bonding in sort of two coats. I'd put the first one on and then leave it for a while before I came back on it with the second coat. If it went on how I wanted then I'd leave it alone but sometimes I had to

fiddle with it to get it right. I left in all of the nice drag marks and I rounded off the corners. Sharp corners are so wrong in a building like this.'

It all sounds so easy but that belies the fact that Pauline and Philip spent most weekdays working on the site and that, from time to time, their children have had to pitch in and help. The attitude of the planners was another thing they had to contend with. The barn is in an Area of Outstanding Natural Beauty and the planners had very strict views about how the barn should be developed. Although they were willing for it to be converted into a dwelling, they did not want it to look 'domestic' and said so, refusing permission for an extension that Pauline and Philip had originally planned. In fact they've interested themselves in every aspect of the build, from the choice and arrangement of external materials, even through to how the garden is to be planted. 'At the moment,' Philip laments, 'we haven't even got planning permission for a garage. However, they did allow the barn across the lane to build one so perhaps we'll be all right.'

As you'd expect, Pauline and Philip took on much of the second-fix carpentry work and the fitting of the kitchen. However, although Philip has done quite a bit of plumbing and electrical work on their previous ventures, they decided that this time, they'd use subcontractors. 'But with the money we saved by me doing the plastering, it means that I have been able to splash out a bit on the fittings and the kitchen,' Pauline proudly boasts. This is one barn that's not going to moulder into the ground and that can and will be brought into the modern age as a lovely dwelling that reflects its history.

A detached house near Bristol

As an example of a couple who, freed from the constraints of family life, were determined to exercise their design wishes with little or no compromise, you'd be hard put to find better than John and Judy Jennings-Chick. But like many, they bought a plot in a village street and then found, to their dismay, that the planners had vastly different ideas from theirs. Whilst John and Judy dreamt of innovative modern architecture, the planners were thinking in terms of a modern copy of the Victorian residence from whose garden the plot had been hived off. Planning, of course, is all about compromise and whilst the authorities had their way with the street elevations, John and Judy were able to achieve what they wanted on the others and, inside the house, they were even able to benefit from the planners' insistence on high-pitched roofs. 'People say it's a big house,' says John, 'but I just think that at 190 square metres, it's comfortable. Certainly it's uncompromising. It makes a statement that you can take it or leave it. That's me all over. That's what I am. It's not arrogance: it's a personality statement just as this house is. Why pretend?'

Whatever kind of statement it makes, the one thing it does is make sound economic sense. At their ages and with a busy local post office and shop to run, they quite sensibly decided that they wouldn't have the time or the inclination to manage any aspect of the work on site, so they went for the option of a local builder. Three quotations were obtained, all within a spit of each other, but they chose the most expensive one as it was from a local firm who regularly used their shop and they knew would be keen to impress and maintain their reputation. It wasn't cheap. The land had cost £67,500 and with build costs of £177,500, that came to a total of around £245,000. But set that against a finished value of £325,000 and it all becomes very worthwhile.

The house was always going to be open plan, at least for the major living areas, and John was always keen to explore, with his designer, Beverley Pemberton

of Design & Materials Ltd, the relationships between different materials such as stone, wood, glass and plaster. 'The shapes that they perform more or less happened. We stated that we wanted an open fire between the lounge and dining areas and that we wanted the lounge to be at the higher level in the front of the house. That meant that the fire in the dining section would have been half way up the wall so rather than just having it stuck there in mid air, we decided to accentuate it as a feature. Not hide it or apologise for it.

'I love the open aspects of the design, the light and the airiness. We could have blocked off the second arch by the staircase but we've left it open and it gives architectural texture. I wanted the eye to be intrigued by differing views. If you sit on one side of the lounge you see the sweep of the room and the archways, plus the oriel window. If you sit on the other side you see the level changes, the staircase and the sky through the coloured glass mezzanine window. One chap who came here said that we could always block off the arch and put doors in. Bloody idiot. Over my dead body!'

Of course, John and Judy do have to think about family to some extent. They have sons who have wives and girlfriends, and grandchildren. But theirs are occasional visits and John's not prepared any longer to have the design of his home predicated on their needs rather than his. 'Yes, there is a mixture of sleeping, living and utility areas,' he admits. 'But that makes perfect sense. We've got fabulous views here so it makes perfect sense to me to have the day room upstairs with a balcony. On the other hand, one day we'll be decrepit so it makes just as much sense to have a bedroom and en-suite downstairs and in the meantime it can double up as a guest suite. You see, we haven't just planned for the medium term. We might not be able to stay here for ever but certainly for the foreseeable future. If I had my wish this would be my last home and I'd go out of here feet first.

'Just walking around the house still excites me. We were determined not just to have a box. I didn't even want squares within the house. Take the doors from the dining room. If we'd put the wall in square we could have got one single door to the day room and the dining area would have been smaller. By

Above: John didn't always see eye to eye with the planners about his new home.

Below: John and Judy love things modern and vibrant such as this corner bath and the heated ladder towel rail.

Right: The full height mezzanine window, with its coloured glass, over the open staircase, floods light down into the split-level living rooms.

Top & above: Joyce and Sally's bungalow, viewed from the churchyard opposite.

Right: Light was so important to both Sally and Joyce. In the background, you can see just how close the bungalow is to the Grade II Listed church.

putting the wall at the angle we get double doors that can be opened to throw light into the whole of the living area. The same applies upstairs. If the wall between the main bedroom and the en-suite had been square, the bedroom would have looked quite small. As it is, by taking the wall at an angle, your eye follows it as you enter the room, to the mirrored wardrobes at the end, the windows and the view.

'I hated having to compromise on the design and it's true to say that I've ended up quite antipathetic towards planners. They hide behind precedent and convention, incapable of understanding design innovation, which they encourage in theory but are unable to accept in practice. I wanted this house to be a statement of our ideals, our needs and requirements and of our whole experience of life and it pains me to have to water that down in any way.'

A replacement bungalow in Gloucestershire

In 1963 Joyce Andrews, with her husband Ron, bought a plot of land overlooking open countryside, just north of Cheltenham racecourse, and had a Woolaway bungalow built on it. 'But I always wanted a proper brick-built bungalow,' Joyce recollects. 'I don't know why my husband wanted to do it another way but at the time he presumably thought it was best.'

They raised a family and lived happily in the bungalow. Ron unfortunately died some time ago and their daughter, Sally, returned home to live with her mother, taking up a lecturing post and holding classes in china painting; something at which she excels. Then five years ago ominous cracks appeared in the bungalow. Alarmed, they called in surveyors who blamed a tree in their beautifully thought-out, Japanese-style garden. The insurers offered a fairly paltry sum in order to effect any necessary repairs and, to be honest, Sally felt that perhaps that's just what they should do. 'Not mother, however,' she recalls. 'Mother had completely different ideas.'

'Well, as I said, I'd always wanted a proper bungalow and I just felt that this was my opportunity. A little while before I'd casually remarked to a friend that I'd like to build and that wasn't it a pity that we couldn't get one on the end piece of our garden. Now this seemed like the right thing to do. He had already built a bungalow for himself and his wife and they were planning to do it again, so he suggested that we contacted the package-deal company he was dealing with.'

'And this chap came along and did his very best to dissuade us,' Sally remembers. 'Yes,' Joyce complains, 'he said that at rising 80 it would be the death of me, that I'd never stand the stress of self-building and that we should just have the old bungalow repaired and made good.' 'He didn't know my mother,' Sally laughs. 'She's a very determined lady. I wasn't so sure. The old bungalow had been my home for much of my life and I felt that we should be more cautious. That's my nature I suppose, whereas Mother is much more get-up-and-go. Now, sitting here in our new home, I know it was the right thing to rebuild and I'm so glad that we did.'

The plot is in a conservation area, bang opposite a Grade II church and yard that basically dominates the street scene. That many of the other bungalows in the village, but particularly their pre-fabricated concrete panelled one, would have no chance of getting planning permission in these enlightened times, there is no doubt. In fact, when the planners were first consulted, they literally jumped at the chance of 'cleaning up' this important corner of the village. But they did, nevertheless, put some stipulations on, the most important of which was that the new dwelling should reflect the local vernacular, should remain as single storey and that it should not be very much bigger than the original.

'In the main that was completely satisfactory for us,' Joyce explains, 'but they still found fault with the design and they sent us a letter saying that their conservation officer had some reservations and enclosing suggested elevations which we didn't like at all. So we went to a meeting with them and we let them outline all of their objections. Then we showed them a photograph of the village school and told them that this was what we had tried to emulate. They looked at it and just changed their minds immediately!

'Our friend put us on to a local builder and he quoted for the weathertight shell, after which we employed the subcontractors such as the plasterer, plumber, electrician and carpenter. We didn't have any trouble with any of that and all of the men who worked here were really nice and accommodating. If anything was wrong it was the pressure that time put upon us. We were in rented accommodation with all of our furniture in store and that gave us time limits. In turn that meant that we sometimes had to make the decision that saved time rather than money. We did all of our own decoration and Sally painted those wonderful *trompe-l'oeil* in the lounge and my bedroom.'

The land, of course, cost them nothing but it was, nevertheless valued at around £70,000. It's not a big bungalow, barely 120 square metres including the garage, but they did manage to build for a cost of £65,000, which, by any standards, was a remarkable achievement but especially so for two single women with no previous experience of the building industry. Now, two years later, they have re-created and enhanced their garden and the value of their new home is conservatively put at £200,000.

Sally sums up their achievement by saying, 'Mother's a sparky woman. She was determined that she was going to do this and that her age was not going to be a barrier. It's taken all of our savings but the return on our investment is well worth while, quite apart from the fact that we now have a 'proper' bungalow that we both love. The only trouble is that once the garden's finished, Mother's going to be at a loose end and looking for another project. World peace, perhaps?'

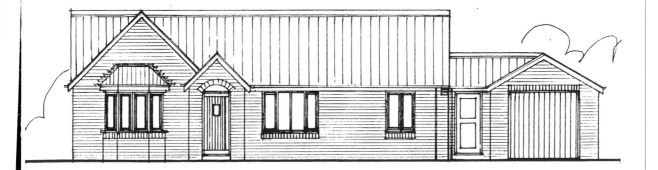

A split-level family house in Wales

Most parents look forward to visits from their grown-up children. Most enjoy it even more when grand-children come along. But most, if they're honest, will admit to heaving a sigh of relief when the visits are over and their homes can get back to normality. Imagine a visit that stretches out for months. Imagine a small quiet home for two suddenly becoming home to two more adults, three children under five, two cats and an exuberant terrier.

Frank and Emma McCarthy lived in London for the first part of their marriage but then, as the children came along, Emma decided that she would prefer to raise them in her native Wales, close to friends and family. They sold up and moved back, buying the house next door to her mother and father whilst Frank commuted once a week to his job with the London Fire Brigade. 'London's not for children,' Emma insists, 'and besides, I wanted to do a law degree and start a Masters in Education.'

Frank, meanwhile, staying during the week with his mother in London, dreamed of self-building. 'I've just always wanted to do it,' he explains. 'Emma only came around to the idea later on.' 'We were going to buy a new house,' says Emma, taking up the story, 'and when it was nearly finished, we went to see it and very quickly realised that it wasn't right. So I started to look into what Frank had been thinking of and I quickly realised that for the money we had, if we self-built, we could get so much more.'

As luck would have it a plot came onto the market just down the road for £55,000. It wasn't an easy plot. It was on an estate where close on a hundred plots had been marked out and given planning for four-bedroom houses, most of which were on steeply sloping land. Their particular plot rose 10 metres from the front kerb line to the rear boundary, but it was a big one and, being opposite a road junction, it would always enjoy fabulous views of the estuary. Their house sold quickly and, with their furniture distributed between the lofts and garages of various friends and family and the store above a local butcher's shop, they all moved in next door with Mum and Dad, Malcolm and Ita.

Now began the hunt for an architect. 'We toyed with the idea of using a package-deal company but, in the end, decided that we'd prefer to use a local arch itect with us being responsible for sourcing the materials and labour,' Frank remembers. 'I'd been reading the magazines for so long and going to all the shows so I knew what we wanted and with Emma's family being from around here, it wasn't difficult to get the names of various tradesmen.' 'Nevertheless,' Emma reminds him, 'we had a few shocks when we went to local architects. We wanted five bedrooms, a big separate lounge, a rumpus room, study, family room and a big kitchen-breakfast room and, with the slope of the land we appreciated that it was going to have to be on three levels with the garage, rumpus room and study in the basement. That meant that it was going to be big but we were still amazed at the cost estimates we received and the price for the architectural work. One chap wanted £8,000!' 'Anyway,' says Frank, 'we saw an advert in the local paper from a designer and he

Above: Self-building with three children under five (plus visitors) deserves a medal.

Above: The house on three floors measures something like 320 square metres and when the loft is fully utilised that will add a further 60 square metres in the form of either a playroom or two further bedrooms.

Right: An essential pre-requisite for both Frank and Emma was a large and well-fitted kitchen with enough room for the family to be able to eat in there.

agreed to do all the drawing office work and make the applications for us for a fixed fee of £1,900. When the drawings came back they were almost exactly what we wanted. The planning was easy. It had to go to committee but the only stipulation was that the windows to the side must be obscure glazed.'

With Frank away all week and with Emma now enrolled at teacher training college, they decided that they really needed a builder for at least the weathertight shell of the building. But they were still insistent that they should buy all of the materials. Work started on site in March 2000. At least 30 loads of spoil were sent away to a local site where they wanted fill, and 65 cubic metres of concrete went back into the foundations. It was a mammoth task but the weathertight shell was complete by the end of July.

Frank and Emma did the electrical work themselves as well as the decoration and ceramic wall and floor tiling. They subbed out the plumbing labour but bought all of the materials themselves. As they've got beam and block floors to all levels except the attic, they opted for underfloor central heating throughout with 12 separate zones fired by a condensing boiler, all of which they supplied. 'The plumber just walked in on the job one day and asked if we were looking for a plumber,' Frank recalls. 'We also engaged a local plasterer and the carpenter was a local guy I knew who came in after the first one just disappeared after hanging a few doors. The P-vcu windows and doors came from a local company. The fitting was in the builder's price but they preferred to fit themselves so we deducted that. Similarly with the kitchen. We went to a local firm and they supplied and fitted it for £4,000 inclusive.'

'I think I need to say that we couldn't have done any of this without Mum and Dad,' Emma points out. 'They put us up and they looked after the kids whilst we were working and building the house. They were wonderful. Now that we're finished, they spend almost as much time here as they do back at home but it's big enough, so who cares? In fact, to be honest it's a little bigger than it needs to be for comfort. All in all it's 320 square metres on three floors and when we've finished fitting out the loft, that'll provide a further 68 square metres and we'll be four storeys high! That's too big really. In some ways I wonder if we'll ever really use that huge lounge and I wish we'd made the family room a little bigger instead.'

'Still, we're happy and proud of our achievement,' Frank insists. 'We moved in, in March 2001 and it took us another seven months to be able to say we'd finished. The total costs, now that I've added up and sent off the VAT reclaim were just under £134,000 which works out at £418 per square metre, not counting the attic space which is all there, ready for us to occupy when and if we want to. If you add those costs to the land costs, that means that we've spent £189,000 to set against a recent valuation of £245,000. Not bad, and suitable recompense for all those months of hard work and disruption.'

An 'Arts and Crafts' house in Oxfordshire

'Buy the worst house in the best street,' was the advice Michael received when he and his wife Emma went looking for a new development project, having sold their first self-build, which was reported on in the last edition of this book.

It is said that Michelangelo could see the finished sculpture within the raw block of marble. Well, when Michael and Emma sat in the car outside the original house and drew thumb-nail sketches on the back of the details, showing just how an ugly Sixties chalet bungalow could be transformed into a modern 'arts and crafts' residence, they certainly displayed the same foresight. It wasn't exactly the worst house in the street but it was certainly up there in the running for the title. Originally built as a two-bedroom property and then extended in 1985 to provide four bedrooms, it had a 55 degree pitched roof with interlocking concrete tiles, was built of cheap brick with timber cladding and had huge single-glazed picture windows. The third and fourth bedrooms were in a new timber-framed section over the carport, supported by an ugly steel pillar and the gardens, whilst neatly kept, were terraced and covered with apple trees, so that they appeared really cramped.

'But it was exactly where we wanted to be,' Michael recalls, 'slap bang in the middle of the village and next door but one to Emma's sister. I knew it was a "pig in a poke" but I could also see what could be done with it and I could see that what we were proposing would be for the good of the area as a whole, and therefore likely to gain the approval of the planners. Five- to six-bedroom houses in this area were fetching £500,000–£600,000 and this was for sale for £200,000.'

They toyed with the idea of knocking it down and starting afresh at one stage but in the end came back to the ideas that they'd first encapsulated in the original sketches, guessing, at that stage, that what they were proposing would cost in the region of £150,000. 'Oh no, it'll cost at least £250,000,' said one

architect that they contacted. 'No, it could be done for the £150,000,' said another, who happened to be the original architect who'd been responsible for the 1985 extension, pleased no doubt to have the chance to put right what had gone before. Of course, for those who've read about Michael and Emma before, he was reckoning without knowledge of their absolute refusal to compromise when it comes to choices of materials, fixtures and fittings and, in the end, the first architect was nearer the mark as far as the costs went.

The design that Michael and Emma had foreseen meant creating a new drawing room where the old carport had been, leaving the two bedrooms above. It also meant lopping 1 1/2 metres off the old lounge to create a new entrance porch and hallway and building a new extension at the back and the side to house the new limestone-flagged kitchen and dining area. Above this there is a new master suite with a vaulted ceiling and this brings the property into the five-bedroom category and price range of other similar homes in the area. But all of that wouldn't have been enough if it hadn't been for the detail. 'We stripped the old walls back to the bare block and brick, both inside and out,' Michael explains, 'and then we re-plastered inside and on the outside, we built a new plinth of handmade bricks from York Handmade Bricks and then rough cast rendered above. All the old cedar wood cladding had to come off, of course and we replaced that with Keymer peg tiles and then we stripped off the roof and re-tiled that with handmade clay Swallow tiles.

'The new central chimney was essential to the design, as were the windows. We tried looking around for off-the-shelf joinery but none of it was right so in the end we opted for purpose-made joinery from a local works. That way we got the right balance in the glazing bars, especially with the new bay, oriel and French windows that allow light to flood in and us to look out to appreciate fully the garden that my mother has planned and planted for us.'

The walls had already been insulated by the previous owners, so Michael decided to leave them alone and, instead, concentrated his efforts on energy conservation by packing the new roof with 90mm Kingspan insulation and putting 50mm under the new floating floor. 'The old house had "Economy 7" electric heating,' Michael remembers. 'We basically started again and re-wired and re-plumbed the house. I wanted the very latest and we went for a top-of-the-range modulating condensing boiler with underfloor central heating from IPECC to the ground floor and the bathrooms and radiators upstairs, all controlled by the very latest in programming technology.'

The planning sailed through as, even though they were increasing the size of the original building by a great deal more than the normal guidelines, the planners were on their side as they could see that what they were being offered was so much better for the street scene. Not so the Parish Council, who, as is usual, objected to everything, almost on principle. 'Happily, though, the planners overruled all of their objections one by one,' says Michael, 'but then we had a scare. We had left one of the dormers with a flat roof but when it came to it, we decided that we really didn't like it, so we instructed the builders to change it to a pitched roof, thinking of course that it could be done under Permitted Development Rights. Then I thought I'd better check with the planners and they told me that I did need retrospective planning permission after all, which they would, of course, support. Well, the Parish Council objected to that and the whole thing had to go to committee, and although they passed it, it gave us a few sticky moments.'

'Yes, and that's not the only one,' Emma interjects. 'We were just having the new front dry stone wall built and this woman turned up claiming that half our front garden was in fact Highways land.' 'Yes, and that meant that not only did we stand to lose the garden but that the Lpg tank would have to come up,' Michael adds. 'She had all these measurements and documents proving that the land had been acquired for road widening but our solicitor kept on insisting that we owned the land. In the end I got out and measured everything from fixed points that hadn't changed for decades, and I found out that this woman had been measuring things up wrongly. She'd been working from the road edge, whereas the road had already been widened and, effectively, she was trying to double up what they'd taken. She had a red face in the end but she certainly gave us a few sleepless nights.'

As before, with their earlier self-build, Michael and Emma chose to use a builder, David Mill on a cost plus basis for the main weathertight shell of the

Above: The original 1960's house that never really fitted into the street scene of this Oxfordshire village.

Below: The completed house from the same viewpoint, taken just after they'd moved in.

building. 'It's not something I could recommend in most circumstances, but it seems to work for Emma and me, especially as we know that we're always going to be changing our minds and because we know Dave so well, we can trust him.' The costs in the end added up to £210,000 including VAT, which they could not unfortunately recover under current legislation. Added to the original cost of the house that means a total outlay of £410,000 to set against a value that creeps up towards the £600,000 mark. All financially well worthwhile and, from the improvement in the street scene, socially desirable to boot!

Above: Now the house has balance. Its proportions, though not by any means symmetrical, are harmonious and the design details and choices of materials reflect the true character of an 'Arts & Crafts' house.

Right: Michael and Emma scoured the local demolition and salvage yards for the details and fixtures such as this Victorian cast iron fireplace.

Further information

Books – available from Ryton Books Ltd.
Tel: 01909 591652

The Home Plans Book by David Snell and Murray Armor, Ebury Press

Plans for a Dream Home by Murray Armor, Ebury Press

The Housebuilder's Bible by Mark Brinkley

Practical Housebuilding by Bob Matthews, Blackberry Books

All About Self-building by Bob Matthews, Blackberry Books

How to Find a Building Plot by Speer and Dade, Stonepound Books

How to Get Planning Permission by Speer and Dade, Stonepound Books

How to Finance Building and Converting your own Home by Speer and Dade, Stonepound Books

The House Restorer's Guide by Hugh Lander, David and Charles

Magazines

Homebuilding & Renovating Tel: 01527 834400 www.homebuilding.co.uk

Build It Tel: 020 7837 8727 www.self-build.co.uk

Self-build and Design Tel: 01283 742950

Planning Inspectorates and Appeal Boards

England – The Planning Inspectorate Tel: 0117 372 8754

Wales – The Planning Inspectorate Tel: 02920 825007

Scotland – The Scottish Executive Inquiry Reporters Unit Tel: 0131 244 5649

Northern Ireland – The Planning Appeals Commision – Tel: 02890 244710

The Republic of Ireland (Eire) – An Bord Pleanala Tel: 00 353 1872 8001

Architectural, design and engineering associations and societies

The Association of Self-builders Tel: 0704 154 4126

Royal Institute of British Architects (RIBA) Tel: 020 7580 5533

Royal Incorporation of Architects in Scotland (RIAS) Tel: 0131 229 7205

Royal Society of Architects in Wales Tel: 02920 874753

Royal Society of Ulster Architects Tel: 028 9032 3760

Royal Institute of Architects in Ireland (RIAI) Tel: 00353 1676 1703 www.riai.ie

Associated Self-build Architects (ASBA) Tel: 0800 387310 www.asba-architects.org

The Architect's Registration Board (ARB) Tel: 0207 278 2206 www.arb.org.uk

Royal Town Planning Institute Tel: 020 7636 9107 www.rtpi.org.uk

The British Institute of Architectural Technologists Tel: 020 7278 2206 www.biat.org.uk

Architectural Designers Association Tel: 0118 941 6571

Institute of Civil Engineers Tel: 020 7222 7722

Architectural practices featured in this book
Julian Owen Associates Tel: 0115 922 9831

Keith Bishop Associates Tel: 01684 566494

David H.Anderson Tel: 028 3833 0632

Building trades associations

Interior Decorators' and Designers' Association
Tel: 020 7307 3700 www.idda.co.uk

Federation of Master Builders
Tel: 020 7242 7583 www.fmb.org.uk

HomePro/Fair Trades Ltd.
Tel: 0870 738 4858 www.HomePro.com

ImprovelineLtd. www.improveline.com

Association of Plumbing and Heating Contractors
Tel: 02476 470626 www.aphc.co.uk

Council for Registered Gas Installers (CORGI)
Tel: 01256 372200 www.corgi-gas.com

National Inspection Council for Electrical Installation
Contractors Tel: 020 7582 7746 www.niceic.org.uk

Federation of Specialist Builders Tel: 020 7436 0387

National Federation of Roofing Contractors
Tel: 020 7436 0387 www.nfrc.co.uk

Guild of Master Craftsmen Tel: 01273 478449

The British Decorators' Association
Tel: 02476 353 776 www.british-decorators.co.uk

The Thatching Advisory Service Tel: 01256 880828

Joint Contracts Tribunal (JCT) Tel: 0121 722 8200
www.buildingcontract.co.uk

Yellow Pages Tel: 0118 959 2111 www.yell.com

Government agencies and establishments

The Building Research Establishment (and BRECSU)
Tel: 01923 664000

National Radiological Protection Board
Tel: 01235 831600

HM Land Registry
Tel: 020 7917 8888 www.landreg.gov.uk

Floodline Tel: 0845 988 1188

Special-interest groups or associations

The Association of Self-builders Tel: 0704 154 4126

The Traditional Housing Bureau Tel: 01344 725757

Timber and Brick Information Council
Tel: 01923 778136

The Basement Development Group
Tel: 01344 725737

The Disabled Living Foundation
Tel: 020 7289 6111

The Society for the Protection of Ancient Buildings
(SPAB) Tel: 020 7377 1644

English Heritage
Tel: 020 7973 3000 www.english-heritage.org.uk

Historic Scotland Tel: 0131 668 8600
www.historic-scotland.gov.uk

Cadw Tel: 02920 500200 www.cadw.wales.gov.uk

The Council for British Archaeology
Tel: 01904 671417

Council for the Protection of Rural England (CPRE)
Tel: 020 7253 0300

The Ancient Monuments Society Tel: 020 7236 3934

The Georgian Group Tel: 020 7387 1720

The Victorian Society Tel: 020 8994 1019

Companies and agencies assisting in land finding

Plotfinder – 24-hour hotline Tel: 0906 557 5400.
Fax back Service 01527 834428 www.plotfinder.net

Landbank Services
Tel: 0118 962 6022 www.landbank.co.uk

Plotsearch Tel: 0870 870 9004
www.buildstore.co.uk/plotsearch

English Partnerships (formerly CNT)
Tel: 01908 692692 www.englishpartnerships.co.uk

Agencies involved in group and community self-build

The Community Self-build Agency
Tel: 020 7415 7092

Wadsworth Landmark Ltd. Tel: 0117 940 9800

The National Housing Federation Tel: 020 7278 6571

The Housing Corporation Tel: 020 7393 2000

The Young Builders' Trust Tel: 01730 266766

The Walter Segal Trust Tel: 020 7388 9582

Exhibitions, shows and self-build courses

The Homebuilding & Renovating Show – every spring at the NEC, summer at Sandown Park and autumn in Harrogate and Edinburgh.
Tel: 01527 834400 www.homebuildingshow.co.uk

The Build It Self-build and Home Improvement Show, held at Alexandra Palace every autumn, Cardiff and Glasgow every spring and with various other regional shows held throughout the year.
Tel: 020 7837 8727

Homebuilding and Renovating with Worcester College of Technology – four-day residential courses with optional three days' practical, held twice a year in spring and autumn.
Tel: 01905 619031

Constructive Individuals – weekend and three-week hands-on courses.
Tel: 020 7515 9299 www.constructiveindividuals.com

Ideal Homes Exhibition – every spring at Earl's Court.

Self-build insurances

DMS Services Ltd – for all self-build insurances
Tel: 01909 591652

Capital Cover – for site insurance in The Republic of Ireland (Eire) Tel: 00353 1491 0210

Warranties

NHBC – 'Buildmark' and 'Solo'
Tel: 01494 434477

Zurich – 'Newbuild' and 'Custombuild'
Tel: 01252 5222000

Project Builder
Tel: 020 7716 5050

Willis (Forest of Dean Scheme)
Tel: 020 7488 8994

NHBG – 'Homebond' Tel: 00353 1021 0149

Package-deal companies and timber-frame manufacturers

Border Oak Design and Construction Ltd.
Tel: 01568 708752

Buildstore Ltd.
Tel: 0870 870 9991 www.buildstore.co.uk

Custom Homes Ltd.
Tel: 01293 822898 www.customhomes.co.uk

T.J. Crump Oakrights
Tel: 01432 353353 www.oakrights.co.uk

Design and Materials Ltd.
Tel: 01909 540123

Fleming Homes Ltd.
Tel: 01361 883785

Frame Homes (South West) Ltd.
Tel: 01872 572882 www.framehomes.co.uk

Guardian Homes
Tel: 01772 614243 and 01252 617754

Maple Timber Frame of Langley
Tel: 01772 683370

Potton Ltd Tel: 01480 401401 www.potton.co.uk

The Self-build House Company Ltd.
Tel: 01342 312513 www.self-buildhouseco.com

Scandia-Hus Tel: 01342 327977

The Swedish House Company Ltd.
Tel: 01892 665007

Southern Timber Frame
Tel: 02380 293062

Scotframe Timber Engineering Ltd.
Tel: 01467 624440

Taylor Lane Timber Frame Ltd.
Tel: 01432 271912 www.taylor-lane.co.uk

Underfloor heating and boiler specialists

Eco Hometec
Tel: 01302 722266 www.eco-hometec.co.uk

Hipkin Heating Systems
Tel: 020 8984 1000

IPECC Systems Ltd.
Tel: 0121 622 4333 and 0141 4017285
www.ipecc.co.uk

Kee Triple Tube Underfloor Heating Ltd.
Tel: 028 4062 4141 www.keeheating.co.uk

Nu-Heat UK Ltd.
Tel: 01404 549771 www.nu-heat.co.uk

Robbins Systems
Tel: 01424 830140 www.underfloorheating.co.uk

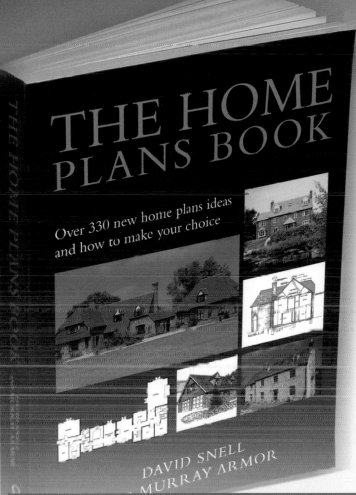

Index

SELFBUILDERS INSURANCES
ASSESSING YOUR INSURANCE REQUIREMENTS

INSURANCE

ENTER PREMIUM REQUIRED

STANDARD COVER

LIABILITIES   Limit of Liability

A. Employers Liability – *no excess*   £10,000,000

B. Public Liability   £2,000,000
   in respect of the site, the natural features on it
   including trees and the work proposed – *excess
   of £250 for property damage*

CONTRACT WORKS

C. Contract Works insurance to the value declared
   in respect of the works and materials for use in
   the works, with a standard excess of £500

Public Liability and Employers Liability premiums account for £100 in the premiums below:

INCLUSIVE PREMIUMS

Rebuild Cost Up to £	Premium £	Rebuild Cost Up to £	Premium £
80,000 (min)	399	90,000	436
100,000	474	110,000	511
120,000	548	130,000	586
140,000	623	150,000	660

Premiums for larger sums on application
Premiums INCLUDE Insurance Premium Tax

OPTIONAL COVER

PLANT

D. Plant and tools owned by the proposer, cover on
   the site only with a standard excess of £500

£2 per £100 of value

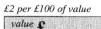
value £

E. Employees tools or plant, cover effective on the
   site only with a standard excess of £50. (Maximum
   2 employees)

Cover for £330 each employee, premium £30

F. Plant and tools hired in by the proposer and NOT
   covered by Hiresafe or other hirers scheme, cover
   for the whole term of the policy with the standard
   excess of £500

£2.50 per £100 of value

value £

G. Plant and tools hired in by the proposer and NOT
   covered by Hiresafe or other hirers scheme, short
   term cover for a 14 day period. (Phone 01909
   591652 to arrange)

Premiums will be quoted after consultation

*The **minimum** total premium for Section D, E & F is £250. It is recommended that proposers requiring this cover telephone 01909 591652 to discuss their requirements*

CARAVAN

H. Caravan on the site, used
   as a site hut or temporary
   dwelling, excess £250

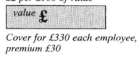
value £

£52.50 per £1,000 value of caravan (Does not include cover for personal possessions)

INCREASED PUBLIC LIABILITY LIMITS

J. Increase Public Liability cover for a 14 day period
   if required by an authority to facilitate a drain
   connection or similar purpose

K. Public Liability to £1,000,000 and Fire Cover to an
   agreed value on existing buildings, walls and other
   structures on the site which are not part of the
   construction project.

REVISED LIMIT OF INDEMNITY
£2,500,000   fixed premium £26
£5,000,000   fixed premium £46

Premiums will be quoted after consultation

The above cover extends for the duration of the building work or 15 months whichever is the sooner. It applies to mainland UK, C. Isles, IoM, and Shetlands. Rates for N. Ireland exactly double the mainland rates above.

TERRORISM – cover only applies for sum insured on works and plant up to £100,000 total sum insured. If additional cover is required premiums will be quoted.

If living within 25 metres of the new building a discount is applicable. Refer to 01909 591652 for amount.

If excesses on Sections C, D & F are to be increased to £1000 a discount is applicable. Refer to 01909 591652 for amount.

REBATES

A rebate of the premium will be made as a credit towards the cost of a Buildings and Contents policy for the finished homes arranged by DMS Services Ltd. or its associates if the building work is finished and the new policy arranged

| within 6 months | 10% of the premium paid for basic selfbuild cover |
| within 9 months | 5% of the premium paid for basic selfbuild cover |

PREMIUM PAYABLE
(Premiums above are inclusive of Insurance Premium Tax at 5%)

PAYMENT – Please tick as appropriate

❏ Cheque for payment enclosed

❏ Payment to be made by credit card

Card No. ☐☐☐☐ ☐☐☐☐ ☐☐☐☐ ☐☐☐☐   expiry ☐☐☐☐

COMPLETED FORMS AND PREMIUMS SHOULD BE SENT TO DMS SERVICES LTD, ORCHARD HOUSE, BLYTH, WORKSOP, NOTTS. S81 8HF
TEL. 01909 591652 FAX. 01909 591031

SELFBUILDERS INSURANCES
PROPOSAL

AXA INSURANCE

Name of proposer: Mr/Mrs/Ms .... Phone number: ....

Full postal address: ....

.... Post Code: ....

Address of property to be insured: ....

....

Name, address and any reference number of any interested party, e.g. Building Society: ....

....

YOUR PROPOSAL

1. Have you made any other proposal for insurance in respect of the risk proposed? **YES/NO**
   If "yes" give details at 10 below.

2. Has any company or underwriter declined your proposal? *If "yes" give details at 10 below.* **YES/NO**

3. Have you been convicted of (or charged but not yet tried with) arson or any offence involving dishonesty of any kind (e.g. fraud, theft, handling stolen goods etc.) *If "yes" give details at 10 below.* **YES/NO**

YOUR PROGRAMME

4(a). Commencing date of insurance ..../........./.........

4(b). Date work commenced if a start has been made on the site? ..../........./.........

4(c). Have there been any incidents on the site which could have given rise to a claim? **YES/NO**
   If "yes" give details at 10 below.

4(d).Target completion date ..../........./.........
   Standard policy is for 15 months.

THE BUILDING

5(a). Is the building a completely new structure? **YES/NO**
   If "no" refer to DMS Services on 01909 591652 or provide details at 10 below.

5(b). State the value of the new building at builders reinstatement cost. (The minimum premium is for the value up to £80,000) **£**

5(c). Will the new dwelling have brick or masonry walls with or without a timber frame under a tile or slate roof? **YES/NO**
   If "no" refer to DMS Services on 01909 591652 or provide details at 10 below.

5(d). Will the building qualify for a warranty, either N.H.B.C., Zurich Custombuild, surveyors or architects progress certificates **YES/NO**
   If "no" refer to DMS Services on 01909 591652 or provide details at 10 below.

THE SITE

6. Is the site and any existing building on it subject to any special hazard such as flooding, subsidence or other ground conditions **YES/NO**
   If "yes" give details at 10 below.

7. Do the Planning Consent or Building Regulation Approvals indicate any special requirements or special precautions to be taken in the construction of the building? *If "yes" give details at 10 below.* **YES/NO**

SECURITY

8. Does the proposer intend to live within 25 metres of the new work during the construction period? **YES/NO**
   If "yes" a discount can be claimed on the proposal form opposite

9. Will security arrangements on site be to good standard practice on building sites in the local area? **YES/NO**
   (A limit of £20,000 will apply to unfixed electrical, plumbing, heating, kitchen and bathroom fitments which must be contained in a locked building, hut or steel container whenever left unattended)

SPECIAL CIRCUMSTANCES

10. State the circumstances of any unusual circumstances or other facts which might influence the decision of the insurer when considering this proposal.
   If insufficient space please continue on a separate sheet.

I/we declare that all the work to which this proposal relates will be carried out in accordance with the Building Regulations, and that arrangements for the approval or certification of the works under the regulations will be made before any works are carried out.

I/we declare that to the best of my/our knowledge and belief all the statements and particulars made with regard to this proposal are true and I/we agree that this proposal shall be the basis of the contract of insurance between me/us and AXA Insurance. I/we consent to the seeking of information from other insurers to check the answers I/we have provided, and I/we authorise the giving of information for such purposes.

Signature _____ Date _____

COMPLETED FORMS AND PREMIUMS SHOULD BE SENT TO DMS SERVICES, ORCHARD HOUSE, BLYTH, WORKSOP, NOTTS. S81 8HF TEL. 01909 591652 FAX. 01909 591031